THE PROCESS OF GOVERNMENT UNDER JEFFERSON

The Process of Government
under Jefferson

by Noble E. Cunningham, Jr.

PRINCETON UNIVERSITY PRESS
PRINCETON, NEW JERSEY

COPYRIGHT © 1978 BY PRINCETON UNIVERSITY PRESS
PUBLISHED BY PRINCETON UNIVERSITY PRESS, PRINCETON, NEW JERSEY
IN THE UNITED KINGDOM: PRINCETON UNIVERSITY PRESS, GUILDFORD, SURREY

ALL RIGHTS RESERVED

LIBRARY OF CONGRESS CATALOGING IN PUBLICATION DATA WILL
BE FOUND ON THE LAST PRINTED PAGE OF THIS BOOK

PUBLICATION OF THIS BOOK WAS ASSISTED BY A GRANT FROM THE
PUBLICATIONS PROGRAM OF THE NATIONAL ENDOWMENT
FOR THE HUMANITIES

THIS BOOK HAS BEEN COMPOSED IN LINOTYPE MONTICELLO

PRINTED IN THE UNITED STATES OF AMERICA
BY PRINCETON UNIVERSITY PRESS, PRINCETON, NEW JERSEY

FOR

HELEN, JANE ANN, AND MARY ALICE

Contents

List of Tables

Preface

This work is based on the assumption that more is known about the life of Thomas Jefferson as President, about the issues and problems of his presidency, and about the legislative record of Congress than is known about the process of government and the mechanisms through which the executive and legislative branches of government operated during this period. It is based on the further assumption that an understanding of the functioning of government is essential to comprehending the history of the republic. The work attempts to depart from the traditional framework of histories of presidential administrations by examining the historical records with a view to determining the process rather than the narrative of events.

The aim of the book is to examine the functioning of Jeffersonian government, not to provide a history of the eight years of Jefferson's presidency. I have sought to explore the operation of the presidential office, the Cabinet, the departments and other offices in the executive, and to examine the procedures of both houses of Congress. The study describes the first transfer of political control from one party to another in the nation's history; it explores the problems that the new administration faced in organizing the executive branch, filling federal offices, and dealing with party pressures; and it traces the operation of the machinery of the national government during the two terms that Jefferson occupied the presidential office. The study is confined to the executive and legislative branches and does not include the judiciary.

In the course of my investigations, I have sought to discover how decisions were made, how policies were formulated, how departments of government operated, and how legislation was enacted and implemented, rather than examining the decisions, policies, or laws themselves. By examining the making of specific decisions, as case studies, it becomes possible to see the decisionmaking process at work. By tracing the preparation of Jefferson's messages to Congress, one can see the process of policy formation and executive initiative. By studying the records of Congress and of the executive departments, it is possible to analyze the functioning of both branches and the relationships between them.

Although the study is concerned with the day-to-day operations of the government, it is not restricted to administrative history and seeks to explore the influences and pressures upon the government, such as petitioning—a much neglected aspect of the governmental process in the early republic. In addition, I have also tried to relate the role of party to the machinery of government. I have been much concerned with the interrelationships among the various elements of the government, especially those between the President and members of his Cabinet and between the heads of departments and the Congress. I have also explored the role of the Attorney General during the Jeffersonian era. While I have followed a topical organization, the interrelationships are such that no chapter is designed to stand alone. In treating the executive branch, I have tried to move beyond the confines of the presidential office and the Cabinet and to look at lower-level government offices. I have sought to discover the roles and the identities of the lesser officials and the clerks in government offices and in this way to broaden the scope of our view of the past. Unfortunately, my efforts in this regard have not been as successful as I had hoped. The task of identifying the government workers in itself is large, and letters, diaries, or other papers left by government clerks are disappointingly rare. Since I could not find in print a complete civil list for any year of Jefferson's presidency, I have compiled a roster of department subordinate officers and clerks for the year 1807 and included it in the appendix as an aid to future researchers whose collective efforts may be able to uncover more about them than I have been able to find.

In looking at Congress, I have been particularly concerned with the committee systems, where much of the work of the legislature was done. The use of largely unexplored Senate records has permitted a detailed analysis of Senate committees that provides evidence for identifying Senate leaders and leadership roles. In my study of the Senate, I decided to use a limited number of quantitative tools in analyzing this large body of data. While impressed with the mass of tabulations that a computer can supply, I have resisted the temptation to publish all of these interesting tabulations and have attempted to incorporate the major findings into the text without greatly interrupting the narrative and unbalancing the basic design of the study. In giving more attention than usual to the Senate, which has commonly been neglected by historians writing about this period, I hope that the new evidence presented about the operation of that body will atone for my own neglect of the Senate in earlier works. In treating the legislative process I have not attempted a roll-call analysis, because the analysis required demands an extended study that is impossible within the framework of the present volume. Such a separate work would supplement the present study, but I do not believe that it is a necessary foundation for my investigation. I have, however, used recorded roll calls to determine the level of participation in the legislative process.

The records of President Jefferson's administration are extensive, but, unlike the records of recent administrations, they can be handled by an individual scholar, who can examine the papers of the President, the files of all of the executive departments, and the records of both houses of Congress. In making this study, I have followed this comprehensive research plan, although I do not claim to have read every document I have seen. It is a six-week task to go through the records in the National Archives of the four Congresses that met during the eight years of Jefferson's presidency, but it is a rewarding experience for anyone who seeks to understand how Congress and the government operated in the first decade of the nineteenth century.

I am indebted to the National Endowment for the Humanities for a Senior Fellowship, which made possible the writing of this book, and to the Research Council of the University of Missouri, Columbia, which provided support for typing and research expenses. In the course of my research I have incurred numerous debts, and I especially want to thank George Perros, Charles South, John Macoll, James Brown, and William Fraley of the National Archives; Paul G. Sifton of the Library of Congress; and Wilcomb Washburn and Herbert Collins of the Smithsonian Institution. My colleague Thomas B. Alexander of the University of Missouri has provided invaluable assistance in matters relating to the use of quantitative methods and statistical data, and Ross Cameron of the National Archives, while a Research Assistant in the Department of History, University of Missouri, directed the preparation of computer data and made all the computer runs. I am greatly indebted to him for his knowledgeable and efficient assistance. I am also indebted to Julian P. Boyd, of Princeton University, Editor of *The Papers of Thomas Jefferson*, for his careful reading of the manuscript. I have profited immensely from his incisive comments and helpful suggestions and am grateful for his generous willingness to share his expert knowledge. I, of course, accept full responsibility for the defects that remain. Finally, I wish to thank my wife, Dana, for her helpfulness during extended periods of research and writing that must have seemed much longer to her than to me.

University of Missouri　　　　　　Noble E. Cunningham, Jr.
Columbia

THE PROCESS OF GOVERNMENT UNDER JEFFERSON

I. A New Administration

INAUGURATION DAY WAS ONLY TWO WEEKS AWAY when on February 17, 1801, the House of Representatives, after nearly a week of balloting, elected Thomas Jefferson the third President of the United States. Not until then did Jefferson know that he would take office on March 4. Although the Republican victory in the presidential election of 1800 had been known since December, the tie between the two Republican candidates, Jefferson and Aaron Burr, had forced the election into the House of Representatives, where balloting had not begun until February 11. The Federalists in the House did not have the votes to elect Burr without Republican aid, but they had the strength to deny Jefferson the required majority. The possibility existed that the House might be deadlocked when John Adams's term expired and the nation faced with a constitutional impasse disastrous to the young republic. Thirty-six ballots were required to defeat Federalist efforts to block the election of Jefferson, and not until February 17 did Jefferson obtain the majority of the states necessary for election. As President-elect, then, Jefferson had but fourteen days to organize his administration before taking the oath of office on March 4, 1801.

Jefferson had begun to plan for his presidency during the weeks of uncertainty, but he could make no definite arrangements, and the constitutional crisis facing the nation required his first attention. As long as the outcome of the election remained in doubt, he was extremely cautious about making any commitments. In December, when for a few days he was under the impression that one vote had been withheld from Burr in South Carolina[1] and that he had been elected, Jefferson had asked a friend traveling to New York to carry a confidential letter to Robert R. Livingston offering him the post of Secretary of the Navy.[2] Livingston declined; and,

---

[1] This was reported to Jefferson by Peter Freneau, Dec. 2, 1800, in a letter which Jefferson received Dec. 12. Thomas Jefferson Papers, Library of Congress. See also Jefferson to Thomas M. Randolph, Jr., Dec. 12, 1800, *Jefferson Papers*, Massachusetts Historical Society, *Collections*, 7th Ser., I (1900), 80.

[2] Jefferson to Livingston, Dec. 14, 1800, Paul L. Ford, ed., *The Writings of Thomas Jefferson*, 10 vols. (New York, 1892-1899), VII, 463-466.

after Jefferson learned of the tie with Burr in the electoral vote, he did not again tender any appointments until the outcome of the election in the House of Representatives was known.

The letters that passed between Jefferson and James Madison during these weeks reveal that an understanding had been reached that Madison would join the new administration as Secretary of State should the election terminate, as they hoped, with Jefferson's success. In one letter, Madison indicated that he had made a commitment to join the new administration in a previous conversation with Jefferson.[3] As early as December 19, by which time Jefferson knew of the tie vote with Burr, Jefferson was urging Madison to be present in Washington a day or two before March 4, when the new administration was expected to take over.[4] But except for the special confidence he shared with Madison, Jefferson kept his plans to himself. While the newspapers speculated upon Cabinet appointments, Jefferson was careful to make no premature moves. Noting that the newspapers had named him Secretary of the Treasury, Albert Gallatin, the Republican floor leader in the House of Representatives, assured his wife at the end of January that he had "received no hint of that kind from Mr. J[efferson]. Indeed, I do not suppose it would be proper in him to say anything on the subject of appointments until he knows whether he shall be elected."[5]

Once the House of Representatives decided the election, Jefferson moved immediately to form his Cabinet. The next day, the President-elect revealed his choices for Cabinet posts to Gallatin. As expected, he offered Gallatin (the leading fiscal expert in Republican ranks) the position of Secretary of the Treasury.[6] On the same day, Jefferson wrote to Madison acceding to Madison's view that it would be improper to arrive in the capital prior to the inauguration but urging him to "come within a day or two after."[7] This letter further confirms that a previous understanding had been made with Madison that he was to be Secretary of State. On the same day, Jefferson wrote to General Henry Dearborn of Massachusetts: "On a review of the different characters in the different states proper for the different departments, I have had no hesitation

[3] Madison to Jefferson, Jan. 10, 1801, Gaillard Hunt, ed., *The Writings of James Madison*, 9 vols. (New York, 1900-1910), VI, 415.

[4] Jefferson to Madison, Dec. 19, 1800, Jefferson Papers, Lib. Cong.

[5] Gallatin to his wife, Jan. 29, 1801, Henry Adams, *The Life of Albert Gallatin* (Philadelphia, 1879), pp. 258-259.

[6] Gallatin to his wife, Feb. 19, 1801, *ibid.*, p. 263.

[7] Jefferson to Madison, Feb. 18, 1801, Jefferson Papers, Lib. Cong.

in considering you as the person to whom it would be most advantageous to the public to confide the Department of war. May I therefore hope Sir, that you will give the country the aid of your talents as Secretary of War?"[8]

Jefferson's hint to Dearborn of a concern for geographical representation in his Cabinet would have been easily recognized by the New Englander, who could appreciate Jefferson's hope of winning support in the area of weakest Republican strength. With the top post in the Cabinet reserved for a fellow Virginian, it was particularly important to fill the other Cabinet positions with persons outside the South. Another New Englander, Levi Lincoln of Massachusetts, was offered the post of Attorney General, a position that had Cabinet rank, though there was no department under his direction. The secretaryship of the Navy, which Livingston had refused, was now tendered to Samuel Smith, a Republican congressman from Maryland and a prominent Baltimore merchant. "You will bring us the benefit of adding in a considerable degree the acquiescence at least of the leaders who have hitherto opposed," Jefferson wrote in trying to convince the reluctant Smith to accept the post. "Your geographical situation too is peculiarly advantageous, and will favor the policy of drawing our naval resources toward the states from which their benefits and production may be extended equally to all parts."[9] Despite strong pressure from Jefferson, Smith persisted in declining the appointment.

Jefferson's prospective nominations for Cabinet appointments appear to have been widely known in the capital before the end of February 1801. William Barry Grove, a Federalist representative from North Carolina, listed on February 27 "the persons spoken of by friends of the *new order* of things to aid and conduct our nation through the new voyage over 'the tempestuous sea of liberty,' " naming all the men to whom Jefferson had offered Cabinet posts.[10]

The President-elect wrote to Army Lieutenant Meriwether Lewis, asking him to become his private secretary. "In selecting one I have thought it important to respect not only his capacity to aid in the private concerns of the household," he wrote to Lewis, "but also to contribute to the mass of information which it is interesting for the administration to acquire. Your kno[w]le[d]ge of the Western country, of the army and of all it's interests and relations

8 Jefferson to Dearborn, Feb. 18, 1801, *ibid.*

9 Jefferson to Smith, Mar. 9, 1801, Ford, ed., *Jefferson Writings*, VIII, 13.

10 Grove to Walter Alves, Feb. 27, 1801, Walter Alves Papers, University of North Carolina.

has rendered it desireable for public as well as private purposes that you should be engaged in that office." While the salary (which came entirely out of Jefferson's own pocket) was only five hundred dollars a year, Lewis would have no expenses of board and lodging "as you would be one of my family," Jefferson assured him, pointing out that the post would "make you know and be known to characters of influence in the affairs of our country."[11] From Pittsburgh, Lewis promptly accepted Jefferson's offer, but it was March 20 before Jefferson received the letter of acceptance.[12] Meanwhile, Jefferson requested that the chief clerk of the State Department be directed to attend him at his lodgings immediately after the inauguration to deliver a message or messages to the Senate.[13] Jefferson made one other appointment before taking office, asking Robert R. Livingston to become minister to France;[14] the New York chancellor, having declined to head the Navy Department, agreed to the French mission.

As soon as the outcome of the election in the House became known, a number of Republican leaders wrote to the President-elect giving their opinions in regard to policies that the new administration should follow and reporting their assessments of public opinion in their respective states or regions. While most of these letters did not reach Jefferson until after his inauguration, they quickly initiated the new President to the pressures that his followers would place upon him. They also reflected the accessibility that had characterized Jefferson's party leadership before his election to the presidency—an accessibility that his assumption of office would not alter.[15] Jefferson was also early introduced to the pressures that could be expected from members of Congress, especially from his Republican supporters. The senators from Tennessee addressed a joint letter to the President-elect on February 26, calling his attention to the fact that Congress had appropriated funds for the President to negotiate a treaty with the Indians south of the Ohio River and reporting that President Adams had never taken steps to carry out the law. They followed with a second letter on March 5, stress-

[11] Jefferson to Lewis, Feb. 23, 1801, Jefferson Papers, Lib. Cong.
[12] Lewis to Jefferson, Mar. 10, 1801, endorsed by Jefferson as received Mar. 20, *ibid.*
[13] Jefferson to John Marshall, Mar. 2, 1801, *ibid.*
[14] Jefferson to Livingston, Feb. 24, 1801, *ibid.*
[15] Examples of such letters include: Pierce Butler to Jefferson, Feb. 26, 1801; John Beckley to Jefferson, Feb. 27, 1801; George Logan to Jefferson, Feb. 27, 1801, *ibid.*

ing the importance of the matter to Tennessee and outlining the position that they thought should be taken by the government in negotiating a treaty.[16] Similar letters began to arrive from other members.[17]

There was some contact between the President-elect and the Adams administration during the transitional period, but it was very limited. On February 25 Secretary of the Navy Benjamin Stoddert "by direction of the President" sent to the President-elect a letter from the Philadelphia Chamber of Commerce (on the subject of British privateers) together with a copy of his reply. On the day before Jefferson took office, Stoddert sent him some additional papers "by permission of the President," including letters just received from the West Indies and a copy of instructions to naval commanders.[18] Jefferson also conferred personally with Samuel Dexter, Adams's Secretary of the Treasury, about staying on until Gallatin could take over that office.[19] The contacts between Jefferson and Adams were few. Jefferson dined with Adams in January, and before Mrs. Adams's departure from the capital in early February, he paid her a farewell visit during which they discussed some details of household management.[20] After Jefferson's election by the House of Representatives, the only contact appears to have been a brief note written by Adams three days after the House decision, informing the incoming President that he would leave seven horses and two carriages with harness, all government property, in the stables of the United States.[21] Soon thereafter Congress discovered that Adams had purchased the horses and carriages out of an appropriation for furnishings and ordered them sold.[22]

Many Republicans felt that President Adams was trying to make the transition as difficult as possible. "Instead of smoothing the

[16] James Anderson and William Cocke to Jefferson, Feb. 26 and Mar. 5, 1801, *ibid*. The letter of Feb. 26 was addressed to "The President-Elect."

[17] See Abraham Baldwin (senator from Georgia) and Benjamin Taliaferro (representative from Georgia) to Jefferson, Mar. 5, 1801, *ibid*.

[18] Stoddert to Jefferson, Feb. 25, 1801, *ibid*.; Stoddert to Jefferson, Mar. 3, 1801, Letters of the Secretary of the Navy to the President, RG 45, National Archives.

[19] Jefferson to Dexter, Feb. 20, 1801, Jefferson Papers, Lib. Cong.

[20] Abigail Adams to Thomas B. Adams, Jan. 3 and Feb. 3, 1801, Adams Papers, Mass. Hist. Soc., microfilm edition, reel 400.

[21] Adams to Jefferson, Feb. 20, 1801, Lester J. Cappon, ed., *The Adams-Jefferson Letters*, 2 vols. (Chapel Hill, N. C., 1959), I, 263.

[22] See Dumas Malone, *Jefferson the President: First Term, 1801-1805* (Boston, 1970), p. 41.

path for his successor," Madison complained, "he plays into the hands of those who are endeavoring to strew it with as many difficulties as possible."[23] The main thing that Adams seemed to be doing was filling vacant offices with Federalists. "More nominations, both military and civil, have been made by the President and confirmed by the Senate, within the last month, than for a year past," protested one Republican congressman at the end of February. "This is merely intended, either with a view to clog the new President with men in whom he has no confidence, and who may take every opportunity to thwart his plans; or with a view to compel him to remove a great number from their places, with a hope of exciting a clamor which may promote the reinstatement of their party in power."[24] Many of the new appointments were made under the judiciary act of February 13, 1801, which provided places for many Federalists in posts not subject to removal by the President. Jefferson himself later protested Adams's "indecent conduct, in crowding nominations after he knew they were not for himself, till 9 o'clock of the night, at 12 o'clock of which he was to go out of office."[25]

During this period, the President-elect also devoted much time to preparing his inaugural address. He made numerous changes in the draft of his speech,[26] wrote a revised copy in which he made further changes,[27] and then prepared a copy from which to read. In this reading copy, he placed separate ideas and key phrases on different lines, varied the numerous indentations from the margin, and used extensive abbreviations. By writing on both sides of the paper, he was able to get the carefully transcribed script on two sheets of paper.[28] Early on the morning of his inau-

[23] Madison to Jefferson, Feb. 28, 1801, Hunt, ed., *Madison Writings*, VI, 417.

[24] Joseph Eggleston to Joseph Jones, Feb. 26, 1801, Joseph Jones Papers, Duke University.

[25] Jefferson to Benjamin Rush, Mar. 24, 1801, Ford, ed., *Jefferson Writings*, VIII, 32.

[26] The earliest known draft, one large sheet of paper written on both sides with numerous interlineations, is in the Jefferson Papers, Lib. Cong., v. 110 with a stamped foliation number 18838.

[27] This copy, consisting of two sheets written on both sides and a small sheet containing ten lines of clean copy cut to fit over a section of revised text on the verso of sheet one, is in the Jefferson Papers, Lib. Cong., v. 110, but has no stamped foliation number.

[28] This copy is on permanent exhibition at the Library of Congress, having been removed from v. 110 of the Jefferson Papers. It bears the stamped foliation numbers 18836 and 18837. This is the copy from which Ford

gural, Jefferson sent a copy of his address to Samuel Harrison Smith, editor of the *National Intelligencer*, who printed it in the issue of March 4, 1801, and had copies ready for distribution immediately after the inaugural ceremonies.[29] "So great was the demand for this address," Smith reported, "and so considerable the number of citizens surrounding the office in expectation of its appearing that the Press could scarcely keep pace with it."[30] Smith also printed the speech in the *Universal Gazette*, the weekly edition of the *National Intelligencer*.[31] All evidence indicates that the copy which Jefferson sent to Smith for publication in his papers was the revised draft from which Jefferson made his reading copy. There are thus two drafts of his inaugural which Jefferson considered as final—the revised draft he sent to Smith for printing, and the copy he used in delivering his address. There are no important differences between the two manuscripts, although there are sufficient minor variations to establish that the contemporaneously printed versions were not printed from the reading copy but from the revised draft. The text printed in the *Senate Journal* was also that of the revised draft rather than the reading copy.[32]

Jefferson himself handled the few necessary arrangements required for his inauguration. On March 2, in separate notes to the President pro tempore of the Senate and the Speaker of the House, he notified the legislature that he would take the oath of office on March 4 at twelve o'clock in the Senate chamber.[33] He sent another note to Chief Justice John Marshall informing him of these arrangements and requesting him to administer the oath. He also suggested that Marshall try to be on time.[34] Upon receipt of Jeffer-

---

printed the text in his edition of *Jefferson Writings*, VIII, 1-6. Ford described the document as the first draft, but textual analysis demonstrates clearly that it is not the earliest known draft.

[29] Mrs. Samuel Harrison Smith to Susan B. Smith, Mar. 4, 1801, Gaillard Hunt, ed., *The First Forty Years of Washington Society, Portrayed by the Family Letters of Mrs. Samuel Harrison Smith* (New York, 1906), p. 26; *National Intelligencer* (Washington, D. C.), Mar. 4, 1801.

[30] *Universal Gazette* (Washington, D. C.), Mar. 12, 1801.

[31] *Ibid.*, Mar. 4, 1801.

[32] *Journal of the Senate of the United States of America, 1st Congress-13th Congress*, 5 vols. (Washington, D. C., 1820-1821), III, 148-150; *Journal of the Executive Proceedings of the Senate of the United States: From the Commencement of the First to the Termination of the Nineteenth Congress*, 3 vols. (Washington, D. C., 1828), I, 392-395.

[33] Jefferson to President pro tempore of Senate, Mar. 2, 1801; Jefferson to Speaker of the House, Mar. 2, 1801, Jefferson Papers, Lib. Cong.

[34] Jefferson to Marshall, Mar. 2, 1801, *ibid.*

son's letter of March 2, the Senate ordered that "seats be provided for such members of the House of Representatives and such of the public Ministers, as may think proper to attend; and that the Gallery be opened to the Citizens of the United States."[35] The Chief Justice also promptly acceded to the request of the President-elect and promised to "make a point of being punctual."[36]

The ceremony on March 4, the first inaugural in the new capital on the Potomac, was unpretentious, although touches of pageantry unplanned by Jefferson were added by others. The President-elect walked to the Capitol from his nearby lodgings at Conrad and McMunn's. "His dress," noted one reporter, "was, as usual, that of a plain citizen, without any distinctive badge of office."[37] Preceded by a detachment of Alexandria militia officers with drawn swords and the marshal and deputy marshals of the District, Jefferson was followed by an escort of members of the House of Representatives. Upon his arrival at the Capitol, the Alexandria rifle company stationed at the door opened ranks and saluted the President-elect as he passed.[38] As Jefferson entered the crowded Senate chamber, members rose, while Vice-President Burr, who had been sworn in earlier in the morning by the President pro tempore of the Senate,[39] relinquished the chair of the Senate to him. With the Vice-President taking a seat on the right and the Chief Justice on the left, Jefferson seated himself and paused briefly before rising to speak. Not present at the ceremonies was former President John Adams, who had left Washington at four o'clock that morning.[40] After delivering his address in tones inaudible to many in the chamber, Jefferson moved to the clerk's table where Chief Justice Marshall administered the oath of office. Immediately thereafter the Alexandria artillery company, which had transported two field pieces to Capitol Hill, fired a salute of sixteen rounds.[41]

Despite Jefferson's effort to keep the ceremony simple, an aura of excitement filled the capital. Some observers noted the high significance of the occasion, among them Mrs. Samuel Harrison Smith, who wrote: "I have this morning witnessed one of the most

[35] Copy of Senate resolution, Mar. 2, 1801, *ibid.*

[36] Marshall to Jefferson, Mar. 2, 1801, *ibid.*

[37] *Examiner* (Richmond), Mar. 13, 1801.

[38] *Times* (Alexandria), Mar. 6, 1801.

[39] *Senate Executive Journal*, i, 392.

[40] Thomas Claxton to Jefferson, Mar. 4, 1801, Jefferson Papers, Coolidge Collection, Mass. Hist. Soc., microfilm edition.

[41] *Examiner* (Richmond), Mar. 13, 1801; *Times* (Alexandria), Mar. 6, 1801.

interesting scenes, a free people can ever witness. The changes of administration, which in every government and in every age have most generally been epochs of confusion, villainy and bloodshed, in this our happy country take place without any species of distraction, or disorder."[42] What Mrs. Smith had witnessed was both a significant scene and a new experience for the young nation: the first transfer of political power in the national government from one party to another. That this transfer was accomplished in an orderly and peaceful manner was a measure of the maturity of the republic's political and party systems. "So complete a *bouleversement* rarely happens in any country," noted another thoughtful observer, "but could happen quietly in no other than this."[43]

Four years earlier, the transfer of power from Washington to Adams had been a succession, and Adams, as if to emphasize the continuity of his administration with that of his predecessor, had retained all of Washington's Cabinet. The formation of a new Cabinet when Jefferson took office thus brought the first complete change in the executive branch since the Constitution had gone into operation. And not only was a new administration in office, but a new party also was in power. The party changeover in the executive was accompanied by a like change in the legislature, where Republican majorities in the House of Representatives and the Senate replaced the Federalist majorities that had controlled both houses of Congress throughout the four years of Adams's presidency. The transfer of power in the national government in 1801 was thus complete.

With his fifty-eighth birthday only a few weeks away when he took office, Jefferson brought to the presidency a background of years of government service that was extremely varied. In his early public career, he had served extensively as a legislator—altogether some twelve years in the Virginia General Assembly and the Continental Congress—experience that would serve him well as President in working with Congress. Jefferson's executive experience had been less extensive, but no less important. He had served as Governor of Virginia for two consecutive one-year terms during the latter years of the Revolution. Although the powers of the Governor of Virginia and those of the President were vastly different, Jef-

[42] Mrs. Smith to Susan B. Smith, Mar. 4, 1801, Hunt, ed., *First Forty Years of Washington Society*, p. 25.

[43] George Tucker to St. George Tucker, Feb. 24, 1801, Tucker-Coleman Collection, College of William and Mary.

ferson had provided effective leadership in meeting the formidable tasks of administration under wartime conditions, and he had displayed many of the administrative abilities that would later characterize his presidency.[44] In the postwar years, Jefferson's five years of service as minister to France immediately preceded his four-year tenure as Secretary of State and together provided extraordinary preparation for the responsibilities of the presidency in the conduct of foreign affairs. The four years in Washington's Cabinet had given Jefferson immensely useful administrative experience that he frequently drew upon as President. Jefferson's most recent experience prior to the presidency had been as Vice-President under Adams. As the head of the Republican opposition and a rival for the presidency, Jefferson was never a part of Adams's administration, but he had been in a position to watch at close range the process of government; and upon becoming President he sought to avoid what he regarded as the failures of Adams as an executive. As Vice-President, Jefferson's duties were entirely legislative; as presiding officer of the Senate, he immersed himself in the procedures of the legislative process, preparing the *Manual of Parliamentary Practice* that became the authority for the Congress.

For the political demands of the presidential office, Jefferson had the advantage of being the recognized and undisputed head of the Republican party. While that party was neither his creation nor his engine, he had inspired and mobilized it against the Federalist regime under Adams and had led the Republicans to victory in 1800. More than anyone else, he spoke for the party. Jefferson was to become the first President to accept the responsibility of being both the head of the nation and the leader of his party.

By inauguration day, Jefferson had received acceptances of all of the Cabinet posts except that of Secretary of the Navy, and on March 5 he submitted the following nominations to the Senate: Madison as Secretary of State, Dearborn as Secretary of War, Lincoln as Attorney General, and Livingston as minister to France.[45] Jefferson did not send the nomination of Gallatin as Secretary of the Treasury for fear that it might be rejected by the Senate that assembled on March 4 in special session. With three of the newly

[44] The charge of ineffectiveness as Governor of Virginia is not supported by the record. See Julian P. Boyd, ed., *The Papers of Thomas Jefferson*, 19 vols. to date (Princeton, 1950-), Vols. II-VI.

[45] *Senate Executive Journal*, I, 395.

elected Republican senators unable to attend and an expected Republican senator from Maryland not yet named, the Federalists still controlled the Senate and manifested great hostility to Jefferson's choice for the Treasury post. Gallatin, who recognized himself as "the most obnoxious to the other party" of any of Jefferson's proposed appointments, believed that President Adams had improperly summoned the special session of the Senate to thwart Jefferson's nominations;[46] but Adams was only following the precedent of Washington, who had called a similar session of the Senate to meet on the day of Adams's inauguration. Rather than risk rejection of Gallatin's name by the Senate, Jefferson decided to delay his appointment until after the Senate adjourned, thus postponing confirmation until the regular meeting of the Senate in December, when Republicans would be in control. Meanwhile, Samuel Dexter, Adams's last Secretary of the Treasury, agreed to stay on until Gallatin could take over the office.[47]

By the time he took office, Jefferson had received three refusals of the post of Secretary of the Navy. In declining that office, Livingston had been the only one of Jefferson's first choices for Cabinet places not to accept appointment. Jefferson next had been turned down by Samuel Smith. After Smith's rejection, he offered the position to John Langdon of New Hampshire, who also declined. Jefferson then pressed Smith to reconsider; when he again declined, an offer was made to William Jones of Philadelphia. After Jones refused, Smith agreed to take charge of the office temporarily, though he never accepted any official commission or compensation that might force him to vacate his seat in the House of Representatives.[48] "I believe I shall have to advertise for a Secretary of the Navy," Jefferson quipped in early May,[49] but he was

[46] Gallatin to his wife, Feb. 19 and Mar. 5, 1801, Adams, *Gallatin*, pp. 263, 265.

[47] Jefferson to Dexter, Feb. 20, 1801, Jefferson Papers, Lib. Cong.; Gallatin to his wife, Mar. 5, 1801, Adams, *Gallatin*, p. 265.

[48] Jefferson to Madison, Mar. 12, 26, 1801; Jefferson to Samuel Smith, Mar. 9, 24, 1801, Ford, ed., *Jefferson Writings*, VIII, 13-14, 28, 34. Jefferson to Thomas Mann Randolph, Jr., Mar. 12, 1801; Samuel Smith to Jefferson, Mar. 17, 1801; William Jones to Jefferson, Mar. 23, 1801; Jefferson Papers, Lib. Cong. On Smith's refusal of the appointment as Secretary of the Navy, see Frank A. Cassell, *Merchant Congressman in the Young Republic: Samuel Smith of Maryland, 1752-1839* (Madison, Wisc., 1971), pp. 106-107.

[49] Jefferson to Gouverneur Morris, May 8, 1801, Ford ed., *Jefferson Writings*, VIII, 49.

masking his growing concern over finding a qualified Republican to accept the office. "The knowledge of naval matters in this country is confined entirely to persons who are under other absolutely disqualifying circumstances," he confessed.[50] Four months after taking office, Jefferson was still without a Secretary of the Navy, though he had made offers to four men and pressed it a second time upon three of them.[51] Finally, on July 9 he tendered the post to Robert Smith, a Baltimore lawyer with a large admiralty practice and the brother of Samuel Smith. At last the President received a prompt acceptance.[52]

In offering the Navy post to Smith, who obviously was aware that he was not the President's first choice, Jefferson explained that his "attention was naturally first drawn to those gentlemen whose line of life led them to an intimacy with shipbuilding and navigation."[53] In reply, Smith expressed regret that the President had "been constrained to turn your attention to a person whose education and habits have not sufficiently prepared him for the various duties of this office. Unqualified, however, as I may be at the beginning, I am disposed to accept the appointment under the persuasion that the requisite information may be acquired."[54] In Smith's modest reply may lie part of the explanation of the low esteem in which he has been held by many historians. But as Smith's administration of the Navy Department would demonstrate, he was a capable administrator, and that record rather than the fact that he was Jefferson's fifth choice for the Navy post deserves the greater emphasis.

With all of the posts filled, the Cabinet appeared to be well formed, and the President could not but have been satisfied with the training and experience they brought to their jobs. The average age of the members of his Cabinet in 1801 was forty-seven. The oldest member was Attorney General Lincoln, who at fifty-two was six years younger than the President. The youngest member

[50] Jefferson to Samuel Smith, Mar. 9, 1801, *ibid.*, p. 13.

[51] Jefferson to William Jones, May 16, 1801; Jones to Jefferson, May 20, 1801; Jefferson to Langdon, May 23, 1801; Langdon to Jefferson, June 10, 1801, Jefferson Papers, Lib. Cong.

[52] Jefferson to Robert Smith, July 9 and 15, 1801, Jefferson Papers, Lib. Cong.; Smith to Jefferson, July 13, 1801, Worthington C. Ford, ed., *Thomas Jefferson Correspondence: Printed from the Originals in the Collections of William K. Bixby* (Boston, 1916), pp. 87-88.

[53] Jefferson to Robert Smith, July 9, 1801, Jefferson Papers, Lib. Cong.

[54] Smith to Jefferson, July 13, 1801, W. C. Ford, ed., *Jefferson Correspondence: Bixby Collection*, p. 88.

was Secretary of the Treasury Gallatin, who had just turned forty. Both Secretary of State Madison and Secretary of War Dearborn were fifty; Secretary of the Navy Smith was forty-four. They were, in the main, the younger men of the Revolution. Only the Swiss-born Gallatin, who arrived in the United States in 1780, had not lived through the whole experience of the Revolution. Dearborn, Lincoln, and Smith had seen military service, Dearborn having served throughout the war, once captured and exchanged. They were a well-educated group, as might have been expected in a Cabinet named by Jefferson. Madison and Smith were graduates of the College of New Jersey (Princeton); Gallatin was a graduate of the University of Geneva and one-time instructor of French at Harvard; Lincoln was a Harvard graduate and a member of the bar. Only Dearborn was lacking in college education, though he was trained in medicine, which he had practiced before entering military service during the Revolution. Smith was a practicing lawyer in Baltimore when he joined the Cabinet.

Jefferson's Cabinet members were also men who had had much experience in government. Madison was the most experienced, with service in the Virginia assembly, the Continental Congress, the Federal Constitutional Convention, the Virginia ratifying convention, and the House of Representatives during the first four Congresses. Gallatin had been a member of the Pennsylvania state constitutional convention of 1789 and had been in the Pennsylvania house of representatives before serving three terms in Congress. Lincoln had been a delegate to the Massachusetts constitutional convention of 1779, served in both houses of the Massachusetts legislature, and was in Congress for one session before resigning his House seat (to which he had been reelected) to become Attorney General. Dearborn had been in the House of Representatives during the Third and Fourth Congresses. Smith had served in both houses of the Maryland legislature in the 1790s. What is most striking when the biographies of the members of Jefferson's administration are viewed collectively is that of all the men who served in the Cabinet, only Robert Smith had not previously been in Congress. Madison with four terms in the House, Gallatin with three, and Dearborn with two, represented considerable experience in a Congress that had been in existence for only twelve years. Madison, Gallatin, and Dearborn also had served together in one Congress—the Fourth Congress—and Lincoln and Gallatin served together during the last session of the Sixth Congress. Subsequent changes in the Cabinet would not reduce the level of political experience. Lincoln's successor as Attorney General, John Breckinridge, served in the Senate for four years prior to taking the Cabinet post, and Caesar A. Rodney, who succeeded Breckinridge, had been in the House of Representatives for one term. The generally smooth relationships between the officers in the Cabinet and the members of Congress owed much to this reservoir of legislative experience.

Jefferson's Cabinet also represented considerable experience in party politics and showed that he recognized his dual responsibility as head of the nation and leader of his party. Nearly all members of the new administration had been active in the Republican opposition during the Federalist-dominated 1790s. In the early Congresses, Madison had led the opposition to Hamilton that became the nucleus of the Republican party. Succeeding Madison as Republican leader, Gallatin had been the minority leader in the House throughout the four Federalist years under John Adams. He was in close contact with Republicans in Pennsylvania and in New York through his father-in-law, James Nicholson. Lincoln had been a leading party activist in the Republican assault on Federalism in Massachusettts. Dearborn had lost his seat in Congress because of his alignment with Madison and the Republicans in the House and had returned to Maine to build the nucleus of the Republican party in that distant district of Massachusetts.[55] Robert Smith was active in party affairs in Baltimore, and his brother Samuel Smith, Republican representative and later senator from Maryland, was the most influential Republican in that state. In terms of party politics, the chief weakness in the Cabinet was the absence of a New York Republican. New York representation in the government might have been provided by Vice-President Burr, but his alienation from the administration led to his exclusion from executive councils from the outset. By the time George Clinton, another New Yorker, replaced Burr as Vice-President, the Republican party was so divided in New York that no single Republican could represent the party in that state. Throughout Jefferson's presidency, the Vice-President's role was limited to that specified by the Constitution—to preside over the Senate.

With two New Englanders, one middle-state member, a Marylander, and a Virginian, the Cabinet had a good geographical distribution, providing the President with a wide range of access to

---

[55] Paul Goodman, *The Democratic-Republicans of Massachusetts: Politics in a Young Republic* (Cambridge, Mass., 1964), pp. 62, 119-121.

opinion throughout the country. The presence in the Cabinet of two members from the stronghold of Federalism in New England was politically shrewd, and, when the Postmaster General was chosen from Connecticut, critics who suspected the Republicans would favor the South were disarmed.

Only Madison and Gallatin were nationally known when appointed to the Cabinet; the other members were dismissed as unimportant and uninfluential by such contemporary observers as Edward Thornton, the British chargé d'affaires, who predicted that only Madison and Gallatin would have any influence outside their own departments.[56] With an outlook perhaps not unlike that of Thornton, Henry Adams later wrote that "neither Dearborn nor Lincoln was so strong, either in political or social connections or in force of character, as greatly to affect the course of the Cabinet."[57] But like the British chargé, Adams missed the point. Jefferson was not in London forming a British ministry. As advisers to the new Republican President of a diverse and extensive young nation, the Cabinet members were well chosen. Gallatin himself saw this. Assessing the strengths that the little-known New Englanders brought to the Cabinet, he noted: "General Dearborn is a man of strong sense, great practical information on all the subjects connected with his Department, and what is called a man of business. He is not, I believe, a scholar, but I think he will make the best Secretary of War we [have] as yet had. Mr. Lincoln is a good lawyer, a fine scholar, a man of great discretion and sound judgment, and of the mildest and most amiable manners." In summing up his evaluation of his two New England colleagues, Gallatin concluded: "Both are men of 1776, sound and decided Republicans; both are men of the strictest integrity; and both, but Mr. L[incoln] principally, have a great weight of character to the Eastward with both parties."[58] That Jefferson would make his strongest appointments to the most important posts was to be expected, and that the secretaries who headed the departments charged with the direction of foreign affairs and the management of the Treasury would be the most influential members of his administration was equally predictable. But this should not detract from the useful roles of

[56] Thornton to Hawkesbury, June 2, 1801, quoted in Malone, *Jefferson the President: First Term*, p. 57.

[57] Henry Adams, *History of the United States of America during the Administrations of Thomas Jefferson and James Madison*, 9 vols. (New York, 1889-1891), I, 220.

[58] Gallatin to Maria Nicholson, Mar. 12, 1801, Adams, *Gallatin*, p. 276.

other members of the Cabinet; under Jefferson all members of the Cabinet were to be active participants in the administration.

The last major appointment that Jefferson made to complete the new administration was that of Gideon Granger to the position of Postmaster General. Jefferson offered the post to the Connecticut Republican on October 14 and had his acceptance before the end of the month.[59] The office of Postmaster General did not carry Cabinet rank, but it was one of considerable responsibility and extensive patronage. The Republicans had long complained of the partisanship of Federalist postmasters, and Jefferson would have been under intense pressure to remove Joseph Habersham, who had been appointed Postmaster General by Washington in 1795, had not Habersham resigned. "On receiving a hint too plain to be misunderstood that my services were no longer wanted," Habersham grudgingly explained, "I resigned to save the administration from the odium of swelling the list of removals, and myself from the mortification of being one of the proscribed."[60] Jefferson was obviously pleased to have Granger's acceptance of the politically sensitive post.

After six months' experience in office, the President seemed confident that he was gathering around him a capable group of administrators. "My wish," he said, "is to collect in a mass around the administration all the abilities and the respectability to which the offices exercised here can give employ. To give none of them to secondary characters. Good principles, wisely and honestly administered cannot fail to attach our fellow citizens to the order of things which we espouse."[61]

Initially the President had trouble assembling the new administration. He had planned to get his administration under way promptly and have the departments organized before his spring visit to Monticello in April. He had urged Madison to be in Washington within a day or two after the inauguration;[62] and he had persuaded Gallatin, who had been in Washington as a member of Congress and who was anxious to get home to move his family to the capital, to stay until Madison arrived so that the general outlines and leading principles of the new administration might be

[59] Jefferson to Granger, Oct. 14, 1801; Granger to Jefferson, Oct. 25, 1801, Jefferson Papers, Lib. Cong.

[60] Habersham to Abraham Baldwin, Mar. 15, 1802, Abraham Baldwin Papers, University of Georgia.

[61] Jefferson to Granger, Oct. 31, 1801, Jefferson Papers, Lib. Cong.

[62] Jefferson to Madison, Feb. 18, 1801, *ibid*.

agreed upon.[63] But five days before the inauguration, Madison's father died, making his early departure for the capital impossible.[64] When this news reached the President, he abandoned his plans for an early organization of the Cabinet. Since Gallatin's appointment to the Treasury had not been submitted to the Senate on March 5 and Dexter was temporarily staying on at that post, Gallatin delayed taking over the department until he could move his family to Washington; this move was not completed until May 13.[65] Without Madison and Gallatin in the two principal departments and with the Navy post unfilled, the President found his first weeks in office a trying experience. "Harrassed with interruptions and worn down with fatigue, I take up my pen at midnight to scribble you a line," the exhausted President wrote to a son-in-law on his third day in office.[66] A week later he was "still at a great loss, Mr. Madison not having been able to come on as yet, Mr. Gallatin not agreeing to join us till my return, and not knowing as yet where to get a Secretary of the Navy."[67]

Meanwhile, Attorney General Lincoln, who had been a member of Congress and was in Washington on March 4, and Secretary of War Dearborn, who had taken over his department immediately after his confirmation by the Senate on March 5, composed the President's Cabinet; and in Madison's absence Lincoln took over the duties of Secretary of State.[68] By the third week in March, with no appointment having been made to the Navy post, Benjamin Stoddert, who had stayed on temporarily, had become impatient to leave. Arguing that everything in the Navy was at a standstill awaiting a new secretary and that ships arriving in port were remaining there with men on board for want of orders, he urged the President to turn the department over to Lincoln or Dearborn in order that "either of these Gentlemen communicating freely with the President and understanding his System, might commence its execution."[69] Soon thereafter Jefferson persuaded Samuel Smith to take over the administration of the Navy Department

---

[63] Gallatin to his wife, Mar. 5, 1801, Adams, *Gallatin*, p. 265.

[64] James Madison, Sr., died Feb. 27, 1801. Irving Brant, *James Madison: Secretary of State, 1800-1809* (Indianapolis, 1953), p. 37.

[65] See Raymond Walters, Jr., *Albert Gallatin: Jeffersonian Financier and Diplomat* (New York, 1957), p. 143.

[66] Jefferson to T. M. Randolph, Jr., Mar. 6, 1801, Jefferson Papers, Lib. Cong.

[67] Jefferson to T. M. Randolph, Jr., Mar. 12, 1801, *ibid.*

[68] See Jefferson to Madison, Mar. 26, 1801, *ibid.*

[69] Benjamin Stoddert [memorandum on conversation with Levi Lincoln], endorsed by Jefferson: Stoddert to L. Lincoln, Mar. 21, 1801, *ibid.*

unofficially and temporarily, and he transferred the official responsibility of the office to Secretary of War Dearborn.[70] With
these temporary arrangements made, the President, who had been
in Washington since Congress had convened in November 1800,
returned to Monticello for his annual spring visit and postponed the organization of his administration until May, when it
was expected that Madison and Gallatin would join Lincoln and
Dearborn in the Cabinet. It was not until May 14 that the President was able to write: "Mr. Gallatin's arrival yesterday, renders
the organisation of our new administration compleat, and enables
us to settle our system of proceeding."[71] Even then the Navy office
was not yet permanently filled.

Despite the difficulties in getting the new Cabinet together, Jefferson had moved ahead with the stock-taking that new management required. Just before Jefferson took office, Madison suggested
to him that one of the first steps of the new administration should
be "to institute returns, particularly in the Navy and war departments, of the precise state in which every circumstance involved
in them, comes into the new hands. This will answer the double
purpose of enabling the public to do justice both to the authors of
past errors and abuses and the authors of future reforms."[72] Jefferson followed Madison's suggestion and expanded it to include
all departments, from each of which he sought information on the
state of the department and its operations. Secretary of War Dearborn had the return of the Army ready for the President by March
30.[73] By early May he also presented a report on the state of military fortifications, public buildings, military stores, the quartermaster department, the manufacture of cannon, military bounty
lands, the general state of the Army, and Indian affairs (also under the jurisdiction of the War Department).[74] This report was not
a full statistical summary, but rather a digested status report on
the state of operations in each of these areas and a summary of what
was currently being done. Jefferson received a similar report from
the Navy Department. Although Samuel Smith was temporarily
administering that department, he provided the President on May

[70] Jefferson to Dearborn, Mar. 31, 1801, *ibid.*

[71] Jefferson to T. M. Randolph, Jr., May 14, 1801, *ibid.*

[72] Madison to Jefferson, Feb. 28, 1801, Hunt, ed., *Madison Writings*,
vi, 418.

[73] "A Return of the Army of the United States, shewing the strength of
each Regiment and Corps . . . March 30, 1801," MSS, Jefferson Papers,
Lib. Cong.

[74] Dearborn to Jefferson, received May 12, 1801, *ibid.*

4 with a report on all of the ships in the Navy as of March 4, 1801, indicating those retained under the law providing for the naval establishment and those the President was authorized to sell, together with a detailed account of the planned and recommended disposition of each ship.[75]

Even before taking over the Treasury Department, Gallatin was supplying the President with information. Ten days after the inauguration, he sent Jefferson some rough sketches on the financial situation, including an estimate of receipts and expenditures for 1801 and an estimate of reductions in the naval and military establishments required to repeal all internal taxes.[76] Some of the memoranda that Jefferson received from department heads in his information-gathering quest were not unlike the papers of task forces appointed by more recent Presidents or Presidents-elect. Perhaps the best example is the report prepared by Gallatin on the operation of the internal revenue system, submitted to the President on July 28. Gallatin described in detail the division of the country into sixteen districts for collecting internal revenues, each district being headed by a supervisor. In turn, the districts were divided into surveys headed by an inspector. Under the inspectors were the collectors of revenue appointed by the supervisor of the district; the collectors were in charge of divisions consisting of one or more towns, townships, or counties. As Gallatin described the operation of the system, the flaw in it was that inspectors did not submit their accounts for any quarter until all of the collectors under them had reported, and the supervisors did not settle their accounts with the Treasury until all inspectors had reported. Gallatin went on to explain:

No correspondence exists between the Collectors and the Supervisors, none between either the Collectors or Inspectors and the Treasury. The Secretary has not yet been able to procure even the dates to which the last accounts of the Inspectors and Collectors have been rendered to the Supervisors for settlement. Whenever the accounts of a Supervisor are not rendered in time, he may always charge the delay to one of the Inspectors. The delinquency of a single Collector stops the settlement of accounts of a whole state without its being possible for this Department to trace the evil to its source. And although the Supervisors, having the exclusive power of appointing and re-

75 Smith to Jefferson, May 4, 1801, *ibid.*
76 Gallatin to Jefferson, Mar. 14, 1801, with enclosures, *ibid.*

moving Collectors, may be supposed to be responsible for their conduct, this responsibility is almost altogether annihilated by the intermediate class of Inspectors who stand between them and the Collectors and have immediate superintendance of that inferior class of officers.[77]

The above procedural details have been cited because Gallatin's memorandum is revealing in several important aspects. It illustrates the type of examination to which the new Republican administrators subjected the existing administrative machinery and the type of information that the President received from his department heads. It also suggests that the much vaunted Federalist administrative machinery had serious defects, that the new Republican administrators had more to do than simply take over a smoothly operating administrative structure, and that Republicans were more concerned with the improvement of administrative mechanisms than was admitted by their detractors who complained of visionary and impractical Republicans.

Much of the attention of the new Republican administration in these early months of fact-finding and internal reforms centered on finances and ways to reduce government expenses. "The summer will be pretty closely employed in procuring the information necessary to enable Congress to reduce the Government to a reasonable scale of expence," Jefferson wrote to his son-in-law Thomas Mann Randolph, Jr., in June 1801. "We are hunting out and abolishing multitudes of useless offices, striking off jobs, etc., etc. Never were such scenes of favoritism, dissipation of treasure, and disregard of legal appropriation seen. Provided they did not spend more than all the appropriations amounted to, they overspent some and neglected others without regard to the legislative will."[78] About the same time, Jefferson was explaining to James Monroe that "the expences of this government were chiefly in jobs not seen; agencies upon agencies in every part of the earth, and for the most useless or mischievous purposes, and all of these opening doors for fraud and embezzlement far beyond the ostensible profits of the agency. These are things of the existence of which no man dreamt, and we are lopping them down silently to make as little noise as possible. They have been covered from the public under the head of contingencies, quartermaster's department, etc."[79] Finding con-

---

[77] Gallatin to Jefferson, July 28, 1801, *ibid.*

[78] Jefferson to T. M. Randolph, Jr., June 18, 1801, *ibid.*

[79] Jefferson to Monroe, June 20, 1801, James Monroe Papers, Lib. Cong., microfilm edition.

siderable laxity in the operation of the administrative machinery left by the Federalists, the President and his department heads, especially the Secretary of the Treasury, took vigorous steps to bring accounts up to date, tighten procedures, and institute reforms.[80]

After the special session of the Senate adjourned on March 5, 1801, Congress was not again in session until the first week of December. The new administration thus had eight months to organize the executive branch and establish control over the administrative agencies of government without legislative pressures. During these first months in office, the administration also had to deal with the pressing problems of appointments and removals. Finally, the administration had to make preparations for the meeting of Congress.

After spending "the bilious months" of August and September at Monticello, as he regularly did,[81] and encouraging his department heads likewise to find refuge from Washington's late summer heat, Jefferson reassembled his administration to prepare for the meeting of Congress. The most important item of business was the preparation of the President's annual message to Congress.[82] In addition, an estimate of expenditures for the following year had to be worked out, and department heads had various reports to prepare for submission to the new Congress. The heaviest workload fell on the Secretary of the Treasury, who by early December had retreated to his home to finish his statements and reports without the interruptions at his office.[83] Much effort went into the preparation of the reports to Congress, and a certain amount of last-minute pressure was evident in the correspondence that passed between the President and his department heads as the deadline approached. Gallatin not only had to work at home but on Sundays as well to get his reports completed.[84]

One of the large projects undertaken by the new administration was a new roll of governmental officers, both civil and military—

[80] See pp. 117-118 below. In a move to keep a closer watch over departmental expenditures, Jefferson in the summer of 1801 instituted the practice of having each department head submit to him weekly a list of warrants issued by his department. Jefferson to Gallatin, Aug. 7, 1801; John Newman to Meriwether Lewis, Aug. 10, 1801, Jefferson Papers, Lib. Cong.

[81] See pp. 45-46 below.

[82] This subject is examined in detail in Chap. v below.

[83] Gallatin to Jefferson, Dec. 7, 1801, Jefferson Papers, Lib. Cong.

[84] Gallatin to Jefferson, received Dec. 13, 1801, ibid.

the last list having been prepared by Alexander Hamilton in 1792.[85] Jefferson had hoped to have this ready for the opening of Congress, but it turned out to be so demanding an assignment that in his annual message he could only promise it at a later date,[86] which turned out to be in February 1802.[87] Gallatin, who prepared the general outlines for the list of officers to be filled in by the different departments, warned that "the whole when done will form a formidable list." "I had no idea," he said, "that it would be so complex and difficult completely to obtain."[88]

In sending Gallatin's plan to the other department heads, Jefferson admitted the difficulties but emphasized its importance. "To compleat the roll of governmental officers on the plan inclosed will give the departments some serious trouble," he wrote. "However it is so important to present to the eye of all the constituted authorities, as well as of their constituents, and to keep under their eye, the true extent of the machine of government, that I cannot but recommend to the heads of departments to endeavor to fill up each, their portion of the roll as compleatly as possible and as early too, that it may be presented to the legislature."[89] The new President wanted both for himself and for the public an accurate idea of the size and scope of "the machine of government," and he pushed to have the report completed. When presented to Congress, the bulky manuscript was ordered printed by the House, and the document printed by William Duane filled 166 octavo pages.[90] Jefferson admitted that the list was not so perfect as could have been wished,[91] but for the first time in a decade there was a civil

[85] Hamilton's list contained only civil officers. It is printed in *American State Papers: Documents, Legislative and Executive of the United States*, 38 vols. (Washington, D. C., 1832-1861), *Miscellaneous*, I, 57-68. Hereafter cited as *ASP*.

[86] *Journal of the House of Representatives of the United States*, 1st Congress-13th Congress, 9 vols. (Washington, D. C., 1826), Dec. 8, 1801, IV, 9.

[87] "Roll of the Officers, Civil, Military, and Naval of the United States," communicated to Congress, Feb. 17, 1802, by message of the President, Feb. 16, 1802, Senate Records, RG 46, Natl. Archives. This document is printed in *ASP, Misc.*, I, 260-319.

[88] Gallatin to Jefferson, Dec. 27, 1801, Jefferson Papers, Lib. Cong.

[89] Jefferson to the Secretary of State, Dec. 29, 1801, marked "circular," *ibid.*

[90] A. W. Greeley, ed., *Public Documents of the First Fourteen Congresses, 1789-1817* (Washington, D. C., 1900), p. 305.

[91] Jefferson, message to Senate and House of Representatives, Feb. 16, 1802, *ASP, Misc.*, I, 260.

list, a military roster, and a summary of offices and compensations. It was an orderly beginning for the new administration.

On December 8, 1801, Jefferson sent copies of his first annual message to the House of Representatives and the Senate accompanied by a letter stating:

> The circumstances under which we find ourselves placed rendering inconvenient the mode heretofore practiced of making by personal address the first communication between the legislative and executive branches, I have adopted that by message, as used on all subsequent occasions through the session. In doing this, I have had principal regard to the convenience of the legislature, to the economy of their time, to their relief from the embarrassment of immediate answers on subjects not yet fully before them, and to the benefits thence resulting to the public affairs.[92]

In sending a written message, Jefferson was thus departing from the precedent set by Washington and followed by Adams of delivering an address in person at the opening of each annual session of Congress. Jefferson is commonly given the credit, or the blame, for the innovation that set the precedent followed until the presidency of Woodrow Wilson, and it has sometimes been suggested that the real explanation for the change was to be found in Jefferson's poor public-speaking abilities.[93] There is evidence, however, that Jefferson was responding to the wishes of his followers, who had likened the annual presidential address and the formal answer from Congress to the monarchical habits of Great Britain. Writing to Jefferson in the opening weeks of his administration, Nathaniel Macon, a North Carolina Republican who had been a member of the House since 1791, offered the new President a list of suggested changes "that the people expect." Near the top of the list was the expectation "that the communication to the next Congress will be by letter not a speech."[94] In his reply to Macon in May 1801, Jefferson assured him that "the first communication to the next Congress will be, like all subsequent ones, by

[92] Jefferson to the President of the Senate, Dec. 8, 1801, Ford, ed., *Jefferson Writings*, VIII, 108; *House Journal*, IV, 7-8.

[93] "He said it was to save time, but we know he hated to speak in public," wrote Marshall Smelser in *The Democratic Republic, 1801-1815* (New York, 1968), p. 2.

[94] Macon to Jefferson, Apr. 20, 1801, Jefferson Papers, Lib. Cong.

message to which no answer will be expected."[95] It is reasonable to assume that Macon, who would be elected to the speakership of the House by the Republican majority in the first Congress that Jefferson was to address, spoke for a wide following of Republicans, and that Jefferson responded to their wishes for reasons that had no bearing on his speaking ability. If he emphasized the convenience of Congress in his letter announcing the change, it was no doubt his wish not to cast aspersions on the practices of his predecessors that any emphasis on the more republican character of the new practice would surely have suggested. In any event, the matter of the form of presentation had been settled by the President long before he began the preparation of the message.

The innovation won warm praise from Republicans. One Republican representative wrote enthusiastically: "All the pomp and pageantry, which once dishonored our republican institutions are buried in the tomb of the Capulets. Instead of an address to both houses of Congress made by a President, who was drawn to the Capitol by six horses, and followed by the creatures of his nostrils, and gaped at by a wondering multitude, we had a message delivered by his private Secretary, containing every thing necessary for a great and good man to say, and every thing which embraced the benefit and comfort of the people."[96] On the other hand, a Federalist member pointed disapprovingly to the change as proof that "under this administration nothing is to remain as it was. Every minutia is to be changed." [97] While more substantive changes were to follow, the new procedure clearly signaled that a new administration had taken power.

[95] Jefferson to Macon, May 14, 1801, *ibid*.

[96] Michael Leib to Lydia Leib, Dec. 9, 1801, Leib-Harrison Family Papers, Miscellaneous Collection, Historical Society of Pennsylvania.

[97] Roger Griswold to David Daggett, Dec. 8, 1801, William Griswold Lane Collection, Yale University.

II. The President as Chief Executive

JEFFERSON BELIEVED THAT UNDER PRESIDENT
Adams the administration of the executive branch of the
government had drifted in the direction of independent departments. Adams, he thought, had "parcelled out the government in
fact among four independent heads, drawing sometimes in opposite
directions."[1] The new President criticized his predecessor for "long
and habitual absences from the seat of government" that removed
him from any share in the daily transaction of business. As President, Jefferson took steps to reverse the trend of Adams's administration. In a "Circular to the heads of the departments," sent in
early November 1801, Jefferson assured his men that he had unqualified confidence in them; but he indicated that he intended to
be a chief executive who was in command of his administration and
in charge of its daily operation. He expected to be "a central point
for the different branches," to be "always in accurate possession of
all facts and proceedings in every part of the Union, and to what-
soever department they related," to participate in the making of
departmental policy decisions, and to assume the responsibility
for whatever was done. To implement this, he asked each department head to make up, once a day, "a packet of all their communications for the perusal of the President." This packet was to contain letters received, together with copies of proposed replies;
letters requiring no answer were to be included simply for the information of the President.[2]

"A very little experience will probably show us what description
of letters, etc., are worth perusal for the sake of information,"
Jefferson explained to Gallatin,[3] who was at first unsure how many
papers of his department the President wished to see.[4] He did not

[1] Jefferson, circular to the heads of the departments, Nov. 6, 1801, Jefferson Papers, Lib. Cong.

[2] *Ibid.* In sending this memorandum, Jefferson explained his procedures
in terms of following practices set by President Washington, but this appears less a description of Washington's administration than a device by
which Jefferson explained his own methods. The circular is printed in Ford,
ed., *Jefferson Writings*, VIII, 99-101.

[3] Jefferson to Gallatin, Nov. 10, 1801, Albert Gallatin Papers, New-York
Historical Society.

[4] Gallatin to Jefferson, Nov. 9, 1801, Jefferson Papers, Lib. Cong.

want to see all of the returns that daily poured into the Treasury office, the President assured the Secretary, but he would like to see such papers as the weekly summaries that were prepared from them for the use of Secretary of the Treasury. Jefferson made it clear that he did not want to examine all of the routine papers of the departments, and from this, Gallatin interpreted Jefferson's request to mean that department heads should communicate to the President "before a decision takes place every letter on which *judgment must be exercised* and also every one which contains useful information."[5] This was a succinct statement of the President's intent. In amplifying his memorandum, Jefferson also explained that he did not expect to see letters requiring an answer until the reply was prepared, unless there was some difficulty that required a conference.[6]

Under these guidelines a considerable amount of paperwork passed through the President's hands. In addition to the daily business, department heads submitted for the President's review both regular and special reports to Congress.[7] The Secretary of State also sent diplomatic instructions for the President's approval.[8] While much departmental business in which the President was directly involved was handled in written communications, private conferences between the President and department heads were frequent. Jefferson commented more than once on how much easier his work was when he was in Washington, where "a short conference saves a long letter,"[9] than when he was at Monticello.

Jefferson's door was always open to his department heads, who were free to bring matters to him at any time and apparently did so. Thomas Tudor Tucker, the Treasurer of the United States, calling on the President on a confidential matter, found that "General Dearborn came in just when I was about to mention the subject and appeared to have come upon business, so that I was obliged to leave them."[10] Congressmen reported waiting to see the Presi-

[5] Gallatin to Jefferson, Nov. 10, 1801, *ibid.*

[6] Jefferson to Gallatin, Nov. 10, 1801, Gallatin Papers, N.-Y. Hist. Soc.

[7] Smith to Jefferson, Dec. 10, 1802, Letters of Sec. of Navy to President, RG 45, Natl. Archives.

[8] Jefferson to Madison, Feb. 22, 1803, James Madison Papers, Rives Collection, Lib. Cong.

[9] Jefferson to Madison, Sept. 1, 1807, Ford, ed., *Jefferson Writings*, IX, 135. See also Jefferson to Gallatin, Aug. 23, 1802, Henry Adams, ed., *The Writings of Albert Gallatin*, 3 vols. (Philadelphia, 1879), I, 94.

[10] Tucker to John Page, July 2, 1808, Thomas Tudor Tucker Papers, Lib. Cong.

dent while he was engaged in conference with a department head.[11] There was little formality and no appointments secretary involved in such conferences, although the President was not always available when a Cabinet member called. When the Secretary of the Navy failed to see the President on two visits in one day, he left a packet of papers and a note explaining that he had called "at your house to inform you in person of these particulars but you were once engaged and the other time you had rode out. I will call upon you tomorrow morning about 10 o'clock."[12] Major conferences, however, were arranged in advance. "I will be fully ready to wait on you any day after Sunday next on the subject of finances," Gallatin wrote the President in November 1801, as they prepared for the convening of Congress.[13] Jefferson was available to his Cabinet advisers any day of the week, including Sunday.[14]

Many conferences resulted from department heads bringing problems to the President, but he also took matters to them. There are various memoranda in Jefferson's papers on topics to be discussed with department heads. One such memorandum contained a list by departments of subjects to be taken up with each secretary and shows that the President checked off the items disposed of.[15] A memorandum dated November 1801 recorded consultations with all four department heads and included such entries as: "Nov. 15. Navy department. Settled with Mr. Smith the following arrangement for the Navy the ensuing year." A listing of the employment or disposition of each ship followed.[16] The President also sent proposals to department heads "for consideration and consultation as soon as we can meet," and he suggested specific agenda, such as when he wrote the Secretary of the Navy: "I wish to consult you on a plan of a regular naval militia."[17] Or he might send a note such as the following to the Secretary of the Treasury: "Th: Jefferson asks the favor of Mr. Gallatin to come half an hour before dinner to-day (say at 3) to consult on a judge for N. York vice

[11] Samuel L. Mitchill to his wife, Jan. 10, 1802, Samuel Latham Mitchill Papers, Museum of the City of New York.

[12] Smith to Jefferson, Nov. 11, 1805, Jefferson Papers, Lib. Cong.

[13] Gallatin to Jefferson, Nov. 19, 1801, *ibid.*

[14] Madison to Jefferson, received Nov. 16, 1801, *ibid.*

[15] Jefferson, memorandum, [1806], *ibid.*, v. 163, p. 28665. A similar memorandum is in *ibid.*, v. 234, p. 41852.

[16] Jefferson, memorandum, Nov. 10-15, 1801, *ibid.*, v. 118, p. 20350.

[17] Jefferson to Smith, Oct. 24, 1805, Ford, ed., *Jefferson Writings*, VIII, 381.

Livingston."[18] Jefferson also assigned to department heads matters to be handled by them without recurrence to the President.[19]

Jefferson's review of the departmental business laid before him was never perfunctory. Having instructed his department heads to submit policies to him for approval, he remained conversant with a wide range of problems and responded with informed opinions. Carefully reviewing their recommendations, he made alterations where he thought necessary, and although he often accepted their proposals without qualification, he never resorted to *pro forma* endorsements. The careful attention, the time, and the informed effort that Jefferson applied to the affairs of state and the business of government day after day, and year after year, is everywhere in evidence in the records of his administration—in his private papers, in those of members of his Cabinet, and in the records of the departments of the government.

As shown by his request to department heads to forward papers "for the sake of information," Jefferson tried to follow procedures that would keep him informed on all matters coming before the departments. He also sought to stay abreast of public sentiment through his Cabinet and personal contacts with legislators while Congress was in session. Friends in Congress such as Speaker Macon, who recognized the President's need "to hear the sentiments of the people in the different parts of the Union," also wrote to him when they returned to their districts.[20]

Members of the administration likewise reported their assessments of public sentiments in their home states and supplied information that came to them. Attorney General Lincoln and Postmaster General Granger were particularly energetic in such matters. "Deeming it of importance that you should know, as fully as possible, the state of the public mind; and the feelings, and opinions of the people, which you are obliged to meet, and to manage, especially in that difficult part of the Country, of which I am an inhabitant," Lincoln wrote of New England, "I have thought proper to submit to your inspection the inclosed letters—They prove, what I am sure has taken place, or will soon take place, in that part of the Country."[21] Postmaster General Granger turned his

---

[18] Jefferson to Gallatin, June 11, 1805, Gallatin Papers, N.-Y. Hist. Soc.
[19] Jefferson to Madison, Apr. 9, 1804, Madison Papers, Rives Collection, Lib. Cong.
[20] Macon to Jefferson, June 17, 1802, Jefferson Papers, Lib. Cong.
[21] Lincoln to Jefferson, June 28, 1802, *ibid.*

trips to Connecticut into expeditions for political intelligence.[22] On May 6, 1803 Granger reported from New York: "I arrived here yesterday noon having taken time to ascertain the state of things in the several States." He followed with an assessment of the Republican situation in Delaware, Pennsylvania, and New York.[23] Again from New York, Granger wrote the President in January 1808: "I tarried two days in Baltimore and also in Philadelphia in both of which places I am fully convinced the Embargo is approved of by the reflecting and most judicious of all parties. Here I have been three days. . . . The Republicans here will give support and countenance to the measures of Government. I have not heard one speak against any measure—yet I am inclined to believe the Embargo does not receive from them an approbation equal to that of the other Cities."[24]

These examples are indicative of the flow of information and opinion to the President and the willingness of his friends and advisers to supply unfavorable as well as favorable news. "I have lately spent some time in Boston," Lincoln wrote in November 1805. "Republicanism there, in my opinion, is retrograde. Among our friends there seem to make but little exertions, and less concert. . . . The federalists have abated none of their virulence towards the principles of the administration of the General Government, nor remitted in their labours to discredit and obstruct its measures."[25] These reports unquestionably influenced administration policy on such matters as the appointment of Federalists to office.

Jefferson corresponded with many people outside the national government—Republican leaders in different states, editors of leading Republican newspapers, and a wide circle of friends throughout the country. He had little correspondence with state governors, except when they were close political or personal friends, such as Governors Thomas McKean of Pennsylvania or James Monroe of Virginia. Jefferson also had a chance to talk with a large number of people who came to Washington from various parts of the country. Numerous visitors to the capital called on the President with letters of introduction from their congressman or from state and local Republican leaders. Many times the letters they carried noted

22 Granger to Jefferson, Sept. 5, 1802, *ibid.*
23 Granger to Jefferson, May 6, 1803, *ibid.*
24 Granger to Jefferson, Jan. 19, 1808, *ibid.*
25 Lincoln to Jefferson, Nov. 6, 1805, *ibid.*

that the President could confer with confidence on the affairs of a particular state with the person introduced.[26] While it is unlikely that the President shared confidences with such callers, they broadened his access to public opinion.

Jefferson's sources of domestic information came largely from within the government, both executive and legislative, or from personal or political friends and supporters, rather than from the public press. Early in his administration he did attempt to use newspapers as a means of keeping abreast of public opinion. He subscribed to the leading Republican newspapers in various parts of the country and saw a number of lesser Republican papers which he took to encourage party editors.[27] He even arranged for the editor of the New York *American Citizen* to send him copies of the *New-York Evening Post*, the leading Federalist paper in the city and one of the nation's major newspapers. "It is proper I should know what our opponents say and do," he explained in asking editor James Cheetham to put the copies under cover with the *American Citizen*.[28] But as time passed, Jefferson became convinced that the Federalist press was largely irresponsible, and he ceased paying it much attention. When he instructed Cheetham to stop sending him the *New-York Evening Post* in 1807, he said he had "scarcely opened one for two years past."[29] Although he continued to read the leading Republican papers, he became increasingly suspicious of newspapers as a reflection of public sentiment or sources of information.[30]

At the same time, Jefferson recognized the importance of the use of newspapers in the governing process, and he relied especially on Samuel Harrison Smith's *National Intelligencer* to reach the public with information on national affairs and administration policy. Jefferson had been instrumental in persuading Smith to move from Philadelphia to Washington after the capital was moved in 1800, and as President he maintained close ties with Smith's

[26] There are numerous such letters in the Jefferson Papers, Lib. Cong. Examples are Christopher Ellery to Jefferson, introducing John Slocum, June 21, 1806; Levi Lincoln to Jefferson, introducing Jonathan Russell, Apr. 21, 1808.

[27] For a list of the newspapers Jefferson received, see Noble E. Cunningham, Jr., *The Jeffersonian Republicans in Power: Party Operations, 1801-1809* (Chapel Hill, N. C., 1963), p. 254n.

[28] Jefferson to James Cheetham, Apr. 23, 1802, Jefferson Papers, Lib. Cong.

[29] Jefferson to Cheetham, Nov. 6, 1807, *ibid.*

[30] See Jefferson to John Norvell, June 11, 1807, *ibid.*

paper. He recommended the *National Intelligencer* as a source of correct information on the proceedings of the administration, supplied Smith with data and extracts from documents and other papers, and on several occasions even wrote pieces to be published in the paper.[31] In 1801 when a Massachusetts Republican leader inquired of Vice-President Burr as to the role of the *National Intelligencer*, Burr replied: "The Washington paper edited by Smith has the countenance and support of administration. His explanations of the Measures of Government and of the Motives which produce them are, I believe, the result of information and advice from high Authority."[32] Although Smith was his own man and Jefferson did not control his paper, Burr's assessment is well supported by the evidence. Jefferson encouraged Smith to publish materials that would promote policies favored by the President—he sent Smith an article on the gunboat policy of Denmark,[33] and asked Madison to send Smith material on militia organization. After reading a pamphlet supporting a plan to classify the militia to provide a select corps ready for national service—a plan that Jefferson strongly advocated—he wrote to Madison: "Could S. H. Smith put better matter into his paper than the 12 pages above mentioned, and will you suggest it to him? No effort should be spared to bring the public mind to this great point."[34] The administration also used the *National Intelligencer* to make information public that it was not prepared to announce officially.[35] Smith enjoyed a close personal relationship with the President, was invited to dinners at the executive mansion, and had easy access to the President and the heads of the departments. His paper played an important role in the governing process, as did other Republican papers, many of which followed Smith's lead. Because of the violent attacks made upon him by the Federalist press, Jefferson became highly distrustful of newspapers, but, while releasing his resentment in private correspondence, he never abandoned his be-

[31] Jefferson to John Wayles Eppes, Mar. 27, 1801, Jefferson Papers, Univ. of Va.; examples are cited in Cunningham, *Jeffersonian Republicans in Power*, pp. 261-263.

[32] Burr to Barnabas Bidwell, Oct. 15, 1801, Henry W. Taft Collection, Mass. Hist. Soc.

[33] Jefferson to Smith, Mar. 2, 1808, Jonathan Bayard Smith Papers, Lib. Cong.; *National Intelligencer*, Mar. 4, 1808.

[34] Jefferson to Madison, May 5, 1807, Jefferson Papers, Lib. Cong.

[35] Madison to Jefferson, Sept. 21, 1807; Jefferson to Madison, Sept. 22, 1807, *ibid.*; *National Intelligencer*, Sept. 28, 1807.

lief in the fundamental importance of the press to a representative form of government.

Jefferson apparently read all of the mail sent to him, even anonymously written letters (including some threats on his life, which he dismissed). When he saw something useful, even in an unsigned letter, he took note of it. After reading an eleven-page letter signed "A Kentucky Citizen," he marked a passage in it and sent it to the Secretary of War. "The letter is chiefly of the sneering kind," he observed, "but among a number of gigantic measures he recommends to procure *fame* for myself, there is one which, as it may *procure public good*, a more legitimate object, appears worthy consideration at this moment while we are about to negociate for roads through the Indian country." He asked the Secretary of War to consider whether the route proposed by the anonymous writer might become an object of the ensuing treaty.[36] Jefferson also read, and carefully endorsed, a great volume of letters relating to appointments—both letters of application and recommendations for office. His policy was to acknowledge none of these, "leaving the answer to be found in what is done or not done on them," and he filed them away in a separate bundle of papers.[37] "Besides that this correspondence would literally engross my whole time," he said, "into what controversies would it lead me."[38]

It has been argued that Jefferson while President gave little attention to administrative matters, that "his was a speculative rather than an administrative mind."[39] A leading student of public administration concluded that "Jefferson was not interested, indeed, in the normal process of day-by-day administration. Apart from disposing of particular cases there is hardly a reference in his public or private papers to the management of the public business."[40] That Jefferson had no narrow "administrative mind" may be granted, but the records of his presidency provide ample evi-

[36] Jefferson to Dearborn, June 26, 1801, enclosing letter signed "A Kentucky Citizen," received June 26, 1801, Jefferson Papers, Lib. Cong.

[37] Jefferson to Aaron Burr, Nov. 18, 1801; Jefferson to Madison, Sept. 14, 1803, Ford, ed., *Jefferson Writings*, VIII, 102, 263. See also Jefferson to Rufus Easton, Feb. 22, 1806, Jefferson Papers, Lib. Cong.

[38] Jefferson to Larkin Smith, Nov. 26, 1804, Ford, ed., *Jefferson Writings*, VIII, 336-337.

[39] Leonard D. White, *The Jeffersonians: A Study in Administrative History, 1801-1829* (New York, 1951), p. 4.

[40] *Ibid.*

dence of his interest and involvement in administrative routine and the day-by-day management of the public business.

Jefferson personally handled an immense amount of correspondence and paperwork. By November 1801 he reported that his office routine had "now got to a steady and uniform course. It keeps me from 10 to 12 and 13 hours a day at my writing table, giving me an interval of 4 hours for riding, dining and a little unbending."[41] A few weeks later, with Congress in session, he found that "my occupations are now so incessant that I cannot command a moment for my friends. 7 hours of close business in the forepart of the day, and 4 in the evening leave little time for exercise or relaxation."[42]

Much of this burden resulted from the fact that Jefferson wrote all of his own letters and state papers. During his first month in office, Jefferson wrote 116 letters, and by the end of his first year as President he had recorded 677 letters sent.[43] Only rarely making a rough draft, he penned finished letters on complex subjects with a clarity of style that seldom betrayed the demands and pressures of his office. He likewise drafted his own messages and communications to Congress, commonly preparing in his own hand copies for both houses of Congress.[44] The only major exceptions were his lengthy annual messages, which, after going through several drafts in his own hand, were copied by his secretary for transmittal in separate copies to the Senate and the House of Representatives. Most of the lists of nominations of persons to office submitted to the Senate were in Jefferson's hand. Toward the end of his presidency, he forwarded, without recopying, lists of army promotions furnished by the Secretary of War; but during most of his administration he prepared even nominations for military commissions.[45] Letters transmitting reports from department heads to

41 Jefferson to T. M. Randolph, Jr., Nov. 16, 1801, Jefferson Papers, Lib. Cong.

42 Jefferson to John Wayles Eppes, Jan. 1, 1802, Jefferson Papers, Univ. of Va.

43 Jefferson docketed 248 letters received during his first month in office and 1,881 letters received during his first year as President. These totals did not include letters and papers addressed to department heads or members of Congress which were passed on to the President. These figures have been compiled from the indexes to his correspondence prepared by Jefferson. Jefferson Papers, Lib. Cong.

44 Original Messages from the President, 7th-10th Congresses, House Records, RG 233, Senate Records, RG 46, Natl. Archives.

45 Messages from the President, 7th-10th Congresses, Senate Records,

Congress, generally of a routine nature, were likewise usually in the President's hand, as were messages accompanying documents or other information sent to Congress. For his own files, Jefferson made copies by means of a letter press until he acquired a polygraph in 1804. The latter device, by which two or more pens could be operated simultaneously to make identical copies, was perfected by the inventive President, and he found it "a most invaluable Secretary, doing it's work with correctness, facility and secrecy."[46]

As he had been in every public office that he had held, Jefferson was concerned about safeguarding public records and insuring their accessibility. Early in his presidency he explained to Madison:

> Having no confidence that the office of the private secretary of the President of the U.S. will ever be a regular and safe deposit for public papers or that due attention will ever be paid on their transmission from one Secretary or President to another, I have, since I have been in office, sent every paper, which I deem merely public, and coming to my hands, to be deposited in one of the offices of the heads of departments. . . . I make the selection regularly as I go along, retaining in my own possession only my private papers, or such as, relating to public subjects, were meant still to be personally confidential for myself.[47]

No American of his time was more zealous than Jefferson in his efforts to protect public records and to insure their completeness. As President, he scrupulously endeavored to leave every official record in the public offices.

Since the President handled all of his correspondence, made most of his own copies, and forwarded all public papers to be filed in departmental offices, his private secretary had little to do of a clerical nature. "The office itself is more in the nature of that of an aid de camp, than a mere Secretary," Jefferson explained in offering the post to William A. Burwell in 1804. "The writing is not considerable, because I write my own letters and copy them in a press." The principal duties of the office, as Jefferson described them, were "the care of our company, the execution of some com-

---

RG 46, Natl. Archives. Jefferson began forwarding the lists from the Secretary of War during the 10th Congress in December 1807.

[46] Jefferson to James Bowdoin, Apr. 2, 1807, Ford, ed., *Jefferson Writings*, IX, 39-40.

[47] See Jefferson to Madison, Dec. 29, 1801, Jefferson Papers, Lib. Cong.

missions in the town occasionally, messages to Congress, occasional conferences and explanations with particular members, with the officers, and inhabitants of the place where it cannot so well be done in writing."[48] The secretary lived in the President's house—the unfinished East room being divided into two rooms for Jefferson's first secretary, Meriwether Lewis.[49] He greeted visitors and was included at the table of the President's frequent dinner parties. His primary responsibility in the procedures of state was in carrying communications to and from Congress. He took Jefferson's annual messages and all other messages and communications to the two houses. He transmitted to the legislature the information that the President had signed bills into law. Whether the latter was always done in writing is unclear, but there are several such communications addressed to the Speaker of the House of Representatives in the handwriting of Meriwether Lewis and signed by him with the identification "P. S. P. U. S." written below his name. In one of these letters, Lewis reported that he had been "directed by the President of the United States to inform the Honorable the House of Representatives that he did this day approve and sign certain acts, which originated with them." The titles of the acts were then listed.[50] Such letters are among the rare instances when the name of the President's secretary appears on official communications.

Jefferson's secretary also carried papers on legislative actions from the Capitol to the President,[51] and he was expected to be informed about debates in Congress. Senator William Plumer reported a before-dinner conversation with the President in which, when Plumer could not answer a question about the proceedings that day in the House of Representatives, the President directed the question to his secretary, who had just returned from the Capitol.[52] Besides maintaining communications between the legislature and the President, Jefferson's secretary aided in making corrections or additions to papers in which Jefferson discovered deficiencies after

[48] Jefferson to William A. Burwell, Mar. 26, 1804, W. C. Ford, ed., *Jefferson Correspondence: Bixby Collection*, pp. 105-106.

[49] William Cranch to John Adams, May 15, 1801, Gallatin Papers, microfilm edition.

[50] Meriwether Lewis to the Speaker of the House, Feb. 19, 1803, forwarded to the Senate, in Senate Records, RG 46, Natl. Archives; another list is in Lewis to the Speaker of the House, Jan. 14, 1803, *ibid.*

[51] Samuel A. Otis to Secretary of State, Feb. 7, 1803, *ibid.*

[52] Everett S. Brown, ed., *William Plumer's Memorandum of Proceedings in the United States Senate, 1803-1807* (New York, 1923), Jan. 5, 1804, p. 100.

their transmittal to Congress.[53] When the President sent Isaac A. Coles to the Senate with documents omitted from a series accompanying a message in 1806, he asked the Secretary of the Senate to allow his secretary "to substitute each paper in it's proper place, as we have been in the habit of correcting errors, and supplying accidental omissions in this informal way, rather than the more embarrassing one of formal messages of correction."[54]

It is clear that the President's secretary was an aide rather than a messenger and that he acted as a liaison between the President and the Congress. The "occasional conferences and explanations with particular members" which Jefferson expected his secretary to handle are difficult to document for the very reason that Jefferson gave for making use of them: they dealt with matters that could not be easily handled by writing. It can be assumed that they took place occasionally as the President indicated.[55]

Jefferson apparently expected Lewis to resume his post after completing the great expedition to the Pacific,[56] but Lewis never did so. Meanwhile, the office was filled by a succession of secretaries: Lewis Harvie (1803-1804), William A. Burwell (1804-1805), and Isaac A. Coles (1805-1809).[57] To none of them did Jefferson delegate many of his clerical burdens.

Jefferson did most of his work in his office in the executive mansion. He used a room on the southwest corner that had been the levee room under Adams and today is part of the state dining room. An antechamber, which Jefferson called his sitting room, connected his office with the Oval Room, which had been a vestibule under Adams but was transformed by Jefferson into a drawing room.[58] Immediately after moving into the President's house,

[53] Jefferson to Otis, Feb. 8, 1802, Senate Records, RG 46, Natl. Archives.

[54] Jefferson to Otis, Jan. 19, 1806, *ibid.*, see also Jefferson to the President of the Senate (private), Jan. 17, 1806, *ibid.*

[55] Jefferson sent Lewis to make private explanations to James Thomson Callender regarding the remission of his fine under the sedition act and to give him fifty dollars to relieve his distress until his fine was refunded. See Jefferson to Monroe, May 29, 1801, Worthington C. Ford, ed., *Thomas Jefferson and James Thomson Callender, 1798-1802* (Brooklyn, N. Y., 1897), p. 38; Cunningham, *Jeffersonian Republicans in Power*, pp. 250-252.

[56] Jefferson to William A. Burwell, Mar. 26, 1804, W. C. Ford, ed., *Jefferson Correspondence: Bixby Collection*, p. 105.

[57] Coles substituted for Burwell in December 1804 during the session of the Virginia General Assembly of which Burwell was a member. William A. Burwell, Memoir [1804-1808], William A. Burwell Papers, Lib. Cong.

[58] See Malone, *Jefferson the President: First Term*, p. 44.

Jefferson closed the south entrance through the Oval Room and made the entrance at the front door on the north side. Visitors thus entered through the grand hall with the entrance to the oval drawing room straight ahead. While one partisan opponent complained that changing the entrance to the President's house was proof that "under this administration nothing is to remain as it was,"[59] William Cranch, a nephew of Mrs. Adams, concluded that "if these household improvements are the prototype of his political improvements, we shall have no cause of complaint."[60] Work continued on the unfinished mansion throughout his presidency, but Jefferson's working quarters remained as arranged by him in 1801.

All of the departmental offices were within a short walk of the President's office. To the east of the President's house, in one of two brick buildings flanking the mansion, was the Treasury Department. The other building to the west housed the departments of State, War, and the Navy. Department heads were thus close enough to be called upon at any time, and conferences could be arranged on short notice. "If Mr. Gallatin will be so good as to call on Th. J. on his arrival at the office," a note from the President began, "the other gentlemen will then attend on being notified, and consider the subject of Mr. Gallatin's letter received yesterday."[61] Although most meetings with department heads were held at the President's house, Jefferson did on occasion go to departmental offices. A note from the President summoning Attorney General Breckinridge to a conference explained: "As soon as Mr. Gallatin comes to his office I have desired him to walk with me to Mr. Madison's office to consult on an important and pressing subject. Can you meet us there, and amuse yourself till Mr. Gallatin comes, the moment of which I am not able to fix."[62]

Jefferson also went to the Capitol on the closing day or days of sessions to sign bills passed by the Congress. In a note to Gallatin on May 1, 1802, arranging a conference with the Secretary of the Treasury, Jefferson explained: "I shall probably be at the Capitol a good part of to-day, if not to-night, if that will facilitate

[59] Roger Griswold to David Daggett, Dec. 8, 1801, William Griswold Lane Collection, Yale Univ.

[60] Cranch to John Adams, May 15, 1801, Gallatin Papers, microfilm edition.

[61] Jefferson to Gallatin, July 16, 1807, Adams, ed., *Gallatin Writings*, I, 337-338.

[62] Jefferson to Breckinridge, Mar. 21, 1806, Breckinridge Family Papers, Lib. Cong.

the rising of Congress to-day."[63] On March 27, 1804, the last day of the session, Senator John Quincy Adams recorded: "The Committee of Enrolled Bills presented to the President, who was in the committee room of the Senate, nine bills for his approbation. They were soon after returned signed."[64]

Jefferson's regular schedule was to rise at five in the morning and conclude the first segment of his work day at one in the afternoon. He devoted the early morning hours to writing, but after nine o'clock, Cabinet officers and members of Congress were free to drop in for consultations.[65] Cabinet meetings were frequently scheduled for noon, though sometimes at one, and in times of crisis might be held at any hour. At one in the afternoon, Jefferson normally went for a ride on horseback. His dinner hour was regularly scheduled for three-thirty, and sometimes he invited particular dinner guests to arrive at three for private conferences.[66] "Could you do me the favor to come a quarter or half an hour before the company, say at three a clock and bring with you the plans of the Capitol, on which and the avenue I wish to consult you?" Jefferson asked in a note to William Thornton, who had drawn the original plans for the Capitol and was now head of the patent office.[67] The day, it might be noted, was a Sunday. After dinner some guests lingered for a while, and at times others dropped by to join the company. Senator Plumer, a dinner guest, said that he "tarried in the evening and drank coffee—and had much conversation with him."[68] Senator Adams, a guest at dinner on another evening, reported that "after dinner, Mr. Macon, the Speaker of the House, and Mr. John Randolph and Mr. Venable, came in. We came home at about six."[69] After his guests departed, the

[63] Jefferson to Gallatin, May 1, 1802, Gallatin Papers, N.-Y. Hist. Soc. Congress adjourned Monday, May 3, 1802.

[64] Charles Francis Adams, ed., *Memoirs of John Quincy Adams, Comprising Portions of His Diary from 1795 to 1848*, 12 vols. (Philadelphia, 1874-1877), Mar. 27, 1804, I, 312.

[65] Senator Plumer reported visiting the President at nine in the morning and spending an hour; Brown, ed., *Plumer's Memorandum*, Apr. 2, 1806, p. 465. See also Robert Smith to Jefferson, Nov. 11, 1805, Jefferson Papers, Lib. Cong.

[66] Jefferson to Gallatin, June 11, 1805, Gallatin Papers, N.-Y. Hist. Soc.; see also Jefferson to Gallatin, July 10, 1807, Ford, ed., *Jefferson Writings*, IX, 104.

[67] Jefferson to Thornton, Sunday, Mar. 6, [1803], William Thornton Papers, Lib. Cong.

[68] Brown, ed., *Plumer's Memorandum*, Dec. 27, 1806, p. 543.

[69] Adams, ed., *Memoirs of John Quincy Adams*, Nov. 7, 1803, I, 272.

President generally spent four hours at his writing desk or with other paperwork.[70] At ten o'clock he went to bed.[71] As Jefferson explained in a formal reply to one social invitation, "for 10 years past he has been in the habit, from considerations of health, of never going out in the evening. His friends have been so kind as to indulge this habit."[72]

The small dinner parties that Jefferson gave on a regular schedule when Congress was in session provided the President with his principal social activity, but these dinners were also very much a part of the process of government. Around the dinner table, the President got to know personally the members of Congress, most of whom were invited to dine and most of whom accepted; and the legislators had a chance to become acquainted with the President. In reply to one representative who declined an invitation to dine, Jefferson explained: "I cultivate personal intercourse with the members of the legislature that we may know one another and have opportunities of little explanations of circumstances, which, not understood might produce jealousies and suspicions injurious to the public interest, which is best promoted by harmony and mutual confidence among it's functionaries. I depend much on the members for the local information necessary in local matters, as well as for the means of getting at public sentiment."[73]

In his customarily efficient manner, Jefferson prepared rosters of members of Congress and checked off their names as he invited them to dine. He also kept lists of the guests at each dinner, since many members were invited to dine several times during the course of a session, and compiled lists showing by each member's name the dates on which he was a dinner guest.[74] At the end of a session,

[70] Jefferson to Eppes, Jan. 1, 1802, Jefferson Papers, Lib. Cong.

[71] A niece of Mrs. Albert Gallatin, Frances Few, who spent the winter of 1808-1809 in the Gallatins' home, where Jefferson's habits must have been well known, wrote: "The President always goes to bed at ten oClock and rises at five works 'till one and then takes a ride on horseback." Noble E. Cunningham, Jr., ed., "The Diary of Frances Few, 1808-1809," *Journal of Southern History*, XXIX (1963), 350.

[72] Jefferson to William Thornton, Feb. 14, 1801, Thornton Papers, Lib. Cong.

[73] Jefferson to David R. Williams, Jan. 31, 1806, Jefferson Papers, Lib. Cong. This letter was in reply to Williams's letter to Jefferson, received Jan. 29, 1806, W. C. Ford, ed., *Jefferson Correspondence: Bixby Collection*, p. 128.

[74] The lists of dinner guests from November 1804 to March 1809 are in Jefferson Papers, Coolidge Collection, Mass. Hist. Soc., microfilm edition.

Jefferson sometimes added up the totals, as he did at the end of the second session of the Eighth Congress. During the period of 110 days from November 5, 1804, to February 22, 1805, the President had 47 dinner parties, averaging twelve guests per dinner. The guests included 153 different persons, 75 of whom dined twice, 52 dined three times, and 26 were present at four dinners, making a total of 563 dinner guests during the 16-week period.[75] Jefferson's records show that he generally had dinner parties three nights each week, either on Monday, Wednesday, and Friday, or on Tuesday, Thursday, and Saturday. While Congress was in session, he directed most of his invitations to members, but he also invited Cabinet officers. He included justices of the Supreme Court while the court was in session. Sometimes foreign diplomats were invited with congressmen and members of the Cabinet. An occasional dinner party was composed largely of foreigners and persons outside the national government, but such dinners were rare while Congress was in session. Since most congressmen came to Washington unaccompanied by wives or family, there were few ladies at dinner while Congress was in session; when members with wives or Cabinet members and their wives were invited, Jefferson always invited several couples on the same evening.[76]

Mrs. Samuel Harrison Smith reported that the President's table was seldom set for more than twelve, and Jefferson's guest lists generally bear this out, although the parties varied from eight to fifteen, not counting the President and his "family," which included his private secretary.[77] Whatever the exact number on any given day, most guests observed that the number was small enough to promote conversation and make a party that was "easy and sociable."[78] "The dinners are neat and plentiful and the cookery good," said Congressman Mitchill. "No healths are drank at table. Nor are any toasts or sentiments given after dinner. You drink as you please and converse at your ease. In this way, every guest feels inclined to drink to the *digestive* or *social* point, and no further."[79]

An interesting aspect of Jefferson's dinner parties scheduled

[75] *Ibid.*   [76] *Ibid.*

[77] Mrs. Smith to Maria Bayard, May 28, 1801, Hunt, ed., *First Forty Years of Washington Society*, p. 29; Jefferson, lists of dinner guests, November 1804, Jefferson Papers, Coolidge Collection, Mass. Hist. Soc., microfilm edition.

[78] Samuel L. Mitchill to his wife, Feb. 10, 1802, Mitchill Papers, Museum C.N.Y.

[79] Mitchill to his wife, Jan. 10, 1802, *ibid.*

on days that Congress was in session was that he issued invitations to members of Congress to dine with him "at half after three, or at whatever later hour the house may rise."[80] When Congress was late in adjourning, dinner was held. Representative Mitchill reported one instance when the House did not adjourn until five o'clock and several members hired a hackney coach to hurry to the President's house.[81] On another occasion he reported that the House did not adjourn until seven-thirty and he did not arrive at the President's house until eight, but the "dinner was kept waiting untill the company came, and between 8 and 9 in the evening we sat down to dine."[82] That there must have been some limit on how long the President held dinner is suggested by the fact that when the House did not adjourn until nine in the evening on a day Mitchill was invited to the President's, he went back to his lodgings for a late supper.[83] The courtesy of the President in adjusting his dinner hour to the adjourning of Congress indicates not only that such dinners were planned for the legislators but also that the members of Congress daily stayed at their posts until adjournment.

At the beginning of his presidency when he was trying to implement the spirit of his inaugural, Jefferson apparently did not consider party affiliations in issuing invitations. "We are literaly, all federalists and all republicans," Mrs. Samuel Harrison Smith elatedly concluded in June 1801. "At the President's table no distinction is made, and a day or two ago, Mr. Smith met there one of his most violent opponents."[84] But when hopes of reconciling Federalists to his administration faded, Jefferson attempted to promote congeniality at his dinner table by inviting Federalists and Republicans on different days. At least, enough guests commented on the practice to indicate that there was some such intention. Representative Simeon Baldwin, a Connecticut Federalist, declared in 1804 that the President was "in the habit of separating the wheat from the chaff, and invites the federal members by themselves."[85]

[80] Jefferson, invitation to Richard Cutts, Jan. 27, 1802, Thomas Jefferson Papers, Chicago Historical Society; Jefferson, invitation to Ebenezer Mattoon, Feb. 1, 1802, Broadside Collection, Rare Book Division, Lib. Cong. Brown, ed., *Plumer's Memorandum*, Dec. 3, 1804, p. 211. Samuel L. Mitchill to his wife, Oct. 25, 1803, Mitchill Papers, Museum C.N.Y.

[81] Samuel L. Mitchill to his wife, Apr. 29, 1802, *ibid.*

[82] Mitchill to his wife, Oct. 27, 1803, *ibid.*

[83] Mitchill to his wife, Dec. 8, 1803, *ibid.*

[84] Mrs. Smith to Mrs. Andrew Kirkpatrick, June 20, 1801, Mrs. Samuel Harrison Smith Papers, Lib. Cong.

[85] Baldwin to his wife, Jan. 5, 1804, Baldwin Family Papers, Yale Univ.

Senator Adams reported dining at the President's "with a company of fifteen members of both Houses, all federalists, and consisting chiefly of the delegations from Massachusetts and Connecticut."[86] Senator Plumer, a New Hampshire Federalist, believed that the President's dinner invitations read *Th: Jefferson requests* rather than *The President requests* so that he would not have to follow an official list and be obligated "to invite gentlemen of different politic's at the same table."[87]

Plumer also charged that Jefferson did not invite those members of Congress who abused him on the floor.[88] Although Jefferson's lists of guests show that he included many strong political opponents, his records reveal that he did not feel obligated to invite every member of Congress to dine with him and that he did not send invitations to some members who attacked him in Congress. Perhaps the clearest example is the case of John Randolph, who dined with Jefferson five times during the second session of the Eighth Congress, and three times during the first session of the Ninth Congress; after that, Randolph's name does not appear on Jefferson's lists of dinner guests for the remainder of his presidency. The last date that Randolph was recorded at dinner with the President was March 1, 1806.[89] Four days later, Randolph opened a violent attack on the administration on the floor of the House. "Never has the *President* been handled so severely in public debate, as by Randolph," one member observed.[90] The attack marked Randolph's break with Jefferson's administration, and he was not again to be among Jefferson's guests.

Jefferson paid the cost of entertaining, the operation of his household and office, and the salary and expenses of his private secretary out of his annual salary of $25,000. During his first year in office, these expenses amounted to over $16,000, including a wine bill of $2,797.38.[91] His total expenditures of some $33,000 during that year exceeded his income from all sources by over

[86] Adams, ed., *Memoirs of John Quincy Adams*, Feb. 25, 1806, i, 415.

[87] Brown, ed., *Plumer's Memorandum*, Dec. 3, 1804, pp. 211-212.

[88] *Ibid.*, p. 212.

[89] According to Jefferson's list, Randolph dined on Nov. 9, 27, Dec. 21, 1804; Jan. 23, Feb. 23, Dec. 9, 1805; Feb. 1, Mar. 1, 1806, Jefferson Papers, Coolidge Collection, Mass. Hist. Soc., microfilm edition.

[90] Timothy Pitkin to Simeon Baldwin, Mar. 10, 1806, Baldwin Family Papers, Yale Univ.

[91] Jefferson, Account Book, Mar. 8, 1802, photostatic copy, Manuscript Division, Lib. Cong.

$4,000.[92] In a detailed calculation of household costs for 1806, Jefferson determined that his average monthly expenses for provisions, groceries (not including wine), servants, fuel, and household contingencies amounted to $674 per month when Congress was in session, compared to $482 per month when he was in Washington at other times, and $439 per month when he was away.[93] There is no indication that Jefferson's careful cost accounting prompted him in any way to curtail his expenditures for entertaining or to restrict that hospitality which he regarded as necessary to the conduct of his office.

After Congress closed its session each spring, generally in March or April, Jefferson regularly made a visit of two or three weeks to Monticello.[94] It took three days each way to travel the 120 miles between Washington and Charlottesville. In late summer each year there was "a general recess of the Executive," Jefferson explained, during which members of his Cabinet were expected "to seek situations in which we have more confidence to pass the months of August and September so trying to health."[95] During these two months, Jefferson moved the President's office to Monticello, where he found the transaction of the public business "infinitely more laborious" than it would have been in Washington and "leaves it in my power to be of little use to my private matters."[96] But he was convinced his health demanded the change. When Federalists raised criticisms of the absence of so many members of the administration from the capital during the first such summer recess,[97] Jefferson indicated that he had no intention of abandoning the practice. "I consider it as a trying experiment for a person from the mountains to pass the two bilious months on the tide-water," he wrote. "I have not done it these forty years, and nothing should induce me to do it. As it is not possible but that the Administration must take some portion of time for their own affairs, I think it best they should select that season for absence. General Washington set the

[92] Jefferson borrowed $4,361; the amount of $33,000 includes payment of previous debts of $3,917.59 during the year. *Ibid.*

[93] Figures were for the period Jan. 4, 1806, to Jan. 3, 1807. *Ibid.*

[94] Jefferson to Maria Jefferson Eppes, Apr. 11, 1801, Thomas Jefferson Miscellany, Lib. Cong.

[95] Jefferson to John Steele, June 30, 1802, Jefferson Papers, Lib. Cong.

[96] Jefferson to Gallatin, Aug. 23, 1802, Adams, ed., *Gallatin Writings*, I, 94.

[97] Gallatin to Jefferson, Sept. 14, 1801, *ibid.*, p. 54.

example of those two months; Mr. Adams extended them to eight months. I should not suppose our bringing it back to two months a ground for grumbling, but, grumble who will, I will never pass those months on tide-water."[98] Jefferson adhered to this resolve throughout his eight years in office.

During the summer recess, the administration of the departmental offices was largely left in the hands of the chief clerks,[99] who sent weekly packets of letters and papers to their chiefs,[100] and the latter kept in contact with the President through a steady exchange of letters. Jefferson himself could get information from Washington within two days and an answer back within a week.[101] Whenever pressing matters were pending, there was usually at least one member of the Cabinet in the city.[102] When decisions could not be postponed until the Cabinet reassembled in the fall, the President solicited their opinions by mail. "The last post brings me the opinions of the Secretaries at War and of the Navy, as well as yours, on our Barbary affairs," he wrote to Gallatin who was still in Washington in August 1802. "I had before asked and received that of the Secretary of State; but as his did not go to all the points arising out of the others, and explanations by letter might lose us a post day or two, I shall immediately on closing my mail for this day's post set out to Mr. Madison's, so that the next post shall carry definitive arrangements to Washington, where it will arrive on Tuesday (24th) at 8 P.M."[103] As this letter indicates, presidential management of the affairs of state continued without interruption during the summer recess, and the heavy increase in Jefferson's correspondence with Cabinet members during these periods testifies to the fact that the President got very little vacation from the burdens of his office. Since he gave his private secretary leave when he was away from Washington, he was without even the little assistance he demanded of that aide.[104]

When both Jefferson and Madison were in Virginia, they were

[98] Jefferson to Gallatin, Sept. 18, 1801, *ibid.*, p. 55.
[99] Jefferson to Dearborn, Jan. 8, 1808, Ford, ed., *Jefferson Writings*, IX, 172.
[100] On the role of the clerks, see pp. 94-96 below.
[101] Malone, *Jefferson the President: First Term*, p. 64.
[102] Henry Dearborn to Caesar A. Rodney, Aug. 5, 1807, Dearborn Papers, Chicago Hist. Soc.
[103] Jefferson to Gallatin, Aug. 20, 1802, Adams, ed., *Gallatin Writings*, I, 93.
[104] Jefferson to William A. Burwell, Mar. 26, 1804, W. C. Ford, ed., *Jefferson Correspondence: Bixby Collection*, p. 106.

but thirty miles apart; Madison could forward to the President the weekly packets from the State Department,[105] and there were frequent visits between them. "I am just returned from a visit to Mr. Madison whom I went to consult on certain matters," Jefferson wrote to Gallatin following one such trip. Among the subjects discussed were appointments in the Louisiana territory. "After waiting to the 12th hour to get all the information I could respecting the government of Orleans," the President explained, "I have, on consultation with Mr. Madison, sent on the commissions by the mail which left Charlottesville yesterday morning for the Westward. It is very much what had been approved by the heads of departments separately and provisionally, with a few alterations shewn to be proper by subsequent information."[106] Similar reports on this action went also to the Secretaries of War and the Navy.[107] In an age accustomed to no means of communication faster than that provided by a horse, the inconvenience and delay caused by the summer recess do not appear to have seriously interfered with the governmental process, and the President was able to fulfill his responsibilities as chief executive from Monticello.

[105] Madison to Jefferson, Sept. 17, 1801; Jefferson to Madison, Aug. 23, 1804, Jefferson Papers, Lib. Cong.

[106] Jefferson to Gallatin, Sept. 1, 1804, *ibid.*

[107] Jefferson to Dearborn, Sept. 6, 1804; Jefferson to Smith, Sept. 6, 1801, *ibid.*

III. Presidential Decisionmaking

FROM THE OUTSET OF HIS ADMINISTRATION, JEF-
ferson included his Cabinet in the decisionmaking process.
"The principles of removal, are to be settled finally when our administration collects about the last of April," the President wrote in
late March 1801;[1] but it was May 13 before all Cabinet members
were in Washington and Jefferson was able "to settle our system
of proceeding."[2] On May 15 a Cabinet meeting was held with all
members present, including Samuel Smith, who was temporarily
performing the duties of Secretary of the Navy. The President laid
before them a major problem. Reports indicated that in March
Tripolitan cruisers had been sent out to attack American shipping,
and Jefferson had ordered a squadron to rendezvous at Norfolk to
prepare to sail for the Mediterranean to protect American commerce. "But as this might lead to war," the President explained,
"I wished to have the approbation of the new administration."[3]

To the assembled Cabinet, Jefferson put the question: "Shall
the squadron now at Norfolk be ordered to cruise in the Mediterranean?" And if so, "what shall be the object of the cruise?" At
issue was the basic question of how far the executive's power extended, when it came to taking military action on his own authority. Following a procedure he would frequently use throughout
his presidency, Jefferson listed on a sheet of paper the opinion of
each Cabinet officer.[4] Gallatin argued that "the Executive can not
put us in a state of war, but if we be put into that state either by
the declaration of Congress or of the other nation, the command
and direction of the public force then belongs to the Executive."
Smith agreed that "if a nation commences war, the Executive is
bound to apply the public force to defend the country." Attorney
General Lincoln took a narrower view. "Our men of war may repel
an attack on individual vessels," he said, "but after the repulse,

[1] Jefferson to Thomas McKean, Mar. 26, 1801, Thomas McKean Papers,
Hist. Soc. Pa.

[2] Jefferson to T. M. Randolph, Jr., May 14, 1801, Jefferson Papers,
Lib. Cong.

[3] Jefferson to Wilson Cary Nicholas, June 11, 1801, Ford, ed., *Jefferson
Writings*, VIII, 63.

[4] Jefferson, notes, May 15, 1801–Apr. 8, 1803, Jefferson Papers, v. 112,
p. 19297, Lib. Cong. See Chap. IV, n. 34 below.

may not proceed to destroy the enemy's vessels generally." The views of Madison and Dearborn were less clear on the President's power, but Madison thought that "the cruise ought to be undertaken, and the object openly declared to every nation." Dearborn similarly said that "the expedition should go forward openly to protect our commerce against the threatened hostilities of Tripoli." Though there was a difference of opinion on the power of the President, Jefferson recorded that all concurred in the expediency of the cruise. The Cabinet then considered the question "whether the captains may be authorized, if war exists, to search for and destroy the enemy's vessels wherever they can find them?" All except Lincoln agreed that they should be so authorized. Madison, Gallatin, and Smith thought that they could *pursue* into harbors, but Madison insisted that they could not *enter* except in pursuit.[5] With the Cabinet unanimous in opinion that the squadron be sent to the Mediterranean, the orders for the expedition were issued in accordance with the majority view that if Tripoli were making war on the United States, then the Navy was authorized to attack the enemy. The major decision to commit naval forces of the United States to battle if Tripoli were found to be attacking American shipping was thus the product of full deliberation by the Cabinet.

Despite the clear decision of the Cabinet to attack the Tripolitan cruisers, when Jefferson reported this action and the subsequent engagements with Tripolitan cruisers in his first message to Congress in December 1801, he emphasized the defensive character of the operation and explained the release of a captured enemy cruiser on that ground. "Unauthorized by the constitution, without the sanction of Congress, to go beyond the line of defence, the vessel being disabled from committing further hostilities, was liberated with its crew," he reported. Then he suggested that the legislature might "consider whether, by authorizing measures of offence, also, they will place our force on an equal footing with that of its adversaries."[6] But if Jefferson allowed his own predilections to influence his later interpretation of this Cabinet decision, he also permitted his Cabinet to act as a check on him. When in the draft of his second annual message to Congress, Jefferson suggested the need for congressional authority to act offensively in case of

---

[5] Jefferson, notes, May 15, 1801–Apr. 8, 1803, Jefferson Papers, v. 112, p. 19297, Lib. Cong. The notes on the May 15, 1801 meeting are inaccurately printed in Ford, ed., *Jefferson Writings*, I, 293-294.

[6] Jefferson, first annual message, Dec. 8, 1801, Ford, ed., *Jefferson Writings*, VIII, 118.

war declared or waged by other Barbary powers, Gallatin objected so strongly that Jefferson omitted the passage from his message. Gallatin told the President that he had never believed it necessary to obtain legislative sanction in such cases. "Whenever war does exist, whether by the declaration of the United States or by the declaration or act of a foreign nation," he explained, "I think that the Executive has a right, and is duty bound, to apply the public force which he may have the means legally to employ, in the most effective manner to annoy the enemy. If the instructions given in May or June, 1801, by the Navy Department to the commander of the Mediterranean squadron shall be examined," he reminded the President, "it will be found that they were drawn in conformity to that doctrine; and that was the result of a long Cabinet discussion of that very ground. It is true," he continued, "that the message of last year adopted a different construction of the Constitution; but how that took place I do not recollect. The instructions given to the commanders to release the crews of captured vessels were merely because we did not know what to do with them."[7] Considering that Jefferson had been vigorously attacked in the Federalist press on this very point following his first message to Congress in December 1801,[8] Gallatin's frankness is evidence of the freedom Jefferson allowed his Cabinet members. While Jefferson often spoke of the harmony within his official family, he did not mean by this an absence of differing opinions.

The decisionmaking process employed by Jefferson as President can be usefully observed in the case of General Arthur St. Clair, governor of the Northwest Territory. On February 20, 1802, Jefferson received from Thomas Worthington, a member of the territorial legislature in Ohio and an active Republican then in Washington promoting statehood for Ohio, a memorandum of charges of illegal and improper conduct by St. Clair. Worthington

[7] Gallatin, notes on Jefferson's second annual message [December 1802], Adams, ed., *Gallatin Writings*, I, 105-106.

[8] In a series of articles on the President's message, Alexander Hamilton, writing as "Lucius Crassus," began with an attack on Jefferson's report on the action against Tripoli. "The first thing in it, which excites our surprise," he wrote, "is the very extraordinary position, that *though Tripoli had declared war in form* against the United States, and had enforced it by actual hostility, yet that there was not power, for want of *the sanction of Congress*, to capture and detain her cruisers with their crews." "Lucius Crassus," No. 1, John C. Hamilton, ed., *The Works of Alexander Hamilton*, 9 vols. (New York, 1850-1851), VII, 745.

listed ten specific charges against the Federalist governor and enclosed a five-page memorandum of explanations and references to documents which supported the charges.[9] As restated more succinctly by Gallatin, Worthington charged Governor St. Clair with:

1. Erecting Counties and fixing Seats of Justice by proclamation.
2. Putting his negative on useful and necessary laws.
3. Taking illegal fees.
4. Negativing the laws annulling those for fees and approving the law giving him 500 dollars as a compensation for the same.
5. Attempting the division of the Territory and the alteration of the Constitutional boundaries of the intended States.
6. Granting to his Son a Commission, as Attorney General, during good behavior, whilst all his other commissions were revokable at will.
7. Improper interference with Judiciary proceedings.
8. Appointing to offices, persons residing out of the County.
9. Neglecting the organisation of the Militia.
10. Hostility to a republican form of Government.[10]

Jefferson gave St. Clair an opportunity to reply to the charges, and, after receiving his defense,[11] he laid the matter before the Cabinet. In a memorandum to all members dated April 29, 1802, the President wrote:

> Th. Jefferson asks the favor of the heads of the departments to examine and consider the charges of Col. Worthington against Govr. St. Clair with the answer of the latter and the documents in support or invalidation of the charges; and to favor him with their opinion in writing on each charge distinctly, whether "established" or "not established," and whether those "established" are sufficiently weighty to render the removal of the Governor proper?[12]

[9] Thomas Worthington to Jefferson, Feb. 20, 1802, Jefferson Papers, Lib. Cong.; printed in Clarence E. Carter, ed., *The Territorial Papers of the United States*, 26 vols. (Washington, D. C., 1934-1962), III, 212-214.

[10] Gallatin to Jefferson, Apr. 30, 1802, Jefferson Papers, Lib. Cong.

[11] See Madison to St. Clair, May 8, 1802, acknowledging the receipt of St. Clair's defense, Carter, ed., *Territorial Papers of the United States*, III, 224.

[12] Jefferson to heads of departments, Apr. 29, 1802, Jefferson Papers, Lib. Cong.

The documents relating to the charges were passed from member to member,[13] and the replies to the President's request for opinions were written over a period of eight weeks. Gallatin, who was anxious to get away on a trip to New York, replied almost immediately. He wrote a five-page memorandum, carefully transcribed by a clerk, in which he concluded:

> Of the preceding charges the 3d, 5th, 6th, and 8th are the only ones which appear established. The two last, although the Acts evince improper partiality for his family, do not seem to afford alone, sufficient grounds for removal. Either of the two others, the taking illegal fees, or attempting to dismember the Territory or State, is in the Secretarys opinion sufficiently weighty to justify the appointment of a Successor. . . .
>
> But although a removal is justified on those grounds, the propriety of that measure under present circumstances appears doubtful. Congress having provided for the admission of the new State in the Union, the age, infirmities, and past services of the Governor, may be a sufficient reason why the mortification of a removal should be spared, if by the assent of the territorial Convention, his office shall of course expire with the colonial form of Government. . . .[14]

In making his recommendation Gallatin took into account the enabling act authorizing Ohio to form a state government just passed by Congress and signed by Jefferson on the same day that Gallatin drafted his reply, April 30, 1802.

The next adviser to reply was Attorney General Lincoln, who had already investigated several of the questions raised by the charges in response to an earlier request from the President for his opinion on the legal powers of the territorial governor.[15] On May 25 Lincoln submitted an eight-page opinion in which he concluded:

> I have no doubt but that there has been that departure from duty, and abuse of power, which will justify the President in a removal. . . . As a question of policy there may be some doubt. In reference to the territory abstractedly considered, I am inclined to think it would be useful, and also in its immediate effects on them, in their connection with the United States. How

[13] See Levi Lincoln to Jefferson, June 9, 1802, Carter, ed., *Territorial Papers of the United States*, III, 227.

[14] Gallatin to Jefferson, Apr. 30, 1802, Jefferson Papers, Lib. Cong.

[15] Jefferson to Lincoln, Jan. 28, 1802; Lincoln to Jefferson, Feb. 2, 1802, Carter, ed., *Territorial Papers of the United States*, III, 207, 208-211.

it would impress the public mind, is uncertain. It would be improved by the opposition to create new, and to strengthen its old prejudices. But these I would risque, rather than the republicanism of the territory, if that is the alternative.[16]

The Attorney General thus raised the political question involved in the issue. The removal of St. Clair would be popular with the Republicans in Ohio, and Lincoln was inclined to believe that the political advantages to the Republican party would outweigh the uses the Federalists might make of the dismissal.

On June 15 Secretary of the Navy Smith sent the President a ten-page memorandum in which he found all but the third and sixth charges not to be established. The "6th charge is established and the explanation of the governor is not satisfactory," he concluded. "And viewing it in connection with the 3d charge I consider it sufficiently weighty to justify his removal from office, provided that such 3d charge upon the proposed further examination of the Territorial Code be established and cannot be softened by extenuating circumstances."[17] Smith's opinion was limited to the evidence examined and did not offer advice on the wisdom of removal as a policy rather than a legal decision.

The last opinion which Jefferson received came from Madison on June 19. No opinion from Secretary of War Dearborn has been found, and the President made his decision shortly after he had Madison's reply. As the department head to whom the governor of the Northwest Territory reported (the territories being a part of the domestic concerns that came under the jurisdiction of the State Department), Madison had handled the correspondence with St. Clair and was more familiar with the case than other members of the Cabinet. These circumstances may explain why he was the last to submit his report and also why his four-page report was the briefest examination offered by any Cabinet member. Any action taken in regard to St. Clair would be communicated through his office so that he would have further opportunity to confer with the President if more elaboration were required. Madison's conclusion was brief but specific. He wrote:

> Upon the whole, it appears that altho' the conduct of the Governor has been highly culpable in sundry instances, and sufficiently so in the particular cases of commissioning his son during good behavior, and in what relates to fees, to plead for

16 Lincoln to Jefferson, May 25, 1802, Jefferson Papers, Lib. Cong.
17 Smith to Jefferson, June 15, 1802, *ibid.*

a removal of him from his office, yet considering the revolutionary and other interesting relations in which he has stood to the public, with other grounds on which some indulgence may be felt for him, it is the opinion of the Secretary of State, that it will be proper to leave him in possession of his office under the influence of a salutary admonition.[18]

With the receipt of Madison's opinion, the President had before him independent examinations of the charges against St. Clair from four of the five members of his Cabinet. All had followed the President's instructions to examine each charge separately and to give an opinion on each, though only Smith had distinctly stated "established" or "not established" on each charge, and Madison refused to give an opinion on several charges. The President could read the opinions of his advisers and find that, while they differed on specifics, there was a consensus that the charges against St. Clair were sufficiently established to justify his removal. He also would find that Gallatin and Madison agreed that as a matter of policy it would be better not to remove the governor, though each man emphasized different considerations for such a decision, Gallatin stressing the practical circumstance that his office would soon come to an end with the admission of Ohio and Madison giving weight to St. Clair's Revolutionary services. Only Lincoln called attention to the political advantages to the Republicans that the removal would have.

An examination of these opinions shows that Jefferson received independent counsel from his advisers. They did not all agree, and they raised different points for the President to consider. There is no evidence of any of them telling the President what they thought he wanted to hear or marshaling evidence in support of a decision that they thought the President had already made. Nor is there any indication that Jefferson made his decision before he received the opinions from his Cabinet members. At the same time, it is interesting to notice in regard to Jefferson's decisionmaking procedures that he also contributed to the analysis that led to the determination of the question. He did not simply call for written opinions from each member of the Cabinet, wait for their reports, and make his decision based solely on the opinions they had submitted. He himself examined the evidence and drew up his own memorandum, noting observations by each charge as he had re-

[18] Madison to Jefferson, June 19, 1802, *ibid.*

quested his advisers to do.[19] Although Jefferson refrained from deciding this question on his own, his observations are no less critical of St. Clair than those of his advisers. The general impression that his memorandum gives, though he did not draw a conclusion in it, is that Jefferson, like his advisers, believed that St. Clair was guilty of misconduct. The President's own judgment was confirmed by the independent judgments of his advisers so far as St. Clair's conduct was concerned. In deciding upon the policy to be adopted, he waited until all of the opinions were in, and then acted in accordance with the dominant view. On June 23, the Secretary of State conveyed by letter to Governor St. Clair the President's displeasure of his conduct, stressing Jefferson's instructions "that his particular disapprobation should be expressed to you, of your conduct in granting to your son an illegal tenure of office; and in accepting yourself illegal fees." The President also wished St. Clair to be informed that his actions in laying out counties and fixing their seats of justice were not in accordance with "the construction put by the Executive on the Ordinance constituting the Territorial Government."[20] The latter point was one which Jefferson had particularly stressed in his own memorandum on the charges.

After careful consideration, the decision in regard to St. Clair was thus for a "salutary admonition" rather than removal. But within six months the issue presented itself again. On November 19, 1802, the President received in separate letters from two leading Ohio Republicans, Thomas Worthington and John Smith,[21] copies of the address that Governor St. Clair had made to the Ohio constitutional convention on November 3, in which St. Clair had declared the enabling act of April 30, 1802, a nullity. The next day Gallatin sent Jefferson another copy of the speech, which he thought was "so indecent, and outrageous that it must be doubtful whether, notwithstanding his approaching political death, it is not incumbent on the Executive to notice it."[22] The President did so immediately, and on November 22 the Secretary of State notified

[19] Jefferson's undated memorandum is filed under June 1802 in the Jefferson Papers, Lib. Cong.

[20] Madison to St. Clair, June 23, 1802, Carter, ed., *Territorial Papers of the United States*, III, 231.

[21] Thomas Worthington to Jefferson, Nov. 8, 1802; John Smith to Jefferson, Nov. 9, 1802, Jefferson Papers, Lib. Cong.

[22] Gallatin to Jefferson, Nov. 20, 1802, Carter, ed., *Territorial Papers of the United States*, III, 259.

Governor St. Clair of his dismissal.[23] The consultation and thorough examination that earlier had been given to the governor's conduct enabled the President to move decisively—a decisiveness which on this occasion endeared him to the Republicans of Ohio. "The removal of Governor St. Clair from office has produced much joy and triumph among the Republicans of this new state," wrote John Smith, who, along with Worthington, was soon to be one of Ohio's first senators.[24] That Jefferson was aware of the political advantage seems clear, but when the long and thorough decision-making process is explored, it is evident that partisan political considerations had not dominated the decision.

The procedures that Jefferson followed in deciding to send a squadron to the Mediterranean in 1801 and in considering the dismissal of Governor St. Clair were employed in principle in making the major decisions of his administration. In crisis situations the time for deliberation was shorter, but the same patterns of procedure were followed, although at an accelerated pace. On June 25, 1807, the President received word of the attack on the *Chesapeake* that had occurred three days earlier, and he immediately issued a call for his Cabinet to assemble. Gallatin and Dearborn, who were out of town, were asked to return to the capital "without a moment's avoidable delay,"[25] and the decision on the course of action to be taken was postponed until the Cabinet could meet. Within a week the Cabinet had assembled and began meeting almost daily. Meanwhile, the President with the help of Madison prepared the draft of a proposed proclamation.[26] As in the drafting of legislative recommendations for his annual and special messages to Congress, Jefferson took the lead in preparing recommendations for consideration by the Cabinet. At the same time, the President did not present proposals that he expected merely to be sanctioned by the Cabinet.

Describing the *Chesapeake* incident to his father in a letter of July 1, 1807, Attorney General Rodney reported that the British action "has excited the spirit of 76 and the whole country is literally in arms." He then went on to explain: "In consequence of the

[23] Madison to St. Clair, Nov. 22, 1802, *ibid.*, p. 260.

[24] Smith to Jefferson, Dec. 27, 1802, Jefferson Papers, Lib. Cong.

[25] Jefferson to Gallatin, June 25, 1807; Jefferson to Dearborn, June 25, 1807, *ibid.*

[26] Jefferson's draft of the proclamation, July 2, 1807, with extensive revisions is in *ibid.*, v. 168, p. 29629; Madison's notes, received by Jefferson, June 29, 1807, are in *ibid.*, p. 29612.

absence of Mr. Dearborn and Mr. Gallatin we have not yet come to a final resolution as to our line of conduct. They have arrived this morning and tomorrow we shall meet in full council and decide. I trust we shall act with firmness spirit and promptitude. I shall give my vote with due consideration and with a safe and honest conscience. But I feel the importance and the delicacy of my situation."[27] Clearly Rodney, the lowest-ranking member of the Cabinet, felt that major decisions were made in the Cabinet and that his vote had meaning and importance.

On the surface, Jefferson's decision not to submit the Monroe-Pinkney treaty of 1806 to the Senate might appear to have been a presidential decision made without time for deliberation or advice. On the last day of the Ninth Congress, March 3, 1807, the British minister received a copy of the treaty, which he carried to Madison's office. During the day, the Secretary of State and the President examined the treaty and then Jefferson informed a Senate delegation that he intended to reject the treaty without submitting it to the Senate.[28] However hasty this decision may have appeared, the crucial decision had been made after due deliberation by the full Cabinet on February 2. At that meeting the Cabinet reviewed communications received from the American envoys in London indicating that they expected to sign a treaty in which the British would not give up the practice of impressment. The President then posed the question "Shall we agree to any treaty yielding the principle of our non-importation act, and not securing us against impressments?" The Cabinet decided: "Unanimously not." The President also raised the question: "Shall we consult the Senate?" The Cabinet decided: "Unanimously not, had the 1st question been decided affirmatively their advice should have been asked."[29] Jefferson's notes on the Cabinet meeting indicate that the questions were fully discussed and the decisions made at that time. The Cabinet had agreed that "we had better have no treaty than a bad one" and had decided that the treaty would not be submitted to the Senate if it did not include an agreement relating to impressment.[30] Thus, all that Jefferson and Madison had to do before announcing that the treaty would not be sent to the Senate was to

[27] Caesar A. Rodney to Thomas Rodney, July 1, 1807, H. F. Brown Collection, Historical Society of Delaware.

[28] Bradford Perkins, *Prologue to War: England and the United States, 1805-1812* (Berkeley, Calif., 1961), p. 135.

[29] Jefferson's notes on the Cabinet meeting of Feb. 2, 1807, Ford, ed., *Jefferson Writings*, I, 322-323.

[30] *Ibid.*

check the document to confirm that the subject of impressment had been omitted. The President's normal decisionmaking process of deliberation and consultation with his Cabinet had been fully followed. Had not Congress been ready to disperse, the President might have assembled the Cabinet to confirm the earlier decisions, but it would not have been necessary.

Jefferson's decisionmaking process was characterized by his willingness to accept counsel. He permitted his initial views to be altered by new information, by the opinions of his advisers, and by changing circumstances. His decision in 1803 not to seek a constitutional amendment to permit the incorporation of Louisiana into the United States, often cited as evidence of Jefferson's willingness to abandon his out-of-power principles of strict construction, might more usefully be noticed as an example of a decisionmaking process in which the executive did not prematurely commit the administration to an inflexible position but left open future options. Thus, although Jefferson drew up two drafts of a constitutional amendment and submitted both to members of his Cabinet, in the end he abandoned the proposed amendment altogether and sent the Louisiana Treaty to the Senate without a recommendation for an amendment. This decision resulted from the opinions of advisers who did not share the President's view of the need for a constitutional amendment and from the course of events which argued persuasively for speedy ratification of the Louisiana Treaty.[31] While Jefferson thought it "important in the present case to set an example against broad construction by appealing for new power to the people," he concluded: "If however our friends shall think differently, certainly I shall acquiesce with satisfaction, confiding that the good sense of our country will correct the evil of construction when it shall produce ill effects."[32] Jefferson's advisers and Republican friends did indeed differ with the President, and in the final decision their views prevailed.

Although Jefferson's decisionmaking process did not include a

[31] Jefferson's views and actions in regard to the constitutional question regarding Louisiana are analyzed in detail in Malone, *Jefferson the President: First Term*, pp. 311-332.

[32] Jefferson to Wilson Cary Nicholas, Sept. 7, 1803, Jefferson Papers, Lib. Cong. Jefferson was replying to Nicholas's letter of Sept. 3, 1803, in which Nicholas had written that upon examining the Constitution, he found the power of the government to acquire territory and to admit new states "as broad as it could well be made" and did not "see anything in the Constitution that limits the treaty making power, except the general limitations of the powers given to the government." *Ibid.*

systematic procedure for consultation with legislative leaders, there was considerable informal consultation by both the President and the members of his Cabinet with Republican leaders in Congress, and the President and his department heads were easily accessible to all members of Congress. Jefferson also relied on members of his Cabinet to serve as conduits for public and party views; and he continued a voluminous private correspondence with political friends and party leaders throughout the country. Since Jefferson regarded the Republican party as representative of public opinion —commanding the support of two-thirds to three-fourths of the voters—and persisted in seeing the Federalists as a misguided faction, he drew no distinctions between majority public opinion and Republican party sentiment. Thus to Jefferson the mechanisms of the Republican party provided a means through which public sentiment could influence public policy.

IV. The President's Cabinet

THE CABINET WAS THE CENTRAL MECHANISM OF the policymaking structure of the presidency under Jefferson. The members of the Cabinet were not only the President's chief administrative officials, they were also his major advisers. His closest political confidant was Secretary of State; his chief consultant on economic and financial matters was Secretary of the Treasury. A very accessible President, Jefferson sought out and received information and opinions from all over the country, but he had no friend or adviser outside his Cabinet to whom he turned in making the decisions of government.

Believing that "those of the cabinet council of the President should be of his bosom-confidence,"[1] Jefferson shared all confidential information with them. "Unless restrained especially to *personal* confidence I always think myself at liberty to communicate things to the head of the department to which the subject belongs," he said.[2] In Madison, his longtime friend, Jefferson had within his Cabinet a colleague with whom he could discuss even the question of his relationship to department heads. Before issuing a circular on departmental procedures in November 1801, Jefferson asked Madison to review it. "Will you consider whether a copy of the inclosed sent to each head of department would be best," he wrote, "or to avail myself of your kind offer to speak to them. My only fear as to the latter is that they might infer a want of confidence on my part. But you can decide on sounder views of the subject than my position may admit. If you prefer the letter, modify any expressions which you may think need it."[3] Madison approved of the President's circular, and Jefferson sent it to the heads of all the departments the next day.[4]

The correspondence that passed between the President and the members of his Cabinet was remarkably open. Members gave their

---

[1] Jefferson to Samuel Dexter, Feb. 20, 1801, Jefferson Papers, Lib. Cong. This letter shows that Jefferson used the term "cabinet" from the outset of his presidency.

[2] Jefferson to Gallatin, Apr. 7, 1802, Gallatin Papers, N.-Y. Hist. Soc.

[3] Jefferson to Madison, Nov. 5, 1801, Madison Papers, Rives Collection, Lib. Cong.

[4] Jefferson, circular to the heads of the departments, Nov. 6, 1801, James Madison Papers, Lib. Cong.

views frankly when the President asked for them and felt free to volunteer unsolicited opinions. Gallatin did not hesitate to advise the President against sending a letter explaining appointment policies to William Duane, editor of the Philadelphia *Aurora*, even though Jefferson had spent considerable effort preparing the letter and said that he was "strongly of opinion it will do good." Gallatin observed that "unforeseen circumstances may produce alterations in your present view of the subject, and if you shall hereafter think proper to act on a plan somewhat different from that you now consider as the best, a commitment would prove unpleasant."[5] On reconsideration, the President did not send the letter. Members of the Cabinet freely gave their advice on the drafts of messages that the President submitted to them, sent recommendations to the President concerning matters that they thought the President should present to Congress, and offered procedural advice.[6]

No record has been found of any Cabinet officer complaining that he was not listened to by the President. Jefferson respected the judgment of his advisers and treated them as equals.[7] "Of your candor and indulgence I have experienced repeated proofs," Gallatin wrote the President in 1806; "the freedom with which my opinions have been delivered has been always acceptable and approved, even when they may have happened not precisely to coincide with your own view of the subject and you have thought them erroneous."[8] Six weeks after joining Jefferson's Cabinet as Attorney General, Caesar A. Rodney wrote to his father: "I had a very high opinion of Mr. Jefferson you know before and indeed it was a matter of habit and affection with me, but I never knew him until I saw his open undisguised frankness to his official advisers whether when singly or in cabinet meeting or council."[9]

Friction among members of Jefferson's Cabinet was infrequent, the principal tension being between the Secretary of the Treasury and the Secretary of the Navy. Gallatin thought that Smith was not strict enough in the administration of Navy expenditures, and

[5] Jefferson to Gallatin, July 25, 1803; Gallatin to Jefferson, Aug. 11, 1803, Adams, ed., *Gallatin Writings*, I, 129, 134.

[6] Dearborn to Jefferson, Dec. 5, 16, 1801; Gallatin, "Outlines, etc.," received Nov. 9, 1801; Madison to Jefferson, received Nov. 16, 1801, Jefferson Papers, Lib. Cong.

[7] See Jefferson to Gallatin, Nov. 28, 1801, Adams, ed., *Gallatin Writings*, I, 74.

[8] Gallatin to Jefferson, Oct. 13, 1806, *ibid.*, p. 310.

[9] Caesar A. Rodney to Thomas Rodney, Mar. 15, 1807, Brown Collection, Hist. Soc. Del.

being opposed to a Navy in the first place, he kept a close watch on that department. Gallatin felt strongly that Congress should be as specific as possible in appropriating funds and that administrators should adhere rigidly to these appropriations.[10] Having advocated specific appropriations and protested Federalist administrative laxity while he was in Congress, he sought from the beginning of Jefferson's presidency to commit the new Republican administration to strict practices. For example, the item "contingency expenses" in a department budget was sure to catch his eye. When Smith included in his proposed budget for 1803 an item of forty thousand dollars for general contingencies, Gallatin protested to the President that there were already contingencies for vessels in service, contingencies for repairs, contingencies for the marine corps, and contingencies for stores. "What those 40,000 dollars, therefore, are for, I am totally at a loss to know; only 16,000 are asked for the military establishment." At most, Gallatin thought that ten thousand dollars should cover general contingencies. "Indeed, I cannot discover any approach towards reform in that department (the navy)," he told the President, "and I hope that you will pardon my stating my opinion on that subject, when you recollect with what zeal and perseverance I opposed for a number of years, whilst in Congress, similar loose demands for money."[11] When in 1805 the Secretary of the Treasury requested that departmental expenditures be kept low for several months in order to accumulate funds to meet certain French bills without borrowing, Gallatin thought the Navy Department did not assist much in the effort. "As I know that there was an equal wish in both Departments to aid in this juncture," he wrote the President, "it must be concluded either that the War is better organized than the Navy Department, or that naval business cannot be conducted on reasonable terms." Again expressing concern about naval expenditures, Gallatin concluded: "On this subject, the expense of the navy greater than the object seemed to require, and a merely nominal accountability, I have, for the sake of preserving perfect harmony in your councils, however grating to my feelings, been almost uniformly silent; and I beg that you will ascribe what I now say to a sense of duty and to the grateful attachment I feel for you."[12]

[10] Gallatin to Jefferson, received Nov. 16, 1801, and notes on message, November 1801, Adams, ed., *Gallatin Writings*, I, 68.

[11] Jefferson to Gallatin, Jan. 18, 1803, *ibid.*, p. 117.

[12] Gallatin to Jefferson, May 30, 1805, *ibid.*, p. 234.

The President's own style of seeking consensus and maintaining harmony set a tone for the administration that his Cabinet members respected, but as Gallatin's letter indicates, there was tension at times within the Cabinet. With all Cabinet officers sharing the President's confidence, he was able to keep friction at a minimum. In retirement Jefferson looked back at his administration as "an example of harmony in a cabinet of six persons, to which perhaps history has furnished no parallel."[13]

President Jefferson consulted with his advisers individually and collectively. "The ordinary business of every day is done by consultation between the President and the Head of the department alone to which it belongs," he explained. "For measures of importance or difficulty, a consultation is held with the Heads of departments, either assembled, or by taking their opinions separately in conversation or in writing."[14] The practice which Jefferson most regularly followed was that of assembling the department heads and the Attorney General in a Cabinet meeting, though at times he did collect separate opinions. The latter procedure was so unusual in the early years of his presidency, however, that when following it in 1804 he felt called upon to explain that in this case he was "beginning the practice of separate consultation, which a host of considerations satisfy me is a very salutary and useful one to be resorted to occasionally." He also asked Madison if he would "be so good as to endeavor, in an unsuspected way, to observe to the other gentlemen the advantages of sometimes resorting to separate consultation? To Mr. Gallatin may be remarked the incipient indisposition which we noted in two of our brethren on a late consultation; and to the others may be suggested the other important considerations in it's favor."[15] Jefferson argued that separate consultation was "most strictly in the spirit of the constitution. Because the President, on weighing the advice of all, is left free to make up an opinion for himself."[16] Nevertheless, he admitted that the procedure he normally followed was that of holding Cabinet meetings. "The harmony was so cordial among us all," he recalled,

[13] Jefferson to Comte Destutt de Tracy, Jan. 26, 1811, Ford, ed., *Jefferson Writings*, IX, 307. In describing the Cabinet as composed of six persons, Jefferson was including himself.

[14] Jefferson to Walter Jones, Mar. 5, 1810, *ibid.*, p. 273. See also Jefferson to William Short, June 12, 1807, *ibid.*, pp. 69-70.

[15] Jefferson to Madison, Apr. 9, 1804, Madison Papers, Rives Collection, Lib. Cong.

[16] Jefferson to Walter Jones, Mar. 5, 1810, Ford, ed., *Jefferson Writings*, IX, 273.

"that we never failed, by a contribution of mutual views on the subject, to form an opinion acceptable to the whole. I think there never was one instance to the contrary, in any case of consequence."[17] Separate consultation was largely resorted to in instances where friction was anticipated. "The method of separate consultation, practised sometimes in the Cabinet," Jefferson observed, "prevents disagreeable collisions."[18]

Although many matters were decided by the President and the head of the department most directly concerned, the President consulted the entire Cabinet on foreign policy. There is no indication that Jefferson considered foreign policy a matter to be worked out by the President and the Secretary of State, nor did he feel it was a responsibility to be delegated to the Secretary of State. Although Madison was Jefferson's closest and most influential foreign-policy adviser, Jefferson took charge of the direction of foreign affairs and included all of his Cabinet in the decisionmaking process in that area. It was the leading subject recorded in Jefferson's minutes of the Cabinet. Except for several meetings devoted to appointment and removal problems early in the administration and a series of Cabinet sessions relating to the Burr conspiracy, most recorded Cabinet meetings were dominated by the discussion of foreign affairs. It may be that Jefferson simply did not record many other matters, which he expected a department head to keep track of. His minutes were kept for his own use, not to provide a record for historians, and the subject on which he most needed to keep notes was foreign affairs. But, while these notes may not reveal the complete scope of Cabinet deliberations, they leave no doubt as to the full involvement of the Cabinet in the making of foreign-policy decisions.[19] Jefferson's correspondence with members of his Cabinet also supports this conclusion.[20]

When news of a breakdown in negotiations with Spain arrived during the summer recess of 1805, packets of papers were shuttled between members, all of whom were asked for advice. "General Dearborn has seen all the papers," the President wrote to Madison who was then in Philadelphia. "I will ask the favor of you to communicate them to Mr. Gallatin and Mr. Smith. From Mr. Gallatin I shall ask his first opinion, preparatory to the stating

[17] *Ibid.*

[18] Jefferson to Joel Barlow, Jan. 24, 1810, *ibid.*, p. 269.

[19] See note 34 below for a list of Jefferson's Cabinet minutes.

[20] Jefferson to Madison, Apr. 11, 1806, Madison Papers, Rives Collection, Lib. Cong.

formal questions for our ultimate decision. I am in hopes you can make it convenient on your return to see and consult with Mr. Smith and Gen. Dearborn, unless the latter should be come on here where I can do it myself. On the receipt of your own ideas, Mr. Smith's and the other gentlemen, I shall be able to form points for our final consideration and determination."[21] This letter reveals much about Jefferson's procedures and the participation of the entire Cabinet in foreign-policy decisions, and it shows how the President directed the process. Had the President and his Cabinet been in Washington, members would have been summoned to a Cabinet meeting rather than consulted through the mail; but whatever the procedure, their counsel was sought—and not as a perfunctory gesture. "I am anxious to receive the opinions of our brethren after their review and consideration of the Spanish papers," Jefferson wrote with obvious sincerity to Madison in late August.[22] Within the next few weeks he received long letters from both Gallatin and Smith,[23] and Dearborn paid a visit to Monticello.[24] Meanwhile, there were exchanges of letters with the Secretary of State,[25] and the Cabinet was scheduled to meet as soon as the administration reassembled.[26]

Meetings of the Cabinet did not take place on any regular schedule. Early in the administration, Gallatin suggested that meetings be held once a week,[27] but Jefferson doubted that matters "out of the common line and presenting difficulty are numerous enough to furnish subjects of conference weekly."[28] He thus followed the practice of summoning the Cabinet when there were subjects demanding consideration, sending notices such as: "At present there is a sufficiency of matter and I propose therefore a

[21] Jefferson to Madison, Aug. 7, 1805, Ford, ed., *Jefferson Writings*, VIII, 375.

[22] Jefferson to Madison, Aug. 25, 1805, *ibid.*, p. 376.

[23] Gallatin to Jefferson, Sept. 12, 1805, with enclosure on Spanish affairs, Adams, ed., *Gallatin Writings*, I, 241-254. Smith to Jefferson, Sept. 16, 1805, Letters of Sec. of Navy to President, RG 45, Natl. Archives. Smith's copy of this letter is in Robert and William Smith Papers, Maryland Historical Society.

[24] Jefferson to Madison, Sept. 16, 1805, Ford, ed., *Jefferson Writings*, VIII, 379.

[25] Jefferson to Madison, Aug. 27, 1805, acknowledging Madison's letter of Aug. 20, *ibid.*, p. 377.

[26] Jefferson to Madison, Sept. 18, 1805, Madison Papers, Rives Collection, Lib. Cong.

[27] Gallatin to Jefferson, Nov. 9, 1801, Jefferson Papers, Lib. Cong.

[28] Jefferson to Gallatin, Nov. 10, 1801, Gallatin Papers, N.-Y. Hist. Soc.

meeting for the day after tomorrow at 12 aclock."[29] The midday hour of meeting was preferred by the President, and Cabinet meetings were scheduled to adjourn in time for him to take his daily horseback ride before dinner at three-thirty. Sometimes, when an early afternoon hour was set, Cabinet members were invited to stay for dinner, as indicated in the following note to John Breckinridge:

> Th: Jefferson asks the favor of the Attorney General to meet him with the heads of department tomorrow at 1 aclock to consult on Tunisian and Tripolitan affairs and to do him the favor to dine with him.

Thursday Mar. 13. 06.[30]

In periods of crisis, the Cabinet was summoned on short notice. "Our government has, it is reported, received Dispatches from England, and the Cabinet was called at three o'clock this day (Sunday)," wrote Senator Samuel L. Mitchill in indicating that he was anxiously awaiting word of what transpired at the Cabinet meeting on December 6, 1807.[31] In such critical times, Cabinet sessions might last all afternoon. During the period of the Burr conspiracy, Senator Plumer recorded in his journal on Sunday, December 21, 1806, that: "At little past twelve the President had all the heads of department at his house, where they remained till near evening. All that I have yet learnt of the result is that dispatches were immediately sent by Expresses into the western country."[32] On occasion the Cabinet met without the President in attendance, although apparently only upon his direction. "The President being too sick to be present at a consultation, wishes one to take place among the Heads of Department without him," Madison wrote to Gallatin in March 1803. "Will you be so good as to join us for that purpose as soon as you can make it convenient today?"[33] It may be assumed from Madison's note that the Secretary of State presided in the President's absence.

The number of Cabinet meetings held during Jefferson's presidency cannot be accurately established. Jefferson kept minutes or

[29] Ibid.

[30] Jefferson to Breckinridge, Mar. 13, 1806, Breckinridge Family Papers, Lib. Cong.

[31] Mitchill to his wife, Dec. 6, 1807, Mitchill Papers, Museum C.N.Y.

[32] Brown, ed., Plumer's Memorandum, p. 536.

[33] Madison to Gallatin, Tuesday, Mar. 29, [1803], Gallatin Papers, N.-Y. Hist. Soc.

made memoranda on at least fifty-four meetings during his eight
years in office,[34] but there is evidence to indicate that he did not
record every meeting or that some minutes have not survived. When
there were major decisions to be made, the Cabinet met frequently,
sometimes every day. There were conferences on three consecutive
days in May 1801, when the administration was just getting under
way and a number of pressing matters had to be decided.[35] The
Cabinet was summoned frequently during the Burr conspiracy.
The British attack on the *Chesapeake* in June 1807 produced almost daily meetings of the Cabinet during the height of the crisis.[36]
After the Cabinet met four times in six days, Jefferson sought to
work out procedures that would make such frequent meetings
unnecessary. "Something now occurs almost every day on which
it is desirable to have the opinions of the heads of departments,"
he explained, "yet to have a formal meeting every day would con-
sume so much of their time as to seriously obstruct their regular
business." He thus proposed that Cabinet officers call on him at
their convenience each day, at which time he could transact regular departmental business, communicate new information that he
had received, and collect their opinions on developments.[37] While
this procedure may have avoided the necessity of some Cabinet sessions, it did not eliminate the need for bringing the whole Cabinet
together for joint consultation, and during July 1807 the Cabinet
met no less than seven times.[38]

Jefferson once said that in Cabinet meetings his vote counted
as one. How often an actual count was made is unclear, but in his

[34] The major series of Jefferson's notes are: Mar. 8-9, 1801, Jefferson
Papers, v. 110, p. 18892, Lib. Cong.; May 15, 1801–Apr. 8, 1803, *ibid.*,
v. 112, p. 19297; May 7, 1803–Nov. 19, 1805, *ibid.*, v. 131, p. 22677;
Mar. 5, 1806–Feb. 25, 1809, *ibid.*, v. 157, p. 27516; and "Notes of Consultations, 1807," *ibid.*, v. 169, p. 29819. Jefferson kept these notes on
separate sheets of paper which were later incorporated along with other
memoranda in the "Anas," printed in Ford, ed., *Jefferson Writings*, I, 291-
339. The Anas make it appear that Jefferson kept a rather jumbled diary
in which notes on Cabinet meetings were mingled with notes on conversations at the dinner table. His papers, however, reveal that he kept separate
series of notes, one on Cabinet meetings and another on various conversations.

[35] Jefferson, notes for May 15, 16, and 17, 1801, printed in Anas, Ford,
ed., *Jefferson Writings*, I, 293-295.

[36] *Ibid.*, pp. 317-325.

[37] Jefferson to Gallatin, July 10, 1807, Ford, ed., *Jefferson Writings*,
IX, 104.

[38] "Notes of Consultations, 1807," Jefferson Papers, v. 169, p. 29819,
Lib. Cong. Printed in Anas, Ford, ed., *Jefferson Writings*, I, 325-330.

minutes of Cabinet meetings Jefferson commonly recorded that decisions were unanimous, or, if they were not, he indicated the exceptions. Most of the time the Cabinet reached decisions which all could approve. But votes were taken at times, as when the number of naval captains was reduced from fifteen to nine "by a vote on each man struck off."[39] In his notes Jefferson made entries such as: "It is determined by unanimous consent (except Mr. Gallatin who dissents),"[40] or "There was no dissent to any article of this plan."[41] Frequently he elaborated on the differing views. The following entry in his minutes for April 14, 1806, is an example of Jefferson's own record of a Cabinet session.

Apr. 14. Present all the heads of departments. The message of this day to both houses respecting Tunis was submitted to them, and approved by all of them except Mr. Gallatin who would rather no communication on the subject should be made. However, he suggested several alterations in the message, which were made.

Information being received that the Spaniards prohibit our vessels passing up the Mobille, I proposed for their consideration whether I should communicate it to Congress. We all were against it, except Mr. Madison and Genl. Dearborne who rather leaned to a communication, but acquiesced. The reasons against it were that it would open anew the sluices of invective which had lately been uttered there, the lateness of the period, Congress being to adjourn in 7 days, the impossibility of their administering a remedy in that time, and the hope that we might get along till we could hear from Paris.[42]

The above example has been selected because its limited agenda and comprehensible decisions make it suitable to illustrate the nature of Jefferson's Cabinet meetings. It should be stressed, however, that the minutes of most Cabinet sessions recorded more critical questions under consideration, reported continuing problems over a period of time, and suggest long agenda and lengthy deliberations.[43]

Jefferson frequently recorded differing views, but more often he

[39] Jefferson, notes for Oct. 22, 1801, printed in *ibid.*, p. 296.
[40] Jefferson, notes for July 8, 1805, *ibid.*, p. 307.
[41] Jefferson, notes for Apr. 25, 1806, *ibid.*, p. 315.
[42] Jefferson, notes for Apr. 14, 1806, Jefferson Papers, v. 157, p. 27516, Lib. Cong.
[43] On Jefferson's notes on Cabinet meetings, see note 34 above.

recorded unanimous decisions. "We sometimes met under differences of opinion," he recalled, "but scarcely ever failed, by conversing and reasoning, so to modify each other's ideas, as to produce an unanimous result."[44] As President, he sought to develop a Cabinet consensus in which he shared. While he might speak of his vote in the Cabinet as counting as one, he did not believe that all were equal in authority. In referring to the unanimity of his Cabinet, he said that he was "not certain this would have been the case, had each possessed equal and independent powers. . . . But the power of decision in the President left no object for internal dissension."[45] Jefferson referred to the members of his Cabinet as his "coadjutors,"[46] and there was never any doubt as to who was in charge of the administration.

Jefferson's Cabinet was unusually stable, with far less turnover than in the Cabinets of either of his predecessors. Excluding the temporary assignments at the beginning of Jefferson's presidency, the first change in the Cabinet came when Attorney General Lincoln resigned at the end of December 1804 after Jefferson's reelection for a second term.[47] The President had been aware of Lincoln's intention, having discussed possible candidates with Gallatin as early as September,[48] and upon Lincoln's resignation, he asked the Cabinet for recommendations for a successor. He received eight names from Gallatin and seven names from Dearborn. Gallatin listed John T. Mason, who lived in Georgetown, as "the best if he will accept" and Senator John Breckinridge of Kentucky, his second choice, as "very good if he will accept." Breckinridge headed Dearborn's list, though Dearborn did not indicate any preference.[49] Smith in a confidential note to the President said that he preferred either Mason or Breckinridge but that if neither would accept he would prefer that office to being Secretary of the Navy.[50] Jefferson's immediate response was that it would be easier to find a new Attorney General than a new Secretary of the Navy, but he suggested

[44] Jefferson to Comte Destutt de Tracy, Jan. 26, 1811, Ford, ed., *Jefferson Writings*, IX, 307-308.

[45] *Ibid.*

[46] Jefferson to William Short, June 12, 1807; Jefferson to Dearborn, June 8, 1808, *ibid.*, pp. 69, 171.

[47] Lincoln to Jefferson, Dec. 26, 1804; Jefferson to Lincoln, Dec. 28, 1804, Jefferson Papers, Lib. Cong.

[48] Gallatin to Jefferson, Sept. 18, 1804, *ibid.*

[49] Gallatin to Jefferson, received Jan. 3, 1805; Dearborn to Jefferson, Jan. 2, 1805, *ibid.*

[50] Smith to Jefferson, Jan. 2, 1805, *ibid.*

that Smith name three candidates for the Navy post and stop by for "a minute's conversation."[51] The outcome was that Jefferson nominated Smith to be Attorney General and Jacob Crowninshield, a representative from Massachusetts, to be Secretary of the Navy. Crowninshield had at first declined, but Jefferson pressed him to reconsider and after a conference with him got his consent to accept the appointment.[52] On March 2, 1805, the Senate approved the nominations of Smith to be Attorney General and Crowninshield to be Secretary of the Navy.[53] For a moment it appeared that Jefferson had made a major shift within his Cabinet, but at the end of March he received word from Crowninshield, who had returned home after the adjournment of Congress, that his wife's health made it impossible for him to accept the post.[54] Jefferson now persuaded Smith to stay on at the Navy Department[55] and continued the search for an Attorney General. In June he offered the appointment to John Julius Pringle, attorney general of South Carolina, who declined.[56] He then pressed the post upon John T. Mason, the person he would "rather have than any other."[57] After Mason refused,[58] Jefferson asked Breckinridge to take the post, explaining: "Your geographical position will enable you to bring into our councils a kno[w]le[d]ge of the Western interests and circumstances, for which we are often at a loss, and sometimes fail in our desires to promote."[59] Although Breckinridge accepted promptly, he did not take up the duties of the office until December 1805.[60] During the year that the office was vacant, Smith apparently performed the necessary duties.

Breckinridge's death a year later in December 1806, at age forty-six, again left Jefferson without an Attorney General. This

---

[51] Jefferson to Smith, Jan. 3, 1805, *ibid.*

[52] Crowninshield to Jefferson, Jan. 24, Feb. 20, 23, 1805, *ibid.*

[53] *Senate Executive Journal*, I, 484.

[54] Crowninshield to Jefferson, Mar. 27, 1805, Jefferson Papers, Lib. Cong.

[55] Henry Adams, *History*, III, 10-12, clarified Smith's continuance in the Navy Department, but Crowninshield's name still appears on many lists of Jefferson's Cabinet during his second term.

[56] Jefferson to Pringle, June 15, 1805; Jefferson to Dearborn, July 14, 1805, Jefferson Papers, Lib. Cong.

[57] Jefferson to Dearborn, July 14, 1805, *ibid.*

[58] John T. Mason to Jefferson, July 20, 1805; Dearborn to Jefferson, July 20, 1805, *ibid.*

[59] Jefferson to Breckinridge, Aug. 7, 1805, Breckinridge Family Papers, Lib. Cong.

[60] Lowell H. Harrison, *John Breckinridge: Jeffersonian Republican* (Louisville, 1969), pp. 188-189.

time he was able to fill the office more quickly. A month later he nominated Caesar A. Rodney, a former congressman from Delaware,[61] who took office promptly—he was recorded at a Cabinet meeting on February 2—and served for the remainder of Jefferson's second term.[62] On his list of possible Attorneys General in 1805, Gallatin had named Rodney as "not equal" to the job. But Jefferson had formed a good opinion of him when Rodney was in Congress, and he was assured by one prominent Pennsylvania Republican that his appointment would be popular both in Pennsylvania and in Delaware.[63]

There were no other changes in the Cabinet during the remainder of Jefferson's presidency. When Secretary of War Dearborn proposed to leave the administration as of July 1808, Jefferson succeeded in persuading him to stay.[64] Thus, during eight years the only resignation from the Cabinet was that of Levi Lincoln, and the only changes in the Cabinet were in the office of Attorney General. No other two-term President in American history has had a more stable Cabinet.

[61] Jefferson to the Senate, Jan. 15, 1807, Jefferson Papers, Lib. Cong.

[62] Jefferson, notes for Feb. 2, 1807, Ford, ed., *Jefferson Writings*, I, 322.

[63] Thomas Leiper to Jefferson, Jan. 11, 1807, Jefferson Papers, Lib. Cong.

[64] Jefferson to Dearborn, Jan. 8 and May 25, 1808, Ford, ed., *Jefferson Writings*, IX, 171-172; Adams, *History*, V, 9.

V. The Making of the Annual Message

AN EXAMINATION OF THE PROCESS BY WHICH JEF-
ferson prepared his annual messages to Congress provides
an excellent opportunity to observe the roles of the President and
his Cabinet in the formulation of policy. A principal means of influencing and directing legislative action, the annual message was
a major vehicle of executive policymaking. The address reported
on the state of the Union, directed the Congress to the consideration of specific problems and questions, and presented recommendations for legislative action. The procedures that Jefferson worked
out in preparing his first annual message were followed with only
minor changes in each of his subsequent years in office.

Jefferson started to work on his first legislative report well in
advance of the meeting of Congress. He began by gathering information from his department heads and then prepared a working
draft of the message, which he submitted to all members of his
Cabinet for their opinions and suggestions for revisions. About
four weeks before December 7, 1801, the day Congress was due
to assemble, Jefferson sent his draft to Madison with a note
asking him to give the paper "a serious revisal, not only as to matter, but diction." While he urged the Secretary of State to correct
both substance and grammar, he said more about the latter in his
brief note, indicating that in compliance with the "purists of New
England," strictness of grammar should be followed if it did not
weaken expression. "But where by small grammatical negligences
the energy of an idea is condensed, or a word stands for a sentence," he said, "I hold grammatical rigor in contempt."[1] He also
asked Madison to collect the documents from the State Department
that should accompany the message. Madison promptly complied
with the President's request, and within two days Jefferson was
able to send the draft on to Gallatin, to whom he wrote:

> Thomas Jefferson asks the favor of Mr. Gallatin to examine
> the enclosed rough draft of what is proposed for his first com-
> munication to Congress; not merely the part relating to finance,
> but the whole. Several paragraphs are only provisionally drawn,

[1] Jefferson to Madison, Nov. 12, 1801, Ford, ed., *Jefferson Writings*,
VIII, 108-109.

to be altered or omitted according to further information. The whole respecting finance is predicated on a general view of the subject presented according to what I wish, but subject to the particular consultation which Th. J. wishes to have with Mr. Gallatin, and especially to the calculation proposed to be made as to the adequacy of the impost to the support of government and discharge of the public debt, for which Mr. G. is to furnish correct materials for calculation. The part respecting the navy has not yet been opened to the Secretary of the Navy. What belongs to the Departments of State and War is in unison with the ideas of those gentlemen. Th. J. asks the favor of Mr. Gallatin to devote the first moments he can spare to the enclosed, and to make notes on a separate paper, with pencilled references at the passages noted on.[2]

Gallatin's reply together with detailed notes on the message filled nine pages, all prepared within two days of the receipt of Jefferson's draft.[3] Gallatin analyzed the President's message paragraph by paragraph, raising questions and offering suggestions. In general, Gallatin's comments indicate his concern that Jefferson was being too optimistic about the state of the nation and its immediate prospects. The Secretary of the Treasury was particularly worried that the President might be presenting too favorable a view of the nation's finances. Concerned about the effects of peace in Europe on American import revenues, he was fearful that revenues would not be sufficient to permit the elimination of the taxes, including all internal taxes, that Jefferson proposed. He sent Jefferson several pages of computations showing projected import duties calculated on the basis of restoration of peace. Gallatin also feared that there could not be the reduction in government expenses that Jefferson envisioned. "You will also see that I lay less stress on savings on the civil list than you do," Gallatin told the President. He had investigated the matter when he was in Congress and found that the savings would be so trifling that "the whole time I was in Congress, eager as we all were to propose popular measures and to promote economy, I never proposed it. . . . It seems to me that the subject may be mentioned, but less stress laid on it."[4] Gallatin also suggested that the President not refer to specific taxes, but

2 Jefferson to Gallatin, Nov. 14, 1801, *ibid.*, p. 109.

3 Gallatin to Jefferson, received Nov. 16, 1801, and notes [November 1801], Jefferson Papers, Lib. Cong.

4 Gallatin to Jefferson, received Nov. 16, 1801, and notes on message, November 1801, Adams, ed., *Gallatin Writings*, I, 71, 66.

propose a general reduction or the elimination of a whole class of taxes, in order not to be charged with "interference with legislative details."[5] In conclusion, Gallatin wrote the President that "there is but one subject not mentioned in the message which I feel extremely anxious to see recommended." This was the need for tighter controls on public funds through more specific appropriations, stricter application of funds to the objects for which they were appropriated, and a single accounting office.[6]

The President accepted the suggestion and added a paragraph making the recommendation. He also made a number of other modifications in light of Gallatin's comments, but he determined the final tone and content of the message. In regard to the decline in revenue from import duties which Gallatin stressed as a consequence of peace in Europe, Jefferson noted in his final draft that "changes of foreign relations now taking place so desirably for the world, may for a season affect this branch of revenue, yet, weighing all probabilities of expense, as well as of income, there is reasonable ground of confidence that we may now safely dispense with all the internal taxes, comprehending excises, stamps, auctions, licenses, carriages, and refined sugars."[7] The final message had the optimistic tone that had made Gallatin fear that rising expectations might be disappointed.

Jefferson's practices in subsequent years suggest that the draft of his message would have been sent after Gallatin's review to Secretary of War Dearborn, but there are no notes from Dearborn on the message in Jefferson's papers. That Dearborn was consulted, however, is evident from Jefferson's comment to Gallatin that the military section was in unison with the ideas of the Secretary of War.

On November 21 the President received more than six pages of comments on his message from the Secretary of the Navy. Smith had studied the message closely, and he sent the President a page-by-page commentary with suggested revisions. As he did in regard to suggestions from other Cabinet members, Jefferson adopted some of Smith's recommendations and rejected others. In recommending a reduction of the fourteen-year residence requirement for naturalization in his message to Congress, Jefferson followed the suggestion of Smith who thought the President ought not to specify a new requirement. "With respect to the Naturalization Laws,

[5] *Ibid.*, p. 65.   [6] *Ibid.*, p. 68.

[7] Jefferson, first annual message, Dec. 8, 1801, Ford, ed., *Jefferson Writings*, VIII, 119.

would it not be better to submit the subject generally without prescribing in detail the modifications?" Smith had asked the President, pointing out that "the opinions of Republicans upon this are various."[8] Jefferson heeded Smith's advice to leave the matter to Congress to decide.

In the case of one of the most significant alterations Jefferson made in his message, Smith's comments are the strongest on record. In his original draft, Jefferson had included a paragraph on the sedition act in which he declared the law "in palpable and unqualified contradiction to the constitution." He explained that "considering it then as a nullity, I have relieved from oppression under it those of my fellow-citizens who were within the reach of the functions confided to me"—a reference to his executive order ending all prosecutions under the sedition law soon after taking office. Jefferson then went on to state that each branch of the government had the right to decide on the validity of an act according to its own judgment, and he proceeded to assert the right of the executive to decide on the constitutionality of the sedition act. "On my accession to the administration," he explained, ". . . called on by the position in which the nation had placed me, to exercise in their behalf my free and independent judgment, I took that act into consideration, compared it with the constitution, viewed it under every aspect of which I thought it susceptible, and gave it all the attention which the magnitude of the case demanded. On mature deliberation, in the presence of the nation, and under the tie of the solemn oath which binds me to them and to my duty, I do declare that I hold that act to be in palpable and unqualified contradiction to the constitution."[9] This was an extraordinary assertion that the President could declare an act of Congress unconstitutional, and Jefferson was prepared to thus invalidate the sedition law, even though the law had expired on the last day of Adams's administration.

In his review of the President's draft of the message, Gallatin had noted: "*Sedition Act:*—The idea contained in the last paragraph had struck me; but to suggest its propriety to the Legislature appears doubtful." Smith's reaction was much stronger. "Altho' I have no doubt of the power of the President to grant in the exercise of a sound discretion a Nolle prosequi," he wrote, "yet I have very serious doubts respecting the ground stated. The prevailing opinion among Constitutional Lawyers will I believe be opposed

8 Smith to Jefferson, received Nov. 21, 1801, Jefferson Papers, Lib. Cong.
9 Jefferson, draft of first annual message, Dec. 8, 1801, *ibid.*

to the principles set forth." Then he asked: "But why make this communication? Does it give to Congress any information of the State of the Union or does it recommend to them any Measure that requires legislative provision? Will it not be hazarding, without necessity, a division of our friends? The claim to such Executive prerogative will not be easily assented to."[10]

These comments indicate that the members of the administration did not hesitate to speak freely to the President, even Smith who never shared a close personal relationship with Jefferson. Moreover, the President listened. On his draft of the message, Jefferson placed brackets around the paragraph on the sedition act, and in the margin he noted: "The whole paragraph was omitted as capable of being chicaned, and furnishing some thing to the opposition to make a handle of. It was thought better that the message should be clear of every thing which the public might be made to misunderstand."[11] Since Gallatin had also expressed doubts about the paragraph, Smith was not alone in questioning the President. But his criticism was the most vigorous on record, and it provides proof that Smith played a far more active role in Jefferson's administration than historians have generally recognized. Certainly there is far more evidence of Smith's influence in Jefferson's decision to strike out the paragraph declaring the sedition act unconstitutional than that of any other member of Jefferson's Cabinet.[12]

In addition to the written critiques on his first annual message from Gallatin and Smith, Jefferson also received a similar memorandum prepared by Attorney General Lincoln, some of whose suggestions he incorporated into the message while rejecting others. The major change prompted by Lincoln's review resulted from his query whether postage on newspapers might be added to the list of taxes to be eliminated. "The means of instruction and of spreading knowledge are generally in all the states, not only exempted from duty, but in whole, or in part aided by public support," Lincoln pointed out. "The measure would be very popular with printers and both popular and useful with the people at large. The postage is too small to be of importance as an item of revenue, and

10 Smith to Jefferson, received Nov. 21, 1801, *ibid.*

11 Jefferson, draft of first annual message, Dec. 8, 1801, *ibid.*

12 Irving Brant, in *James Madison, Secretary of State*, curiously credits Madison with convincing Jefferson to omit this paragraph, concluding: "Since nothing was said to Madison on the subject, it is obvious that the advice to omit came from him" (p. 58).

yet so large as to prevent in some degree the circulation of papers."[13] The influence of Lincoln's recommendation is visible on the draft of Jefferson's message. Following the list of taxes that were to be abolished, Jefferson carefully interlined this addition: "to which the postage on newspaper may be added to facilitate the progress of information."[14] A New Englander, Lincoln also questioned the statement that Jefferson proposed to make in regard to the carrying trade. "We cannot indeed but all feel an anxious solicitude for the difficulties under which our carrying trade will soon be placed," Jefferson wrote, "but whether it can be relieved, otherwise than by time, is a subject for consideration."[15] Lincoln thought that this wording could be improved "considering the importance that agriculture and manufactures are to our country and the ideas, too prevalent in the northern states, that the administration and the southern states, are hostile to our navigation and commerce." He suggested that some such general expressions as the following would have a good effect:

> It is with Congress to consider whether the agriculture and manufactures of our country require immediate attentions, beyond the private patronage of individuals, and whether any legislative efforts are necessary or practicable for the securing, encouraging, or preventing the abridgement of the carrying trade particularly important to the prosperity of the northern states.[16]

Jefferson did not incorporate the above paragraph into his message, but he did go back and alter the language of the passage quoted earlier. Instead of saying "but whether it [the carrying trade] can be relieved, otherwise than by time, is a subject for consideration," he changed the passage to read: "How far it can be relieved, otherwise than by time is a subject for important consideration." This small textual revision altered considerably the tone and meaning of the passage.

Although he promised that additional documents, reports, and separate messages would be presented to Congress in the course

[13] [Levi Lincoln, suggested revisions in Jefferson's first annual message], Jefferson Papers, v. 109, p. 18686, Lib. Cong.

[14] Jefferson, draft of first annual message, Dec. 8, 1801, Jefferson Papers, Lib. Cong.

[15] *Ibid.*

[16] [Lincoln, suggested revisions in Jefferson's first annual message], Jefferson Papers, v. 109, p. 18686, Lib. Cong.

of the session, the President used the annual message to outline his major legislative recommendations. In 1801 Jefferson recommended the abolishment of all internal taxes; the reduction of the Army, the Navy, and the civil establishment; the revision of the judiciary structure; the revision of militia laws; the restructuring of the accounting offices; and the reduction of the residence requirement for naturalization. He also mentioned other matters, such as naval yards and harbor fortifications, that Congress might need to reexamine.[17] The leading recommendations of Jefferson's first annual message followed the broad policy positions that he had outlined in his inaugural address and the Republican party had advocated in the campaign of 1800.

In preparing his second annual message, Jefferson introduced several changes. One of these was a Cabinet consultation on the message after it had been individually examined by each member. While such discussion may have taken place in 1801, no record of it has been found; and the letters Jefferson wrote in 1802 suggest that he was initiating, or at least formalizing, the procedure at that time. In sending his second message to Madison for review, Jefferson instructed: "Will you give the inclosed a serious perusal, and make such corrections in matter and manner as it needs, and that without reserve, and with as little delay as possible, as I mean to submit it in like manner to the other gentlemen, singly first, and then together."[18] In a similar note enclosing the draft of the message to Dearborn, Jefferson wrote that "when individually examined by all the gentlemen, I propose to submit it to them collectively."[19] This procedure apparently left some of the more controversial subjects to be determined in a Cabinet meeting. On the subject of Louisiana, Gallatin noted in his comments on the 1802 message: "this being the most delicate part of the speech, will, I presume, be the subject of a Cabinet consultation."[20]

Beginning in 1802, Jefferson included in his annual messages a summary of government finances, indicating the payments on the national debt, the balance in the treasury, and the outlook for receipts and expenditures. This summary, which Jefferson and Gallatin came to refer to as "the financial paragraph," was an

[17] Jefferson, first annual message, Dec. 8, 1801, Ford, ed., *Jefferson Writings*, VIII, 108-125.

[18] Jefferson to Madison, Nov. 18, 1802, Madison Papers, Rives Collection, Lib. Cong.

[19] Jefferson to Dearborn, Nov. 22, 1802, Jefferson Papers, Lib. Cong.

[20] Gallatin to Jefferson, received Nov. 21, 1802, *ibid.*

advance look at the Secretary of the Treasury's annual report submitted to Congress early in each session. Washington and Adams had not included such a paragraph in their annual addresses, but Jefferson's messages being in written form and longer than those of his predecessors offered more opportunity for citing statistics. Gallatin furnished the President the "sketches from which to make the financial paragraph," and in 1806 the summary he provided was included in the message with only minor rewording and rearrangement.[21] In 1807 Jefferson sent to Gallatin "the form in which I would wish to place the financial paragraph, with blanks which I must ask you to fill up."[22] He followed the same practice the next year in preparing his last annual message.[23]

The correspondence that passed between the President and members of his Cabinet shows that each year Jefferson followed the procedure of submitting the draft of the message to the heads of the departments in the order of the ranking of the departments. Thus, the draft of the message went first to the Secretary of State, then to the Secretary of the Treasury, the Secretary of War, the Secretary of the Navy, and finally to the Attorney General, who headed no department but who had Cabinet status. Such attention to procedure illustrates the careful and systematic process the President followed in preparing his annual messages.[24]

Jefferson's manuscript papers show also that all members of his Cabinet contributed to his annual messages.[25] His papers contain comments and suggestions on drafts of his annual messages from every member of his Cabinet except Attorney General Breckinridge, who assumed office too late in 1805 to contribute and was

[21] Gallatin to Jefferson, Nov. 26, 1806, *ibid.*

[22] Jefferson to Gallatin, Oct. 21, 1807, Adams, ed., *Gallatin Writings,* I, 357-358. On Oct. 14, 1807, Jefferson had written to Gallatin: "Can you give me the materials for the financial paragraph of the message?" Jefferson Papers, Lib. Cong.

[23] Gallatin to Jefferson, Nov. 2, 1808, Adams, ed., *Gallatin Writings,* I, 421.

[24] The evidence does not support the statement in Walters, *Gallatin,* that Jefferson "made a practice of submitting messages and other important state papers to Gallatin first among the cabinet members" (p. 145).

[25] This fact has been obscured by the publication of numerous notes by Gallatin and Madison, but few by other Cabinet members. In printing Jefferson's annual messages, Paul L. Ford included selected notes and revisions primarily from Gallatin and Madison; he included several brief comments by Dearborn, and one set of notes by Rodney, but he printed no comments from Smith and gave no hint that any such papers existed. Ford, ed., *Jefferson Writings,* VIII and IX, *passim.*

on his deathbed in 1806 when the message of that year was pre-pared.[26] While Gallatin's notes are the only ones that can be found for all eight messages, on five out of the eight messages Jefferson received written comments from at least four of the five members of his Cabinet, and only on the last message in 1808 are the comments of Madison and Gallatin the only such memoranda in his papers. While Secretary of War Dearborn's observations were generally brief, he responded in writing to the President's request for review of the annual message in at least six of the eight years, and the memoranda by Secretary of the Navy Smith, who wrote detailed critiques, can be found in the President's papers for five years—the same number for which written commentaries by Madison are known. There are suggestions for revisions from Attorney General Lincoln on three messages and from Attorney General Rodney on one, thus providing additional evidence of the wider participation of the Attorney General in the councils of the administration than is generally recognized.[27]

An analysis of the commentaries provided to the President by his advisers shows that those by Gallatin were consistently the most detailed and analytical and that year after year the Secretary of the Treasury assumed the heaviest burden of reviewing the President's messages. It also shows that Dearborn regularly made the least contribution. In 1806 on the letter from Jefferson enclosing the draft of his message and asking for Dearborn's suggested alterations, the Secretary of War simply wrote: "H. Dearborn has looked over and considered the inclosed without observing any thing that he can consider as a defect, or requiring alteration."[28] He returned the message on the same day that he received it.

The greatest revelation of Jefferson's papers relating to his annual messages is the important contribution of Secretary of the

[26] Breckinridge arrived in Washington on Dec. 7, 1805, to assume the duties of Attorney General; he died Dec. 14, 1806. Harrison, *John Breckinridge*, pp. 189, 198.

[27] The Jefferson Papers, Lib. Cong., contain letters or notes submitted to President Jefferson on his annual messages as follows: 1801, from Gallatin, Smith, and Lincoln; 1802, from Gallatin, Dearborn, Smith, and Lincoln; 1803, from Madison, Gallatin, Dearborn, and Lincoln; 1804, from Madison, Gallatin, Dearborn, and Smith; 1805, from Madison, Gallatin, Dearborn, and Smith; 1806, from Madison, Gallatin, and Dearborn; 1807, from Gallatin, Dearborn, Smith, and Rodney; 1808, from Madison and Gallatin.

[28] Jefferson to Dearborn, Nov. 17, 1806; Dearborn to Jefferson, received Nov. 17, 1806, Jefferson Papers, Lib. Cong.

Navy Smith, whose role in Jefferson's administration has been commonly denigrated. Smith consistently made valid criticisms of Jefferson's messages; Jefferson clearly took them under advisement, and a number of alterations can be traced directly to Smith's objections. In the draft of his 1805 message, Jefferson had made reference to American harbors being blockaded and beleaguered by private and public armed ships. Smith pointed out that "Blockade is a technical term and has an appropriate meaning. In that sense it is not intended I trust, to state that our harbours have been molested. Would not some other word be more proper. . . . Besides the blockading of our harbours could not be considered but as an act of publick War."[29] Neither Madison nor Gallatin, who had already reviewed the message, had caught this slip.[30] Jefferson changed "blockaded" to "watched," and in response to Smith's further objections to "beleaguering," he struck it out.[31]

Smith's active participation in the preparation of the annual messages suggests that the description of Jefferson's administration as a triumvirate of Jefferson, Madison, and Gallatin needs revision.[32] The Attorney General also, as has been noted, participated in the drafting of the message. Madison and Gallatin were certainly Jefferson's closest advisers, but all members of Jefferson's administration had a part in the formulation of policy.

At times, Cabinet members offered so many suggestions and made so many criticisms regarding the annual message that they were apparently somewhat embarrassed to be giving the President of the United States so much advice, even if he had asked for it. Lincoln explained in 1802: "In obedience to directions I have stated without reserve the doubts which occurred to me—am sensible of the impropriety of expressing positively ideas, as substitutes for the ones objected to. The design was only the more fully to explain my difficulties."[33] Even Gallatin, who took the President's messages apart line by line and did not hesitate to give such blunt opinions as "*Dry dock*—I am *in toto* against this recommendation," felt compelled to conclude five pages of frank comments on

[29] Smith to Jefferson, received Nov. 27, 1805, *ibid.*

[30] Madison's notes, received Nov. 24, 1805, are printed in Ford, *Jefferson Writings*, VIII, 386. Ford also mistakenly printed Madison's notes on Jefferson's message of 1804 with the 1805 message. Gallatin's notes of Nov. 25, 1805, are in Adams, ed., *Gallatin Writings*, I, 264-265.

[31] The draft with corrections is printed in Ford, ed., *Jefferson Writings*, VIII, 389, 390.

[32] See Walters, *Gallatin*, p. 145.

[33] Lincoln to Jefferson, Nov. 25, 1802, Jefferson Papers, Lib. Cong.

Jefferson's message of 1802 with the explanation that "the President's directions to make free remarks have been very freely followed." Then he added one last sentence: "As to style I am a bad judge, but I do not like, in the first paragraph, the idea of limiting the quantum of thankfulness due to the supreme being; and there is also, it seems, too much said of the Indians in the enumeration of our blessings in the next sentence."[34]

The drafts of Jefferson's messages and the notes on them by members of his Cabinet show that Jefferson year after year paid close attention to their suggestions. On the manuscripts of some of the notes from his advisers there are marginal marks by items that were incorporated into his message or used to revise it. Some of the proposed stylistic revisions he ignored, such as Dearborn's suggestion in 1804 that instead of using the word "war" he write "that scurge to the human race, which has so frequently laid waste many of the best parts of the world."[35] But he gave attention to substantive objections, though he did not always accept the recommendations offered. His department heads checked on the accuracy of statements in relation to their departments, and he regularly made modifications to meet their objections. In the draft of his message of 1804, Jefferson wrote that "in pursuance of the views of Congress in their act of Feb. 28, 1803 a number of gunboats have been built and are now ready for service."[36] Secretary of the Navy Smith objected: "The language respecting gun Boats is rather too strong. The truth is—two of the gun Boats have been built and equipped for service—Eight more are building and most of these will be launched in the course of next Month."[37] Jefferson did not provide Congress with these details; he simply altered his message to read: "The act of Congress of Feb. 28, 1803 for building and employing a number of gunboats is now in a course of execution to the extent there provided for."[38] This change suggests Jefferson's efforts to keep his message honest while presenting the administration in a favorable light.

There is ample proof that the reactions of the members of Jefferson's Cabinet to drafts of his message influenced the President

[34] Gallatin to Jefferson, received Nov. 21, 1802, *ibid.*

[35] Dearborn to Jefferson, received Oct. 29, 1804, *ibid.*

[36] Jefferson, draft of fourth annual message, Jefferson Papers, v. 144, p. 25106, Lib. Cong.

[37] Robert Smith to Jefferson, received Oct. 31, 1804, Jefferson Papers, Lib. Cong.

[38] Jefferson, draft of fourth annual message, Jefferson Papers, v. 144, p. 25106, Lib. Cong.

to make major alterations. One of the best documented examples is the message of 1807, which reported on the critical events that had followed the attack on the *Chesapeake* in June 1807 and indicated administration policy in regard to the crisis with Great Britain. Jefferson's early draft of this message struck several members of his Cabinet as being excessively warlike. "I have kept your message longer than usual," Gallatin wrote the President in October 1807, "because my objections being less to details than to its general spirit, I was at a loss what alterations to submit to your consideration." Then he went on to explain that "the message appears to me to be rather in the shape of a manifesto issued against Great Britain on the eve of a war, than such as the existing undecided state of affairs seems to require."[39] Smith reacted in much the same way, writing the President: "As peace is our favorite object, as it is not intended to excite Congress to a declaration of war, or to present to them a ground upon which to found any war measures and especially as there is at this moment a pending negotiation for the adjustment of all our differences with G. Britain upon every point, I could wish the Message had less of the air of a Manifesto against the British government."[40] Gallatin stressed "that recommendations or incitements to war should not, under our Constitution, be given by the Executive without much caution; and, above all, that the precise manner and time of acting which Congress should adopt are subjects which have not yet been sufficiently examined." While convinced that Great Britain would prefer war to any retaliation short of war that the United States might attempt, he thought world and national opinion would support the United States if the nation did not rush into war before an answer was received and Britain refused to disavow or make satisfaction for the outrage on the *Chesapeake*. "Public opinion abroad is to us highly valuable; at home it is indispensable," he noted. "I feel strongly impressed with the propriety of preparing to the utmost for war," he wrote in conclusion, ". . . but in the mean while persevering in that caution of language and action which may give us some more time and is best calculated to preserve the remaining chance of peace and most consistent with the general system of your Administration."[41] While Gallatin and Smith were the most

[39] Gallatin to Jefferson, Oct. 21, 1807, Adams, ed., *Gallatin Writings*, I, 358.

[40] Smith to Jefferson, received Oct. 19, 1807, Jefferson Papers, Lib. Cong.

[41] Gallatin to Jefferson, Oct. 21, 1807, Adams, ed., *Gallatin Writings*, I, 359, 361.

outspoken, Dearborn also suggested that Jefferson's message contained some expressions that were "rather stronger than may be necessary" and others that seemed to indicate the intention of offensive operations.[42] In view of these criticisms, Jefferson sharply modified his message, making major alterations in its content and tone. Gallatin felt that he was largely responsible for this. "The President's speech was originally more warlike than was necessary," he told his wife, "but I succeeded in getting it neutralized; this between us; but it was lucky; for Congress is certainly peaceably disposed."[43]

Although Jefferson retained and exercised the authority to make the final determination of what went into his reports to Congress, he sought to present to Congress the policy that best represented a consensus of his Cabinet. "There was not a single paragraph in my message to Congress, or those supplementary to it," Jefferson wrote of his message of 1805, "in which there was not an unanimity of concurrence in the members of the administration."[44] Jefferson drew the members of his Cabinet into the task of preparing special messages in much the same manner as he did in writing annual messages.[45] He also submitted his second inaugural address to his advisers for review, and they offered their suggestions on this occasion with the same freedom that characterized their criticisms of other messages.[46]

All of the evidence relating to Jefferson's annual messages—the notes in his private papers, the letters to and from Cabinet members, their detailed critiques of his drafts, and the revisions that Jefferson made before sending his message to Congress—documents a pattern of close attention to content, to wording, and to the general tone of the messages. What was said was carefully weighed as to how it might be interpreted not only by members

[42] Dearborn to Jefferson, received Oct. 17, 1807, Jefferson Papers, Lib. Cong.

[43] Gallatin to his wife, Oct. 30, 1807, Adams, *Gallatin*, pp. 363-364. Madison's role in regard to the revision of this message is unknown. It may be assumed that there was consultation between the President and the Secretary of State, but there are no notes from Madison on the message.

[44] Jefferson to William Duane, Mar. 22, 1806, Ford, ed., *Jefferson Writings*, VIII, 432.

[45] See confidential message on Spain, Dec. 6, 1805, and accompanying notes, Ford, ed., *Jefferson Writings*, VIII, 397-402; Gallatin, remarks on Spanish message [Dec. 3, 1805], Adams, ed., *Gallatin Writings*, I, 275.

[46] See Madison's comments, Feb. 8 and 21, 1805, in Ford, ed., *Jefferson's Writings*, VIII, 342; Gallatin's comments [Feb. 12, 1805], in Adams, ed., *Gallatin Writings*, I, 227-228.

of Congress but also by the Federalist opposition and by Republicans in various parts of the country. The review of the messages by Cabinet members from different sections of the country helped the President avoid statements that might create alarm in particular quarters. Lincoln was especially concerned in his reviews of the messages about public reaction; he sought to anticipate responses that might be expected from his native New England and to warn the President against statements that he thought the Federalists might use to attack the administration.[47]

The annual message was not only a means of putting the President's program before Congress, it was also a way of getting his program before the country at large. The message received considerable coverage in the press, the text being printed in newspapers and broadsides. Republicans reprinted and circulated additional copies for partisan political purposes. "Your message to Congress at the opening of the Session, has had a wonderful operation here," Caesar A. Rodney wrote to the President from Wilmington, Delaware, after Jefferson's first annual message. "It answers the most sanguine expectations of all our friends, and we consider it of so much importance that we are about publishing in pamphlets three thousand copies thereof to be distributed among the people in the three counties."[48] Republican party leaders throughout the country warmly applauded Jefferson's first annual message and uniformly predicted that it would have a useful political effect. Philip Norborne Nicholas, chairman of the Republican state committee in Virginia, reported: "The presidents communication to congress has met the warmest approbation of the Republicans here both on account of the manner and the matter. The idea of such a diminution of the taxes will secure to the administration the hearts of the people more than any thing which could happen. This is an argument which will have weight in every part of the Union and with all parties."[49] In addition to anticipating the political advantages to be gained at the polls, some Republican leaders also recognized the importance of Jefferson's message in strengthening the President's political support to the point where he might, if he chose, display less partisanship without endangering his party leadership. James Monroe explained: "Your last communication

[47] Lincoln to Jefferson, Nov. 25, 1802, and Oct. 10, 1803, Jefferson Papers, Lib. Cong.

[48] Rodney to Jefferson, Dec. 27, 1801, *ibid.*

[49] Philip N. Nicholas to Wilson C. Nicholas, Dec. 14, 1801, Wilson Cary Nicholas Papers, Univ. of Va.

to the Congress has placed your administration on such ground with the republican party, as to leave it in your power to act with respect to removals from office, as you may judge expedient; by which I mean that if you are disposed in any case where the merit of the party interests you, to indulge feelings of benevolence towards him or them, your so doing will excite no uneasiness among the republicans."[50]

The relationships between the President, the Cabinet, and the Congress, the interaction of policy and party politics, and the dual role of Jefferson as the leader of the nation and the head of the Republican party were all clearly displayed in the making of the annual message.

[50] Monroe to Jefferson, Dec. 21, 1801, Stanislaus M. Hamilton, ed., *The Writings of James Monroe*, 7 vols. (New York, 1898-1903), III, 323.

VI. The Four Departments

THE DEPARTMENTS OF STATE, THE TREASURY, War, and the Navy constituted the central administrative apparatus of the national government during Jefferson's presidency. Although organized much like a department, the General Post Office had a distinct status, and the Postmaster General was not a member of the President's Cabinet. The Attorney General was a member of the Cabinet, but there was no department of justice, and the Attorney General had no administrative duties. The heads of the four departments were both Cabinet policymakers and working administrators. There were no assistant secretaries in any of the departments, and only the Treasury Department had a staff of subordinate officers. The Secretary of State and the Secretary of the Treasury each earned $5,000 per year—the top salary in government except for that of the President—indicating the primary importance of the two departments. The salaries of $4,500 paid to the heads of the War and the Navy departments reflected lesser duties and status. The departments performed not only the functions assigned to them by the laws creating them and by subsequent statutes, but they also had responsibilities given to them by the President, by congressional resolutions, and by the call of legislative committees. Since neither the President, nor members of Congress, nor congressional committees had staffs, all staff work, whether legislative or executive, was done by the departments. Departments also maintained the only files of executive records.[1]

The government establishment was small and each department largely autonomous. There were no general services, central purchasing agents, or uniform personnel policies. Each department head hired his own clerks or delegated the authority to a subordinate officer. Each office provided for its own housekeeping functions out of funds appropriated for those purposes, buying its own furniture and equipment, wood and coal, stationery, sealing wax, and red tape. The State Department bought oats to feed a horse kept for the use of the department and paid for horseshoeing out of its contingent fund.[2] The Treasury provided its own watch-

---

[1] Jefferson to Madison, Dec. 29, 1801, Jefferson Papers, Lib. Cong.

[2] Daybook of the Department of State for Miscellaneous and Contingent Expenses, Jan. 20, 1802, May 12, 1803, microcopy T-903, Natl. Archives.

men. The development of a bureaucracy, however, was foreshadowed by increasing attention to procedures. Congress was becoming more systematic in its requirements for reports from departments; the number of periodic specialized reports presented to Congress was steadily rising.[3] A move toward more uniform personnel policies was signaled in 1806 when Congress introduced the requirement of an annual report from each department listing names, salaries, and duties of the clerks employed in each office.[4]

The legislature was well served by the executive departments. Formal reports to Congress were accurate, often elaborately detailed, and generally useful. Answers from department heads to inquiries from congressional committees were normally prompt, straightforward, and informative, and they were often accompanied by copies of relevant documents or summaries of data abstracted from departmental files by painstaking clerks. In that age of slow communications, candlelight, and quills, department offices little resembled the computer centers of modern bureaucracy, but the mass of surviving evidence indicates that they effectively served the process of government in a young and growing nation.

THE DEPARTMENT OF STATE

The Department of State was first in rank but smallest in size of the four departments. During most of Jefferson's presidency, the Secretary of State had a staff consisting of a chief clerk, six other clerks (one of whom was in charge of the patent office and had no other duties), and a messenger.[5] When Madison submitted an estimate of the expenses for operating his office during 1803, he listed the following:[6]

[3] For the 10th Congress, 2nd Session, there is a compilation of printed annual reports from the executive departments—the first such printed series of reports in the National Archives. House Records, RG 233, Natl. Archives.

[4] Required by act of Apr. 21, 1806. *The Debates and Proceedings in the Congress of the United States, 1789-1824*, 42 vols. (Washington, D. C., 1834-1856), 9 Cong., 1 Sess., 1280-1282. Hereafter cited *Annals of Congress*.

[5] See Appendices I and II.

[6] The total proposed departmental budget was $271,426.67. This included salaries and expenses for ministers abroad, and expenditures in relation to treaties, captures, relief of seamen, the consular service, and other foreign and domestic functions. Estimates for 1803, Nov. 13, 1802, Domestic Letters of the Department of State, microcopy M-40, Natl. Archives.

Salaries in the Department of State

Secretary of State	$ 5,000
Clerks	5,950
Messenger	410
	$11,360

Contingent expenses in the Department of State

Fire and candles	$ 200
Newspapers for the office and public agents abroad	150
Mediterranean passports, printing and parchment	1,350
Patents, personal passes, circulars and other blanks	1,000
Purchasing books	400
Stationery	600
For purchasing maps and charts	500
Miscellaneous	500
	$ 4,700

Although the department was not organized to reflect its different functions, it was both a foreign office and a home office. The conduct of foreign affairs was the primary function, but the department was also charged with administering a diverse group of domestic matters which Congress or the President had assigned to it. Generally, all functions not related to finances or military and naval affairs were placed under the Secretary of State, but in a few cases —notably that of the mint—duties were assigned to his office that might more logically have been delegated to the Treasury Department.

The Department of State handled all correspondence with and instructions to ministers and consuls and all negotiations with foreign governments. The routine correspondence with ministers abroad was not extensive, since after Jefferson became President he reduced the diplomatic establishment to three ministers—at London, Paris, and Madrid—and the staff of each consisted of a secretary of legation.[7] There were two commissioners in England on the spoliations commission under the seventh article of the

---

[7] "Salaries and Compensation to the Secretary of State, his Clerks, and the Officers acting in connection with the Department of State" [December 1801], Jefferson Papers, v. 119, p. 20522, Lib. Cong.

Jay Treaty and a secretary to the commissioners.[8] In the consular service there were forty-eight consuls, four vice-consuls, and eleven commercial agents at the end of 1801, but only four (the consul general at Algiers and consuls at Tunis, Tripoli, and Morocco) received salaries. All others were allowed commissions on their services. The consul at London also acted as agent for managing claims for spoliations and received a small salary in that capacity. Agents in London and Jamaica for the relief and protection of American seamen completed the overseas roster.[9] This was not a large number of persons with whom to maintain contact. However, in the course of Jefferson's presidency a series of major problems in foreign relations placed a heavy administrative burden on the Department of State.

Madison in 1807 reported that his clerks were assigned "a considerable quantity of copying, particularly of correspondence with our ministers and agents abroad, frequently including voluminous documents."[10] In both 1807 and 1808 he asked Congress for additional office help, calling attention to the progressive increase in the business of the department and in 1808 to the "peculiar increase in the business growing out of our foreign relations."[11] The matter of impressed seamen required a growing amount of time and paperwork. One list covering applications made to the British government in cases of impressment for a nine-month period in 1804-1805 filled forty-five pages in a record book,[12] and in 1806 Madison reported that "the business attending the impressment of American seamen" had "much increased."[13] The State Department also issued passports for citizens going abroad. Since all clerks in the Secretary of State's office assisted in the copying of papers relating to foreign affairs "according to the

[8] *ASP, Misc.*, I, 306-307. The fifth commissioner on the mixed board was an American, and half of his salary was paid by the United States.

[9] *Ibid.*, pp. 307-308.

[10] *Report of the Secretary of State, Inclosing a List of the Persons Employed as Clerks in His Office, during the Year 1806*, Jan. 14, 1807 (Washington, D. C., 1807), Rare Book Division, Lib. Cong.

[11] Report enclosed in Madison to the Speaker of the House, Jan. 22, 1808, Original Reports of the State Department, House Records, RG 233, Natl. Archives.

[12] The list presented to Congress Mar. 8, 1806, covered the period Sept. 1, 1804, to May 18, 1805. Reports of the State Department, III, 393-437, *ibid.*

[13] *Report of the Secretary of State . . . Clerks in His Office . . . 1806.*

state of their other engagements,"[14] it is impossible to determine what portion of each clerk's time was devoted to foreign, and what to domestic, duties. But each clerk had one or more specific assignments in relation to the domestic duties of the department. These included the collating of the laws and their publication, the making out and recording of land patents, and the preparing of all commissions issued by the President.[15] The Secretary of State also had the responsibility for taking the census every ten years, but the census schedule did not require one during Jefferson's eight years in office.

The publication of the laws was a sizeable operation. Congress required that all acts of Congress be published in at least one newspaper in each state and authorized the Secretary of State to publish them in as many as three, if necessary, to insure extensive circulation.[16] This placed in the hands of the Secretary of State considerable patronage, which Madison directed exclusively to Republican presses.[17] The heaviest work in relation to the publication of the laws came at the end of each session of Congress, when the laws for that session were printed in pamphlet form and distributed. There was always considerable pressure for the work to be done promptly. Five thousand copies of the laws passed at each session were distributed among the states,[18] copies going to federal, state, and local officials, county courthouses, and similar public offices. At the beginning of every session of Congress, each member was supplied with a copy of the laws passed at the preceding session; a new member received a complete set of the laws of the United States. The back copies and sets of the laws were kept in the office of the Secretary of State, who furnished them to the Secretary of the Senate or the Clerk of the House of Representatives for distribution to the legislators.[19]

The seal of the United States was in the custody of the Department of State, and all commissions issued by the President were prepared in that office. This meant, for example, that after the Secretary of the Treasury and the President had agreed upon an appointment for a collector or other officer under the Treasury

[14] *Ibid.*   [15] *Ibid.*

[16] Act of Mar. 2, 1799, *Annals of Congress*, 5 Cong., 3 Sess., 3933.

[17] See Cunningham, *Jeffersonian Republicans in Power*, pp. 247-249.

[18] Act of Mar. 2, 1799, *Annals of Congress*, 5 Cong., 3 Sess., 3933.

[19] Jacob Wagner to Samuel A. Otis, Dec. 16, 17, 1801, Nov. 29, 1802, Senate Records, RG 46, Natl. Archives.

Department, his commission then had to be prepared in the State Department.[20]

The business of recording land patents required an increasing amount of time. Early in 1806, Gallatin sent the Secretary of State a copy of a letter from the Register of the Treasury reporting certain inconveniences arising from delays in obtaining patents for lands. He also noted that "complaints of a similar nature have been made by individuals; and it is necessary that you should be informed that the number of applications for Patents daily increases, and will probably be much greater during this year than it has heretofore been."[21] Gallatin suggested that Madison might need to employ an additional clerk to handle the work.

In 1802 the business of granting patents for useful inventions and copyrights was separated from the other functions of the Department of State by placing Dr. William Thornton in charge of a patent office. Thornton officially was appointed as a clerk in the State Department, but he assumed the title "superintendent of the patent office." Madison listed him separately in his reports on clerks employed in the State Department, reporting "for services rendered by Dr. Thornton, in superintending and issuing patents for useful inventions and discoveries; in securing copy-rights, etc., etc., a compensation has been allowed him of $1,400."[22] Thornton headed his letters "Department of State, Patent Office," and corresponded directly with congressional committees.[23] Although his salary was that of a clerk, Thornton's professional and social standing enabled him to move comfortably among the officers of government. From 1794 to 1802, Thornton, who had submitted the winning design for the Capitol, was one of the commissioners of the District of Columbia. The Madisons and the Thorntons were close friends; in fact, Madison lived next door to Thornton in a house on F Street near Fourteenth Street that Thornton had had built for him.[24]

Thornton had a separate office in the building housing the State, War, and Navy departments, and he kept there the models and drawings of inventions for which patents had been issued and

[20] See Gallatin to Madison [1801], Madison Papers, v. 23, p. 112, Lib. Cong.

[21] Gallatin to Madison, Jan. 15, 1806, Albert Gallatin Papers, Lib. Cong.

[22] *Report of the Secretary of State . . . Clerks in His Office . . . 1806.*

[23] Thornton to Jacob Crowninshield, Nov. 21, 1807, House Records, RG 233, Natl. Archives.

[24] Brant, *Madison, Secretary of State*, p. 43; White, *Jeffersonians*, p. 208.

copies of the books for which copyrights had been granted. By 1807 the models and the books were overflowing the small office. Senator Plumer reported: "The floors and shelves are covered with models thrown together without any order or regularity. The books lie in an irregular confused pile on shelves and window stools covered with dust. The room is too small for the purpose; but a little money and labor would procure a convenient and useful book case, and arrange the models and drawings in order."[25] Thornton did keep his records in order, however, and in 1805, at the request of the House of Representatives, he furnished a list of all "persons who have invented any new and useful arts, machine, manufacture or composition to whom patents have been issued."[26] The establishment of the patent office, which Thornton would head until his death in 1828, began the process of placing the different functions of the Department of State in separate offices, but no other steps were taken in that direction during Madison's tenure as Secretary of State.

The routine domestic duties assigned to the State Department were largely performed by the clerks under the supervision of the chief clerk with little actual involvement of the Secretary of State. Something of the routine in the department can be seen in the following letter written by Daniel Brent to Madison while the latter was absent from the capital in May 1802. Brent, who had been left in charge of the office due to the illness of chief clerk Jacob Wagner, wrote:

> I shall not trouble you with any of the letters that have been received for you since your departure, as they are generally unimportant, and not one of them requires your attention. No private or foreign ones have been received. Mr. Dallas has furnished the Copy of the proceedings of the District Court of Pennsylvania, in the case of the Magicienne, and I have sent it to the Secretary of the Treasury's Office, as you directed. The printing of the laws goes on very well; and no attention, on the part of your Office, will be wanting to accelerate a completion of the work. Two Clerks, of other Offices, who write very good hands, are employed every after-noon on our Records, and I flatter myself that they will nearly bring them up by your Re-

[25] Brown, ed., *Plumer's Memorandum*, Jan. 3, 1807, p. 556.
[26] Original Reports of the Secretary of State, Feb. 18, 1805, House Records, RG 233, Natl. Archives. This list is printed in *ASP, Misc.*, I, 423-431.

turn, notwithstanding their being so much in arrear. Most of us, at the same time, are closely occupied, in arranging the papers etc. belonging to the Office. A duplicate Copy of the late Convention with England goes to the President today, to be ratified by him. The public prints accompanying this contain all the news we have.[27]

The duties of the chief clerk were described in a memorandum to Jefferson in 1801 in the handwriting of Jacob Wagner and undoubtedly prepared by him. This job description—a rare document for this early period—provided the following information:

J. Wagner has been employed in filing away the papers, making copies of the most confidential of them, when necessary; receiving applications about the current business and having them executed; collating the laws and superintending their publication and distribution; the receipt and management of complaints for captures and impressments of American citizens, when they do not embrace such peculiar circumstances as render them worthy of the particular attention of the Secretary; drafting commissions, formal official papers and answers to such letters of inferior consequence, as the Secretary may charge him with, etc., etc. It is not easy to comprehend every particular of his duty in a concise sketch: but the above will serve to give a view of the general nature of his usual employment, the design of which is, by saving the attention of the Secretary, as much as possible, from matters of routine and small importance, to enable him to devote his time to objects of greater magnitude.[28]

Wagner may have exaggerated his own importance, but the chief clerk of the State Department did serve as something of an assistant secretary of state. Senator John Quincy Adams, in fact, referred to the chief clerk as the "Under-Secretary of State,"[29] and John Randolph regarded the holder of the post as one "in whom a high confidence is necessarily reposed."[30] During the summer recess in August and September, when, as Jefferson explained, "we are in the habit of leaving things to the chief clerks,"[31] Wagner

[27] Daniel Brent to Madison, May 18, 1802, Madison Papers, Lib. Cong.
[28] Memorandum [1801], Jefferson Papers, v. 235, p. 42188, Lib. Cong.
[29] Adams, ed., *Memoirs of John Quincy Adams*, I, 475.
[30] *ASP, Misc.*, I, 385.
[31] Jefferson to Dearborn, Jan. 8, 1808, Ford, ed., *Jefferson Writings*, IX, 172.

took charge of the State Department with far more assertiveness than did chief clerks or subordinate officers in other departments.[32] Although Wagner referred all policy matters to the Secretary of State for decision, he gave his opinion on them and prepared drafts of letters for Madison to approve.[33] "I transmit a copy of the enclosed very important letter from the Spanish Minister, by this mail to Monticello, lest the President might not receive it with the greatest celerity," he wrote to Madison in September 1803. "If I entered into a reflection upon it, it would be that orders have doubtless issued to the Spanish officers in Louisiana to delay the delivery to France."[34] Such observations were not the customary deferential remarks of a clerk, but of a man who was acting as an assistant secretary. Many other letters from Wagner to Madison reflect this role.[35] In a letter which also provides a summary of his direction of the department in the absence of the Secretary of State, Wagner wrote to Madison in August 1801 that:

> I have the honor to enclose you various letters, some of them merely for your information, and others which will perhaps require answers. Among them are the three letters you received from Mr. Thornton [British chargé], with sketches of answers, I have drafted. They seemed to me to present a fit, if not a necessary occasion of explaining to him our right to admit French privateers and prizes to an equal footing with those of Great Britain. At least I am satisfied that we cannot avoid the decision much longer, and it is so important, that it will be convenient to take it up as early a possible for consideration. You will notice at the end of Mr. Thornton's letter of the 23rd July a promise to communicate to us further information respecting the prize at Boston, which will serve as a cover for any delay that may be necessary in making the decision.
>
> By the next post I shall send you some topics to enter into a letter for Mr. Pinckney, to be forwarded by Mr. Brown.
>
> I have made a memorandum on the letter from George Helmbold which shews the footing on which the printing of the laws stands in Pennsylvania. I think the idea of printing the laws in German in one of the papers in Pennsylvania, an important one.

32 See Wagner to Madison, Aug. 24, 1803, Madison Papers, Lib. Cong.
33 See Wagner to Madison, Aug. 21, 1804, *ibid.*
34 Wagner to Madison, Sept. 9, 1803, *ibid.*
35 See the following letters from Wagner to Madison during the summer recess in 1801: Aug. 3, 10, 17, 24, 31, Sept. 7, 12, 14, 25, 1801, *ibid.*

The legislature of that State prints its journals in German as well as in English; and I am not certain, whether the laws of the State are not also reprinted in the same manner.[36]

Wagner's letter shows his readiness to advise the Secretary of State, but it is important to note that the chief clerk's advice was not necessarily followed. In regard to the drafts of the letters to Thornton, which Madison forwarded to Jefferson, the President took a quite different approach. "When we consider that our minister has to wait months and years for an answer to the most trifling or the most urgent application to his government," he wrote to Madison, "there would be no indecency to decline answering so crude an application as this respecting the prize, which he does not know if it be prize or not, brought into Boston *as the newspapers say*. I think it better to avoid determining, with foreign ministers, hypothetical cases." Jefferson then went on to outline what he thought the answer to Thornton should be, in effect saying that Thornton raised questions "which it cannot now be necessary to determine."[37] Foreign policy was not being made by the chief clerk of the State Department, though he did relieve the Secretary of State of many routine chores.

At times, Wagner went further in acting on the Secretary of State's behalf than some ministers to the United States thought proper. When in Madison's absence Wagner wrote to British minister Anthony Merry about American seamen, Merry, who was unusually touchy about protocol, protested by asking whether Wagner was authorized to correspond with ministers of foregin nations. In reporting the incident to Madison, Wagner explained: "Had Mr. Merry been here I should in all probability have made these requests verbally, when he would not have questioned my authority more than he has heretofore, either in making communications to me on your behalf or in receiving them from me in like manner. As you were both absent I did by writing what I should otherwise perhaps have transacted personally."[38] Although in this case Merry thought Wagner was acting improperly, Wagner's comments indicate that the chief clerk regularly served as an aide to the Secretary in communicating with foreign ministers.

While the Secretary of State's principal energies were directed

[36] Wagner to Madison, Aug. 3, 1801, *ibid.*

[37] Jefferson to Madison, Aug. 12, 1801, Ford, ed., *Jefferson Writings*, VIII, 80-81.

[38] Wagner to Madison, Sept. 1, 1804, Madison Papers, Lib. Cong.

to matters of foreign affairs, the responsibilities of superintending the domestic duties assigned to his office required considerable attention. He handled correspondence with state governors, administered territorial governments, and directed federal marshals and district attorneys. His department received petitions for pardons and prepared recommendations in consultation with the Attorney General for consideration by the President.[39] Congress regularly referred various petitions to the Secretary of State; and legislative committees turned to him for information and recommendations, though the burden of such requests was generally less than on the other departments. The Secretary of State presented an annual return on the relief and protection of American seamen and was increasingly called upon for reports on impressed seamen.[40]

As the ranking member, the Secretary of State presided at Cabinet meetings in the President's absence, but there is no evidence that Madison attempted to be a first minister, or that the Department of State sought to expand its role or to intrude in other departments. The critical problems of foreign affairs which Madison faced as Secretary of State, together with the diverse domestic responsibilities of his department, kept him fully engaged. Nor did he assume the party role that might have been expected of one who had been so active in the early organization of the Republican party. While Madison advised the President on party matters and remained sufficiently engaged in partisan politics to win the presidential nomination as Jefferson's successor, the Department of State did not become the Republican party headquarters, and Madison was not directly engaged in the management of the party. The Department of State under Madison was primarily devoted to fulfilling its statutory responsibilities and the duties delegated to the Secretary of State by the President.

THE DEPARTMENT OF THE TREASURY

The Department of the Treasury had the most extensive administrative responsibilities of any of the departments, was the most elaborately organized, and employed by far the largest number of

[39] Leonard D. White, *The Federalists: A Study in Administrative History* (New York, 1948), p. 133; Domestic Letters of the Department of State, 1802-1808, M-40, Natl. Archives. The letter books of domestic correspondence show a considerable volume of such correspondence.

[40] Original Reports of the Secretary of State, 7th-10th Congresses, House Records, RG 233, Natl. Archives.

persons in its central offices and throughout the country. Of the 127 officers and employees in the Washington offices of the four departments and the General Post Office in 1801, 73 were in the Treasury Department. In 1808, at the end of Jefferson's presidency, the figures were only slightly different, with the Treasury employing 67 out of 123.[41] Outside the Washington offices, the Treasury employed in 1801 in the external revenue (customs) service 704 persons as collectors, naval officers, surveyors, masters and mates of revenue cutters, port inspectors, measurers, weighers, and gaugers. At many ports, one person filled several jobs; a port inspector was often also a weigher, measurer, and gauger. About one-fourth of those employed in the external revenue service were located in Massachusetts. The internal revenue service employed 500 persons as supervisors, inspectors, collectors, and auxiliary officers in the different states. The greatest number of internal revenue officers were located in Virginia, the state with the largest population, where 133 persons were employed.[42] When Congress repealed all internal taxes after June 30, 1802,[43] the entire internal revenue service was abolished, reducing the number of Treasury employees outside Washington by 40 percent. The elimination of the internal revenue service enabled the Treasury Department to absorb the increase in work brought about by the normal growth of the country and the extraordinary expansion of the nation by the Louisiana purchase without expanding the staff at headquarters.

The organization of the Treasury Department when Gallatin took office was basically that which had been established under Hamilton. In addition to the office of the Secretary, the department included the offices of the Comptroller, the Auditor, the Treasurer, the Register, the Commissioner of the Revenue, and the Superintendent of Stamps. "This constellation of great men in the treasury department was of a piece with the rest of Hamilton's plans," Jefferson insisted. "He took his own stand as a Lieutenant General, surrounded by his Major Generals, and stationing his Brigadiers and Colonels under the name of Supervisors, Inspectors, etc., in the different States."[44] Gallatin, however, was not prepared to dismantle the structure. He felt that "coming all new in the Adminis-

[41] See Appendix I.

[42] "Roll of the Officers, Civil, Military, and Naval, of the United States," Feb. 17, 1802, *ASP, Misc.*, I, 260-288.

[43] Act of Apr. 6, 1802, *Annals of Congress*, 7 Cong., 1 Sess., 1323-1326.

[44] Jefferson to Gallatin, Apr. 1, 1802, Ford, ed., *Jefferson Writings*, VIII, 141.

tration, the heads of Departments must obtain a perfect knowledge of all the details before they can venture on a reform. The number of independent officers attached to the Treasury renders the task still more arduous for me. I assure you that it will take me twelve months before I can thoroughly understand every detail of all those several offices. . . . Until I know them all I dare not touch the machine."[45]

The elimination of the internal revenue service ended the offices of the Commissioner of the Revenue and the Superintendent of Stamps, and Jefferson thought that "it remains to amalgamate the comptroller and auditor into one, and reduce the register to a clerk of accounts; and then the organization will consist, as it should at first, of a keeper of money, a keeper of accounts, and the head of the department."[46] But Gallatin did not adopt the President's suggestion, and the offices of the Comptroller, the Auditor, the Treasurer, and the Register remained unchanged. In fact, the Auditor and the Register—who had been appointed under Washington—remained throughout Gallatin's tenure as Secretary of the Treasury. New appointments of a Comptroller and a Treasurer were made within the first two years of Jefferson's presidency.

The most important of these offices was that of the Comptroller. John Steele, a Federalist appointed to the post by Washington in 1796, was retained by the new Republican administration, and he was soon assuring his Federalist friends that he had been treated "with respect" and "with a degree of confidence which cannot but be gratifying to an ingenuous mind. The kind, indeed I may say friendly deportment of the President himself had laid me under great obligations to him."[47] When Steele resigned in September 1802, it was due neither to his dissatisfaction with the administration nor to the administration's dissatisfaction with him but to illness in his family.[48]

The office that Steele vacated was not only the most important subordinate office in the Treasury Department, it was also the most important office outside the Cabinet. The Comptroller had a wide

[45] Gallatin to Jefferson, received Nov. 16, 1801, Adams, ed., *Gallatin Writings*, I, 72.

[46] Jefferson to Gallatin, Apr. 1, 1802, Ford, ed., *Jefferson Writings*, VIII, 141.

[47] Steele to John Haywood, July 12, 1801, Ernest Haywood Collection, Univ. of N. C.

[48] Steele to Jefferson, Sept. 30, 1802; Jefferson to Steele, Dec. 10, 1802, *ibid.*

range of responsibilities and considerable discretionary authority. His salary of $3,500—exceeded only by the heads of departments and the Chief Justice of the Supreme Court—reflected the responsibilities of his office.[49] With the Secretary of the Treasury, the Comptroller countersigned all warrants for money to be drawn from the Treasury, though his authority extended only to the legality of warrants not to their expediency. With the Auditor, the Comptroller was responsible for the settlement of all public accounts. The Auditor examined accounts submitted for settlement, examined the vouchers and supporting documents, and certified the balances to the Comptroller. His authority was subordinate to the Comptroller, but in making the initial examination of accounts, the Auditor exercised considerable discretionary responsibility. The Comptroller reviewed the accounts settled by the Auditor and certified the balances for recording by the Register. Any decision regarding the settlement of an account by the Auditor might be appealed to the Comptroller, whose decision was final.[50]

It was the duty of the Comptroller to see that regular and punctual payments were made into the Treasury of all moneys collected; in this connection he was authorized to initiate prosecutions against delinquent collectors for debts due the United States. In supervising the collectors, the Comptroller carried on considerable correspondence with them, sent out printed circulars of instructions over his name,[51] and assumed the responsibility of keeping them informed of new laws, of changes in laws affecting their duties, and decisions of the Supreme Court. He also ordered a halt to practices which he regarded as misinterpretations of acts of Congress and answered questions in regard to interpretation of laws relating to the customs service.[52]

Gallatin placed particular emphasis on the legal functions per-

[49] The heads of departments received $4,500 to $5,000; Associate Justices of the Supreme Court, $3,500; the Chief Justice, $4,000; the Postmaster General, $3,000; and the Attorney General, $3,000. *ASP, Misc.*, i, 302-305.

[50] The duties of the Comptroller as they had become fixed in the 1790s are well covered by White, *Federalists*, pp. 337-345. Hamilton described the duties of all Treasury officers in a report, Mar. 4, 1794; Harold C. Syrett, ed., *The Papers of Alexander Hamilton* (New York, 1961-), xvi, 114-115.

[51] A series of these circulars is in the Nicholas Gilman Papers, Lib. Cong.

[52] Gabriel Duvall, circulars, Mar. 18, 1803, Dec. 22, 1804, Mar. 9, 1805, *ibid.*; Duvall, circular, Sept. 5, 1806, Papers of U. S. Treasury Relating to Customs, Lib. Cong.

formed by the Comptroller. When he outlined the qualifications for the position after Steele had resigned in 1802, he said that "a certain degree of legal knowledge is the most essential qualification." Indeed, he thought it preferable to appoint a person with legal training "who had only a general idea of accounts, than a perfect accountant without law knowledge." He was led to this conclusion, he said, both by the duties of the office and by the fact that he was not a lawyer. "The law questions which arise in the Treasury (exclusively of those relating to the settlement of accounts) are numerous: during the Comptroller's absence, nearly one-half of my time is occupied by questions directed to me by collectors and which I would refer to him if he was present, or directed to him and which his clerks refer to me during his absence. If we have a Comptroller who is not a lawyer, it will considerably increase my labor, or rather prevent its being applied in the most proper manner." The Comptroller must also possess "method and great industry," Gallatin stressed, and "he should write, if not with elegance, at least with precision and great facility, for his correspondence is very extensive, and consists principally of decisions, instructions, and explanations." Protesting his own inadequacy to write "even a decent letter without great labor," the Secretary of the Treasury argued strongly for a Comptroller who could write with facility. "For the duties of the two offices are so blended in what relates to the collection of the impost," he said, "that a great part of the correspondence with collectors may fall either on the one or the other, as may be agreed on between them."[53] While Gallatin's observations suggest the difficulty of precisely defining the duties of the office of Comptroller, they leave no doubt as to the importance of the office.

In appointing a successor to Steele, Jefferson followed Gallatin's advice by naming a lawyer, Gabriel Duvall, who was a judge of the supreme court of Maryland. A former congressman, Duvall had been an active supporter of Jefferson in the campaign of 1800.[54] In offering the position to Duvall, Jefferson explained that the nature of the office was "partly Executive, and partly judiciary, as the Comptroller decides in the first instance all questions of law arising in matters of account between the U.S. and individuals.

[53] Gallatin to Jefferson, Oct. 26, 1802, Adams, ed., *Gallatin Writings*, I, 103-104.

[54] See Noble E. Cunningham, Jr., *The Jeffersonian Republicans: The Formation of Party Organization, 1789-1801* (Chapel Hill, N. C., 1957), pp. 191-195.

The office hours are from 9 A.M. to 3 P.M. during which it furnishes pretty steady daily occupation. The Salary is 3500 D." Urging Duvall to accept the post, the President indicated that the Treasury Department "suffers while wanting so important an officer in it's organisation."[55] Duvall assumed the office in mid-December of 1802, and despite offers to return to the Maryland judiciary, which he came to regard as preferable to the "arduous office" of Comptroller,[56] he remained in the Treasury post until 1811. Duvall has received little notice by historians,[57] but the records indicate that he was an important member of Jefferson's administration. He was rewarded for his devotion to his office when President Madison in 1811 named him an Associate Justice of the Supreme Court of the United States.

Of the subordinate positions in the Treasury Department, the least demanding office was that of the Treasurer, who was charged with receiving, keeping, and disbursing the moneys of the United States government. Since funds were disbursed only upon warrants from the Secretary of the Treasury, his duties were purely administrative. "The office itself requires only perfect integrity and correctness," Gallatin said.[58] But both he and the President believed in "the idea of collecting men of talents about us, even in offices which do not need them,"[59] and, when the office became vacant in 1801, it went to Thomas Tudor Tucker, former congressman from South Carolina and brother of St. George Tucker of Williamsburg. Tucker also had the family connections to post the considerable security bond required of the Treasurer.[60] When Tucker took up the duties of the office in December 1801, he found himself baffled by the routines of the post. "I seem to myself to be almost intirely without intellect for I understand nothing that I am doing," he wrote, "and the consciousness of high responsibility whilst I am transacting important business in utter darkness or as a mere automaton increases my stupidity. . . . I sign my name because I am told to do it, but without knowing for what reason, so that I am intirely dependent on others to keep me in the right

[55] Jefferson to Duvall, Nov. 5, 1802, Papers of Gabriel Duvall, Lib. Cong.
[56] Gabriel Duvall to Edmund B. Duvall, Jan. 25, 1806, *ibid.*
[57] Duvall is not included in Allen Johnson and Dumas Malone, eds., *Dictionary of American Biography*, 22 vols. (New York, 1928-1944).
[58] Gallatin to Jefferson, Oct. 1, 1801, Gallatin Papers, microfilm edition.
[59] Jefferson to Gallatin, Oct. 3, 1801, *ibid.*
[60] The magnitude of the security required was given as the principal reason for declining the post when it was previously offered to Richard Harrison, the Auditor. John Steele to Gallatin, Oct. 12, 1801, *ibid.*

way. Such is my present condition, and my comfort only is that what others have found extremely easy, I think cannot be forever incomprehensible to me."[61] Although he found the first weeks in office difficult, Tucker was soon in command of his duties and ultimately found them so manageable that he retained the office until his death in 1828 at age eighty-three. Throughout Jefferson's administration, the staff in the Treasurer's office consisted of three clerks and a messenger, the smallest staff of any Treasury or departmental office. Other than the annual submission to Congress of the general account of the office and the accounts of the War and the Navy departments,[62] for which he served as Treasurer, few demands for reports or information were made upon the Treasurer.

The Register's office was the recording office of the Treasury Department and maintained an elaborate series of books. Register Joseph Nourse, who had managed the office since its establishment under the Confederation,[63] furnished a view of the work of the office in 1801 by describing the most important records; these were:

> Revenue Journal—The Entries in this Book relate to all accounts originating from the Impost and Tonnage duties, and the Internal Revenue, they are made direct from the report of the Auditor of the Treasury (approved by the Comptroller) and exhibit in the usual form of bookkeeping the several debits and Credits as designated in the Report.
>
> Revenue Ledger—Exhibits the individual accounts of the Collectors of the Customs, Supervisors of the Revenue and Postmaster General, also the General Accounts of each particular object of the Revenue as well as those which form deductions therefrom, viz Drawbacks, Bounties, allowances to vessels employed in the Fisheries, Revenue Cutters and Expenses attending the Collection thereof; into which are regularly posted the several Items detailed in the Journal Entry; the aggregate of all these correspond with the printed Statement annually presented to Congress.
>
> Impost Book—This Book shows in detail the quarterly en-

---

[61] Thomas Tudor Tucker to St. George Tucker, Dec. 3, 1801, Tucker-Coleman Collection, College of William and Mary.

[62] Tucker to the Senate, Dec. 23, 1802, Dec. 23, 1803, Jan. 21, 1805, Senate Records, RG 46, Natl. Archives.

[63] See Merrill Jensen, *The New Nation: A History of the United States During the Confederation, 1781-1789* (New York, 1950), p. 360.

tries into the several districts of the value of Merchandize paying a *duty advalorum* and the various articles paying a specific duty arranged under their proper heads (as stated by the Auditor on the Settlement of a Collectors Account) in appropriate Columns are also exhibited the gross amount of duties collected, the several deductions therefrom and the nett amount of Revenue in each district.

Tonnage Book—Exhibits the Tonnage entered quarterly into each district distinguishing that of the United States employed in foreign trade and in the coasting and fishing trade, also the Tonnage belonging to each foreign Nation together with the duties thereon.

Expost Books general and particular to each State—The general Book exhibits the aggregate of the Exports to each foreign Country from the United States, distinguishing the several species thereof,—the particular ones shew the quantity and value exported from the States individually, from these the annual Statement for Congress is made out.[64]

In describing other records, Nourse noted that "a new sett of books for the Receipts and Expenditures are annually opened; from these books certificates of the monies charged against Individuals are daily called for from the Auditors Office and other extracts from the Books are occasionally required by the Heads of Departments. It is a regulation of office that the books be kept as nearly posted as the course of the Business will possibly admit."[65]

The Register's office prepared the major reports that the Secretary of the Treasury annually submitted to Congress. These detailed and elaborate documents were models of penmanship and draftsmanship.[66] One statement on importations into the United States sent to Congress in December 1801 was inscribed on sheets of paper two feet by four feet.[67] The statements and reports an-

[64] Joseph Nourse, "Report of the State of the Office and Duties thereof, May 16, 1801," Treasury Dept., Register's Office, Estimates and Statements, x, 22-23, RG 56, Natl. Archives.

[65] *Ibid.*, p. 27.

[66] Original Reports of the Treasury Department, 7th-10th Congresses, House Records, RG 233, Natl. Archives.

[67] "A General Statement of Goods, Wares, and Merchandise, Imported into the United States in Foreign Vessels, Commencing October 1799 and ending September 30, 1800," enclosed in Gallatin to the Speaker of the House, Dec. 16, 1801, received Dec. 17, 1801, House Records, RG 233, Natl. Archives.

nually prepared in the Register's office, as listed by Nourse in 1801, were as follows:

An Account of the Receipts and Expenditures of the United States, stated in pursuance of the standing order of the House of Representatives passed the 30 December 1791.

Statements in relation to the Sinking Fund, under the provisions of an Act passed the 8 May 1792.

The Annual Estimates for the services of the year ensuing that in which the Estimate is formed.

Annual Statement of the Receipts and Expenditures of the United States for the year preceding the 30 September together with the Balances of Appropriations unexpended on the 1 October in each year. This Statement accompanies the Estimate for an annual appropriation of monies.

A Statement of the district Tonnage of the United States.

An account of the Expenditures of Monies granted to defray the Contingent Charges of Government, and which are exclusively subject to the orders of the President of the United States.

An annual Statement made in conformity with the Act of 2 April 1792 establishing a Mint and regulating the coins of the United States.

Statement shewing the amount of Duties and Drawbacks on the several Articles imported into the United States and exported therefrom, each including the three years respectively immediately preceding that year in which it shall be made, per order of the House dated 3 March 1797.

Statement shewing the quantity and value of Goods, Wares and Merchandize imported into the United States in American Vessels, distinguishing the Countries from whence imported, per order of 28 May 1798.

Statement similar to the above in Foreign vessels, per same order.

Statement of the Exports of the United States together with a summary of their value and destination, also a summary of the value from each State.

Statement of the Tonnage of vessels entered into the United States, shewing the American Tonnage employed in Foreign Trade and in the coasting and Fisheries, also the Tonnage amount belonging to each foreign nation, per order of Senate February 10, 1796.

Note—The four last Statements are made up from the 1 October in each year to 30 September following.[68]

This list, which the Register prepared for the information of the new Secretary of the Treasury when he took over the department in May 1801, not only shows the work of the Register's office but also throws considerable light on the process of government. It indicates that the executive branch kept efficient and useful records and supplied Congress with extensive information at each session on all matters of finance and commerce. The legislative process in those areas requiring statistical data was well served.

Although Gallatin did not restructure the Treasury offices, he proposed to eliminate the offices of the accountants of the War and the Navy departments and to replace them with a second auditor of the Treasury to handle the Army and Navy accounts, thus bringing all accounting procedures under the Treasury Department.[69] Under the existing system, the War and the Navy departments each had an account in the Treasury in the name of its accountant. Individuals receiving funds from the Treasurer on warrants of either of these departments were accountable to the accountant of the department issuing the warrant. The accountants provisionally settled these subordinate accounts and reported quarterly to the Treasury, their accounts being ultimately adjusted and settled by the Auditor and the Comptroller in the same manner as all others.[70] What Gallatin was proposing was that all accounts be settled directly with the Treasury Department in the Auditor's and the Comptroller's offices. This procedure had been instituted in the Department of State at Madison's request soon after he took over that office.[71] Although there had never been an accountant of the State Department, all accounts under that department had earlier been accounted for to the Secretary of State, who in turn settled the account for the department with the Treasury. A year after Madison became Secretary of State, the accounts of former

[68] Nourse, "Report of the State of the Office, May 16, 1801," Treasury Dept., Register's Office, Estimates and Statements, x, 20-21, RG 56, Natl. Archives.

[69] *Communication from the Secretary of the Treasury, to the Chairman of the Committee, Appointed to Investigate the State of the Treasury, in Answer to the Enquiries Made by the Committee*, Mar. 1, 1802 (Washington, D. C., 1802), p. 20. Rare Book Division, Lib. Cong.

[70] *Ibid.*, p. 14.

[71] Gallatin to Jefferson, received Nov. 16, 1801, Adams, ed., *Gallatin Writings*, I, 72.

Secretaries of State John Marshall and Timothy Pickering were still unsettled, though both had been rendered; and a suit was still pending against Edmund Randolph.[72] To avoid these difficulties, Madison and Gallatin made an arrangement in June 1801 whereby the Secretary of State no longer received any money; the Treasury made all payments for that department and settled all accounts directly. "It is proposed generally," Gallatin explained to Congress, "to place the expences, which relate to the war and navy departments, precisely on the same footing now established for those under the controul of the department of state."[73] A bill to carry out Gallatin's recommendations was reported in the House of Representatives in 1802 but was not acted upon;[74] and the War and the Navy accounting offices remained in existence throughout Jefferson's presidency.

Until the creation of the general land office as a bureau within the Treasury Department in 1812, the Secretary of the Treasury had direct administrative responsibility for the sale of public lands. Under the land act of 1800, four district land offices had been established in the Northwest Territory, and a register and a receiver of public moneys appointed for each office.[75] These offices were under the jurisdiction of the Treasury, and the registers and the receivers corresponded directly with the Secretary of the Treasury, who assigned clerks to assist in the routine business. The number of clerks engaged in land-office duties increased from one in 1801 to five in 1808,[76] reflecting the rise in land sales, which jumped from 67,751 acres in 1800 to 497,939 acres in 1801 and surpassed 500,000 acres in both 1805 and 1806. In only one year of Jefferson's two terms did the quantity of public lands sold drop under 200,000 acres.[77] Between 1801 and 1808, eight new land districts were created by Congress and district land offices estab-

---

[72] *Communication from the Secretary of the Treasury, to the Chairman of the Committee, Appointed to Investigate the State of the Treasury,* Mar. 1, 1802, pp. 16-17.

[73] *Ibid.,* pp. 15, 19.

[74] "A Bill to provide more effectually for the due application of public money, and for the accountability of persons entrusted therewith," reported Apr. 8, 1802, House Bills, 7 Cong., 1 Sess., microfilm edition, Lib. Cong.; *Annals of Congress,* 7 Cong., 1 Sess., 1157, 1254.

[75] Malcolm J. Rohrbough, *The Land Office Business: The Settlement and Administration of American Public Lands, 1789-1837* (New York, 1968), pp. 49, 23.

[76] See Appendix i.

[77] Rohrbough, *Land Office Business,* p. 48.

lished in each by the Secretary of the Treasury. Gallatin found the administration of the public domain increasingly troublesome and his time occupied with petty problems of errors in purchase, lost certificates, surveys, claims, and similar matters. By the time Congress freed him from the burden in 1812, he was directing the work of eighteen district land offices and supervising an annual inspection of each office, as required by Congress in an act of 1804.[78]

Since there were few matters of government that did not in some way involve finances, the Secretary of the Treasury had the heaviest administrative load of any member of the President's Cabinet, and no one was more conscientious than Gallatin in performing his duties. After two months in office, he wrote: "I find there is not much mystery in the mere routine of official duties and that I will be able to go on well enough with that part of the business without as much labor as I apprehended; but the apprenticeship costs me about 8 hours close attention every day and will continue so for some time. I find myself also involved in more correspondence of a general nature than I would wish."[79] Before the end of the year, with Congress about to assemble, the Secretary of the Treasury was so pressed with reports that he stayed away from his office, working at home to escape interruptions. In reference to his first annual report, he explained to the President (who was checking to see if all reports were ready) that "in this I have been obliged to do so much of the clerk work and correct so many details, that the tables in relation to it are not yet transcribed."[80] After eleven more years in the office, Gallatin found himself "fairly worn out." When President Madison asked him to return to the post in 1816, he replied that "there is, for what I conceive a proper management of the Treasury, a necessity for a mass of mechanical labor connected with details, forms, calculations, etc., which having now lost sight of the thread and routine, I cannot think of again learning and going through."[81] Later when Gallatin looked back at his early years as Secretary of the Treasury, he recalled that "to fit

[78] *Ibid.*, pp. 30, 48. For further details of Gallatin's administration of the land system, see *ibid.*, pp. 26-50.

[79] Gallatin to James W. Nicholson, July 17, 1801, Gallatin Papers, microfilm edition.

[80] Gallatin to Jefferson, Dec. 7, 1801, Jefferson Papers, Lib. Cong.

[81] Gallatin to Madison, Apr. 18, 1816, Adams, ed., *Gallatin Writings*, I, 694-695.

myself for it, to be able to understand thoroughly, to embrace and to controul all its details took from me, during the first years I held it, every hour of the day and many of the night."[82] While clerks and subordinate officers worked from nine to three, Gallatin arrived at the office at eight and stayed until four or five o'clock in the evening.[83]

A rare opportunity to observe the daily correspondence of Gallatin's office is provided by the record made of the business of the office by the Register during late August and September 1802. On August 27, Gallatin wrote to Nourse saying that he was ill and planned to leave Washington as soon as he was able to travel. Explaining that his chief clerk was absent and that the second-ranking clerk in the office was sick, Gallatin asked the Register to take over the management of the office until one of these clerks could relieve him.[84] Nourse, who had a habit of recording miscellaneous business in a letter book designated "Estimates and Statements," made a list of each day's mail, noting the disposition of each letter, and he sent almost daily reports to Gallatin in New York informing him of the business of the office. These reports show that the Secretary of the Treasury received on August 27 twenty-three letters, nine of which were forwarded for his attention. On August 30, twenty-one letters arrived; five were forwarded and the remainder handled and filed by Nourse. For the two-week period from Monday August 30 through Saturday September 11, with mail six days each week, the volume of letters varied from nine to twenty-two pieces per day, with an average of fifteen letters per day.[85] This was the mail for the Secretary's office only; it did not include the other offices in the Treasury Department. It should also be noted that August and September were the months of the normal summer recess of the executive offices; and it was also a period when Congress, which made heavy demands on the Secretary of the Treasury, was not in session. The data thus suggest the minimum volume of incoming mail that Gallatin faced daily, most of which he handled himself. "No letter directed to me is opened by the Clerks," he explained, "unless . . . endorsed with the

[82] Albert Gallatin to James Gallatin, Feb. 10, 1825, Gallatin Papers, microfilm edition.

[83] Gallatin to James W. Nicholson, July 17, 1801, *ibid.*; Cunningham, ed., "The Diary of Frances Few, 1808-1809," *Jour. So. Hist.*, XXIX, 354.

[84] Gallatin to Nourse, Aug. 27, 1802, Treasury Dept., Register's Office, Estimates and Statements, IX, 280-281, RG 56, Natl. Archives.

[85] *Ibid.*, pp. 282-302.

words 'Custom house,' which designate the species of letters called *public*, meaning thereby the weekly or monthly returns."[86] Treasury Department letter books show a considerable volume of correspondence from the Secretary to custom collectors and other officials throughout the country.[87]

In preparing for the meetings of Congress and while Congress was in session, the Secretary of the Treasury faced greater demands than any other department head. In establishing the Department of the Treasury, Congress had provided that the Secretary of the Treasury report directly to the legislature when called upon. For information respecting other departments, Congress applied to the President asking him to direct a particular department head to provide a report. "The distinction, it is presumable, has been made in order to leave to Congress a direct power, uncontrolled by the Executive, on financial documents and information as connected with money and revenue subjects," Gallatin explained, but he wondered "whether this remarkable distinction, which will be found to pervade all the laws relative to the Treasury Department, was not introduced to that extent in order to give to Mr. Hamilton a department independent of every executive control?"[88]

By the time Gallatin took office, Congress had specified a series of reports which the Secretary of the Treasury was required to make at each session. As he faced the task of preparing his first group of such reports, Gallatin wrote the President that "it would at present be much more convenient to follow a different course; if instead of six or seven reports called for by the standing orders of one or the other House I could throw them all into one, to be made to you, it would unite the advantages of simplicity and perspicuity to that of connection with the reports made by the other Departments, as all might then be presented to Congress through you and by you; but I fear that it would be attacked as an attempt to dispense with the orders of the Houses or of Congress if the usual reports were not made in the usual manner to them."[89] Thus, Gallatin continued to submit the reports in the usual manner. These included three reports that were expected at the beginning of each session: an estimate of appropriations required for the coming year;

[86] Gallatin to Jefferson, Dec. 26, 1801, Jefferson Papers, Lib. Cong.

[87] Letters Sent by the Secretary of the Treasury to Collectors of Customs, RG 46, microcopy M-175, Natl. Archives.

[88] Gallatin to Jefferson, notes on the President's annual message, November 1801, Adams, ed., *Gallatin Writings*, I, 66-67.

[89] *Ibid.*, p. 67.

an account of the receipts and expenditures for the preceding year; and the Secretary of the Treasury's annual report. In December 1801 Gallatin sent the first two of these reports to the House four days after the President sent his annual message to the new session of Congress;[90] a week later he submitted his annual report[91] made in accordance with the supplementary act of May 10, 1800, which required the Secretary of the Treasury "to digest, prepare, and lay before Congress, at the commencement of every session, a report on the subject of finance."[92] This report contained suggestions for legislative measures together with supporting documentation in extensive tables and statements. Among the documents accompanying Gallatin's 1801 report was a statement relating to the public debt which would become the basis for the 1802 act appropriating $7,300,000 annually to eliminate the national debt within sixteen years.[93]

Although the annual report of the Secretary of the Treasury, like the annual message of the President, offered opportunities for the Treasury head to submit legislative recommendations to Congress, Gallatin did so only with the President's approval. "This report with all its tables, is intended of course to be submitted to you before it is transmitted to Congress," he assured the President while the report was in preparation.[94] A major conclusion to be drawn from Gallatin's first annual report was that expenditures would have to be reduced if Congress expected to carry out the President's recommendation to repeal all internal taxes. Since Jefferson had proposed the reduction of military, naval, and civil expenses, the Secretary of the Treasury's report was not in conflict with the annual message. But Gallatin made clearer than the President the necessity of reducing expenditures before reducing taxes.[95]

The Treasury's estimates of appropriations corresponded to what in later years would be known as the budget. The preparation of the estimates began in the Register's office. In early October

[90] Gallatin to the Speaker of the House, Dec. 12, 1801, presented Dec. 14, 1801, House Records, RG 233, Natl. Archives.

[91] Gallatin to the Speaker of the House, Dec. 18, 1801, presented Dec. 21, 1801, ibid.

[92] Annals of Congress, 6 Cong., 1 Sess., 1523-1524.

[93] Statement accompanying the report of the Secretary of the Treasury of Dec. 18, 1801, Senate Records, RG 46, Natl. Archives.

[94] Gallatin to Jefferson, Dec. 7, 1801, Jefferson Papers, Lib. Cong.

[95] Reports of the Secretary of the Treasury of the United States, Prepared in Obedience to the Act of May 10, 1800 (Washington, D.C., 1837-   ), I, 221-223.

1801, Nourse addressed a letter "by direction of the Secretary of the Treasury" to department heads and other officers in charge of separate offices requesting that an estimate of the funds required for the ensuing year be transmitted by November 1 "for the purpose of enabling the Secretary of the Treasury to lay before the Legislature a General Estimate of Monies for the services of the year 1802."[96] The estimates received from the different departments and offices were put into one report by the Register and turned over to the Secretary of the Treasury for transmittal to Congress. In 1801 Gallatin referred to the estimates and the statement of receipts and expenditures as "matters of form prepared by the Register, and to which for the present year I have concluded to make no alteration in point of form."[97] No change was made during the subsequent years of Jefferson's administration, and the Register continued to prepare the estimates of appropriations in the usual manner. On the 1801 request for estimates transcribed in the Register's letter book is the notation that the same form was used in 1802;[98] similar letters in later years requested "the usual Estimates."[99]

The estimates prepared by the Register were reviewed by the Secretary of the Treasury who rounded off figures and made small changes but did not revise departmental requests. However, when the President reviewed the estimates, Gallatin made recommendations to him on departmental figures.[100] The President on occasion obtained modifications in the estimates before they were submitted to Congress. This was the case in regard to the estimates for 1804, when Jefferson wanted to cut expenses before asking Congress for funds for the Louisiana purchase. The absence of Secretary of the Navy Smith—called to Baltimore by family illness—caused Jefferson to put on paper what under normal circumstances would have been worked out in an unrecorded conference, thereby providing a rare glimpse of early budget cutting. "You know the importance

[96] This letter with the list of persons to whom copies were sent is in Treasury Dept., Register's Office, Estimates and Statements, x, 119, RG 56, Natl. Archives.

[97] Gallatin to Jefferson, received Nov. 15, 1801, Adams, ed., *Gallatin Writings*, I, 61.

[98] Treasury Dept., Register's Office, Estimates and Statements, x, 119, RG 56, Natl. Archives.

[99] Joseph Nourse to James Madison and other officers, Oct. 6, 1804, *ibid.*, p. 249; Nourse to Madison, Oct. 3, 1806, Gallatin Papers, Lib. Cong.

[100] Gallatin to Jefferson, Nov. 19, 1801, Jefferson Papers, Lib. Cong.

of our being enabled to announce in the message that the interest
of the Louisiana purchase (800,000 Dollars) can be paid without
a new tax, and what advantage the necessity of a new tax would
give the opposition to the ratification of the treaty, where two or
three desertions would reject it," Jefferson wrote to Smith a week
before Congress was to assemble in October 1803. "To avoid a
new tax we had a deficiency (on the estimates as given in) of about
400,000 Dollars. Our colleagues have bent their shoulders heartily
to the work: Mr. Madison has struck off 100,000 Dollars. Genl.
Dearborn something upwards of that, and we still want 180,000
Dollars to be quite secure. The estimate received from your office,
which I enclose you, amounts probably to 770 or 780, and were
it possible to reduce it to 600, it would place us at ease."[101] The
pressure from the President was effective; the estimate sent to
Congress for the naval establishment on October 25 was $650,-
000.[102]

Gallatin continued to work for changes which he favored even
after estimates had been sent to Congress. When he sent the President "a modification of the navy estimates" early in 1803, he explained: "It is extremely desirable that before the subject shall
be taken up in the house, every part should be fully agreed on
between the heads of the Departments; and I wish you would return the proposed modifications with such alterations as, after
conversing with the Secretary of the Navy, you shall think proper.
Please to let me know whether you wish to confer again with me
on the subject before you decide."[103] In seeking modifications in
the estimates, Gallatin worked openly. For example, Smith was
aware of the changes that Gallatin sought in Navy requests, and
certainly Jefferson consulted with him about the appropriations.
However, the final decision was left to the President. "The corrected navy estimates are much wanted," Gallatin pressed the
President at the end of January 1803. "Whatever you will decide
shall be recommended to the Committee of Ways and Means."[104]
In response, Jefferson contacted Smith, who confessed: "I did not
understand from Mr. Gallatin that I was to send to him an additional Estimate of Navy appropriations. I will however see him

---

[101] Jefferson to Smith, Oct. 10, 1803, Jefferson Papers, v. 135, p. 23366,
Lib. Cong.
[102] ASP, Finance, II, 48.
[103] Gallatin to Jefferson, Jan. 22, 1803, Jefferson Papers, Lib. Cong.
[104] Gallatin to Jefferson, Jan. 29, 1803, ibid.

this morning."[105] Many of the details in regard to the estimates were no doubt worked out in other such conferences.

While appropriations were under consideration by Congress, Gallatin worked directly with the House Ways and Means Committee. In April 1802 he wrote to the committee chairman, John Randolph: "I enclose the appropriation bill with the blanks filled and a few necessary amendments. The estimates which accompany it, with the marginal notes, will, I believe, explain the whole."[106] The close working relationship between Gallatin and Randolph indicated by this note continued as long as Randolph headed the committee; and when he was replaced in 1807, Gallatin confided to his wife: "Varnum has, much against my wishes, removed Randolph from the Ways and Means and appointed Campbell, of Tennessee. It was improper as related to the public business, and will give me additional labor."[107]

Viewing his position as imposing upon him the obligation to see that expenditures did not exceed appropriations, Gallatin sought stricter control by the Treasury over the expenditures of other departments. The first step was for Congress to be specific in appropriations, and at Gallatin's suggestion Jefferson recommended in his first annual message that Congress appropriate "specific sums to every specific purpose susceptible of definition."[108] In the annual appropriations act "for the support of Government," which included the civil establishment and general expenditures, the appropriations were itemized in considerable detail, such as "For expense of stationery and printing in the office of the Auditor, five hundred dollars."[109] But in the acts making appropriations for the Army and the Navy, the itemization was broad, permitting wide discretion on the part of the secretaries of War and the Navy in making expenditures. "It seems to have been generally understood," Gallatin explained, "that the whole of the monies, appropriated for the annual support of the army and navy, respectively, were to be considered as making but one general appropriation for each of those two objects; and that the sums, thus appropriated, were in-

[105] Smith to Jefferson, Jan. 29, 1803, *ibid.*

[106] Gallatin to Randolph, Apr. 13, 1802, Joseph H. Nicholson Papers, Lib. Cong. (misfiled under 1805).

[107] Gallatin to his wife, Oct. 30, 1807, Adams, *Gallatin*, p. 363.

[108] Jefferson, message, Dec. 8, 1801, Ford, ed., *Jefferson Writings*, VIII, 121.

[109] Act of May 1, 1802, *Annals of Congress*, 7 Cong., 1 Sess., 1363-1364.

discriminately applicable to every distinct object of expenditure, embraced under those two general heads." On the other hand, "the appropriations made in relation to the public debt, to the civil department, to domestic expences of a miscellaneous nature (such as the mint establishment, light-houses, census, etc.) and to foreign expences, have been generally considered as constituting . . . a specific distinct appropriation, the amount of which was applicable only to that specific object for which it was appropriated."[110] Gallatin recommended that Congress pass a general law "that every distinct sum, appropriated by any law, for an object distinctly specified in the law, shall be applicable only to that object."[111]

In response to the recommendations from the President and the Secretary of the Treasury, Congress inserted in the enacting clauses of the military and naval appropriations acts of 1802 a statement that the sums specified for the different items were "respectively appropriated."[112] Although some changes were made in the classifications of appropriations, the itemization was not noticeably greater than in previous years. The bill for specific expenditures that Gallatin proposed was also reported,[113] but Congress adjourned without taking action on it. However, the debates in the House of Representatives indicate that members felt that the manner in which the military and naval appropriations bills were written in 1802 provided for specific appropriations and represented a departure from previous practice.[114]

Following the passage of the 1802 acts, Gallatin began to demand that requisitions from the War and the Navy departments for warrants specify the purpose for which the money was to be used. This led to some friction between Gallatin and the Secretary of the Navy. As Smith pointed out, "heretofore these specific appropriations have been disregarded in the drawing of warrants."[115] Under the old system, Smith had requested the Secretary of the Treasury to issue warrants, commonly in sums of $50,000, "for

[110] *Communication from the Secretary of the Treasury, to the Chairman of the Committee, Appointed to Investigate the State of the Treasury*, pp. 8-9.

[111] *Ibid.*, p. 19.

[112] *Annals of Congress*, 7 Cong., 1 Sess., 1356, 1361.

[113] Bill reported Apr. 8, 1802, House Bills, 7 Cong., 1 Sess., microfilm edition, Lib. Cong.; Gallatin to Joseph H. Nicholson, Apr. 27, 1802, Nicholson Papers, Lib. Cong.

[114] *Annals of Congress*, 7 Cong., 1 Sess., 1243-1246.

[115] Smith to Christopher Ellery, Apr. 22, 1802, Letters from the Secretary of the Navy to Congress, RG 45, Natl. Archives.

the maintenance of the Navy" or "the support of the Navy" without specifying the purposes for which the money was to be spent.[116] Once the Navy appropriation act of 1802 was passed, Gallatin called a halt to this practice and required that specific purposes be designated in requesting warrants to be drawn. When he questioned Smith's requisition for $5,000 for the Marine Corps, Smith replied: "I had in view no particular objects to which the 5000 dollars were to be applied. I have sent Circular letters to the several Navy agents enclosing copies of the appropriations Law of the last session with positive directions to them to make it the rule of their Conduct to conform their expenditures and their Accounts to it. If however you should be of the Opinion that my requisitions and my warrants should be as much in detail as the numerous specifications of the Act I will not adhere to my own arrangement as communicated in my Circular instructions but I will adopt what will suit the Treasury Department. In *practice* such a proceeding under the Law will have rather ridiculous appearance."[117] Smith's irritation was due to his having already sought to implement the specific provisions of the appropriations act. Informing Navy agents that the remittances made to them by the Navy Department would be classified according to the appropriation law, he instructed: "In your requisitions for remittances you will designate the particular objects upon which the expenditures are to be made, so as to enable us to ascertain upon what appropriation it will be proper to draw, and you will expend the public money so remitted to you, upon such specific objects, or under such specific appropriations only."[118] While Smith had been attentive to the provisions of the law, Gallatin insisted on the specification of the objects for which warrants were drawn; and Smith complied. He directed that his requisition for $5,000 for the Marine Corps be charged to the appropriation for pay and subsistence of the marines;[119] and in subsequent requisitions he specified the purposes in detail. The itemization of a request for a warrant for $60,000 on May 13, 1802, filled two pages.[120]

[116] Smith to Gallatin, Feb. 8, Mar. 2, 20, Apr. 10, 14, 28, 1802, Gallatin Papers, microfilm edition.

[117] Smith to Gallatin, May 6, 1802, *ibid.*

[118] Smith to Daniel Ludlow and others, circular, May 4, 1802, Miscellaneous Letters Sent by the Secretary of the Navy, microcopy M-209, Natl. Archives.

[119] Smith to Gallatin, May 7, 1802, Gallatin Papers, microfilm edition.

[120] Smith to Gallatin, May 13, 1802, *ibid.*

Although Gallatin maintained closer control over the expenditures of the Army and the Navy than the Treasury had ever done before, it was not until the final days of Jefferson's presidency that Congress passed specific legislation requiring that "all warrants drawn by the Secretary of the Treasury, or of War, or of the Navy, upon the Treasurer of the United States, shall specify the particular appropriation or appropriations to which the same should be charged." The act also provided that moneys paid under such warrants were to be charged to such appropriations in the books of the Comptroller and the accountants of the War and the Navy departments.[121] While restricting the departments to specific appropriations, the act allowed the President during the recess of Congress to permit the transfer of funds from one category of expenditures to another within the same department, reporting such transfers to Congress during the first week of the next session.

Gallatin sought also to improve the efficiency of operations within the Treasury Department. During his first months in office in 1801, he made vigorous efforts to bring government accounts up to date, settle delinquent ones, and introduce greater punctuality on the part of collectors and other revenue officers. By August 1801 he acknowledged "real satisfaction" in the improvement in the customs service. At the same time, he sent a circular to all collectors indicating that the remissness of some collectors "renders it incumbent on me to impress on the minds of all, the absolute necessity of conforming to those regulations which have been heretofore prescribed, either by law, or by this department. Of those, a punctual transmission of accounts to the Comptroller . . . is deemed to be of the first importance; and the President has accordingly directed me to say, that a rigid adherence to the regulation of rendering each quarterly account, previously to the expiration of the next ensuing quarter, shall, hereafter, be considered as indispensably necessary."[122]

Having impressed upon collectors the necessity of punctuality, Gallatin sought to eliminate the delays in settling their accounts in the Treasury. He found the accounts in the Auditor's offices "most shamefully in arrears," with the settling of revenue accounts on the average about fifteen months in arrears.[123] "It is self evident,"

---

[121] Act of Mar. 3, 1809, *Annals of Congress*, 10 Cong., 2 Sess., 1833.

[122] Gallatin, circular, Aug. 20, 1801, U. S. Finance Collection, Manuscripts Division, Lib. Cong.

[123] Gallatin to Jefferson, Aug. 24, 1801, Jefferson Papers, Lib. Cong.

Gallatin told the Auditor, "that punctuality from officers at a distance in rendering their accounts can neither be expected nor enforced unless they shall find similar regularity here in their settlement."[124] Auditor Richard Harrison, who had been in office under Hamilton, protested that the situation had resulted from the removal of the capital from Philadelphia to Washington in 1800 and to the death, resignation, or sickness of his best clerks.[125] While not blaming Harrison personally, Gallatin was convinced that "the delay must be owing either to some defect in the general system, or to want of proper assistance to your office. Whatever the cause may be," he wrote the Auditor, "the effect however, is the same: it should be removed, and you may in your endeavours towards it, rely on every assistance which it is in my power to give."[126] Gallatin authorized Harrison to employ additional temporary clerks or to provide extra pay for extra work by the clerks already employed in order to bring the accounts up to date. "Little doubt remains but what accounts will hereafter be rendered with regularity every quarter," he observed in reference to the collectors; "it is important that they should hereafter be settled with equal regularity."[127]

Throughout Jefferson's presidency the demands on Treasury officers from Congress for reports and information were greater than on any other department, and the President depended on the Secretary of the Treasury for statistical data and technical information. The acquisition of Louisiana required a considerable amount of work on the part of the departments, especially the Treasury. In New Orleans the United States not only had to take over an administrative structure instituted by the Spanish and the French, but had to assume control of a major port. The incorporation of Louisiana into the United States was a test of the administrative capabilities of the national government; the successful extension of the government and administrative machinery of the United States to Louisiana demonstrated the government's capacity to respond to unusual demands and showed that national administrative machinery was well organized. The President assumed the major responsibility for directing the process of incorporating Louisiana

[124] Gallatin to Richard Harrison, Aug. 21, 1801, *ibid*.
[125] Harrison to Gallatin, Aug. 21, 1801; Gallatin to Jefferson, Aug. 24, 1801, *ibid*.
[126] Gallatin to Harrison, Aug. 21, 1801, *ibid*.
[127] Gallatin to Harrison, Aug. 19, 1801, *ibid*.

into the United States, but much of the administrative burden fell on the Secretary of the Treasury.[128]

The major task of enforcing the embargo enacted in December 1807 and repealed fifteen months later in the final days of Jefferson's presidency also fell to the Treasury Department, with the Navy Department assisting. Something of the magnitude of the administrative responsibility can be seen in the fact that during the first eleven months of the embargo, 584 circulars or letters of instructions were sent by the Secretary of the Treasury to collectors and other officers in relation to the embargo.[129] More trying than the volume of work was the frustrating task of enforcing an unpopular measure that was widely evaded. By the summer of 1808, Gallatin was convinced that "Congress must either invest the Executive with the most arbitrary powers and sufficient force to carry the embargo into effect, or give it up altogether." Writing the President this opinion from New York during the summer recess, Gallatin added: "I am so much overwhelmed even here with business and interruptions, that I have not time to write correctly or even with sufficient perspicuity."[130] The administrative structure of the Treasury Department was not designed for the type of controls that the enforcement of the embargo required, but the embargo's failure must be charged to the measure itself, not to the organization or management of the Treasury.

THE DEPARTMENT OF WAR

The Department of War, originally charged with the responsibility for all matters relating to military and naval affairs, was relieved of naval concerns when the Department of the Navy was created in 1798. The administration of military affairs embraced the Army, arsenals, armories, fortifications, military pensions, and

[128] For detailed letters relating to the establishment of the administrative machinery of the Treasury Department in New Orleans, see Gallatin to Hove Browse Trist, Nov. 14, 1803, Feb. 27, Apr. 9, 14, 1804, Treasury Circulars and Letters, U. S. Finance Collection, Lib. Cong. On the transition in regard to law in Louisiana, see George Dargo, *Jefferson's Louisiana: Politics and the Clash of Legal Traditions* (Cambridge, Mass., 1975).

[129] Original Reports of the Treasury Department, bound in two volumes entitled "Embargo Violations," 10 Cong., 2 Sess., House Records, RG 233, Natl. Archives.

[130] Gallatin to Jefferson, July 20, 1808, Adams, ed., *Gallatin Writings*, I, 399.

the granting of bounty lands for military service. In addition, the Department of War was in charge of the administration of Indian affairs. Many of the areas of responsibility of the Secretary of War were subsequently placed under the immediate supervision of subordinate officers or delegated to bureaus created to handle specific functions, but at the beginning of Jefferson's administration there were no subordinate units. The movement in that direction began, however, in 1806, when the office of the superintendent of Indian trade was created.

In 1801 the War Department consisted of the office of the Secretary of War—staffed by a chief clerk, four subordinate clerks, and a messenger—and the office of the accountant of the War Department, employing a chief clerk, eight lesser clerks, and a messenger. The new Republican administration eliminated one clerkship in the office of the accountant. After this slight retrenchment, the size of both staffs remained unchanged during Jefferson's presidency;[131] but by 1809 the accountant was asking for two additional clerks in his office, pointing out "that the business of the Office has very materially increased and that further assistance has become necessary."[132] Besides the War Department offices in Washington, the Purveyor of Public Supplies in Philadelphia was under the administration of the War Department. Gallatin explained to the President in 1803 that "the purveyor is by law the officer who should make all the purchases of clothing, stores, etc., for the War and Navy Departments. . . . He is practically employed principally by the Secretary of War, the Navy Department having, improperly in my opinion, continued to employ, in Philadelphia, agents . . . to whom a commission is paid for services which the purveyor ought to perform."[133] Whatever Gallatin's understanding of the position, the purveyor was included by the Secretary of War in his budget requests,[134] and the office was listed under the War Department in congressional appropriation acts.[135]

Although Gallatin proposed that the offices of the accountants in the War and the Navy departments be eliminated and a second

[131] See Appendix I.

[132] Report of William Simmons, Feb. 14, 1809, in report of the Secretary of War to Congress, Feb. 16, 1809, Reports of the War Department, IV, 219-221, House Records, RG 233, Natl. Archives.

[133] Gallatin to Jefferson, June 21, 1803, Adams, ed., *Gallatin Writings*, I, 124.

[134] Dearborn to Gallatin, Oct. 31, 1801; Nov. 4, 1802; Oct. 5, 1803, Gallatin Papers, microfilm edition (filmed under date May 15, 1801).

[135] *Annals of Congress*, 9 Cong., 1 Sess., 1280.

auditor be added to the Treasury Department to perform their functions, Congress did not act on his suggestion. William Simmons, who was the accountant of the War Department when Dearborn became Secretary of War in 1801, remained in that post throughout Dearborn's eight-year tenure. His staff was one of the stablest in any government office. Peter Hagner, the principal clerk in the office, was employed in that capacity throughout the period; and five of the seven other clerks employed in the office in 1808 had been working there in 1800.[136] In his annual reports on the clerks hired in his office during the years 1807 and 1808, Simmons provided a description of their duties, which offers not only a useful summary of the work of that office but also indicates the principal areas administered by the War Department. Simmons reported that the principal clerk was "employed in the correspondence of the office which is voluminous, and in the general superintendence of the examination and statement of the accounts for entry on the books of the office." Five clerks were employed in the examination of the accounts of the War Department, including "the voluminous accounts of the paymaster and district paymasters of the army; those of the contractors for army supplies; those of the purveyor for purchases made for the army and Indian department; those of the superintendent of Indian trade; the military agents and assistants; agents of fortifications; Indian agents; and generally all accounts arising out of monies appropriated for the War department."[137] Two clerks kept the books in which these accounts were entered and prepared quarterly reports for transmittal to the Treasury. Simmons pointed out that "the duties of the Clerks in this Office are of a nature to require men possessing a complete knowledge of accounts, and on whose accuracy much must depend, because the accounts are adjusted and paid before they are sent to the Treasury for inspection and revision."[138]

In the management of Indian affairs the War Department's duties included carrying out treaties and administering trade. While Indian treaties were negotiated by special commissioners appointed by the President, their implementation generally required the at-

[136] See Appendix II.

[137] Statement of clerks employed in the office of the accountant of the War Department during 1807, enclosed in Henry Dearborn to the Speaker of the House, Jan. 23, 1808, Reports of the War Department, IV, 198-199, House Records, RG 233, Natl. Archives.

[138] Statement of clerks employed in the office of the accountant of the War Department during 1808, enclosed in Dearborn to the Speaker of the House, Feb. 16, 1809, *ibid.*, pp. 219-221.

tention of the Secretary of War.[139] Territorial governors (who reported to the Secretary of State) and Army officers at frontier posts shared and sometimes disputed the management of Indian relations; but the ultimate responsibility rested with the Secretary of War. In 1796 Congress had established a system of government trading houses; though only two trading houses were established prior to 1801,[140] the system was expanded considerably under Jefferson. By the spring of 1809, when Jefferson left the presidency, twelve trading houses were in operation on the frontiers, three of which had been established during the preceding year.[141] The importance of the growing system of trading houses was reflected in the creation of the office of superintendent of Indian trade in 1806.[142] Although under the direction of the Secretary of War, the superintendent managed a separate office, employed two clerks,[143] and headed his correspondence "Office of Indian Trade."[144] Seeking a larger appropriation in 1808, he reminded the Secretary of War that in addition to corresponding with the trading houses, he had "to supply them with goods from time to time, to receive and sell their peltries, to receive and settle their accounts quarterly, and to keep an extensive set of books, and a considerable correspondence with others, on the business of this establishment."[145] Congress responded with additional funds for the agency.[146]

The principal function of the Secretary of War remained the administration of the Army. Since this involved dealing with organized, uniformed, and disciplined military units, his adminis-

[139] Dearborn to William Henry Harrison, Feb. 21, 1803; Dearborn to John Milledge, Oct. 6, 1803, Henry Dearborn Papers, Chicago Hist. Soc.

[140] White, *Federalists*, p. 381.

[141] John Mason, superintendent of Indian trade, to Thomas Newton, Jan. 16, 1809, House Records, RG 233, Natl. Archives.

[142] Act of Apr. 21, 1806, *Annals of Congress*, 9 Cong., 1 Sess., 1288; *ASP, Indian Affairs*, I, 756.

[143] *Ibid.*, pp. 774-775.

[144] John Mason to Thomas Newton, Jan. 16, 1809, House Records, RG 233, Natl. Archives.

[145] Mason to Dearborn, Jan. 18, 1808, *ASP, Indian Affairs*, I, 774. Instructions sent to factors detailing their duties can be found in Mason to Mathew Irwin, Sept. 9, 1808, in Reuben G. Thwaites, ed., "Fur-Trade on the Upper Lakes—1778-1815," State Historical Society of Wisconsin, *Collections*, XIX (1910), 326-330. The history of Indian trading houses is traced in George D. Harmon, *Sixty Years of Indian Affairs: Political, Economic, and Diplomatic, 1789-1850* (Chapel Hill, N. C., 1941), pp. 94-133. For a more detailed study, see Ora Brooks Peake, *A History of the United States Indian Factory System, 1795-1822* (Denver, 1954).

[146] Act of Mar. 3, 1809, *Annals of Congress*, 10 Cong., 2 Sess., 1845.

trative task was different from that of other department heads, such as the Secretary of the Treasury, who directed only civilian employees. Although Dearborn had seen extensive military service in the Revolutionary War—even the President addressed him as General—his civilian status was clear, and the civilian supremacy over the military was firmly maintained. Throughout eight years as Secretary of War, Dearborn carried the major burden of Army administration with little help from the commanding general of the Army, James Wilkinson. While personally handling such details as the design of buttons for Army uniforms, he also gave much attention to the arming, equipping, and supplying of the Army. He encouraged Eli Whitney's manufacture of muskets which employed the principle of standardized parts, and patiently worked with him in fulfilling his contract to supply muskets for the Army. He also sought to introduce Whitney's methods in the national armories. Dearborn also introduced new gun carriages and horse-drawn artillery, thereby establishing the first properly equipped light artillery.[147]

There was no Army staff in the capital to advise or assist the Secretary of War in military administration. The Army had no general staff. The Jeffersonian act of March 16, 1802, fixing the military peace establishment, eliminated the quartermaster general, the paymaster general, the inspector of the Army, the inspector of artillery, the inspector of fortifications, brigade inspectors, and the judge advocate.[148] The peacetime military force as established in 1802 was headed by one brigadier general; he was the commanding general of the Army and was stationed in the field rather than in Washington. His staff consisted of one aid-de-camp taken from the line.[149] One adjutant and inspector of the Army, also taken from the line of field officers, was quartered at Fredericktown, Maryland.[150] The only Army staff in the capital was the paymaster of the Army, who received $120 per month and was provided with an office and enough funds for two clerks.[151] In addition to the paymaster of the Army, the act of 1802 provided for seven paymasters

[147] Richard A. Erney, "The Public Life of Henry Dearborn" (Ph.D. Dissertation, Columbia University, 1957), pp. 68, 56, 83. Erney's study provides a detailed treatment of Dearborn's role in administering the Army.

[148] The Army establishment prior to the reductions of the act of 1802 is reported in ASP, Military Affairs, I, 155. For the act of Mar. 16, 1802, see Annals of Congress, 7 Cong., 1 Sess., 1306-1312.

[149] Ibid., 1306.

[150] ASP, Military Affairs, I, 175, 176.

[151] Annals of Congress, 7 Cong., 1 Sess., 1307; 8 Cong., 1 Sess., 1272.

and two assistants, taken from the line of commissioned officers and attached to such districts as the President might direct, "who, in addition to their other duties, shall have charge of the clothing of the troops." Also authorized were three military agents and such assistant military agents as the President might deem necessary but not exceeding one agent to each military post. The military agents were to purchase, receive, and forward to their proper destination all military stores and other articles for the troops in their respective districts.[152]

The Army as fixed by Congress in 1802 consisted of one regiment of artillery, two regiments of infantry, and a corps of engineers, totaling 3,312 officers and enlisted men.[153] Most of the Army was scattered in small units along the western frontier.[154] The newly formed corps of engineers was stationed at West Point, where the corps became a military academy with the principal engineer acting as superintendent. The Secretary of War was directed to procure the necessary books, implements, and apparatus for the new academy.[155] The authorized strength of the military peace establishment fixed in 1802 remained essentially unchanged until 1808, when the growing tension with Great Britain following the attack on the *Chesapeake* led to a rapid expansion of the Army, whose strength in May 1809, shortly after Jefferson left office, was reported at 6,732.[156]

The Army's small size and lack of efficient centralized machinery reflected the Republican attitude toward standing armies that prevailed in the executive and legislative branches alike. President Jefferson had expressed that position during the political campaign of 1800: "I am for relying, for internal defence, on our militia solely, till actual invasion . . . and not for a standing army in time of peace, which may overawe the public sentiment," he had affirmed in 1799.[157] On March 4, 1801, he renewed the pledge

[152] *Ibid.*, 7 Cong., 1 Sess., 1306-1307, 1310.

[153] This was a reduction from the previous authorized strength of 5,438. *ASP, Military Affairs*, I, 155, 177.

[154] Francis Paul Prucha, *The Sword of the Republic: The United States Army on the Frontier, 1783-1846* (London, 1969), p. 60.

[155] *Annals of Congress*, 7 Cong., 1 Sess., 1312.

[156] Report of Secretary of War William Eustis, May 26, 1809, Reports of the War Department, IV, 224-225, House Records, RG 233, Natl. Archives. On the organization of the Army, see James R. Jacobs, *The Beginning of the U. S. Army, 1783-1812* (Princeton, N. J., 1947), pp. 244-279.

[157] Jefferson to Elbridge Gerry, Jan. 27, 1799, Ford, ed., *Jefferson Writings*, VII, 327-328.

in his inaugural, when he spoke of "a well disciplined militia, our best reliance in peace, and for the first moments of war till regulars may relieve them."[158] In the campaign of 1800, Republicans had said much about the dangers of standing armies and had spoken ominously about the expansion of the Army under President Adams. The act of 1802 reducing the military establishment reflected the Republican party position. Although the President and the Republican majority in Congress agreed on the reduction of the Army, Jefferson's understanding of "a well disciplined militia" was not shared by Congress, which never enacted the President's proposals for organizing the militia into classes. Jefferson's plan, worked out with Secretary of War Dearborn in the fall of 1805, would have provided for a class of trained and equipped militia ready for national service.[159] Although Dearborn worked with the President in drawing up this and other proposals, he was less involved than the Secretary of State or the Secretary of the Treasury in the formation of policy. In the Cabinet he shared in the general formulation of administration policy, but the administrative duties of his office occupied most of his time, which was often devoted to routine details.[160]

Unlike the Secretary of the Treasury, who could call for assistance from subordinate officers, particularly the Comptroller and the Register, in administering the department and preparing reports, the Secretary of War had only clerks; the one subordinate officer in the War Department was the accountant, whose duties were limited to his special responsibility of maintaining and settling accounts. The War Department head had few regular reports to make to Congress, but he was called upon from time to time to prepare special reports such as that submitted in December 1801 furnishing "a statement of the present military establishment of the United States, and an estimate of all the posts and

[158] Jefferson, first inaugural address, Mar. 4, 1801, Jefferson Papers, Lib. Cong.

[159] Jefferson drafted "An act for classing the militia and assigning to each it's particular duties," Jefferson Papers, v. 137, p. 23703, Lib. Cong.; see also Dearborn's "Outlines of a sistem for organizing the Militia in 3 classes," ibid., v. 169, p. 29854; Dearborn to Jefferson, received Nov. 18, 1805, ibid., v. 154, p. 26939. For a summary of Jefferson's military policy, see Dumas Malone, *Jefferson the President: Second Term, 1805-1809* (Boston, 1974), pp. 507-523.

[160] Dearborn to Stephen Moylan, Jan. 5, 1806; Dearborn to Henry A. Dearborn, Aug. 11, 1807; Dearborn to George R. C. Floyd, June 7, 1808, Henry Dearborn Papers, Chicago Hist. Soc.

stations for which garrisons will be expedient, and of the number of men, requisite . . . for each garrison."[161]

The Secretary of War carried on a voluminous correspondence with government officials, military officers, and civilians. Something of the main areas in which the War Department functioned and the regular lines of communication maintained can be seen in the organization of the records of the department. In the new series of letter books started after the fire in the Secretary's office on November 8, 1800, there were six categories of letters sent by the Secretary of War, organized under the following headings: "Letters Sent to the President," "Letters to the Secretary of the Treasury," "Letters Sent, Indian Affairs," "Military Pensions," "Military Books," and "Miscellaneous Letters Sent." A seventh category entitled "Reports to Congress" was begun in 1803. The "Military Books" contained copies of letters addressed to military personnel. Letters to persons outside the Army, filed under "Miscellaneous Letters Sent," related to the manufacture, procurement, and transportation of arms, clothing, stores, and other supplies and equipment; also grouped in this category were letters concerning fortification of harbors, the building of arsenals, land claims based on military service, and other matters.[162] Some routine correspondence of the Secretary's office was handled by the chief clerk. When the Secretary was absent, letters addressed to him were answered over the signature of the chief clerk or another clerk. Many such letters consisted of explanations of the Secretary's absence and assurances that the matters would be brought to his attention upon his return.[163]

Although the President appointed all military officers with the approval of the Senate, he delegated the nominating responsibility to the Secretary of War and depended upon him to recommend the nominations that were sent to the Senate. Since the military establishment was being reduced during the first years of Jefferson's presidency, the problem was less one of making appointments than of making dismissals. Jefferson participated in making the

[161] Dearborn to the Speaker of the House, Dec. 23, 1801, transmitting the report, Original Reports of the War Department, House Records, RG 233, Natl. Archives.

[162] *Pamphlet Accompanying Microcopy No. 370: Miscellaneous Letters Sent by the Secretary of War, 1800-1809* (Natl. Archives, 1962).

[163] See letters signed by John Newman, July 18-Oct. 10, 1801; by Joshua Wingate, Aug. 5-20, 1803; and by John Smith, Hezekiah Rogers, and Andrew McClary, July 27-Sept. 27, 1804, Miscellaneous Letters Sent by the Secretary of War, microcopy M-370, Natl. Archives.

reductions called for by the act of March 16, 1802, fixing the peacetime military establishment, for his papers contain a roster of all officers in the Army, with annotations indicating their military qualifications and political attachments, if any. The key to the symbols designating these evaluations is in the handwriting of Jefferson's private secretary, Meriwether Lewis. An examination of the list shows that in making the dismissals of the eighty-seven officers discharged on June 1, 1802, under the act of March 16, military qualifications rather than political affiliations were the first consideration.[164] When new appointments did become available with the expansion of the Army in 1808, Secretary of War Dearborn gave decided preference to Republicans. "We have at present a sufficient proportion of our political opponents in the Army, to render any new appointments, in the small body of additional troops, of that class, unnecessary, if not inexpedient . . . ," he indicated. "If I recommend any such to the President, it will be from the effect of deception."[165]

A close adviser to the President on the political situation in New England, Dearborn, like other department heads, was a political person; but he was also a competent administrator, though frequently overburdened with petty details. The acquisition of Louisiana brought new responsibilities to the Secretary of War and to the Army. In the task of taking possession of the new land and establishing the authority of the United States government over its people, the Army played an indispensable role and demonstrated that the regular Army on the frontier was not exclusively an Indian fighting force.[166] To the routine administration of military and Indian affairs was added during Dearborn's last eighteen months in office the responsibility for supervising the increased defense preparations that followed the *Chesapeake* crisis of the summer of 1807. In building fortifications, enlarging the Army, and increasing arms production, Dearborn accomplished more than has sometimes been recognized.[167] With the advent of the possibility of war in 1807, Dearborn sought release from his duties, arguing that "in time of peace, a tolerable portion of com-

[164] The roster is in the Jefferson Papers, v. 114, p. 19697, Lib. Cong. and is analyzed in detail in Cunningham, *Jeffersonian Republicans in Power*, pp. 66-68.

[165] Dearborn to William Eustis, May 2, 1808, William Eustis Papers, Lib. Cong.

[166] Prucha, *The Sword of the Republic*, p. 63.

[167] Dearborn's accomplishments are detailed in Erney, "Public Life of Henry Dearborn," pp. 192, 216-243.

mon understanding with some practical knowledge and pure intentions, may be sufficient qualifications for the ordinary duties of the office," but that in the event of war superior talents to his own were needed.[168] Jefferson, however, persuaded him to stay on, assuring him that "the integrity, attention, skill, and economy with which you have conducted your department, have given me the most compleat and unqualified satisfaction."[169]

THE DEPARTMENT OF THE NAVY

Throughout Jefferson's presidency the Navy was small. The new Republican administration began by carrying out the substantial naval reductions which had been authorized by Congress in the final days of Adams's presidency. By the act of March 3, 1801, Congress authorized the President to sell all but thirteen frigates and to take all except six out of service.[170] By the time he sent his first annual message to Congress in December 1801, Jefferson could report that five frigates had already been laid up and two additional ones would soon be taken out of service.[171] He followed with a progress report on the sales of ships which showed that by December 1801 fifteen vessels had been sold for a total of $275,000.[172] The officers authorized for the naval peace establishment under the act of March 3, 1801, totaled 9 captains, 36 lieutenants, and 150 midshipmen.[173] To meet these limits, the positions of nineteen captains had to be eliminated, and in October 1801 the Cabinet made the final reduction from fifteen to nine by voting on each officer.[174]

In 1799 when the Federalists under President Adams were building naval power, Jefferson had declared himself "for such a naval force only as may protect our coasts and harbors from such depredations as we have experienced; and not for . . . a navy, which, by it's own expenses and the eternal wars in which it will implicate us, will grind us with public burthens, and sink us under them."[175] But Jefferson had long favored using naval force

---

[168] Dearborn to Jefferson, Dec. 29, 1807, Jefferson Papers, Lib. Cong.

[169] Jefferson to Dearborn, Jan. 8, 1808, Ford, ed., *Jefferson Writings*, IX, 171.

[170] 2 *Statutes at Large*, 110.   [171] *House Journal*, IV, 10.

[172] Report of Robert Smith, Dec. 8, 1801, *ASP, Naval Affairs*, I, 80.

[173] Act of Mar. 3, 1801, 2 *Statutes at Large*, 110.

[174] Malone, *Jefferson the President: First Term*, p. 103.

[175] Jefferson to Elbridge Gerry, Jan. 26, 1799, Ford, ed., *Jefferson Writings*, VII, 328.

against the Barbary pirates,[176] and one of the first actions of his administration was to send a squadron of frigates to the Mediterranean. In his first annual message he told Congress that "a small force will probably continue to be wanted, for actual service, in the Mediterranean."[177]

Although actions against the Barbary pirates required the maintenance of a small naval force in the Mediterranean, there was no substantial increase in the naval establishment until Jefferson's second term, and then the major additions were gunboats designed to protect the coasts and harbors.[178] In November 1807 when Congress, in the wake of the *Chesapeake* incident, called on the Secretary of the Navy to report on the state of the nation's naval forces, he listed a total of ten frigates of thirty-two to forty-four guns. Of these, two were in service, two ready for service, three under repair and soon ready for service, and three in need of at least three months of repairs. Eight smaller vessels, mounting from seven to sixteen guns, were in service, two were ready for service, and two were being repaired and would soon be ready for service. In addition, sixty gunboats were in service, one was ready for service, and seven were being built.[179] The authorized naval strength under the act of April 21, 1806, up modestly from 1801, allowed for 13 captains, 9 masters commandant, 72 lieutenants, 150 midshipmen, and 925 seamen and boys.[180] As the crisis with Great Britain continued, Congress in January 1809 added 300 midshipmen and 3,600 seamen and boys to the existing authorization.[181]

The Department of the Navy, created in 1798, was the youngest of the four departments and the only one that had been added since the initial organization of the new government under the Constitution in 1789. Similar to that of the War Department, the Navy headquarters consisted of the offices of the Secretary of the Navy and the accountant. Employing three to four clerks, the Secretary of the Navy had the smallest staff of any departmental office. For

176 For Jefferson's efforts as Secretary of State to get such a policy adopted, see Boyd, ed., *Papers of Thomas Jefferson*, XVIII, 369-445.

177 *House Journal*, IV, 10.

178 For a summary of Jefferson's naval policy during his second term, see Malone, *Jefferson the President: Second Term*, pp. 491-506.

179 Robert Smith to Thomas Blount, Nov. 16, 1807, ASP, *Naval Affairs*, I, 168-169.

180 *Annals of Congress*, 9 Cong., 1 Sess., 1273; Charles W. Goldsborough, *The United States Naval Chronicle*, I (Washington, D. C., 1824), p. 332.

181 Act of Jan. 31, 1809, *Annals of Congress*, 10 Cong., 2 Sess., 1808.

several years, Navy Secretary Robert Smith attempted to staff his office with three clerks; finding that "the Business of the Department however is more than ought to be imposed on 3 Clerks,"[182] he raised the permanent force to four in 1806. One of these was the chief clerk, who managed the office of the Secretary and during his absence took charge of his desk, answering routine correspondence addressed to the Secretary of the Navy and holding substantive matters until his return.[183] In promoting Charles W. Goldsborough from a clerkship to chief clerk in 1802, Smith described the duties of the office. The chief clerk, he explained, "shall have under the superintending control of the Secretary, the custody and charge of all Books, Papers and Documents of every description belonging to the Department." He was responsible for the accuracy of all records and "must see that the Business of each day be brought up during that day and that all the books and papers of the Office are arranged in the most regular order." He was charged also with apportioning the duties of the subordinate clerks. Smith believed that "to classify the several duties of each subordinate Clerk and to confine their attentions exclusively to such respective duties would produce much embarrassment. The public business would, under such an arrangement, frequently be subject to considerable delay in consequence of the pressure of unequal and disproportionate duties." Having placed the chief clerk in charge of the office, Smith's practice was to communicate only with him, and he expected him to "be duly prepared at all times when called upon."[184]

The accountant of the Navy employed eight clerks in 1808, one less than when the Republicans assumed power in 1801.[185] Like the accounting office in the War Department, the Navy accountant's office changed little under Republican control. Thomas Turner continued to head the office, and in 1808 only one of the clerks had not been working in the office prior to Jefferson's inauguration.[186] The elimination of one clerkship paralleled a similar retrenchment in the War Department. In reporting to Congress on the clerks employed in his office, the accountant described their assignments and in so doing provided a brief summary of the areas of administration that occupied the Navy Department. Most of the

[182] Smith to Uriah Tracy, Mar. 29, 1806, Letters from the Sec. of Navy to Congress, RG 45, Natl. Archives.

[183] Abishia Thomas to Daniel Ludlow, Sept. 18, Oct. 14, 1801, Misc. Letters Sent by Sec. of Navy, M-209, Natl. Archives.

[184] Smith to Charles W. Goldsborough, Apr. 1, 1802, *ibid.*

[185] See Appendix I.   [186] See Appendix II.

clerks were "employed in examining, adjusting and making office statements of accounts with the Department, embracing the voluminous accounts of the Navy Agents, Pursers, Commanders of Gun Boats, Pay Master to the Marine Corps, etc., etc." These duties, the accountant stressed, "require particular investigation and accurate calculation and it is important that the Clerks employed should be men of business and good accountants." One senior clerk was "employed in examining and adjusting the store accounts of Navy agents and Store keepers: which accounts are very important, and require in the adjustment great attention, labour and correctness."[187]

The naval accountant and his staff were confined to accounting duties, leaving the office of the Secretary of the Navy with all other administrative responsibilities. The Secretary had no professional naval advisers or aides and no chief of naval operations. He issued orders directly to ship commanders, each ship usually being an independent unit.[188] Although the Navy was small, the duties of the Secretary were burdensome. Early in 1801 Benjamin Stoddert reported to Congress that "the business of the Navy Department embraces too many objects for the superintendence of one person, however gifted," and recommended that a board of three or five experienced Navy officers be established "to superintend in subordination to the Head of the Department, such parts of the duties as nautical men are best qualified to understand and to direct."[189] Congress, however, did not respond favorably to the suggestion. The Secretary of the Navy did assign some administrative duties to the commandant of the Marine Corps, delegating to him, for example, the responsibility of preparing the annual estimate of anticipated expenditures for the marines.[190]

The Navy Department administered six naval yards. In addition to the Washington yard, there were installations at Portsmouth, Boston, New York, Philadelphia, and Norfolk. Under Smith, the

[187] Report of Thomas Turner, accountant of the Navy, Jan. 29, 1807, in report of Robert Smith, Feb. 2, 1807, Letters of the Sec. of Navy to Congress, RG 45, Natl. Archives.

[188] White, *Jeffersonians*, p. 269. The direct role of the Secretary of the Navy in naval operations can be seen in Dudley W. Knox, ed., *Naval Documents Related to the United States Wars with the Barbary Powers, 1785-1807*, 6 vols. (Washington, D. C., 1939-1944); most of these documents relate to the period of Smith's tenure as Secretary of the Navy.

[189] Report of Jan. 12, 1801, *ASP, Naval Affairs*, I, 75.

[190] Smith to Col. William W. Burrows, Oct. 14, 1801, Misc. Letters Sent by Sec. of Navy, M-209, Natl. Archives.

responsibilities of superintending the yards were combined with the duties of Navy agents at all ports except Boston. The duties of the Navy agent at Georgetown were transferred in October 1801 to Captain Thomas Tingey, who thereafter served as both Navy agent and superintendent of the Washington naval yard. In appointing Tingey, Smith stated that: "Your duty will be to superintend all the public improvements that may be making there from time to time: to receive all public property of what nature soever, that may be deposited there into your custody and to be responsible for the safe-keeping and expenditure thereof." He also explained that "all the officers and others on board of the Ships in ordinary at Washington are to consider you as the agent of this Department, and to respect your authority as such."[191] Captain Tingey remained in charge of the Washington naval yard throughout Smith's tenure as Secretary. At Portsmouth, New York, Philadelphia, and Norfolk, the Navy yards were placed in the hands of Navy agents, each of whom was authorized to employ an assistant. Only at Boston was there both a superintendent and a Navy agent.[192] In his first annual message to Congress, Jefferson reported in reference to Navy yards that he had "in certain cases suspended or slackened these expenditures, that the legislature might determine whether so many yards are necessary as have been contemplated."[193] But Congress retained all of the yards.

In the building, fitting, and supplying of a naval force, Navy agents were a major element of the administrative structure of the Navy Department. The Secretary carried on extensive correspondence with a varying number of such agents, who acted as purchasing agents and performed other services in the principal ports, receiving as compensation a commission on transactions.[194] All Navy agents were appointed and dismissed at the pleasure of the Secretary of the Navy, and during the first year of Republican control, Federalist Navy agents were replaced by Republicans in all of the chief naval agencies in the United States except at Philadelphia.[195]

[191] Smith to Tingey, Oct. 23, 1801, *ibid.*

[192] Smith to Woodbury Langdon, Oct. 26, 1801, *ibid.*; Charles O. Paullin, "Naval Administration under Smith, Hamilton, and Jones, 1801-1814," United States Naval Institute, *Proceedings*, XXXII (1906), 1,297.

[193] Ford, ed., *Jefferson Writings*, VIII, 122.

[194] Smith to William Smith and Co., Charleston, S. C., Sept. 25, 1801; Smith to Col. John Stricker, Baltimore, Sept. 26, 1801, Misc. Letters Sent by Sec. of Navy, M-209, Natl. Archives.

[195] Paullin, "Naval Administration under Smith, Hamilton, and Jones," United States Naval Institute, *Proceedings*, XXXII, 1,295.

The Secretary of the Navy had a heavy load of administrative correspondence, and Smith handled this with careful attention to the details of administering the department. Indeed, he appears to have been directly involved in everything down to ordering rations for the Navy.[196] Smith's correspondence contains numerous letters relating to Navy stores, lumber for shipbuilding, and similar routine matters. In sending an official to inspect timber contracted for by the Navy Department, Smith provided detailed written instructions on inspecting the lumber and on marking and recording each board.[197]

Although Smith's administrative efforts were little recognized by the Secretary of the Treasury, who continued to complain about the lack of reform in the Navy Department, the records show that Smith took steps to improve the efficiency of the department.[198] Often seen as a weak appointee, Smith proved to be a competent administrator. Charles W. Goldsborough, the chief clerk of the Navy Department who worked directly under Smith for seven years from 1802 to 1809, regarded him as "preeminently qualified for the station." In later years, with the naval exploits of the War of 1812 a matter of record, Goldsborough recalled that Smith "was particularly happy in discovering the merits of the most promising young officers of the Navy."[199] Smith's difficulties as Secretary of State under President Madison and his break with the Madison administration have clouded his record as Jefferson's Secretary of the Navy. With the exception of the Department of the Treasury—the best administered department—the Navy Department was no less well managed than other departments. When the four departments are viewed together, Jefferson appears more successful than either of his two predecessors or his successor in the presidential office in maintaining effective administrative direction of the departments throughout the full period of his presidency.

[196] Smith to Constant Taber, Feb. 13, 1802, Misc. Letters Sent by Sec. of Navy, M-209, Natl. Archives.

[197] Smith to Samuel Humphreys, Mar. 23, 1802, *ibid.*

[198] See Smith to Samuel Brown, Aug. 28, 1801; Smith to Caleb Gibbs, Aug. 29, 1801, *ibid.*

[199] Goldsborough, *Naval Chronicle*, I, 212.

VII. The Executive Complement

THE ACT OF CONGRESS CREATING THE OFFICE OF the Attorney General of the United States called for a person "learned in the law," and prescribed the duties of that officer as being "to prosecute and conduct all suits in the Supreme Court in which the United States shall be concerned, and to give his advice and opinion upon questions of law when required by the President of the United States, or when requested by the heads of any of the departments, touching any matter that may concern their departments."[1] These remained the Attorney General's primary responsibilities throughout Jefferson's administration. In addition, he supplied opinions to Congress and congressional committees when requested.[2] While serving as the legal counsel to the President and department heads, he was at the same time a full member of the Cabinet and participated in all its deliberations. The Attorney General did not head a department; he had no office, no clerk, nor any funds beyond his salary. He kept no records, no letter books, no files of his official opinions. Nor did he have any administrative responsibilities in federal law enforcement. An attempt by the House of Representatives in 1792 to give the Attorney General jurisdiction over the district attorneys had failed to win support in the Senate.[3] Thus, the district attorneys and federal marshals were still administratively under the Department of State. This lack of administrative duties and staff has produced a common assumption that the Attorney General actually did not have much to do and that the office was not very important.[4] While the absence of official files makes the task of

[1] Act to establish the judicial courts of the United States, Sept. 24, 1789, 1 *Statutes at Large*, p. 73, Sec. 35.

[2] See letter of Caesar A. Rodney, Dec. 2, 1807, endorsed "Document accompanying the bill to punish conspiracies to commit treason against the United States, Presented the 2d March 1808," House Records, RG 233, Natl. Archives.

[3] Julius Goebel, Jr., *The Oliver Wendell Holmes Devise History of the Supreme Court of the United States*, Volume I: *Antecedents and Beginnings to 1801* (New York, 1971), pp. 545-546.

[4] See Smelser, *Democratic Republic*, p. 47.

tracing the activities of Jefferson's Attorneys General difficult, there is sufficient evidence scattered among the files of other offices and in extant official opinions to show that the men who held that office had considerable demands made upon them and were an important part of the executive branch.

The annual salary of the Attorney General was three thousand dollars, which was less than the other members of the Cabinet who were also heads of departments; but it was in line with the salaries of other officers of the government and hardly "a tiny stipend," as it has been described.[5] While a successful lawyer in Philadelphia might expect to earn six or seven thousand dollars per year,[6] an associate justice of the Supreme Court of the United States earned only five hundred dollars per year more than the Attorney General. The Attorney General was permitted to continue his private law practice and could even take private cases before the Supreme Court. William Mitton of Georgia employed Attorney General Breckinridge as counsel in a private land suit, and after Breckinridge's death, he engaged Attorney General Rodney.[7] The fee paid in this instance was only one hundred dollars; and evidence indicates that the private law practice of Jefferson's Attorneys General suffered rather than prospered while in office. During his early months in office, Rodney, confessing that "my own family of eight children increasing daily in expense of dress and education consumes every copper I can make" and finding that his salary as Attorney General "will not in pecuniary matters balance the loss" from private practice, hoped "at the next term of the District Court to get some handsome fees in private cases."[8] But the duties of his office kept Rodney in Washington more than he had expected. He wrote from the capital in July 1807, a month of exceptional demands made by the *Chesapeake* crisis and the approaching trial of Aaron Burr: "I have been detained here much longer than I had contemplated, by events as unexpected as they are unexampled. It is very uncertain when I shall get a furlough from head-quarters, tho I never was so anxious to see home, because I came here unprepared for a summer's residence after having spent the winter at this place. It is extremely inconvenient to me at this time to abandon as it were my family and my business

[5] *Ibid.*

[6] Gallatin to Jefferson, Sept. 18, 1804, Jefferson Papers, Lib. Cong.

[7] Mitton to Rodney, July 2, 1807, Rodney Collection, Hist. Soc. Del.

[8] Caesar A. Rodney to Thomas Rodney, Mar. 15, 1807, Brown Collection, Hist. Soc. Del.

at the Court, for I stand in need of the profits of every term; but at such a crisis, there is no personal sacrifice I would not make rather than desert my post in a perilous season."[9]

Jefferson did not have the problems that his predecessors and his successor had in keeping the Attorney General in Washington.[10] His Attorneys General spent a considerable portion of each year in the capital. Their presence was not limited to the short Supreme Court sessions; they were also generally present during sessions of Congress and are recorded as being at some Cabinet meetings when neither the Supreme Court nor Congress was meeting. Attorney General Breckinridge, who served only one year, felt that he was expected to be in Washington while Congress was meeting. The comments that he made about his duties in letters to his wife throw light both on this matter and on the demands of the office. In December 1805, after two weeks in office, the former senator wrote to his wife that he had "been but twice at the Capitol; my time being a good deal occupied with the business of my office since I came."[11] On February 6, 1806, he reported that the Supreme Court had met on February 3, but since two justices were ill and one had not yet arrived, the court was not able to proceed.[12] Meanwhile, the demands on him as a member of the Cabinet continued, and as long as Congress remained in session he was kept busy. "It is impossible for me to get off untill they do adjourn," he wrote his wife on March 14, "and even then it will require a struggle."[13] Two weeks later he complained: "Am drudging on in the usual way; am generally employed, and that closely, and fear it is to be my lot while I live."[14] Finally, he wrote on Thursday April 24: "Congress adjourned on Monday night. I expected to be detained a few days after the adjournment, knowing that the president wished himself to go to Monticello, and that there would be some matters of importance to be laid before the Cabinet, before his departure. They are now preparing, and I still hope I shall get off on Saturday."[15] Both

[9] Rodney to George Read, July 21, 1807, Rodney Collection, Hist. Soc. Del.

[10] On the Attorneys General under Washington, Adams, and Madison, see White, *Federalists*, pp. 164-168; White, *Jeffersonians*, pp. 336-337.

[11] Breckinridge to his wife, Dec. 24, 1805, Breckinridge Family Papers, Lib. Cong.

[12] Breckinridge to his wife, Feb. 6, 1806, *ibid*.

[13] Breckinridge to his wife, Mar. 14, 1806, *ibid*.

[14] Breckinridge to his wife, Mar. 25, 1806, *ibid*.

[15] Breckinridge to his wife, Apr. 24, 1806, *ibid*.

Breckinridge's private letters and public records substantiate the demanding nature of the office. Breckinridge wrote at least five opinions during March and April 1806, the preparation of which required considerable investigation.[16] The demands of the office reported by Breckinridge were similarly felt by his successor, Caesar A. Rodney, who wrote to his father after two weeks in office that "such have been the duties of my office as Attorney General U. S. and the pressure of publick business, that I have really not a moment I could call my own."[17] Two weeks later he was still "incessantly occupied,"[18] and after six weeks in office he confessed: "I have a very laborious time here indeed with Executive and legal duties."[19]

Jefferson regularly submitted questions to the Attorney General for his legal opinion, and the heads of the departments did so with even more frequency. Sending Levi Lincoln a copy of the executive proceedings of Governor St. Clair of the Northwest Territory "for the consideration of the Attorney General, with a view to the power exercised by the Governor," the President indicated that "the Attorney General is desired to give an opinion whether his exercise of these powers be lawful under the acts establishing the Northwestern territory?"[20] On another occasion Jefferson endorsed an eight-page opinion by the Attorney General on a prize case: "Mr. Lincoln's opinion at what moment property taken vests in the Captor [and] on the right of bringing prizes into our ports."[21] As these examples show, the Attorney General was expected to give opinions on both national and international law. The Secretary of State frequently called upon him for opinions in both areas, referring problems of territorial laws, land laws, and other domestic matters to him, along with international questions.[22] The Secre-

[16] Opinions of Mar. 18, Mar. 18, Mar. 22, and Apr. 28 are in Letters from and Opinions of Attorneys General, microcopy T-326, Natl. Archives. An opinion of Apr. 5, 1806 is in House Records, RG 233, Natl. Archives.

[17] Caesar A. Rodney to Thomas Rodney, Feb. 12, 1807, Brown Collection, Hist. Soc. Del.

[18] Caesar A. Rodney to Thomas Rodney, Feb. 26, 1807, ibid.

[19] Caesar A. Rodney to Thomas Rodney, Mar. 15, 1807, ibid.

[20] Jefferson to Lincoln, Jan. 28, 1802, Carter, ed., Territorial Papers of the United States, III, 207.

[21] Lincoln, opinion on prize ship Betsy Cathcart [July 3, 1801], Jefferson Papers, v. 119, p. 20584, Lib. Cong.

[22] Letters from and Opinions of Attorneys General, T-326, Natl. Archives. See also John T. Mason to Madison, July 28, 1807; Robert Williams to Madison, Oct. 5, 1807, Rodney Collection, Hist. Soc. Del.; Madi-

tary of the Treasury referred numerous questions to the Attorney General.[23] In some instances, opinions which a department head obtained from the Attorney General were passed on to congressional committees and used in seeking new legislation or changes in existing laws.[24] Although congressional committees did call upon the Attorney General directly for opinions, more frequently the committees directed their inquiries to a department head who in turn consulted the Attorney General.[25] His opinions were sometimes included in committee reports. A report of the Committee on Public Lands, dated February 26, 1806, contained an opinion of the Attorney General, March 10, 1801, that the Secretary of the Treasury had transmitted to the committee.[26]

Since many opinions of the Attorneys General under Jefferson never found their way into the later collected official opinions of the Attorneys General of the United States, that source is an unreliable indicator of their work. In 1841 when the first collection of opinions by the Attorneys General was printed by the House of Representatives, Attorney General Henry D. Gilpin explained that he was supplying such opinions as he had been able to locate. "Previous to the year 1817," he pointed out, "no records of such opinions were preserved. It has therefore been necessary to procure them, as far as practicable, from the different departments to which they were sent; but many that were, no doubt, given before that period, are not now to be found."[27] For the period of Jefferson's

---

son to Lincoln, June 13, 1802, Domestic Letters of the Department of State, M-40, Natl. Archives.

[23] A series of letters illustrating this practice is Gallatin to Rodney, Feb. 9, 1807, Feb. 6, July 5, and Sept. 8, 1808, in Gallatin Papers, Lib. Cong.

[24] Granger to the Committee on Post Roads, Jan. 7, 1802, enclosing Granger to Lincoln, Jan. 1, 1802, and Lincoln to Granger, Jan. 5, 1802, Letter Book of the Postmaster General, RG 28, Natl. Archives; Gallatin to John Boyle, Feb. 6, 1807, Treasury Dept., Letters and Reports to Congress, "E" Series, v, 29, RG 56, Natl. Archives.

[25] Gallatin to Jonathan O. Moseley, Dec. 4, 1807; Rodney to Gallatin, Dec. 1, 1807, House Records, RG 233, Natl. Archives. See also opinion of Breckinridge, Apr. 5, 1806, on case of ship *Manhattan*, addressed to Gallatin and forwarded to House by Gallatin, Gallatin Papers, microfilm edition.

[26] Gallatin to Andrew Gregg, chairman, Jan. 31, 1806, Reports of the Committee on Public Lands, I, 29, House Records, RG 233, Natl. Archives.

[27] *Opinions of the Attorneys General of the United States, from the Commencement of the Government down to the 1st March, 1841*, House Document 123, 26 Cong., 2 Sess., p. 1.

administration, most of the opinions located in 1841 came from the files of the State Department. With the exception of three opinions addressed to the President and two sent to the Secretary of the Navy, the opinions were addressed to the Secretary of State. Missing were all of the opinions written for the Secretary of the Treasury, the Secretary of War, and the Postmaster General. Some of the major opinions prepared for the President were also lacking, including a thirty-five page opinion from Attorney General Rodney that was submitted in August 1807[28] and another Rodney opinion which the Comptroller sent as a circular to all collectors in July 1808.[29] From this it can be seen that the collected official opinions of Jefferson's Attorneys General are definitely misleading in regard to the extent of their work and the scope of their activities. The importance of the office clearly went beyond what has commonly been accepted as the record of that office.[30]

Not only was the Attorney General consulted by all executive officers, he was also called upon by Congress to furnish reports and opinions. The practice in such cases was for a resolution of the House or Senate to request the President to direct the Attorney General to carry out such duties. Some of these assignments required extensive work.[31] In April 1802, the Senate directed Lincoln "to examine into the contract entered into between the United States and John Cleves Symmes, Esq. and others, bearing date on the 15th of October, 1788, and all the contracts and laws relative thereto; and all the transactions which may legally or equitably affect the same, as far as they may come to his knowledge; and to make a report of the same to the Senate, at their next session,

[28] Rodney to Jefferson, Sept. 15, 1807, Jefferson Papers, v. 171, p. 30148, Lib. Cong.

[29] Rodney to the President, printed circular, July 15, 1808, ibid., v. 179, p. 31694; a copy of the circular and Comptroller Duvall's covering letter, July 21, 1808, is in Papers of U. S. Treasury Relating to Customs, Manuscript Division, Lib. Cong.

[30] The standard collection most commonly used is Benjamin F. Hall, ed., Official Opinions of the Attorneys General of the United States, Advising the President and Heads of Departments in Relation to Their Official Duties, Volume I, 1791-1825 (Washington, D. C., 1852). While this collection is based on the 1841 collection cited in note 27 above, it contains fewer opinions for the period of Jefferson's presidency than the 1841 collection.

[31] Senate Journal, Apr. 12, 1802, III, 210; Jefferson to Lincoln, Apr. 17, 1802, Jefferson Papers, Lib. Cong.; Lincoln to the President of the Senate, Mar. 3, 1803, Senate Records, RG 46, Natl. Archives.

together with his opinion whether the said John Cleves Symmes has any claims, and what, upon the United States."[32] Three days after making this request Congress adjourned, but the Attorney General did not get home to Worcester until July.[33] When he submitted his report on the Symmes claim in January 1803, "together with such other documents as I could obtain having a legal, or an equitable relation to the subject,"[34] the manuscript filled nineteen folio pages in the Senate's volume of "Reports from Heads of Departments to the Senate."[35]

In 1801 Jefferson named Attorney General Lincoln as one of the federal commissioners to serve with the Secretary of State and the Secretary of the Treasury to negotiate an agreement with Georgia for the cession of her western lands. After reaching an agreement with Georgia in 1802, the commissioners undertook an examination of the claims which the United States assumed with the cession, including the controversial claims of the Yazoo land companies; in 1804 they proposed to Congress a compromise settlement to be made to the claimants. Since the commission's task involved extensive legal work, the burden fell upon the Attorney General. After Congress refused to sanction the commissioners' recommendations, the complicated issue remained unsettled throughout the remainder of Jefferson's presidency.[36]

Until May 1802 the Attorney General had certain duties in connection with the commission created by the sixth article of the Jay Treaty to settle prewar debts with Great Britain, and he received six hundred dollars additional compensation per year for these services.[37] The duties had been largely suspended after

[32] *Senate Journal*, Apr. 30, 1802, III, 228-229; Jefferson to Lincoln [May 1802]; Jefferson Papers, v. 123, p. 21281, Lib. Cong.

[33] Lincoln to Jefferson, May 25, June 28, July 25, 1802, Jefferson Papers, Lib. Cong.; Lincoln to Madison, May 12, 1802, Letters from and Opinions of Attorneys General, T-326, Natl. Archives.

[34] Lincoln to the President of the Senate, Jan. 26, 1803, Reports and Communications from the Attorney General, Senate Records, RG 46, Natl. Archives.

[35] Reports from the Heads of Departments to the Senate, I, 208-226, *ibid.*

[36] On the Yazoo land question, see Brant, *Madison, Secretary of State*, pp. 234-240; Thomas P. Abernethy, *The South in the New Nation, 1789-1819* (Baton Rouge, La., 1961), pp. 136-168.

[37] An act of June 30, 1797, instructed the Attorney General to assist the commissioners when his legal advice was sought and gave him the direction of an agent at Philadelphia and such other agents throughout the

July 1799 when the commission reached an impasse, and all offices connected with the commission ended in May 1802 upon the ratification of the convention with Great Britain of January 8, 1802.[38] The Attorney General was also a member of the Commission of the Sinking Fund; and, though the commission did not meet frequently, he might expect an occasional summons such as the following sent to Breckinridge, February 3, 1806: "The Secretary of the Treasury presents his compliments to the Attorney General of the United States, and will thank him to meet the Commissioners of the Sinking Fund, on Wednesday Morning next, at ten O'Clock, in the Committee Room of the Senate."[39]

Although the Attorney General ordinarily was not involved in actions in the lower federal courts, he was involved in the treason charges against Aaron Burr, who was brought before the circuit court in Richmond in June 1807. When Attorney General Breckinridge died in December 1806 in the midst of the Burr conspiracy crisis, Jefferson moved immediately to appoint Rodney as his successor. In informing Rodney that his nomination had been sent to the Senate and urging him to hurry to Washington, the President indicated that "the Supreme Court meeting on Monday will require necessarily the presence of the Attorney General and we have also an Executive matter calling for his immediate agency."[40] The "Executive matter" was the Burr conspiracy, and Rodney had been recommended to the President as the vigorous person needed to prosecute the government's case.[41] Though it was unknown to the President, Burr had been apprehended on the same day that he informed Rodney of his nomination to be Attorney General. Confirmed by the Senate on January 20 and sworn into office on January 29,[42] Rodney was soon deeply involved in the business relating to Burr. Jefferson turned over to Rodney the papers that

---

country as the business of the commission might make necessary. John Bassett Moore, ed., *International Adjudications: History and Documents*, Modern Series, 6 vols. (New York, 1929-1933), III, 16-17.

[38] *Ibid.*, pp. 328, 346.

[39] Gallatin to Breckinridge, Feb. 3, 1806, Breckinridge Family Papers, Lib. Cong.

[40] Jefferson to Rodney, Jan. 17, 1807, Ford, ed., *Jefferson Writings*, IX, 12.

[41] Thomas Leiper to Jefferson, Jan. 11, 1807, Jefferson Papers, Lib. Cong.

[42] *Senate Executive Journal*, II, 48. Rodney's commission and the affidavit of his taking the oath of office are in Brown Collection, Hist. Soc. Del.

he had assembled on the conspiracy,[43] and Rodney took charge of the government's case.

At the end of March, Rodney set out for Richmond to direct the proceedings. On March 27, George Hay, the United States District Attorney for Virginia, reported that Burr had been brought to Richmond the previous evening, that he expected the arrival of Rodney the following morning, and that he would take no steps to procure the commitment of Burr until Rodney reached Richmond.[44] Rodney was present when Burr was examined by Chief Justice John Marshall on March 30, and he participated in the preliminary hearings that immediately followed. Hay opened the government's argument, and Rodney presented the closing summation.[45] Rodney did not linger in Richmond after Burr was bound over for trial, and he was back in Washington by April 6.[46] But while in Richmond, as he later noted, he "took care to employ able counsel to assist in the prosecution" to be conducted by District Attorney Hay.[47] The assertion by one writer that "Rodney peremptorily retired from the case"[48] is inaccurate. However, when he made a trip home to Delaware in mid-April, he was detained there by the illness of his son Caesar and did not get back to Washington until late June.[49] Meanwhile, he sent a steady stream of documents and depositions to Hay in Richmond.[50]

During this period, Jefferson took direction of the proceedings that would have been left to Rodney had he been in Washington. In instructing Hay to obtain a full record of all testimony, Jefferson wrote: "Go into any expense necessary for this purpose, and meet it from the funds provided by the Attorney general for the other expenses. He is not here, or this request would have gone from

[43] Jefferson to George Hay, June 12 and 17, 1807, Ford, ed., *Jefferson Writings*, IX, 55, 56.

[44] Hay to Rodney, Mar. 27, 1807, Brown Collection, Hist. Soc. Del.

[45] Joseph P. Brady, *The Trial of Aaron Burr* (New York, 1913), pp. 9-11.

[46] The record of Rodney's trip to Richmond is in Rodney's notebook headed "United States vs. Aaron Burr," Hist. Soc. Del.

[47] Caesar A. Rodney to Thomas Rodney, July 1, 1807, Brown Collection, Hist. Soc. Del.

[48] Francis F. Beirne, *Shout Treason: The Trial of Aaron Burr* (New York, 1959), p. 66.

[49] Caesar A. Rodney to Thomas Rodney, July 1, 1807, Brown Collection, Hist. Soc. Del.

[50] These communications are listed in Rodney's notebook headed "United States vs. Aaron Burr," Hist. Soc. Del. See also George Hay to Rodney, Apr. 28, 1807, Brown Collection, Hist. Soc. Del.

him directly."[51] Writing a week later, the President indicated that "while Burr's case is depending before the court, I will trouble you, from time to time, with what occurs to me."[52] In a letter a few days later he explained more fully: "My intention in writing to you several times, has been to convey facts or observations occurring in the absence of the Attorney General."[53] Between May 20 and June 23, Jefferson wrote ten letters to Hay,[54] but after reporting in his letter of June 23 that Rodney was back in Washington, the letters ceased until August, suggesting that Rodney resumed management of the case. Rodney's papers confirm this and also indicate that he had planned to return to Richmond. "As soon as I arrived here," he wrote his father from Washington on July 1, "I tendered myself ready to proceed to Richmond and take my regular station in the line of battle, but such was the pressure of business here that the President could not spare me from head-quarters."[55] At that moment the administration was in the midst of the crisis following the attack on the *Chesapeake* that had occurred on June 22, and it seems evident that the President wanted some relief from the Attorney General's duties which he had been handling in Rodney's absence.

Rodney's papers show that the Attorney General was active in seeking witnesses against Burr during the summer of 1807[56] and that he was planning to be in Richmond in August for the beginning of the trial. Writing on July 1 to his father, Judge Thomas Rodney, in the Mississippi territory, he indicated that he expected him to testify against Burr and promised to "send new subpoena's on for all material witnesses and earnestly wish that they will repair in the soonest possible time to Richmond where I shall expect to meet them."[57] But the Attorney General did not return to Richmond to participate in the trial.[58] Instead, after spending

---

[51] Jefferson to Hay, May 26, 1807, Ford, ed., *Jefferson Writings*, IX, 52.

[52] Jefferson to Hay, June 2, 1807, *ibid.*, p. 53.

[53] Jefferson to Hay, June 5, 1807, *ibid.*, p. 55.

[54] These letters are printed in *ibid.*, pp. 52-64.

[55] Caesar A. Rodney to Thomas Rodney, July 1, 1807, Brown Collection, Hist. Soc. Del.

[56] Rodney to James Taylor, July 2, 1807; Taylor to Madison, Aug. 4, 1807; Taylor to Rodney, Aug. 10, 1807, Brown Collection, Hist. Soc. Del.; Robert Williams to Rodney, Aug. 7, 1807, Rodney Collection, Hist. Soc. Del.; Rodney's notebook, "United States vs. Aaron Burr," Hist. Soc. Del.

[57] Caesar A. Rodney to Thomas Rodney, July 1, 1807, Brown Collection, Hist. Soc. Del.

[58] *Trial of Aaron Burr for Treason*, printed from the report taken in shorthand by David Robertson, revised ed., 2 vols. (New York, 1875).

more of the summer in Washington than he had anticipated, he returned home where his wife was expecting their ninth child.[59] His absence had the approval of the President to whom Rodney expressed gratitude for "acts of parental kindness I shall never forget."[60] After Burr's acquittal in Richmond, Rodney was directly engaged in the efforts to bring Burr to trial in Ohio.[61]

In addition to his involvement in the Burr trial, there are other indications that the Attorney General had more to do with the judicial establishment than is indicated by the statutory definition of his duties. In 1806 the Senate called upon him for a report on the fees and compensation of attorneys, officers, jurors, and witnesses of the courts in each state.[62] That the Senate directed its request to the Attorney General suggests that that body thought these matters lay within his area of responsibility or knowledge; the fact that he furnished the report indicates that he did not consider it outside his duties.[63]

Whatever may have been true in regard to Attorneys General who served other early Presidents, the idea that the Attorney General was a part-time lawyer kept on retainer by the government and that his most important business involved private clients[64] is not valid for Jefferson's presidency. That Jefferson expected the Attorney General to devote his primary attention to government business is perhaps nowhere better revealed than in a letter which he wrote to Attorney General Rodney in October 1807 congratulating him on the birth of a child and expressing a hope that Mrs. Rodney's situation would enable him to return to Washington. "The approaching convention of Congress would render your assistance here desirable," he wrote, as he went on to explain the most pressing matters:

> Besides the varieties of general matter we have to lay before them, on which we should be glad of your aid and counsel, there

[59] Rodney to George Read, July 21, 1807, Rodney Collection, Hist. Soc. Del.; Caesar A. Rodney to Thomas Rodney, Oct. 25, 1807, Brown Collection, Hist. Soc. Del.

[60] Caesar A. Rodney to Thomas Rodney, Oct. 25, 1807, *ibid.*

[61] George Hay to Rodney, Nov. 2, 9, Dec. 6, 7, 1807; William Wirt to Rodney, Nov. 8, Dec. 5, 1807; Rodney to Wirt, Nov. 25, 1807, *ibid.*

[62] *Senate Journal*, IV, 89.

[63] The lengthy report was laid before the Senate, Dec. 28, 1807. *ASP, Misc.*, I, 656-700.

[64] See White, *Federalists*, pp. 164, 172; White, *Jeffersonians*, pp. 336-337.

are two subjects of magnitude in which your agency will be peculiarly necessary. 1. The selection and digestion of the documents respecting Burr's treason, which must be laid before Congress in two copies (or perhaps printed, which would take 10 days). 2. A statement of the conduct of Great Britain towards this country, so far as respects the violations of the Maritime Law of nations. Here it would be necessary to state each distinct principle violated, and to quote the cases of violation, and to conclude with a view of her vice-admiralty courts, their venality and rascality. . . . Everything we see and hear leads in my opinion to war; we have therefore much to consult and determine on, preparatory to that event.[65]

It is clear that Jefferson regarded the Attorney General as a working member of his administration and that he expected him to participate fully in decisions concerning the government.

THE GENERAL POST OFFICE

The General Post Office was not one of the executive departments and the Postmaster General was not a member of the President's Cabinet, but the position of Postmaster General was an administrative post of responsibility and extensive patronage. Jefferson's Postmaster General, Gideon Granger, was also a member of the President's inner circle of political counselors and a principal adviser to the President on party affairs in New England. In 1801 the Postmaster General's office, officially known as the General Post Office, was staffed by an Assistant Postmaster General, a chief clerk, six subordinate clerks, and a messenger. Despite his title, the Assistant Postmaster General was regarded by Congress as holding a position inferior to the chief clerks of the State and the Treasury departments, and his salary was kept below their salaries.[66] By 1803 the staff of the General Post Office had increased by three clerks,[67] and another clerk was added by 1806,[68] bringing the total to eleven, where it remained until after

[65] Jefferson to Rodney, Oct. 8, 1807, Ford, ed., *Jefferson Writings*, IX, 144.

[66] *ASP, Misc.*, I, 305, 385.

[67] Granger to John Randolph, Dec. 8, 1803, Letter Book of the Postmaster General, RG 28, Natl. Archives.

[68] *Letter from the Post Master General, Transmitting a Report of the Persons Employed as Clerks in His Office during the Year 1806*, Jan. 6, 1807 (Washington, D. C., 1807), Rare Book Division, Lib. Cong.

1808.[69] With the continuing expansion of the postal service, the work of the office constantly increased. Granger reported in 1803 that the "labours of the Department have nearly doubled" in four years.[70]

The Postmaster General in 1803 listed the duties of the ten clerks then employed as follows: a chief clerk, a bookkeeper, a clerk who kept returns of the arrivals and departure of all the mails, a clerk who handled the location of offices and the course of post roads and assisted in the Postmaster General's correspondence, a clerk charged with the returns of the postmasters, a copying clerk to the Postmaster General, a copying clerk to the Assistant Postmaster General, and three clerks without specified duties.[71] To keep up with the work of the office, it was normally necessary to hire part-time clerks or to pay the regular clerks to work extra hours. The Postmaster General's annual reports on the clerks employed in his office generally contained a statement such as the one in his report for 1806 stressing that "from the extension of the post roads, the establishment of new offices, and the increase of population, wealth, and business through the United States, the business of this office and the labours of every person employed herein, are constantly and rapidly increasing."[72]

Occasionally the demands of Congress for reports strained both the staff and the patience of the Postmaster General. When the House of Representatives called upon him in December 1803 for a detailed report for the preceding three years showing the amount of postage in each state, the cost of transporting the mails on all the roads in each state, the commissions of postmasters, and all other expenses of the Post Office, the Postmaster General had to hire an additional clerk. Besides, he complained to the chairman of the House Committee of Ways and Means, the request "has engrossed nearly the whole time of all the other Clerks employed; insomuch that all the ordinary business, except only such as could not at all be delayed has been postponed, and will remain to be performed after the report which the resolution calls for is completed."[73]

---

[69] See Appendix I.

[70] Granger to Randolph, Jan. 29, 1803, Letter Book of the Postmaster General, RG 28, Natl. Archives.

[71] Granger to Randolph, Dec. 8, 1803, *ibid.*

[72] *Letter from the Post Master General . . . Clerks in His Office . . . 1806*, Jan. 6, 1807.

[73] Granger to Randolph, Feb. 16, 1804; Granger to Macon, Mar. 1, 1802,

The letter books of the Postmaster General attest to a considerable volume of correspondence between Granger and local postmasters and mail contractors, who carried the mail for fixed annual sums. To this was added correspondence with members of Congress and state officials. In a Senate debate on a bill to set salaries for government officers in 1803, Senator Stephen R. Bradley supported raising the salary of the Postmaster General from three to four thousand dollars because "the duties of that officer are greatly encreased—He is frequently obliged to write all night till one oClock in the morning." Bradley further insisted that Granger was "a great man, his duties and *patronage* are great— and if his salary is not raised it will not be possible to retain him in office; and it will be difficult to find his *equal*."[74] Senator John Smith of Ohio, who wanted to go even further and raise Granger's salary to five thousand a year, which would have equaled that of the Secretary of State or the Secretary of the Treasury, joined in confirming Granger's application to his work. "The postmaster General has wrote *two quires and three sheets* of paper in one day in his office," he asserted.[75] Although the Senate voted in support of Bradley's motion to raise the Postmaster General's salary to four thousand, the House of Representatives refused to accept the Senate's action, contending that such a raise would give the Postmaster General—whose office was "of very inferior consequence to that of Comptroller of the Treasury"[76]—a salary higher than that of the Comptroller. The act left the Postmaster General's salary at three thousand dollars per year, the equivalent of the Auditor and the Treasurer, but less than the Comptroller, who received thirty-five hundred dollars.[77] Congress thus made it clear that the General Post Office ranked with subordinate offices rather than with executive departments.

The operation of the Post Office revealed much about the government of the nation. It was the one real service agency of the early republic, and more than any other agency of the national government, it directly touched ordinary people in all parts of the country. Its ability to respond to their needs, to their move-

---

Letter Book of the Postmaster General, RG 28, Natl. Archives; *House Journal*, Dec. 5, 1803, iv, 468.

[74] Brown, ed., *Plumer's Memorandum*, Dec. 6, 1803, pp. 73-74.

[75] *Ibid.*, p. 74.

[76] *ASP, Misc.*, i, 385.

[77] Act of Feb. 20, 1804, *Annals of Congress*, 8 Cong., 1 Sess., 1253.

ments into newer areas, to the rapid growth of the country, and to the dispersion of the population was a reflection of the ability of the government to serve its constituency. When Jefferson took office in 1801, there were 957 post offices and 21,840 miles of post roads in the United States. At the end of 1808, his last full year in office, there were 1,944 post offices and 34,035 miles of post roads.[78] In 1807 the Postmaster General calculated that the daily transportation of the mails in coaches, in sulkies, and on horseback exceeded 12,327 miles.[79]

The President himself took a direct interest in improving postal service. During his first months in office and before the appointment of a new Postmaster General, Jefferson wrote to Secretary of State Madison, noting that he had observed that a large number of contracts for carrying the mails were being advertised and that the notices were proposing four-year contracts. "I have long been persuaded that we might greatly increase the rapidity of the movement of the mails; and have had it in contemplation to propose this when we get ourselves a little clear of more pressing business," he explained. "But we shall be precluded by the 4 year contracts. I suggest to your consideration therefore the expediency of making the ensuing contracts for one year only, to give us time to try whether a more rapid conveyance be not practicable."[80] The pressure from the President to improve the speed of communication by mail continued. After a year in office, Jefferson assured his son-in-law, Thomas Mann Randolph, Jr., that "within 3 years from this time the stages will pass from Richmond to Georgia in 6 days; as we mean to endeavor to make all the principal mails travel 100 miles the 24 hours."[81] By the fall of 1802 an agent of the Post Office was traveling in the South with letters of introduction to members of Congress living along his route announcing that the purpose of his visit was to ascertain the condition of the Post Office in the southern states and to establish a line of stages from Virginia to Georgia.[82] This was a rare example of an official from Washington going into the countryside to arrange for the improvement of government services. His efforts resulted in the establishment of connecting lines of stages from Petersburg to Augusta.[83]

[78] ASP, Post Office, pp. 28, 43.   [79] Ibid., p. 41.
[80] Jefferson to Madison, June 20, 1801, Madison Papers, Lib. Cong.
[81] Jefferson to Randolph, Mar. 12, 1802, Jefferson Papers, Lib. Cong.
[82] Granger to Macon, Sept. 20, 1802, introducing Phineas Bradley, Letter Book of the Postmaster General, RG 28, Natl. Archives.
[83] Granger to James Jackson, Nov. 22, 1803, ASP, Post Office, p. 29.

Republicans had long complained about political abuses in the Post Office. During the campaign of 1800, Jefferson trusted none of his letters relating to political subjects to the Post Office "believing that the postmasters will lend their inquistorial aid to fish out any new matter of slander they can to gratify the powers that be."[84] In 1801 Ephraim Kirby, a prominent Connecticut Republican, reminded the new President that "the Post offices in this part of the United States have for years past been almost universally in the hands of violent political partizans." He charged that "this department has been a monstrous engine of private abuse, and public deception. Correspondence between persons of known Republican character has been altogether unsafe. Republican Newspapers conveyed by Mail have been either suppressed, or ridiculed at the office of delivery, in such manner as to deter many from receiving them."[85] Responsive to such concerns, the new Republican President charged the Postmaster General with remedying the situation. By August 1802 Granger could report to the President that "the department in my opinion (a few cases excepted) is in a hopeful situation. The changes are as rapid as the prompt execution of the duties and the safety of the Department will admit."[86]

Soon after taking office, Granger explained in a letter of dismissal to the postmaster of Augusta, Georgia:

Upon entering on the duties of this office my mind was impressed with an unusual anxiety and solicitude. Knowing as I did that most of the officers under me, from their official stations, had been in the habits of associating and corresponding as well on politics as on business with those lately in authority, from whom the people had withdrawn their confidence and elevated to office men whose political principles they believed better calculated to preserve the constitution and public prosperity, and having a general knowledge of the most prominent recent events, it occurred to me that some removals would become necessary as well to effect an equal participation and enjoyment of office by the two great classes of citizens who are

[84] Jefferson to John Taylor, Nov. 26, 1799, *Jefferson Papers*, Mass. Hist. Soc., *Colls.*, 7th Ser., I, 67-68.

[85] Kirby to Jefferson, Nov. 10, 1801, Letters of Application and Recommendation during the Administration of Thomas Jefferson, 1801-1809, RG 59, Natl. Archives.

[86] Granger to Jefferson, Aug. 23, 1802, Jefferson Papers, Lib. Cong.

designated by the terms federalists and republicans as to preserve and maintain confidence in the department.[87]

The ground upon which the postmaster of Augusta was dismissed was that he was the printer of a newspaper.[88] Granger explained that he was "convinced that as a general rule the printers of newspapers ought not to be employed as postmasters because they have a special interest in suppressing for a time the intelligence forwarded to rival printers, which generate suspicions, mutual recriminations and party bickerings . . . and because they have an uncommon interest in using the right of franking to an extent never contemplated by law if not to the destruction of a fellow craftsman." He insisted that he had "refused to appoint a republican printer postmaster in every instance where application has been made although they have been neither few nor badly supported."[89] In adopting this position, Granger was following a policy which had been urged on the administration by other Republican leaders, among them Nathaniel Macon of North Carolina, who had written the President in the early weeks of the new administration recommending a general regulation "that no person concerned in a printing office, especially where news papers are printed, should hold any appointment in the post office." "Things of this small kind are mentioned," Macon suggested, "on a supposition, that while you are attending to the great interest of the nation, they may possibly escape your attention."[90] The prompt actions of the new Postmaster General[91] suggest that the problem did not escape the attention of the President.

During his first nine months in office, Granger appointed 379 new postmasters.[92] In making these appointments and others during subsequent years, he relied on the recommendations of Republican members of Congress and on state and local Republican

[87] Granger to William J. Hobby, Jan. 16, 1802, Letter Book of the Postmaster General, RG 28, Natl. Archives.

[88] Hobby was associated with the Augusta *Herald*, a "moderately Federalist" paper. David H. Fischer, *The Revolution of American Conservatism: The Federalist Party in the Era of Jeffersonian Democracy* (New York, 1965), p. 422.

[89] Granger to Hobby, Jan. 16, 1802, Letter Book of the Postmaster General, RG 28, Natl. Archives.

[90] Macon to Jefferson, Apr. 23, 1801, Jefferson Papers, Lib. Cong.

[91] See also Granger to Augustine Davis, Jan. 27, 1802, replacing Davis as postmaster of Richmond because he was the printer of a newspaper. Letter Book of the Postmaster General, RG 28, Natl. Archives.

[92] Granger to Jefferson, Aug. 23, 1802, Jefferson Papers, Lib. Cong.

leaders. If there was no Republican member of Congress, as in the case of Delaware in 1801, he called for assistance from members from neighboring states. "The immediate appointment of a Postmaster at St. George's *Delaware* is essentially necessary," he wrote to Representative Joseph H. Nicholson of Maryland. "As I am wholly ignorant of the people there, and there is no gentlemen here from Delaware with whom *I can advise*, and you live in the neighbourhood, I pray you to nominate some suitable person as soon as may be for that office."[93] In the same letter Granger also asked Nicholson for recommendations for vacancies in several towns in Maryland and questioned him about several postmasters, requesting Nicholson "to consult with your friends and suggest to me such alterations as the public interest and the restoration of public confidence require." In his home state of Connecticut, which had no Republican member in either the House or the Senate, Granger relied on state and local Republican leaders such as Ephraim Kirby, whom Granger asked in 1802 "to select the proper stands for Post Offices on the new Post Road between New Haven and Litchfield and give me information together with the list of the name of a proper candidate for each office."[94]

At times Granger sent blank appointment papers to a member of Congress or a trusted political friend and requested him to name a postmaster and fill in the papers. He sent such papers to Senator DeWitt Clinton in 1803, asking him to name a postmaster at Fishkill, New York.[95] To Representative John Smith of New York he wrote similarly: "The postmaster at Suffolk C. H., N. Y., has resigned and recommended his assistant Benjamin Brewster for his successor. I inclose you the necessary papers for an appointment—if Mr. Brewster is a suitable character I pray you to fill them with his name—if not to select a suitable one."[96] In another case Granger sent the necessary blanks for the appointment of three postmasters in Delaware to the Postmaster of Wilmington with instructions that "in case they should be found to be destitute of integrity or revilers of the Government of their Country, I desire you to substitute such names as you may think proper."[97] While indeterminable numbers of Federalist postmasters were dis-

[93] Granger to Nicholson, Dec. 21, 1801, Nicholson Papers, Lib. Cong.

[94] Granger to Kirby, Apr. 12, 1802, Ephraim Kirby Papers, Duke Univ.

[95] Granger to Clinton, Mar. 24, 1803, Letter Book of the Postmaster General, RG 28, Natl. Archives.

[96] Granger to Smith, Apr. 23, 1803, *ibid.*

[97] Granger to Postmaster, Wilmington, Del., Oct. 7, 1803, *ibid.*

missed on political grounds, Granger, like Jefferson, found that "it is easier to restore to the friends of the Administration their just proportion of office by judicious appointments than by removals."[98]

Samuel Harrison Smith, editor of the *National Intelligencer*, reported privately that Granger "is a man of great dignity and propriety of conduct, and possesses none of that intolerance ascribed to him by his enemies."[99] Although Granger sought to rid the postal service of opponents of Jefferson, he was equally vigorous in preventing Republican postmasters from allowing partisanship to influence the execution of their duties as officers of the Post Office. In 1802, he wrote to the editor of the Philadelphia *Gazette of the United States*, one of the leading and most partisan Federalist newspapers in the country, that it had been reported to him that certain letters addressed to the editor had been purloined and blank covers forwarded instead of the letters. "The importance of preserving the channels of correspondence and communication free and unpolluted and also even unsuspected induces me to inquire whether these letters or either of them were intrusted to any one officer of this department," he wrote in asking for a statement about the matter. Granger promised that "no exertion of mine shall be wanting to prevent any such detestable practice," and that any person found guilty would be dismissed and subjected to the full penalty of the law.[100] Under Granger, the Post Office was not to be used as a political instrument. It was a source of extensive minor patronage, but in the performance of their duties, postmasters were expected to keep open a neutral channel of communication.

As Postmaster General, Granger was not only intolerant of partisan interference, he was also intolerant of inefficiency. He did not hesitate to tell postmasters when they were not performing their duties nor to dismiss anyone who was negligent. "A complaint is lodged against you for not arriving with the mails at Fryburg in good season according to contract," he wrote to one Maine contractor, "and on account of your employing mere boys instead of men whereby the public mail is left and transported in an unsafe and insecure manner. Pray remove these causes of complaint. The public service must be safely and well performed."[101]

[98] Granger to Postmaster, Albany, N. Y., Apr. 1, 1803, *ibid.*

[99] Smith to his wife, May 21, 1803, Mrs. Samuel Harrison Smith Papers, Lib. Cong.

[100] Granger to Enos Bronson, Jan. 4, 1802, Letter Book of the Postmaster General, RG 28, Natl. Archives.

[101] Granger to Josiah Paine, Portland, Jan. 25, 1802, *ibid.*

It is significant that Granger used the words "public service," for the record of his management of the Post Office shows that he regarded the Post Office as an agency that operated for the benefit of those it served. Thus, he worked closely with members of Congress in fixing post roads and establishing post offices, investigating matters brought to his attention by members of Congress, recommending alterations in post roads, and, in general, working to improve postal service. "I take the liberty of forwarding the enclosed letter on the subject of a new post road," he wrote to the chairman of the House committee on post roads in one of many similar letters, "and of remarking that it is believed the alteration minuted on the back of the letter and subscribed by me would be useful to the public."[102] Decisions by Congress on the establishment of post roads were often the products of innumerable pressures from constituents, but the Postmaster General sought to provide assessments of proposed changes with a view to public service. After Congress established post roads, it was the responsibility of the Postmaster General to establish offices along the route and work out the contracts for carrying the mail. He reported annually on the post roads that had been in operation more than two years and were not producing one-third of the expense of the route.[103] While some post roads were discontinued, the failure of a route to be self-supporting did not necessarily mean that it would be dropped, since post roads were seen as contributing to the development of the country.

Despite the fact that he had a large number of postmasterships to keep filled, many of which offered little prospect of gain to the appointees, Granger was diligent in attempting to keep them filled. He was thus disturbed when he was accused by a newspaper in Wilmington, Delaware, in September 1803, of having failed to appoint postmasters to six vacant offices in the state. "In July last I carefully examined my list of offices and filled as I thought every vacancy," he wrote to the Republican Governor of Delaware. "I have this day examined every office in Delaware and do not find a single vacancy." He went on to explain: "If Sir you know of any vacancies or any places where the establishment of new offices would be useful I solicit the necessary information and the names

[102] Granger to the Chairman of the Committee on Post Roads, Jan. 26, 1802, *ibid*.

[103] Granger to the Senate and House of Representatives, Dec. 23, 1801, Jan. 24, 1803, Senate Records, RG 46; Letter Book of the Postmaster General, RG 28, Natl. Archives.

of suitable characters to appoint."[104] This letter and numerous others in the records of the Post Office show that the Postmaster General regarded it as his duty to provide service to the public, and the operations of the department demonstrated a responsiveness to public need.[105]

COMMISSIONS

Most of the operations of the executive branch came under the supervision of one of the four departments, the Postmaster General, or the Attorney General; and most administrative duties were assigned to one department or officer rather than made the joint responsibility of two or more departments. An exception was the Commission of the Sinking Fund which was composed of the President of the Senate, the Chief Justice of the United States, the Secretary of State, the Secretary of the Treasury, and the Attorney General. This commission met regularly though not frequently and submitted an annual report to Congress. The administrative work of the commission was handled by the Secretary of the Treasury, and the chief clerk of the Treasury Department served as secretary to the commissioners, for which he received an extra compensation of $250 per year.[106] In their annual report submitted in 1808, the commissioners specified that the measures authorized by the commission were "fully detailed in the report of the secretary of the treasury to this board . . . and in the statements therein referred to, which are herewith transmitted, and prayed to be received as part of this report."[107] Thus, in practice the sinking fund was administered by the Secretary of the Treasury.

From time to time, special commissions were appointed by the President and given specific assignments. Indian treaties were normally negotiated by special commissions. The federal capital had been laid out and its construction supervised until 1802 by three commissioners appointed by the President; in 1802 these commis-

[104] Granger to David Hall, Sept. 30, 1803, *ibid.*

[105] On the operation of the Post Office throughout the country, see Wesley E. Rich, *The History of the United States Post Office to the Year 1829* (Cambridge, Mass., 1924), Chaps. 5-10.

[106] *ASP, Misc.,* I, 304.

[107] *Report of the Commissioners of the Sinking Fund, Accompanied with Sundry Statements, Exhibiting the Proceedings Which Have Been Authorized by the Board, since Their Report, of the Fifth of February, 1807,* Feb. 6, 1808 (Washington, D. C., 1808), Executive Papers, 10 Cong., 1 Sess., House Records, RG 233, Natl. Archives.

sioners were replaced by a superintendent appointed by the President and under his control.[108] The commission appointed by President Adams to negotiate the cession of western lands from Georgia was reconstituted by Jefferson, who named the Secretary of State, the Secretary of the Treasury, and the Attorney General as its members. The commission arranged the Georgia cession in 1802 and subsequently examined the complicated claims which the United States assumed. As previously noted, the Attorney General did most of the legal work of this commission.[109]

Though these commissions performed useful services, such boards, special commissions, and independent agencies were not widely employed during Jefferson's presidency. The closest thing to an independent agency was the United States Mint at Philadelphia which Congress had placed directly under the President's control, but President Washington had assigned its supervision to the Secretary of State;[110] it remained there throughout Jefferson's presidency.

GOVERNMENT CLERKS

At the end of 1801, Jefferson's first year in office, there were ninety-four clerks in the four departments and the General Post Office. In 1808, his last year as President, the same offices employed ninety-seven clerks.[111] Repeal of all internal taxes in 1802 had eliminated four clerkships in the Treasury Department when the offices of the Commissioner of the Revenue and the Superintendent of Stamps were abolished, but this was offset by an increase in the business of the land office. In the Navy Department, one of the clerkships eliminated early in Jefferson's administration was restored in 1806.[112] The only overall increase was in the Post Office, where the number of clerks rose from seven in 1801 to eleven in 1808. Thus, the number and the distribution of departmental clerkships in 1808, as shown in Table 1, were only slightly different from 1801.

When Jefferson in his first annual message to Congress suggested reductions in the civil list, the Secretary of the Treasury

[108] Act of July 16, 1790, 1 *Statutes at Large*, 130; Act of May 1, 1802, 2 *Statutes at Large*, 175.

[109] See p. 140 above.   [110] White, *Federalists*, p. 140.

[111] See Appendix I.

[112] See Smith to Uriah Tracy, Mar. 29, 1806, Letters from the Secretary of the Navy to Congress, RG 45, Natl. Archives.

TABLE 1. NUMBER OF CLERKS IN THE OFFICES OF THE FOUR
DEPARTMENTS AND THE GENERAL POST OFFICE, 1801 AND 1808[a]

	1801	1808
Department of State	7	7
Department of the Treasury	53	54
Department of War	14	13
Department of the Navy	13	12
General Post Office	7	11
TOTAL	94	97

[a] See Appendix i for the detailed compilation upon which this summary is based.

warned that not much was to be expected in that area. The civil list had been closely watched and had grown little since the establishment of the government under the Constitution. "I am confident," Gallatin said, "that no department is less susceptible of reform."[113] The figures in Table 1 show that Gallatin's prediction that the civil list could not be much altered was accurate. At the same time, considering the growth of the country and the new demands made on the administrative offices by the acquisition of the Louisiana territory, Republican attention to economy in government and the elimination of the internal revenue service kept the staffs of departmental offices from expanding. While in the early years of his administration it was Jefferson who sought to reduce the civil establishment, in the latter years of his presidency it was the Congress which kept the civil list from growing by refusing to increase appropriations.

The total expenditures for salaries of clerks in the four departments changed little in the course of Jefferson's presidency, as shown in Table 2. Salaries ranged in 1801 from a low of $525 per year, received by two clerks in the Treasury Department, to a high of $1,800 received by the chief clerk of the Treasury Department. In 1807 the salary range was from $525 received by one of the same clerks as in 1801 to $2,000 paid to the chief clerk of the State Department.[114] There were nine clerks with the title of chief clerk or principal clerk among the ninety-five clerks listed in the records of the four departments and the General Post

[113] Gallatin, notes on the President's message, November 1801, Adams, ed., *Gallatin Writings*, i, 65-66.
[114] These figures are from the sources listed in Appendix ii.

TABLE 2. COMPENSATION PAID TO THE CLERKS IN THE FOUR DEPARTMENTS, 1801 AND 1807[a]

	1801	1807
Department of State	$ 6,509.94	$ 7,100.00
Department of the Treasury	49,723.75	51,118.37
Department of War	17,065.98	15,610.94
Department of the Navy	14,556.47	14,600.00
TOTAL	$ 87,856.14	$ 88,429.31

a The figures in this table are taken from the departmental reports to Congress listed as the sources for Appendix II.

The clerks in the Post Office in 1807 received compensation totaling $11,150; a comparable figure for 1801 has not been found. The figures for 1807 are in Report of the Postmaster General to the House of Representatives, Jan. 7, 1808, Original Reports, Post Office, House Records, RG 233, Natl. Archives.

Office for 1807.[115] Their annual salaries ranged from $1,450 to $2,000. Five other clerks without such titles but performing similar duties drew salaries in the range from $1,350 to $1,800. These included the clerk in charge of handling the business of the land office at a salary of $1,500 and William Thornton, who was in charge of the patent office and received $1,450 per year. In this group of fourteen key clerks, the median salary in 1807 was $1,625. For all other clerks in the four departments and the Post Office in 1807, the median annual salary was $900. If all clerks, principal and subordinate, are grouped together, the median annual salary was $1,000.[116]

Although the salaries of clerks had been raised across the board after the capital was moved to Washington in 1800,[117] clerks found that living costs exceeded the gain. Edward Jones, the chief clerk of the Treasury Department, who earned $1,500 per year at the beginning of 1801, declared: "That the expense of living in the District of Columbia is greater than in Philadelphia, is a

115 See Appendix II.

116 These figures are from the sources listed in Appendix II and from "A Comparative Statement of the Salaries Paid the Clerks in the Several Departments for the Year 1807, Shewing the Additional Compensation each Clerk Received," in House Records, RG 233, Natl. Archives.

117 Statement of the Application of the Appropriations made by Congress for Clerk-hire in the Treasury Department for the years 1799, 1800, and 1801, enclosed in Gallatin to the Speaker of the House, Apr. 6, 1802, Original Reports, Treasury Dept., House Records, RG 233, Natl. Archives.

fact not to be doubted, and I am prepared to shew if necessary, that my expenditures in the articles of house rent, wood, servants, coach hire to the office, etc., etc., have been encreased more than three hundred dollars, in consequence of the removal."[118] Before the end of 1801, Jones's pay had risen to $1,800. Another clerk, earning about $800 per year, sought an allowance of $40 per year for the expense of having to hire a carriage each day because of the distance he lived from his office;[119] there is no indication that he received the requested allowance. "Under the present circumstances of this place," Gallatin told the President in 1801, "we must calculate on paying higher all the inferior officers, principally clerks, than in Philadelphia." He also reported that "my best clerk next to the principal, and who had twelve hundred dollars, has left me to take one thousand in Philadelphia." In discussing the clerkships in the Treasury Department, Gallatin noted that "transcribing and common ones are easily obtained; good book-keepers are also everywhere to be found: it is difficult to obtain faithful examining clerks, on whose correctness and fidelity a just settlement of all the accounts depends, and still more difficult to find men of talents."[120]

There was no uniform salary scale for clerks, and the amount each received was determined, within the limits of a general appropriation, by the head of the office in which the clerk was employed. Congress appropriated an aggregate sum for clerks for each office and authorized the heads of the four departments and the Postmaster General "to apportion the compensations for clerks in their respective departments in such manner as the services to be performed shall, in their judgment, require."[121] While the department heads were responsible for handling the compensation of clerks in all offices within their departments, in practice they delegated all arrangements in regard to clerks outside their own immediate offices to the subordinate officers. These officials did the hiring, firing, and granting of raises. As a result, although certain general practices prevailed (copyists, for example, were the lowest-paid clerks in all departments), clerks doing similar

[118] Edward Jones to Samuel Smith, May 12, 1801, Gallatin Papers, microfilm edition.
[119] Thomas Waterman to Gallatin, July 3, 1801, ibid.
[120] Gallatin to Jefferson, received Nov. 16, 1801, Adams, ed., Gallatin Writings, I, 72.
[121] Act of Apr. 21, 1806, Annals of Congress, 9 Cong., 1 Sess., 1280-1282.

tasks in different offices received unequal pay. When Gallatin took over the Treasury Department in 1801, he found that clerks in the offices of the Comptroller and the Auditor were paid less than those in the offices of the Register and the accountants of the War and the Navy departments.[122] He attempted to rectify the situation by providing additional allowances to clerks in the offices of the Comptroller and the Auditor, but in 1807 he pointed out to Congress that despite such allowances "the compensations received by the clerks employed in those two offices are generally less in proportion than those of clerks belonging to other accounting offices."[123]

When Granger became Postmaster General in 1801, he found that clerks in the General Post Office were receiving 30 to 40 percent less than in the four departments. "Why this difference should exist I cannot decide," he wrote the Secretary of the Treasury. "It is true that the amount of money transactions are much less; but it is believed that it requires as much skill, activity, knowledge and industry to serve with reputation and usefulness in this office as in others and when viewed in all its parts it is of great, tho' probably not equal importance." Granger made a strong plea for a larger allocation for the Post Office. "I wish my Clerks to meet with the same treatment with others of equal usefulness," he concluded, "that they may feel contented and acknowledge the impartial hand of justice."[124] Granger had some success in obtaining salary adjustments, and by 1807 the median pay of $1,000 in the Post Office was the same as the median pay of all clerks in all offices.[125] However, the average pay in the Post Office was still lower than in other offices, and Granger was citing the average figure to the chairman of the House Ways and Means Committee in 1808 in support of increased appropriations for the Post Office.[126] A principal reason for the average pay being lower in the

[122] Gallatin to Jefferson, received Nov. 16, 1801, Adams, ed., *Gallatin Writings*, I, 71-72.

[123] Report accompanying letter from Gallatin to the Speaker of the House, Jan. 19, 1807, Original Reports, Treasury Dept., House Records, RG 233, Natl. Archives.

[124] Granger to Gallatin, Jan. 9, 1802, Letter Book of the Postmaster General, RG 28, Natl. Archives.

[125] "A Comparative Statement of the Salaries Paid the Clerks in the Several Departments for the Year 1807," House Records, RG 233, Natl. Archives.

[126] Granger to George W. Campbell, Jan. 7, 1808, Original Reports, Post Office, House Records, RG 233, Natl. Archives.

Post Office, however, was because the pay of the Assistant Post-master General was not averaged with that of the clerks. In other offices such as the State Department, where the chief clerk was essentially the assistant secretary, his salary, which was comparable to that of the Assistant Postmaster General, was averaged with that of the clerks.

Because salary adjustments had to be made within the limits of congressional appropriations, any major revision of salary scales depended upon legislative action. Increasingly, the matter of differing salary scales was brought to the attention of Congress. One document before the House of Representatives in 1808 listed all the clerks who were doing the work of accountants in the various offices and noted the considerable discrepancies in salary scales. The author of the report, who has not been identified, concluded: "In taking a comparative view of the compensation allowed clerks in the different departments it is proper to observe that the last clerk on the Comptroller's list at 800 dollars per annum, examines and revises the whole of the Treasury accounts, pension and part of the General Post office accounts. It is therefore evident that the lowest grade of accountants in the Comptroller's office is nearly hundred fifty per cent less than in the other accounting offices."[127] Presumedly the author of this statement was not an accountant, since the percentage figure is inaccurate; but the lowest-paid accountant in other offices did earn $1,220.[128]

The normal workday for clerks in government offices was six hours, though they were expected to work longer if the business of the office made this necessary. "By the established custom and usage of this office," the Secretary of War reported to the chairman of the House Ways and Means Committee in 1803, "the Clerks are employed from 9 o'clock A.M. to 3 o'clock P.M. each day; but whenever a pressure of business renders it necessary the time is extended."[129] In a similar report the Secretary of the Navy explained that "the hours of attendance at this office are from 9 till 3 O'Clock, but . . . when business requires it (which is frequently the case) the attendance is not confined to particular

[127] "A Comparative Statement of the Salaries Paid the Clerks in the Several Departments for the Year 1807," House Records, RG 233, Natl. Archives.

[128] *Ibid.*

[129] Dearborn to John Randolph, Dec. 9, 1803, Misc. Letters Sent by Sec. of War, M-370, Natl. Archives.

hours."[130] In the Post Office—where, according to the Postmaster General, "the labors of this office must be continually increasing" —it became a regular practice for clerks to work in the evening. "For some time past in consequence of a great press of business the Clerks in this office have been required to attend in the evening and they have accordingly performed nearly three hours more service than usual," the Postmaster General reported at the beginning of 1803.[131] Since such additional work came to be regularly scheduled, the clerks were allowed the option of working in the evenings for additional compensation. The Postmaster General explained at the end of 1803: "All the clerks in this office labor faithfully six hours a day. This is far short of the labour necessary in the Department. To supply the deficiency as far as was practicable an allowance has been made of forty cents per hour to such clerks as could and would return and labour after dinner."[132]

The Post Office was the only office where clerks received hourly wages for overtime work, but most clerks expected that they would be rewarded for extra duties. In 1802, after chief clerk Jacob Wagner had been out ill for three months, three of the clerks in the State Department wrote to Madison noting that four clerks were now doing the work that had been performed by eight clerks under Adams and reminding the Secretary that Congress had left the distribution of the appropriations for clerks to department heads. "We submit to your candor and liberality whether an increase of duty, more than double, does not demand a consideration," they concluded, "and whether we may not be deemed, in strict justice to the Public, duly entitled to as liberal compensation as the Congress have authorized, and have left to your discretion."[133] Although a record of Madison's actions in this case has not been found, it was the practice to distribute the salaries of vacated positions among the clerks whose workloads had been increased. In reporting the compensation of clerks in the State Department during 1807, Madison explained that "the absence of a Chief Clerk for 1 quarter this year, having necessarily in-

[130] Smith to Randolph, Dec. 8, 1803, Letters from Sec. of Navy to Congress, RG 45, Natl. Archives.

[131] Granger to Randolph, Jan. 29, 1803, Letter Book of the Postmaster General, RG 28, Natl. Archives.

[132] Granger to Randolph, Dec. 8, 1803, *ibid.*

[133] Stephen Pleasonton, William Crawford, and Christopher S. Thom to Madison, July 1, 1802, Madison Papers, Lib. Cong.

creased the duties of all the others, the sum of 500 dollars thus left in hand was distributed among them at the end of the year, in proportion to their respective salaries."[134] Each department had funds for hiring temporary clerks or paying clerks for additional work; if unexpended at the end of the year, these funds were used for bonuses. The Postmaster General complained in 1802 that in his office there was "never any surplus fund here for a New Years present."[135]

Throughout Jefferson's presidency, Congress kept a close watch on the appropriations for the salaries of clerks in government offices. During the first session under Jefferson, the House of Representatives called upon the Secretaries of the four departments for statements showing the expenditures for clerks during the preceding three years and the names and salaries of all clerks.[136] Although it was not until 1806 that another such general request was made, the Ways and Means Committee did collect similar information from department heads periodically.[137] In 1806 Congress passed legislation requiring each department head and the Postmaster General to submit an annual report furnishing the names of all clerks in each office and their compensations during the preceding year. The reports also were to indicate "whether the business for clerks increases or diminishes in their respective departments, that Congress may be enabled to make further arrangements by law respecting clerk hire."[138] The initial reports under this act, which for the first time provided for an annual civil list of government clerks, were submitted to Congress early in 1807 and reported on the preceding year.[139]

[134] Report enclosed in Madison to the Speaker of the House, Jan. 22, 1808, Original Reports, State Department, House Records, RG 233, Natl. Archives.

[135] Granger to Gallatin, Jan. 9, 1802, Letter Book of the Postmaster General, RG 28, Natl. Archives.

[136] *House Journal*, Mar. 25, 1802, IV, 159-160. The reports are listed in Appendix II.

[137] Smith to Randolph, Dec. 8, 1803, Letters from Sec. of Navy to Congress, RG 45; Dearborn to Randolph, Dec. 9, 1803, Misc. Letters Sent by Sec. of War, M-370, Natl. Archives; Granger to Randolph, Dec. 8, 1803, Letter Book of the Postmaster General, RG 28, Natl. Archives.

[138] Act of Apr. 21, 1806, *Annals of Congress*, 9 Cong., 1 Sess., 1281.

[139] The originals of these reports can be found under the dates indicated in the following collections, all of which are in the National Archives: Original Reports of the Secretary of State, Jan. 1, 1807, Reports of the War Department, Jan. 14, 1807, IV, 159-161, Original Reports, Treasury Dept., Jan. 19, 1807, all in House Records, RG 233; Letters of Sec. of Navy to

Most reports for 1806 indicated increased workloads and a need for larger appropriations. The Secretary of State noted that "the business of the Department generally is in a state of progressive increase." In seeking funds for an additional clerk, he pointed to a rise in business relating to patents for useful arts (which had doubled in four years), land patents, and matters involving the impressment of American seamen.[140] The Secretary of the Treasury reported that "it will be necessary on account of the great encrease of business connected with the adjustment of claims and sales of public lands, to employ hereafter a greater number of clerks for that object." He also reported an increase of business in the Comptroller's and Auditor's offices that left those offices insufficiently staffed for the "prompt and regular settlement of all the public accounts."[141] The Secretary of War remarked that "the extension of our relations with the Indians has within two years past, made a considerable addition to the business for clerks."[142] The Secretary of the Navy transmitted a report from the accountant of the Navy stating that "from the encrease of the business in consequence of the additional number of Gun Boats and the vessels employed in actual service at Orleans, it is expected that it will be necessary to employ at least another Clerk."[143] The Postmaster General concluded his report with a request for a larger appropriation and the statement that "from the extension of the post roads, the establishment of new offices, and the increase of population, wealth, and business through the United States, the business of this office and the labours of every person employed herein, are constantly and rapidly increasing."[144]

Despite these pleas for additional personnel, no new positions were created in any of the offices in 1807; and in their reports for that year most of the department heads renewed their previous

Congress, Feb. 2, 1807, RG 45; Letter Books of the Postmaster General, Jan. 6, 1807, RG 28.

[140] Madison to the House of Representatives, Jan. 1, 1807, enclosing report on clerks employed during the year 1806, Original Reports of the Secretary of State, House Records, RG 233, Natl. Archives.

[141] Report accompanying letter from Gallatin to the Speaker of the House, Jan. 19, 1807, Original Reports, Treasury Dept., *ibid.*

[142] Dearborn to the Speaker of the House, Jan. 14, 1807, Reports of the War Department, IV, 159-161, *ibid.*

[143] Report enclosed in Smith to the Speaker of the House, Feb. 2, 1807, Letters of Sec. of Navy to Congress, RG 45, Natl. Archives.

[144] *Letter from the Post Master General . . . Clerks in His Office . . . 1806,* Jan. 6, 1807.

requests. Madison reported that increased demands on his office had made it "impracticable to bestow that prompt and regular attention to titles, and to the issuing patents for lands, which is desirable, especially at a period of peculiar increase in the business growing out of our foreign relations." He concluded by repeating his opinion "that the public service would be promoted, as stated in the report made to the last Congress, by a provision, at least sufficient for the employment of another Clerk."[145] The Secretary of the Treasury in his report for 1807 respectfully called attention to his report of the previous year in regard to the number and compensation of clerks in the Comptroller's and Auditor's offices.[146] The Secretary of War also reported that business for clerks in his department had "from various causes, considerably encreased, within a few months past."[147] And the Postmaster General repeated his plea of the preceding year.[148] The failure of Congress to respond to the requests from department heads for additional funds to expand their office staffs indicates that the legislature rather than the executive was responsible for keeping the size of departmental offices from growing in the latter years of Jefferson's presidency. Despite the assertions by the heads of departments that administrative efficiency was being impaired by the shortage of personnel, Congress did not respond.

Little is known about most of the men who held the clerkships in the government offices of Washington—many of them men who had moved with the government from Philadelphia and continued at their posts after the transfer of power from the Federalists to the Republicans in 1801. But they provided a much needed continuity; and they left behind a mass of records and documents, many of them filled with extensive compilations of data, painstakingly assembled and meticulously transcribed. The availability of information for both the legislature and the executive, so essential in a republic, was dependent upon this staff of clerks, bookkeepers, and copyists. Without their unheralded labors the process of government would surely have faltered.

[145] Madison to the Speaker of the House, Jan. 22, 1808, Original Reports, State Dept., House Records, RG 233, Natl. Archives.

[146] Gallatin to the Speaker of the House, Jan. 15, 1808, Original Reports, Treasury Dept., *ibid*.

[147] Dearborn to the Speaker of the House, Jan. 23, 1808, Reports of the War Department, IV, 198-199, *ibid*.

[148] Granger to the House of Representatives, Jan. 7, 1808, Original Reports, Post Office, *ibid*.

VIII. Appointments and Removals

"**N**OTHING PRESENTS SUCH DIFFICULTIES OF AD-ministration as offices," Jefferson said before his first month as President had passed.[1] After three months, he insisted that "it is the business of removal and appointment which presents the serious difficulties. All others compared with these, are as nothing."[2] After eight years he would leave the presidency believing that "the ordinary affairs of a nation offer little difficulty to a person of any experience, but the gift of office is the dreadful burthen which oppresses him."[3]

The change in administration that occurred for the first time when Jefferson took office raised new questions in regard to federal officeholders. Should the change in the highest office of the nation be accompanied by changes in the subordinate posts of government? Should Federalist officeholders, favored under President Adams, be replaced by Republicans who had made Jefferson President? Large numbers of Republicans thought these questions should be answered in the affirmative, and most Federalists feared that they would be. The editors of the New York *American Citizen* argued: "It is rational to suppose that those who removed John Adams from office, because of his manifold transgressions of the constitution, and his pointed hostility to liberty . . . would naturally expect the removal of lesser culprits in office. If this should not be the case, for what, in the name of God, have we been contending? Merely for the removal of John Adams, that Mr. Jefferson might occupy the place which he shamefully left?"[4] Another newspaper piece, widely reprinted in the Republican press, similarly declared that "the unequivocal wish" of the Republicans was "that *the board should be swept. . . .* It is what the people expect, what both parties struggled for and expected to see;—it was as well understood previous to the elections, that men who had advocated the baleful measures of several years past, who had been per-

[1] Jefferson to Gideon Granger, Mar. 29, 1801, Ford, ed., *Jefferson Writings*, VIII, 44.

[2] Jefferson to John Dickinson, June 21, 1801, Jefferson Papers, Lib. Cong.

[3] Jefferson to James Sullivan, Mar. 3, 1808, *ibid.*

[4] *American Citizen* (New York), June 5, 1801.

secutors of the friends of republicanism, were to be removed and the offices filled by men of republican principles, if they succeeded in their candidates, as if it had been reduced to a written contract."[5] From the Federalist side, Thomas Boylston Adams, son of the former President, resignedly concluded: "It begins to be well understood by both or *all* parties and us, that success in obtaining a Candidate of their own at the head of government, is sufficient to authorize a system of proscription with regard to the opponents. This is Republicanism."[6]

In his inaugural address Jefferson seemed to suggest a policy of moderation when he affirmed: "We have called by different names brethren of the same principle. We are all republicans: we are all federalists." So conciliatory did the President sound that a number of Republican leaders wrote to him expressing their concern. "A pretty general purgation of office, has been one of the benefits expected by the friends of the new order of things," wrote Congressman William B. Giles of Virginia, "and although an indiscriminate privation of office, merely from a difference in political sentiments, might not be expected; yet it is expected, and confidently expected, that obnoxious men will be ousted."[7] Though Jefferson initially hoped to reconcile the Federalists to his administration by a moderate course in regard to removals, he never suggested that there would be no removals, and he was soon explaining to Giles and other Republicans the policy he proposed to follow. First, he considered as nullities all appointments to civil offices held at the President's pleasure that Adams had made after the outcome of the election was known to him on December 12, 1800. These officers would be removed as a matter of course. In addition, all federal marshals and attorneys would be removed. "The courts being so decidedly federal and irremovable," he explained, "it is believed that republican attorneys and marshals, being the doors of entrance into the courts, are indispensably necessary as a shield to the republican part of our fellow citizens, which, I believe, is the main body of the people." While removals would be made for official misconduct, "good men, to whom there is no

[5] *American Mercury* (Hartford), July 30, 1801, printed in Noble E. Cunningham, Jr., ed., *The Making of the American Party System, 1789 to 1809* (Englewood Cliffs, N. J., 1965), pp. 173-175.

[6] Adams to Joseph Pitcairn, Mar. 27, 1801, "Letters of Thomas Boylston Adams," Historical and Philosophical Society of Ohio, *Quarterly Publications*, XII (1917), 44.

[7] Giles to Jefferson, Mar. 16, 1801, Jefferson Papers, Lib. Cong.

objection but a difference of political principle, practised on only as far as the right of a private citizen will justify, are not proper subjects of removal, except in the case of attorneys and marshals."[8] Under these guidelines, the early changes in offices took place, with new appointments going only to Republicans. "I have given, and will give only to republicans, under existing circumstances," Jefferson said.[9] "It is now perfectly just that the republicans should come in for the vacancies which may fall in, until something like an equilibrium in office be restored."[10]

From the beginning of his presidency, Jefferson recognized the difficulty of determining how far to go in removing Federalists. "That some ought to be removed from office, and that all ought not, all mankind will agree," he thought. "But where to draw the line, perhaps no two will agree."[11] During his first week in office he confided to Monroe: "Where we shall draw the line between retaining all and none, is not yet settled, and will not be till we get our administration together; and perhaps even then, we shall proceed *à talons*, balancing our measures according to the impression we perceive them to make."[12] No better description of the removal policy that Jefferson would follow can be drawn. His decisions were based on day-by-day deliberations, which in turn were determined by pressures upon his office, including even the conflicting views of members of his Cabinet. Demands for removals from Republicans in particular states sometimes reached proportions that could not be ignored. Most Republicans preferred that moderation be exercised in removing Federalists in other states, while seeing widespread removal as the logical course in their own state. Jefferson's policy was determined to a considerable extent by Republican pressures to which he was responsive as the leader of the party; but he balanced these demands with the responsibilities of the presidency. The mass of papers in Jefferson's files relating to appointments shows that he was concerned not only with maintaining the political support of his party followers but also with building a competent administrative structure. This

8 Jefferson to Giles, Mar. 23, 1801, Ford, ed., *Jefferson Writings*, VIII, 25.

9 Jefferson to Monroe, [Mar.] 7, 1801, *ibid.*, p. 10.

10 Jefferson to Benjamin Rush, Mar. 24, 1801, *ibid.*, p. 31.

11 Jefferson to Giles, Mar. 23, 1801, *ibid.*, p. 25. Jefferson wrote in a similar vein to T. M. Randolph, Jr., Mar. 27, 1801, Jefferson Papers, Univ. of Va.

12 Jefferson to Monroe, [Mar.] 7, 1801, Ford, ed., *Jefferson Writings*, VIII, 10.

was no easy job. "The task of removing and appointing officers continues to embarrass the Executive . . . ," Madison noted in July 1801. "The degree, the mode, and the times of performing it are often rendered the more perplexing by the discord of information and counsel received from different persons whose principles and views are the same."[13]

The pressures upon the President were greatest, as might be expected, during his opening months in office, and they early produced a modification of his initial policies. He could not fail to notice the views expressed by twenty-four leading Connecticut Republicans in a letter to Attorney General Lincoln.[14] In passing the letter on to the President, Lincoln pointed out that "all the principal Republicans in the State have signed it excepting two or three who are also in the same sentiments."[15] The Connecticut Republican leaders declared that "the peculiar state of politics in Connecticut has prevented our perception of the policy of Mr. Jefferson in delaying the removals from office, a Measure which appears to us absolutely necessary to the progress of republicanism here." They admitted that "republicans are not unanimous as to the extent and proper season of removals. . . . But, Sir, even if it should be judged good policy in all other States, to retain federalists in office, yet in this State, we could contemplate, in such policy only the certain ruin of republicanism. . . . The republicans he[re] expect that the President will remove the federalists from office, nor is the expectation confined to candidates for office, it is general as far as we can judge. They are mortified to see their enemies triumphing in a day when they expected triumph and to be daily insulted and abused as not having merited the confidence of the administration, whose advocates they have been."[16] After a visit to New England and conferences with Republican leaders, Attorney General Lincoln, Jefferson's chief adviser on New England politics, reported that in his opinion "it will be necessary to make the proposed removals in Connecticut, at some future time, in accommodation to the particular circumstances of that State, and the great merits of the Republicans there, and their strong feelings and Sentiments on the Subject. But when, and in what manner,

[13] Madison to Wilson Cary Nicholas, July 10, 1801, Hunt, ed., *Madison Writings*, VI, 426n.

[14] Pierpont Edwards and others to Levi Lincoln, June 4, 1801, Jefferson Papers, Lib. Cong.

[15] Lincoln to Jefferson, June 15, 1801, *ibid.*

[16] Edwards and others to Lincoln, June 4, 1801, *ibid.*

whether gradually, or at once, are questions likewise of some importance."[17] Lincoln's report confirmed Jefferson's decision that in Connecticut "a general sweep seems to be called for on principles of justice and policy."[18]

Similar pressures came from Republicans in other states. Jefferson admitted in June 1801 that "in Pennsylvania there is a strong pressure on me, and some discontent," and that demands for removals in Delaware and New Jersey were "moderately importunate."[19] From Virginia, Representative Giles wrote that "the soundest republicans in this place and throughout the country are rising considerably in the tone which they think ought to be assumed by the administration."[20] From New York, editors David Denniston and James Cheetham, who were taking a firm line in the New York *American Citizen* in favor of removals, wrote the President that "the people of this City and State look to the new administration with full Confidence for a thorough Change in the different offices. . . . We wish respectfully to express to you our firm opinion that a measure of this sort is absolutely necessary to preserve that republican majority in this State which has contributed so essentially towards placing you in that elevated Situation which you now hold. . . . Republican exertions will certainly be relaxed in this quarter if unhappily the people ever be convinced that all their efforts to Change the Chief Magistrate, have produced no consequent effects in renovating the Subordinate Stations of our government."[21] Not all segments of the Republican party in New York were so insistent on removals as the editors of the *American Citizen*, and Jefferson, recognizing the internal Republican divisions there, decided to "yield a little to their pressure, but no more than appears absolutely necessary to keep them together."[22] Jefferson assured Denniston and Cheetham that he was "endeavoring to proceed in this business with a view to justice, conciliation, and the best interest of the nation taken as a whole,"[23] but he was yielding to the pressures from his supporters. He made

[17] Lincoln to Jefferson, June 15, 1801, *ibid*.

[18] Jefferson to Nicholas, June 11, 1801, Ford, ed., *Jefferson Writings*, VIII, 64.

[19] *Ibid*.

[20] Giles to Jefferson, June 1, 1801, Jefferson Papers, Lib. Cong.

[21] Denniston and Cheetham to Jefferson, June 1, 1801, *ibid*.

[22] Jefferson to Nicholas, June 11, 1801, Ford, ed., *Jefferson Writings*, VIII, 64.

[23] Jefferson to Denniston and Cheetham, June 6, 1801, Jefferson Papers, Lib. Cong.

changes, however, only after his own investigation of the circumstances; by refusing to comply with some very insistent demands in particular cases,[24] he demonstrated the independence of his judgment and kept the final power of decision firmly in his own hands.

While there was some validity in Jefferson's complaint that his inaugural address had been misconstrued to mean that Federalists would remain undisturbed in office, he was compelled by the pressures from his supporters to issue a new public statement on his appointment and removal policy in July 1801. He found the occasion for the new pronouncement in answering a memorial from a group of merchants of New Haven, Connecticut, protesting against the removal of Elizur Goodrich, one of Adams's "midnight appointments," as collector of New Haven. In his reply to the New Haven remonstrance, Jefferson took the opportunity to explain his broad policies in regard to appointments and removals and in so doing revealed that he had modified the position that he had taken during the first weeks of his administration. In his July statement he emphasized the exclusion of Republicans from office under Adams and the right of Republicans to their "proportionate share" of public places. "If a due participation of office is a matter of right, how are vacancies to be obtained?" he asked. "Those by death are few; by resignation, none. Can any other mode than that of removal be proposed? This is a painful office; but it is made my duty, and I meet it as such. I proceed in the operation with deliberation and inquiry, that it may injure the best men least . . . that it may be thrown, as much as possible, on delinquency, on oppression, on intolerance, on incompetence, on ante-revolutionary adherence to our enemies."[25] Not only was such language far different from that used in his inaugural address, it also indicated a much broader policy of removals than Jefferson had explained in letters written in the early weeks after his inauguration. It reflected both the pressures from Republicans and the fading prospects of reconciling Federalists to his administration.

Jefferson concluded his New Haven statement by observing: "It would have been to me a circumstance of great relief, had I found

---

[24] See Cunningham, *Jeffersonian Republicans in Power*, pp. 44-49; John A. Munroe, *Louis McLane: Federalist and Jacksonian* (New Brunswick, N. J., 1973), pp. 30-31.

[25] Jefferson to Elias Shipman and others, July 12, 1801, Ford, ed., *Jefferson Writings*, VIII, 69-70.

a moderate participation of office in the hands of the majority. I would gladly have left to time and accident to raise them to their just share. But their total exclusion calls for prompter correctives. I shall correct the procedure; but that done, disdain to follow it, shall return with joy to that state of things, when the only questions concerning a candidate shall be, is he honest? Is he capable? Is he faithful to the Constitution?"[26] As President, Jefferson never reached the point where these questions would control his appointment decisions. He came to define the Republican "just share" of offices in terms of their proportionate strength in the electorate, which he judged to be between two-thirds and three-fourths.[27] Since Republicans never gained this proportion of federal offices, Jefferson never became willing to appoint a Federalist, except when no Republican could be found. When difficulty arose in locating a Republican for a particular post, he preferred "to defer it as long as can be admitted in the hope of hearing of some good republican to invest with it."[28] Jefferson never publicly announced, however, that he would appoint no Federalist to office, and he was careful to issue such instructions only to those he trusted. He did not hesitate to remind Monroe "not to recommend a single federalist, as I am determined to confine appointments to republicans until a due proportion be held by each in the public offices."[29] But before making a similar request of Thomas Newton, collector at Norfolk, he asked Monroe's advice as to whether he could "confide to him my purpose to appoint no federalist?"[30] Monroe's opinion was that "it may have its good effect that the avowal of that sentiment should be known as rarely as possible otherwise than by the act."[31] Jefferson followed that advice.

While Jefferson remained adamantly against appointing Federalists, in making removals he followed a policy less sweeping than his reply to the New Haven remonstrance suggested. Jefferson himself thought that his statement had "given more expectation to the *sweeping* Republicans than I think its terms justify," but he

[26] *Ibid.*, p. 70.

[27] See the article written by Jefferson, published in *Independent Chronicle* (Boston), June 27, 1803, in Ford, ed., *Jefferson Writings*, VIII, 236n.

[28] Jefferson to Gallatin, Nov. 6, 1801, Gallatin Papers, N.-Y. Hist. Soc. See also Jefferson to Gallatin, Nov. 12, 16, 1801, *ibid.*

[29] Jefferson to Monroe, May 9, 1802, James Monroe Papers, New York Public Library.

[30] *Ibid.*

[31] Monroe to Jefferson, May 17, 1802, Hamilton, ed., *Monroe Writings*, III, 350.

defended the pronouncement as "indispensably necessary."[32] In carrying out the policy announced in the New Haven statement, he continued to follow a day-by-day practice of deliberation and determination. Responding to conflicting pressures, he made removals for political purposes in some cases; in other instances he tried to check Republican clamor for removals lest a spirit of intolerance become too widespread. Jefferson was also careful to distinguish between active Federalist opposition by officeholders and the act of voting. "I have never had a wish to controul the right of private opinion or of suffrage in the officers of the government," he explained. "I have only believed it wrong, where they disapproved those principles of administration which the will of the nation has sanctioned, that they should employ the influence of their office in aid of an active opposition to them. No person, not doing this has ever been disturbed in the right of his personal suffrage."[33] That the President tried to steer a middle course in the removal of Federalists is shown not only by his actions in individual cases but also by actual number of Federalists removed and the number left in office after two years of Republican control.

Jefferson kept close track of the changes he made in those offices subject to his appointment and removal. His files contain numerous papers in his handwriting recording appointments and removals, classifying the reasons for vacancies, and figuring the totals of Republicans and Federalists holding office. Not all of these memoranda agree, since Jefferson sometimes listed the same person or office under different classifications.[34] Perhaps the most useful summary is a memorandum compiled in 1803 showing the totals of offices subject to the President's pleasure in both the general government and the states. By Jefferson's calculation the number of offices subject directly to his appointment and removal was 316; appointments to all of these offices required the approval of the Senate. This figure did not include judicial appointments, which were not subject to the President's removal. Of the 316 offices, 109 were in the general government; these included the offices in Washington and several outside the capital, such as at the mint in Philadelphia, the diplomatic and consular services,

[32] Jefferson to Gallatin, Aug. 14, 1801, Adams, ed., *Gallatin Writings*, I, 57.

[33] Jefferson to C. Parker, Nov. 3, 1806, Jefferson Papers, Tucker-Coleman Collection, College of William and Mary.

[34] See Cunningham, *Jeffersonian Republicans in Power*, pp. 60-63.

and the territorial offices. Jefferson supplied the following breakdown of these offices in the general government:[35]

	Republican	Neutral	Federalist
Head of departments	5		
Secondaries	3	1	1
Purveyer	1		
Mint officers	1		1
Foreign ministers	3		
Secretaries of legation	2		
Consuls	34	20	12
Governors of territories	2		
Secretaries of territories	1		1
Attorneys [District of Columbia]	1		
Marshals [District of Columbia]	1		
Collectors	4		1
Director of Marine hospital[a]			
Surveyor General	2		
Receivers	2		4
Registers	3		3
	65	21	23

[a] The remainder of this line is blank in Jefferson's memorandum.

In the states, Jefferson counted 207 offices subject to his appointment and removal. These were primarily revenue officers
(including collectors, naval officers, and surveyors) and officers
of federal courts (marshals and district attorneys). The President provided the following totals:

	Republican	Neutral	Federalist
New Hampshire	6		3
Massachusetts	13	1	24
Rhode Island	6		6
Connecticut	7		5
Vermont	3		1
New York	10		5
New Jersey	6		3

[35] Jefferson, memorandum, [1803], Jefferson Papers, v. 234, p. 41919,
Lib. Cong.

(*Cont. from p. 173*)

	Republican	Neutral	Federalist
Pennsylvania	3	1	5
Delaware	2		2
Maryland	4		13
Virginia	10	1	16
North Carolina	9	1	12
South Carolina	1		9
Georgia	5		5
Tennessee	4		
Kentucky	2	1	
Ohio	2		
	93	5	109 = 207
General	65	21	23 = 109
	158	26	132 316

Thus, when the President added together the state and general government figures, he found that of the total of 316 offices, exactly one-half were in the hands of Republicans.[36] This list corresponds closely to the statistic that Jefferson cited in July 1803 when he wrote that "of 316 offices in all the U. S. subject to appointment and removal by me, 130 only are held by federalists."[37]

Jefferson's figures show the elite appointments under the federal government; there were numerous lesser federal offices subject to appointment and removal by department heads or their subordinates. Each department head had full control over the appointment and dismissal of clerks in his office, and similar authority was enjoyed by second-level administrators such as the Comptroller, Auditor, and Register. When Jefferson was solicited for these posts, he directed the office seeker to his subordinates with explanations about "the nomination of the principal officers of the government only resting with me, and all subordinate places being in the gift of those immediately superintending them."[38] Appointments of officers in the Army and Navy, while reviewed by the

[36] See Carl E. Prince, "The Passing of the Aristocracy: Jefferson's Removal of the Federalists, 1801-1805," *Journal of American History*, LVII (1970), 563-575.

[37] Jefferson to William Duane, July 24, 1803 (not sent), Ford, ed., *Jefferson Writings*, VIII, 258.

[38] Jefferson to William Gardiner, Sept. 11, 1801, Jefferson Papers, Lib. Cong.

President and submitted to the Senate, were largely left to the recommendations of the Secretary of War and the Secretary of the Navy; military and Indian agents were likewise named by the Secretary of War. When such offices were included in compilations of officeholders, the proportion of Republicans to Federalists was greatly different from that of presidential appointees. Secretary of War Dearborn prepared for the President, probably in 1803, a memorandum on party affiliations of officeholders in which he included clerks in departmental offices and military officers and arrived at totals showing that Federalists outnumbered Republicans by more than two to one when these offices were included. Dearborn provided the following breakdown: [39]

	Republican	Federalist
Heads of Departments—including the Postmaster General	6	0
Secondary officers in the above departments	2	5
Clerks in said Departments	19	77
Foreign Ministers	3	0
Judges	8	25
District Attorneys	17	2
Marshals	16	3
Territorial Officers	4	6
Surveyors General	1	1
Collectors of the customs	23	41
Other officers in the customs who receive considerable pay	25	50
Loan officers	4	9
	128	219
Officers of the Army	38	140
Officers of the Navy	7	70
Marine Corps	0	29
	173	458
Indian Agents	6	4

[39] Undated memorandum in Dearborn's handwriting, Jefferson Papers, v. 235, p. 42199, Lib. Cong. The manuscript shows the Republican total as 176; this mistake in addition has been corrected above.

Within the Treasury Department there were numerous persons employed by subordinate officials, subject to the approval of the Secretary of the Treasury. In large ports, the offices filled at the discretion of collectors were, as Gallatin reported, "numerous, influential, and sometimes lucrative."[40] Most numerous of all were the appointments made by the Postmaster General, who named all postmasters and negotiated all contracts for carrying the mail.

Jefferson rarely involved the presidential office in the filling of subordinate posts, but he laid down guidelines to be followed and carefully reviewed appointments submitted to him for approval by department heads. In July 1801 Gallatin submitted to the President a draft of a circular to be sent to all collectors. Among the instructions contained in the circular was a statement of the policy to be followed by collectors in filling subordinate offices. Gallatin proposed to inform the collectors "that the door of office be no longer shut against any man merely on account of his political opinions, but that whether he shall differ or not from those avowed either by you or by myself, integrity and capacity suitable to the station be the only qualifications that shall direct our choice."[41] This was intended, Gallatin explained in an accompanying letter to Jefferson, "to let them know that it is expected that they will, although Federal, divide the offices in their nomination. . . . And it is supposed that there is no danger in avowing the sentiment that even at present, so far as respects subordinate officers, talent and integrity are to be the only qualifications for office."[42] Gallatin's proposed circular also contained another paragraph indicating that, while officers were free to exercise their individual suffrages, any use of their official positions to influence elections would not be tolerated. "The idea intended to be conveyed," Gallatin wrote the President, "is that an electioneering collector is commonly a bad officer as it relates to his official duties. . . . If it is thought better not to touch the subject, let both paragraphs be erased."[43]

After reviewing Gallatin's circular and discussing it with Madison, the President decided that it would be best if the paragraphs were struck out, particularly in view of his recent statement made

[40] Gallatin to Jefferson, July 25, 1801, Adams, ed., *Gallatin Writings*, I, 28.
[41] Draft of circular enclosed in Gallatin to Jefferson, July 25, 1801, *ibid.*, pp. 28-29.
[42] Gallatin to Jefferson, July 25, 1801, *ibid.*, p. 28.
[43] *Ibid.*

in reply to the New Haven remonstrance. After that answer "got into possession of the public," some further statement might be made, he thought, but then "it should go further and require an equilibrium to be first produced by exchanging one-half of their subordinates, after which talents and worth alone to be inquired into in the case of new vacancies."[44] A few weeks later, Jefferson reminded Gallatin that "we must be inflexible against appointing Federalists till there be a due portion of Republicans introduced into office."[45]

The party changeover in 1801 did not result in wholesale dismissal of government clerks in the capital, though strong pressures for extensive removals came from some prominent Republicans. Among them was William Duane, editor of the Philadelphia *Aurora*. In 1801 Duane sent to Gallatin a roster of the clerks in each office with comments by each name. Since this roster was stitched together into a leaflet with "Citizen W. Duane" elaborately lettered on the cover page, the supposition is that it was sent to Duane, who in turn passed it on to Gallatin.[46] Filled with such biting and derogatory comments as "complete picaroon," "nincumpoop," and "notorious villain" and some milder labels such as "Adamite," "high toned Federalist," and occasionally "Republican," the general tenor of the paper was a call for a clean sweep. The intemperate comments are worthy of notice only as an illustration of the pressures for widespread removal of clerks; they should not be viewed as informed comments on any of the individual clerks listed. Edward Jones, the chief clerk of the Treasury Department, for example, appears on this list as a "notorious villain." Meanwhile, Gallatin was receiving assurances from the Republican Congressman from Philadelphia that Jones was recommended by "a Merchant of the first respectability [and] a firm republican" and was "worthy of your protection and good offices."[47]

Most of the clerks were Federalists when Jefferson took office, but the new administration made no effort to apply a political test. Attorney General Lincoln informed one applicant for a clerkship in May 1801 that he believed that most of the clerks then employed

[44] Jefferson to Gallatin, July 26, 1801, *ibid.*, pp. 29-30.

[45] Jefferson to Gallatin, Aug. 14, 1801, *ibid.*, p. 37.

[46] The paper, endorsed by Gallatin, "1801 Clerks in offices given by W. Duane," is in the Gallatin Papers, N.-Y. Hist. Soc. Some excerpts are in Adams, *Gallatin*, pp. 277-278.

[47] William Jones to Gallatin, May 14, 1801, Gallatin Papers, microfilm edition.

would be retained, with only supernumeraries being discharged.[48] When Jacob Wagner, the chief clerk of the State Department, indicated to Madison that he would be willing to resign if a "conformity of political sentiment was indispensable," Madison told him that from the information he had gathered, Wagner was qualified for the office and that "honor and delicacy should stand in the place of a coincidence of general sentiment."[49] An acknowledged Federalist, Wagner wrote to Timothy Pickering, who as Secretary of State had appointed him to his clerkship, that the only concession he intended to make to retain his post was "a neutrality of *conduct* between the belligerent parties. My opinions shall never be sacrificed." Wagner also expected that the other clerks in the State Department would be retained. "Mr. Madison is certainly an amiable, and, considering the temper of parties, a moderate man," he confessed, "and so far as he is concerned, I expect nothing but justice: yet there is not a removal from office, which does not admonish me 'be you also ready.' "[50] Wagner remained in the post until early in 1807, when he resigned to become editor of a Federalist electioneering newspaper, the Baltimore *North American*, in whose pages he was soon attacking the administration in virulent editorials.[51]

Some Republicans vigorously criticized Madison for retaining Federalist clerks in the State Department and later used the issue against him in the election of 1808. "You cannot conceive what injury it has done Mr. Madison here his keeping Waggoner, Brent and Forrest in his office," a Philadelphia Republican wrote to Jefferson in August 1808, "and you may rely on it his election was a very up hill business 'till the republican members of Congress give the vote in his favor. Many is the time I have heard the cry Clinton was the man he would sweep from office all the old Tories and federalists."[52] That such sentiments were more than one man's opinion is supported by other evidence. Wilson Cary Nicholas wrote confidentially to Madison in the summer of 1806 of the concern among Madison's "personal and political friends" that he

[48] Samuel Morse to Madison, June 4, 1801, James Madison Papers, N. Y. Pub. Lib.

[49] Wagner to Timothy Pickering, May 30, 1801, Timothy Pickering Papers, Mass. Hist. Soc., microfilm edition.

[50] *Ibid.*

[51] Fischer, *Revolution of American Conservatism*, p. 369.

[52] Thomas Leiper to Jefferson, received Aug. 18, 1808, Jefferson Papers, Lib. Cong.

was sympathetic to a third party of Federalists and Republicans, and he cited as a principal basis for this fear Madison's retaining Wagner "who is said to have been the confidential clerk of Pickering." Nicholas also revealed that it was believed that much of the scurrility that appeared in the *Washington Federalist* was written by Wagner.[53]

Wagner's known friendship with Pickering and his open Federalism made him a convenient target of attack. Although the State Department may have been the most sensitive department and Wagner the most politically objectionable clerk in the administration, the criticism of retaining Federalist clerks in office could have been directed with equal validity against all other department heads. Edward Jones, the chief clerk of the Treasury Department when Gallatin took over, was still there when Jefferson's second term came to an end. So also were the chief clerks in the offices of the accountants of the War and the Navy departments and in the Post Office, all of whom were in office when Jefferson became President. Indeed, at the end of Jefferson's presidency there was only one chief clerk in any of the departmental offices who had not been appointed to a clerkship prior to Jefferson's taking office.

A comparison of the lists of clerks in 1807 with the department rosters for 1801 reveals that of the ninety-five clerks in departmental offices and the Post Office in 1807, forty-nine had held clerkships on March 4, 1801, most of them in the same offices.[54] How many of the clerks were Federalists is difficult to determine. The memorandum that Secretary of War Dearborn prepared for the President, probably in 1803, reported 77 Federalist and 19 Republican clerks.[55] Whether any preference was given to Republicans in promotions and salary increases is impossible to establish. At least one of the Republicans holding a clerkship in the Treasury Department when Jefferson took office was recommended to Gallatin for preferment by influential Republican friends who suggested that "his political principles have been the only obstacle to the attainment of his wishes under the late administration."[56] This clerk, John Banks, was transferred

[53] Nicholas to Madison, July 7, 1806, Madison Papers, Rives Collection, Lib. Cong.

[54] These figures are based on Appendix ii.

[55] See p. 175 above.

[56] William Jones to Gallatin, May 9, 1801; Alexander Boyd and fifteen others to Gallatin, May 9, 1801, Gallatin Papers, microfilm edition.

from the Comptroller's office to the office of the Secretary of the Treasury in 1801,[57] where he remained until 1807, but his salary of $850 was little more than he had earned in 1801.[58] No evidence has been found of clerks complaining that they were discriminated against on political grounds, and the record of advancement of Federalist-appointed clerks suggests that they were not. Indeed, the fact that many clerks were under the immediate direction of subordinate officers who also had been appointed under previous administrations made such discrimination unlikely.

The President himself, though he made it clear to department heads that he expected new appointments to go to Republicans, did not interfere in appointments to clerkships.[59] In one unusually politically sensitive case where his advice was sought, he allowed himself to be overruled. This was the case of Anthony Campbell and William P. Gardner, two former clerks in the Auditor's office who in 1800 supplied William Duane with copies of delinquent accounts of Federalists Timothy Pickering and Jonathan Dayton, which Duane published in the Philadelphia *Aurora*. In 1801 both men applied to Gallatin for reinstatement, Campbell furnishing an affidavit from three active Philadelphia Republicans stating that in revealing the documents Campbell had been "actuated by a pure regard to the public good, and thereby rendered an essential service to the United States."[60] When Gallatin asked the President's advice on the applications,[61] Jefferson replied that he thought justice should be done to the two men and "cannot suppose the Auditor will think hard of replacing them in their former berths. . . . Specific restitution is the particular measure of justice which the case calls for."[62] When Gallatin took the matter up with Auditor Richard Harrison, he found him adamantly opposed to rehiring either man. Harrison protested that if he reinstated clerks upon their application to another person, he would be unable to perform his official duties in directing and controlling the clerks in his

[57] Statement enclosed in Gallatin to the Speaker of the House, Apr. 6, 1802, Original Reports, Treasury Dept., House Records, RG 233, Natl. Archives.

[58] Statement enclosed in Gallatin to the Speaker of the House, Jan. 19, 1807, *ibid*.

[59] Jefferson to William Gardiner, Sept. 11, 1801, Jefferson Papers, Lib. Cong.

[60] Affidavit signed by John Beckley, Israel Israel, and Samuel Israel, Aug. 10, 1801, Gallatin Papers, N.-Y. Hist. Soc.

[61] Gallatin to Jefferson, Aug. 18, 1801, Jefferson Papers, Lib. Cong.

[62] Jefferson to Gallatin, Aug. 28, 1801, *ibid*.

office. "Mr. Harrison seemed hurt at the supposition that he had been guilty of any act of wanton injustice or political intolerance," Gallatin reported to Jefferson.[63] Indeed, the Auditor made his position clear in a letter to Gallatin: "As Mr. Harrison has been hitherto left entirely free and uncontrolled in the choice of clerks, he thinks it a fit occasion, and but justice to himself, now to declare that he has made it a general rule, as well from private as public considerations, to prefer such as he supposed best qualified to assist him; and that so far from dismissing, he has never objected to employ any one on mere *political* grounds."[64] Embarrassed for having brought the matter to Harrison's attention, Gallatin made no attempt to overrule him; nor did the President overrule the Secretary of the Treasury. Instead, the two applicants received other appointments; Campbell was given a commission in the Army and Gardner was appointed to a consulship.[65]

Despite the President's view that only Republicans should be appointed to offices, such a rule was never actually applied to clerks. Nor is there anything to indicate that department heads ever instructed their subordinate officers to adopt such a policy. Neither Gallatin nor Jefferson repudiated Auditor Harrison's assertion that he was "entirely free and uncontrolled in the choice of clerks." Joseph Nourse, the Register, made no mention of politics when he outlined the application process to one job seeker. "The mode of application for a Clerkship in any of the Public offices, is this," he explained. "The applicant should address a letter to the Head of each Department, and to each of the Heads of offices offering his Services and stating his former employment in life. He should at the same time inclose a Copy of Recommendation of some respectable Person, setting forth his Qualifications and his general Character, the original of which he might keep himself to shew if necessary."[66] Nourse regarded himself as a nonpolitical civil servant,[67] and neither the President nor the Secretary of the Treasury interfered with his employment practices in the Register's

[63] Gallatin to Jefferson, Sept. 14, 1801, Adams, ed., *Gallatin Writings*, I, 50.

[64] Harrison to Gallatin, Sept. 8, 1801, Gallatin Papers, microfilm edition.

[65] Jay C. Heinlein, "Albert Gallatin: A Pioneer in Public Administration," *William and Mary Quarterly*, 3rd Ser., VII (1950), 92-93.

[66] Nourse to Joseph Brumley, July 15, 1801, Treasury Dept., Register's Office, Estimates and Statements, x, 107, RG 56, Natl. Archives.

[67] Nourse to Jefferson, Feb. 24, 1801, Letters of Application and Recommendation, RG 59, Natl. Archives.

office, where as late as 1807 eleven of the fifteen clerks had been appointed before Jefferson took office.[68]

Clerks obviously did not have the power, influence, and political importance attached to most of the positions which the President filled directly. Unlike federal officials in the various states, they were not in positions to be politically useful. Jefferson put Republicans into the most political influential posts, but a fully developed spoils system would have swept clean the government offices in the capital as well and filled them with partisans. The record shows that this did not happen under Jefferson.

Jefferson exercised the dominant voice in determining administration policy on appointments and removals, but the members of his Cabinet, collectively and individually as department heads, participated in his decisions. At the beginning of his presidency when many places had to be filled, long lists of candidates were discussed at Cabinet meetings and decisions made regarding them.[69] Individual members were assigned specific tasks of gathering information or opinions on candidates and writing to particular persons about removals. General policies regarding appointments and removals were also agreed upon at Cabinet meetings. The Cabinet approved the removal of Adams's last appointments and the dismissal of Federalist marshals and attorneys—policies that had originated with Jefferson. In the latter case, the Cabinet was responsible for modifying Jefferson's rules. Jefferson earlier had indicated that all Federalist marshals and attorneys would be removed;[70] but, when he recorded the Cabinet decision, he noted that those officers were to be removed "except in particular cases" and that it was decided that the Federalist marshal in New Hampshire "ought not to be removed because of his connections."[71] The Cabinet also decided to retain the marshal in Massachusetts, who, though a Federalist, was "moderate and prudent and will be republican."[72] Obviously these exceptions were made because Jefferson respected his advisers who were better informed than he about persons and politics in New England.

[68] See Appendix II.

[69] See Jefferson's notes on Cabinet meetings, May 15, 1801–Apr. 8, 1803, Jefferson Papers, v. 112, p. 19297, Lib. Cong.; see also Ford, ed., *Jefferson Writings*, I, 291-295.

[70] See Jefferson to William B. Giles, Mar. 23, 1801, *ibid.*, VIII, 25.

[71] Entry for May 17, 1801, *ibid.*, I, 295.

[72] *Ibid.*

Jefferson spent a great deal of time making appointments and removals, and the voluminous papers relating to offices during his administration testify to the system he employed.[73] There was a steady exchange of letters between Jefferson and his department heads on the details of appointments. The President kept numerous lists of persons proposed for offices, with information as to the qualifications and politics of the candidates and the names of the persons recommending them. The careful endorsements Jefferson made on the hundreds of appointment papers that passed through his hands indicate the attention that he gave to each appointment and the enormous number of papers he reviewed before making decisions. In many cases he prepared a memorandum on a particular vacancy, recording the candidates recommended, by whom they were supported, and the major points in favor of or in opposition to each candidate.[74] When a vacancy occurred on the Supreme Court in 1804, Jefferson drew up such a memorandum before making his first appointment to the court. Headed "Character of the lawyers of S. C.," the memorandum described William Johnson as "a state judge, an excellent lawyer, prompt, eloquent, of irreproachable character, republican connections, and of good nerves in his political principles."[75] No other candidate had such high recommendations, and Johnson received the appointment.[76]

Information on candidates for offices came from a variety of sources, some unsolicited, much of it at the request of the President. Republican members of Congress and Republican party leaders in the states and localities where appointments were contemplated were the principal sources of information and recommendations. While numerous people wrote directly to the President or to members of his Cabinet recommending themselves or others for offices, the administration did not depend on unsolicited applications. The President and department heads alike were careful to consult with Republicans in Congress; in states with no Republi-

[73] The largest collection relating to appointments is the file of Letters of Application and Recommendation, 1801-1809, RG 59, Natl. Archives. Numerous additional papers relating to offices are in Jefferson Papers, Lib. Cong., Gallatin Papers, N.-Y. Hist. Soc., and Madison Papers, Lib. Cong.

[74] See Jefferson to Gallatin, Oct. 28, 1802, Gallatin Papers, N.-Y. Hist. Soc., printed in Cunningham, *Jeffersonian Republicans in Power*, p. 35.

[75] Memorandum, Feb. 17, 1804, in Gaillard Hunt, "Office-Seeking during Jefferson's Administration," *American Historical Review*, III (1898), 282.

[76] See Donald G. Morgan, *Justice William Johnson: The First Dissenter* (Columbia, S. C., 1954), pp. 49-51.

can member, they sought out state and local Republican leaders. Jefferson relied on members of his Cabinet for advice concerning appointments in their home states or states in which they had connections.[77] Many members of Congress passed on to the President or to department heads letters which they received from their constituents relating to offices, commonly adding their own opinions in covering letters. In numerous instances a group of members sent a joint recommendation to the President.[78] When Congress in 1807 added one associate justice to the Supreme Court, the delegations from the three western states to be included in the new circuit held a caucus to agree on a recommendation.[79] Like the President, department heads relied heavily on the advice of Republican members of Congress in making appointments in their departments and in the Army and Navy. As one member explained to a Tennessean seeking an Army commission: "Your success probably will depend on the recommendation of the delegation of the State of Tennessee, as that is the Channel from whence information is sought by the Executive in this case."[80]

The files of successful applicants for office demonstrate the importance of a candidate having the support of party leaders, members of Congress, and influential local Republicans. They also show that it was essential for a candidate to be known as a Republican in politics. Jefferson regularly asked for information on party attachments.[81] When a letter of recommendation "says nothing of the politics of the candidate," Jefferson observed, "[it] generally authorizes a presumption that they are not with the government."[82] Under instructions from the President to appoint

[77] See Lincoln to Jefferson, June 15, 1801, Jefferson Papers, Lib. Cong.; Granger to Jefferson, Aug. 28, 1803, Letters of Application and Recommendation, RG 59, Natl. Archives; Jefferson to Gallatin, Aug. 14, 20, 23, Adams, ed., *Gallatin Writings*, I, 85-86, 92, 94.

[78] For examples see Wade Hampton, John B. Earle, Thomas Moore, Levi Casey, William Butler, and Richard Winn to [Jefferson], Nov. 21, 1803; Robert Brown, Isaac Van Horne, and John Stewart to Jefferson, Mar. 30, 1802, Letters of Application and Recommendation, RG 59, Natl. Archives.

[79] John Randolph to Joseph H. Nicholson, Feb. 17, 1807, Joseph H. Nicholson Papers, Lib. Cong. The nomination of Thomas Todd of Kentucky as an associate justice was made to the Senate on Feb. 28, 1807, and approved Mar. 2, 1807. *Senate Executive Journal*, II, 53-54.

[80] Thomas Sumter to Andrew Butler, July 17, 1808, George W. Campbell Papers, Lib. Cong.

[81] See Jefferson to James Jackson, May 28, 1801, Jefferson Papers, Lib. Cong.

[82] Jefferson to Nicholas, Aug. 8, 1804 (photostatic copy), Jefferson Papers, Univ. of Va.

only Republicans, department heads also sought information on party affiliations. "I wish you had added what his political standing is," Secretary of War Dearborn wrote to former Representative William Eustis of Massachusetts in reply to his recommendation of a candidate for a commission in the Army. "We have at present a sufficient proportion of our political opponents in the Army. . . ."[83] Most correspondents did not need to be reminded to recommend only Republicans. "In every recommendation I shall carefully endeavor to select such as can discharge the duty of the office, and have been uniformly Democratic," Representative Macon of North Carolina wrote the President, "although I do not wish any person turned out of office, who was a whig in the Revolutionary war, for any opinions he may now hold, yet I would not recommend one for office who had not been always Republican."[84] In sending a list of recommendations to Gallatin, Senator John Breckinridge of Kentucky added: "It is unnecessary for me to mention, that all these Gentlemen are well informed republicans, and feel strong interest in the present order of things; for none other have I yet recommended to office, and what is more, I am sure I never shall."[85]

Although Jefferson was at times misled by his informants, he was not credulous and evaluated the source of information. "I know nothing of Chisman, proposed as collector of Hampton," he wrote to Gallatin, "and our friend Mr. [John] Page, from the benevolent and unsuspicious cast of his mind, is the most unsafe recommender we can possibly follow. He never sees but the good qualities of a man, those through the largest magnifiers. As the case will, I suppose, admit of some delay, I will write to persons of the neighborhood for further information."[86] When Jefferson did not receive sufficient information on prospective candidates, he reminded those making recommendations that he sought details on "residence, character, politics, [and] standing in society."[87] When he received strong recommendations in favor of a particular candidate from the principal Republican leaders in a state, he gave them great weight and the respect of prompt action. "I had thought

[83] Dearborn to Eustis, May 2, 1808, William Eustis Papers, Lib. Cong.

[84] Macon to Jefferson, May 24, 1801, Jefferson Papers, Lib. Cong.

[85] Breckinridge to Gallatin, Apr. 25, 1805, Breckinridge Family Papers, Lib. Cong.

[86] Jefferson to Gallatin, Aug. 14, 1801, Adams, ed., *Gallatin Writings*, I, 36. After further checking, Mount Edward Chisman was appointed collector of Hampton, Va., Aug. 31, 1801. Jefferson Papers, v. 119, p. 20545, Lib. Cong.

[87] Jefferson to Gallatin, Apr. 15, 1806, Gallatin Papers, N.-Y. Hist. Soc.

we might let the appointment of the Collector of New Haven lie till our return to Washington: but the recommendations of Abraham Bishop are already as strong as they can be," Jefferson wrote to Gallatin from Monticello in the summer of 1803. "Granger, Kirby, Woolcot, Edwards and others concur with earnestness to sollicit it, and I do not suppose we ought to consider any opposition which can be raised, as equal to this in respectability. In fact if we do not rely on those characters, to what others in Connecticut shall we give our confidence. . . . If you think with me that Abraham Bishop should be appointed, I will on receiving your letter, direct a commission, and give no further time for forming combinations of other interests to embarras us."[88] Bishop, who had already made a favorable impression on the Secretary of the Treasury,[89] was accordingly appointed. In general, Jefferson recognized the advantages of quick action when vacancies occurred. "After a good candidate is known," he observed, "delay only gives time to intrigue, to interest a greater number of persons and consequently to make more malcontents by disappointment."[90]

In making appointments, Jefferson took into consideration local political factors, including the time of elections. "Their election does not come on till at the end of two years," he noted in regard to making changes in South Carolina. Some delay could be tolerated "provided the proper changes are made in time to prevent official weight being then thrown into the federal scale." In this instance, Jefferson sought broader consultation with South Carolina Republicans. "If we can wait till Congress meets," he reasoned, "it will be better that arrangements should be made on the broad counsel we can then have, than on the very limited information we now possess."[91] Here, as in so many of Jefferson's actions, multiple considerations motivated his actions, and partisan interests merged with genuine efforts to make strong appointments. He was alert to Republican partisan advantages, but he was also concerned with consulting members of Congress and anxious to make appointments that would be respected. This can be seen in other instances. In asking Archibald Stuart for a recommendation for a

[88] Jefferson to Gallatin, Aug. 30, 1803, *ibid*. Gideon Granger, Ephraim Kirby, Alexander Wolcott, and Pierpont Edwards were all leading Connecticut Republicans.

[89] See Gallatin to Jefferson, Aug. 13 and 20, 1803, Adams, ed., *Gallatin Writings*, I, 138, 140.

[90] Jefferson to Gallatin, Aug. 30, 1805, Gallatin Papers, N.-Y. Hist. Soc.

[91] Jefferson to Gallatin, Aug. 7, 1801, Jefferson Papers, Lib. Cong.

marshal for the western district of Virginia, Jefferson requested the name that "would be most respected by the public, for that circumstance is not only generally the best criterion of what is best, but the public respect can alone give strength to the government."[92] Concern for maintaining public respect also explained Jefferson's policy of not appointing to office any person related to him.[93]

Jefferson tried to view the country as a whole and not to take steps in one state that might arouse opposition in others. He also was conscious of the need to distribute offices geographically. In October 1801, he pointed out to Samuel Harrison Smith, editor of the *National Intelligencer*, that federal offices were so overfilled with persons from Pennsylvania, Maryland, and Virginia that "on a principle of distribution, no office respecting the union generally can be given in those states till something more of an equilibrium has been obtained. Offices exerciseable within a state are always filled within the state."[94] Jefferson was indeed partisan in filling offices and in making pronouncements about them. He no doubt took pleasure in judgments such as that of a Republican friend who predicted that his answer to the New Haven remonstrance would have "a very happy effect on the approaching elections throughout the United States."[95] But Jefferson was also a conscientious administrator, and he applied orderly and responsible procedures to the task of filling offices.

[92] Jefferson to Archibald Stuart, Apr. 25, 1801, Archibald Stuart Papers, Virginia Historical Society.

[93] Jefferson to Horatio Turpin, June 10, 1807, Jefferson Papers, Lib. Cong.

[94] Jefferson to Smith, Oct. 25, 1801, Jonathan Bayard Smith Papers, Lib. Cong.

[95] Caesar A. Rodney to Jefferson, Aug. 11, 1801, Jefferson Papers, Lib. Cong.

IX. Executive-Congressional Relations

THE REPUBLICAN MAJORITY IN CONGRESS LOOKED to President Jefferson for direction, and, except during his final months in office after his successor had been elected, he supplied strong leadership. All major legislative programs originated in the executive branch. Jefferson's annual and special messages presented numerous recommendations for action; and, while these messages contained only broad outlines, he privately communicated specific details to legislative leaders and members sympathetic to presidential proposals. At the same time, he respected the authority of Congress and in eight years as President never employed the veto, which he regarded as a device to be used only when the President deemed a legislative action unconstitutional.[1]

In seeking a working relationship with Congress, Jefferson attempted to establish an administration spokesman in the House of Representatives. When John Randolph, chairman of the Committee of Ways and Means, emerged as the majority leader in the House, Jefferson took him into his confidence (as did the Secretary of the Treasury) and encouraged him to assume the role of administration spokesman. Randolph, however, had come to his position of leadership not through the influence of the President but through the mechanisms of the House, and he remained independent of executive domination. At the same time, his support of the administration became essential to the maintenance of his party leadership in Congress. When Randolph refused to support the President's policy in the House and openly attacked the administration in 1806, he was abandoned by the Republican majority and soon deprived of his leadership position. On the floor of the House, Randolph denounced the "back-stairs influence—of men who bring messages to this House, which, although they do not appear on the Journals, govern its decisions."[2] With this attack, as Senator Plumer noted, Randolph crossed the Rubicon and could "no longer

---

[1] *Presidential Vetoes: Record of Bills Vetoed and Action Taken Thereon by the Senate and House of Representatives, First Congress through the Ninetieth Congress, 1789-1968*, compiled by the Senate Library (Washington, D. C., 1969), p. 1. Washington vetoed two bills; Adams, none; Madison, seven. *Ibid.*, pp. 1-3.

[2] *Annals of Congress*, 9 Cong., 1 Sess. (Mar. 5, 1806), 561.

be considered as the confident, the friend or advocate of Mr. Jefferson."[3]

Although his relationship with Randolph had never been wholly satisfactory, Jefferson appreciated the value of a spokesman in Congress, and he tried, with little success, to find a replacement for Randolph. During the summer of 1806, he urged Barnabas Bidwell, a member from Massachusetts, to assume that role. In a detailed letter, Jefferson explained his view of an administration spokesman and floor leader: "I do not mean that any gentleman relinquishing his own judgment, should implicitly support all the measures of the administration," he wrote, "but that, where he does not disapprove of them he should not suffer them to go off in sleep, but bring them to the attention of the house and give them a fair chance. Where he disapproves, he will of course leave them to be brought forward by those who concur in the sentiment." Obviously referring to Randolph, the President went on to say that "when a gentleman, through zeal for the public service, undertakes to do the public business, we know that we shall hear the cant of backstairs counsellors. But we never heard this while the declaimer was himself a backstairs man as he called it, but in the confidence and views of the administration as may more properly and respectfully be said." In a revealing statement of his view of executive-legislative relations, Jefferson affirmed that "if the members are to know nothing but what is important enough to be put into a public message, and indifferent enough to be made known to all the world, if the Executive is to keep all other information to himself, and the house to plunge on in the dark, it becomes a government of chance and not of design."[4]

In conversations and written memoranda, Jefferson informally communicated information and detailed proposals for legislation to friendly members. "I thought I perceived in you the other day a dread of the job of preparing a constitution for the new acquisition," the President wrote to Senator Breckinridge regarding Louisiana in November 1803. "With more boldness than wisdom I therefore determined to prepare a canvass, give it a few daubs of outline, and send it to you to fill up. I yesterday morning took up the subject and scribbled off the inclosed. In communicating it to you I must do it in confidence that you will never let any person know that I have put pen to paper on the subject and that if you

[3] William Plumer to William Plumer, Jr., Mar. 11, 1806, Plumer Papers, Lib. Cong.

[4] Jefferson to Bidwell, July 5, 1806, Jefferson Papers, Lib. Cong.

think the inclosed can be of any aid to you you will take the trouble to copy it and return me the original. I am this particular, because you know with what bloody teeth and fangs the federalists will attack any sentiment or principle known to come from me."[5] Breckinridge copied the bill, returned the original, and promised secrecy as to the President's authorship.[6] A short time later, the Senate passed a motion for the appointment of a committee to prepare a bill for the government of Louisiana, and Breckinridge was chosen to head the committee.[7] The bill presented by this committee was to all practical purposes the bill that Jefferson had drafted, although it underwent considerable amendment before its final passage.[8]

On another occasion Jefferson wrote to Breckinridge: "I think the inclosed may properly furnish grounds for an amendment to the judiciary law, whenever it is before Congress; to be proposed by a member. Judge Innis inclosed it to me with an idea that the proposition might go from me to Congress: but this is hardly within the regular compass of [a] message. I therefore turn it over to you."[9] Jefferson's relationship with friends in Congress in whom he confided is similarly revealed in a note from Senator Wilson Cary Nicholas in 1802 telling the President: "I have had the pleasure to receive your notes of this date, with their enclosures. The subject was not acted upon today, nor do I presume it will be for several days. In the meantime I hope to have the pleasure of conversing with you more fully upon the subject, to which your notes refer."[10]

At times, Jefferson prepared complete bills for submission to Congress. One well-documented example is the bill "for the more effectual preservation of the peace in the harbors and waters of the United States and on board vessels," introduced in the House of Representatives by Joseph H. Nicholson in November 1804. In a letter to Randolph, Jefferson explained: "I mentioned to you in a cursory way the other evening that before the meeting of Congress I had conferred with my executive associates on the subject of insults in our harbors, and that we had settled in our own minds

[5] Jefferson to Breckinridge, Nov. 24, 1803, Ford, ed., *Jefferson Writings*, VIII, 279-280.

[6] Breckinridge to Jefferson, Nov. 26, 1803, Jefferson Papers, Lib. Cong.

[7] *Senate Journal*, III, 316, 320-321.

[8] Malone, *Jefferson the President: First Term*, pp. 348-356.

[9] Jefferson to Breckinridge, Feb. 17, 1803, Breckinridge Family Papers, Lib. Cong.

[10] Nicholas to Jefferson, Jan. 26, 1802, Jefferson Papers, Lib. Cong.

what we thought it would be best to do on that subject, which I have thrown into the form of a bill. I meant to have communicated this to you: but on the reference of that part of the message to a special committee it was thought necessary to communicate it without delay to a member of the committee."[11] The bill which Jefferson sent to Nicholson had been carefully drafted by the President, who in October had circulated a draft among members of his Cabinet. The orignal text in Jefferson's own hand has marginal notes indicating changes proposed by Gallatin.[12] Jefferson's papers also contain a six-page memorandum on the President's bill from Secretary of the Navy Smith, with some brief penciled comments on Smith's remarks in the handwriting of Secretary of State Madison.[13] Secretary of War Dearborn also offered some suggestions, although he began his reply to the President by stating: "Not having been conversant with the detailed forms of Bills, it will be with diffidence that I shall suggest any alterations in the draught of the proposed Bill you have been pleased to submit to my perusal."[14] After the first draft of the bill was reviewed by his Cabinet, Jefferson made some revisions[15] and had the revised text copied by his private secretary, William A. Burwell, who gave a copy to Nicholson.[16] On the manuscript in Nicholson's papers is an endorsement by Nicholson indicating: "Mr. Jefferson's draft of a Bill, which I *foolishly* reported in his form, and had to recommit it twice."[17] The act as finally passed contained the basic provisions found in Jefferson's draft, but his clear and simple language had been recast in legalistic terms.[18]

The documentation tracing the route by which Jefferson's proposed legislation became law in this instance is complete. There

[11] Jefferson to John Randolph, Nov. 19, 1804, Ford, ed., *Jefferson Writings*, VIII, 333-334.

[12] Jefferson Papers, v. 144, p. 25069, Lib. Cong. The document is inaccurately printed in Ford, ed., *Jefferson Writings*, VIII, 333-334.

[13] Jefferson Papers, v. 144, p. 25066, Lib. Cong.

[14] Dearborn to Jefferson, received Oct. 22, 1804, Jefferson Papers, Lib. Cong.

[15] Jefferson Papers, v. 144, p. 25069, Lib. Cong.

[16] Burwell wrote in regard to the events of November 1804: "I remained in Washington during this month, and remember well to have copied and given to J.H.N. a Bill drawn by the President to protect our ports and harbors." William A. Burwell Memoir [1804-1808], Burwell Papers, Lib. Cong.

[17] Joseph H. Nicholson Papers, v. 2, pp. 1184-1184B, Lib. Cong.

[18] Act of Mar. 3, 1805, *Annals of Congress*, 8 Cong., 2 Sess., 1694-1698.

is also evidence of contact between Jefferson and Nicholson while the matter was before his committee. After presenting Jefferson's bill to the committee, Nicholson wrote the President: "I have this morning laid before the Committee a short sketch of the several provisions contained in the bill which you sent me. These are fully approved of, but as the business of the gun boats is likewise committed to us, I think it would be better to engraft the whole in the same bill." Nicholson then asked for "such information" on gunboats "as will enable me to meet your wishes."[19] In response Jefferson promised to supply Nicholson with the desired information, but recommended that the gunboats be handled in a separate bill —a suggestion that Nicholson followed.[20]

Other bills were drafted by Jefferson,[21] but in no case were these bills submitted openly to Congress. Jefferson was always careful to warn those in whom he confided to keep his role hidden from public view. Sending the draft of a bill to Representative John Dawson, the President requested that Dawson "be so good as to copy the within and burn this original, as he is very unwilling to meddle personally with the details of the proceedings of the legislature."[22] Jefferson also sought to reassure his friends in Congress that he was not trying to interfere in legislative business. "This is meant merely as a private suggestion to hasten the proceedings of the committee on Indian affairs of which you are chairman," he wrote to Representative Samuel Smith in 1802, urging that the committee revive a recently expired act regulating trade with the Indians.[23] In regard to the administration-drafted act to preserve peace in American harbors that Jefferson had sent to Nicholson, the President assured Randolph: "These were our ideas suggested from practice and a kno[w]le[d]ge of facts: and the communication of them in form of a bill is merely as a canvass or

[19] Nicholson to Jefferson, Nov. 19, 1804, Jefferson Papers, Lib. Cong.

[20] Jefferson to Nicholson, Nov. 20, 1804, Nicholson Papers, Lib. Cong.

[21] Examples of bills drafted by Jefferson include: "A bill for establishing a naval militia," Jefferson Papers, v. 137, p. 23702, v. 173, p. 30685, Lib. Cong.; "An act for classing the militia and assigning to each class its particular duties," *ibid.*, v. 137, p. 23703. Jefferson's role in drafting legislation is extensively covered in Everett L. Long, "Jefferson and Congress: A Study of the Jeffersonian Legislative System, 1801-1809" (Ph.D. Dissertation, University of Missouri, 1966), Chap. 5.

[22] Jefferson to Dawson, Dec. 19, 1806, enclosing "A Bill authorizing the employment of the land or naval forces of the U. S. in cases of insurrection" [polygraph copy], Jefferson Papers, Lib. Cong.

[23] Jefferson to Smith, Mar. 5, 1802, *ibid.*

premiere ebauche for Congress to work on, and to make of it whatever they please. They cannot be worse for knowing the result of our information and reflection on the subject, which has been privately communicated as more respectful than to have recommended these measures in the message in detail as the Constitution permits. With the same view I state them merely as subjects for your consideration."[24]

As his practice of inviting members of Congress to dinner demonstrated, Jefferson worked to keep the channels open to the legislative branch. "I have believed that more unreserved communications would be advantageous to the public," he explained. "This has been, perhaps, prevented by mutual delicacy. I have been afraid to express opinions unasked, lest I should be suspected of wishing to direct the legislative action of members. They have avoided asking communications from me, probably, lest they should be suspected of wishing to fish out executive secrets."[25] The dilemma of trying to provide leadership without being charged with dictation became painfully clear to Jefferson in the course of his presidency. "Our situation is difficult; and whatever we do is liable to the criticisms of those who wish to represent it awry," he confessed in 1806. "If we recommend measures in a public message, it may be said that members are not sent here to obey the mandates of the President, or to register the edicts of a sovereign. If we express opinions in conversation, we have then our Charles Jenkinsons, and back-door counsellors. If we say nothing, 'we have no opinions, no plans, no cabinet.' "[26]

Federalists charged Jefferson with undue influence over Republicans in Congress. "Never were a set of men more blindly devoted to the will of a *prime Mover* or *Minister* than the Majority of both Houses to the will and wishes of the Chief Magistrate," wrote Senator James Hillhouse of Connecticut.[27] Senator Timothy Pickering of Massachusetts insisted that Jefferson "*behind the curtain*, directs the measures he wishes to have adopted; while in each house a majority of puppets move as he touches the wires."[28] Sev-

24 Jefferson to Randolph, Nov. 19, 1804, Ford, ed., *Jefferson Writings*, VIII, 336.

25 Jefferson to Randolph, Dec. 1, 1803, *ibid.*, p. 281.

26 Jefferson to William Duane, Mar. 22, 1806, *ibid.*, p. 433.

27 Hillhouse to Simeon Baldwin, Feb. 11, 1803, Baldwin Family Papers, Yale Univ.

28 Pickering to his wife, Jan. 31, 1806, quoted in Edward H. Phillips, "Timothy Pickering's Portrait of Thomas Jefferson," Essex Institute, *Historical Collections*, XCIV (1958), 313.

eral Federalists explained the measures passed by the Seventh Congress in terms of the President's influence. "The Internal taxes will be abolished," Archibald Henderson, a representative from North Carolina, wrote in January 1802. "The President has said it must be done and that is a sufficient reason for doing it. The majority are determined .that his views shall be carried into effect."29 In February 1802 Senator Gouverneur Morris protested that the repeal of the judiciary act of 1801 would "be carried on the triumphant vote of a great majority (many of them inwardly cursing their leaders) because the President has recommended it."30 At the beginning of the next session, Henderson wrote again: "The President has only to act and the Majority will approve. I do not believe that in any Country there ever was more implicit obedience paid to an administration than in this. I do not mean to say that Mr. Jefferson has this uncontrolled authority, but that when the Cabinet determines on measures they will be passed."31

The Federalist charges were overdrawn, but there is ample evidence that Jefferson exerted strong presidential leadership. He also had considerable leverage in Congress because of his immense popular support. Only 14 out of 176 electoral votes were cast against him in 1804. "The President's popularity is unbounded, and his will is that of the nation," Nicholson wrote in 1807. "His approbation seems to be the criterion by which the correctness of all public events is tested." Referring to the President's dissatisfaction with the treaty negotiated by William Pinkney and James Monroe with Great Britain, Nicholson suggested that popular approval of any treaty would depend on the President's opinion. The Federalists would oppose "a literal copy of Jay's Treaty, if ratified by the present administration," he concluded, "while the same instrument, although heretofore so odious to some of us, would now command the support of a large body who call themselves Democrats. Such is our present infatuation."32 By 1807, Nicholson, like Randolph, was not in full accord with the President and had come to resent his great popularity; but he was well aware of the

29 Henderson to Duncan Cameron, Jan. 5, 1802, Cameron Family Papers, Univ. of N. C.

30 Morris to Nicholas Lowe, Feb. 22, 1802, Morris Letter Book, Papers of Gouverneur Morris, Lib. Cong.

31 Henderson to Samuel Johnston, Dec. 16, 1802, Hayes Collection, transcript, North Carolina Department of Archives and History.

32 Nicholson to Monroe, Apr. 12, 1807, Monroe Papers, Lib. Cong.

influence that popularity had on the decisionmaking process of Congress.

Whether Federalist or Republican, members of Congress who disagreed with the President tended to see others as uncritically accepting his recommendations. The records of Congress, however, show that proposals coming from the President received careful scrutiny; some were rejected, and others emerged from the legislative process in quite different form. One example, at the height of Jefferson's popularity, may be cited. Prior to the meeting of Congress in November 1804, Jefferson circulated within his Cabinet a draft of a bill to regulate the clearance of armed merchant vessels trading with St. Domingo;[33] and in his annual message he recommended that Congress take action on the subject.[34] The recommendation was referred to a House select committee, and a bill was promptly reported. Then began a legislative process that did not terminate until the final day of the session, March 3, 1805, when the President approved the act that had been agreed upon by the two houses on the preceding day. The act implemented the President's recommendation that armed merchant vessels trading with the West Indies be regulated, and rejected congressional proposals that would have prohibited trade with St. Domingo and prevented merchant vessels from arming. However, these final provisions were considerably different from those in the bill originally introduced in November 1804.[35] Indeed, the bill had undergone modification at nearly every step in the legislative process. The House made so many changes after the second reading that a new printing was required, and a further altered version was finally passed.[36] When the bill reached the Senate, the President was asked to provide more information and documents; all of the issues were again debated, and the bill was completely rewritten.[37]

During the long process of congressional deliberation, the administration kept in touch with the proceedings. Senator Plumer

[33] Madison, memorandum, Oct. 23, 1804; Robert Smith, memorandum, received Oct. 27, 1804; Henry Dearborn to Jefferson, Oct. 28, 1804, Jefferson Papers, v. 144, pp. 25038, 25098, 25054, Lib. Cong.

[34] Jefferson, message, Nov. 8, 1804, Ford, ed., *Jefferson Writings*, VIII, 325-327.

[35] *Annals of Congress*, 8 Cong., 2 Sess., 636-684, 698, 722-723, 1698-1699.

[36] *Ibid.*, 724, 811-812. The printed copy with interlined penciled changes is in House Records, RG 233, Natl. Archives.

[37] Bill, Dec. 26, 1804, with accompanying motions and amendments; committee report, Jan. 21, 1805, Senate Records, RG 46, Natl. Archives.

noted in February 1805: "I scarce ever meet with a member of the Administration, but he expresses his anxious wishes that this bill may pass."[38] As the bill neared final passage, William B. Giles, the Republican leader in the Senate, sent a copy of the bill to the Secretary of State with a note advising: "If you can suggest any amendment to it in its present form be pleased to notice it in the course of the day."[39] At the same time, Congress listened to voices other than those that came from the executive branch. When a petition was received from the Philadelphia Chamber of Commerce seeking revisions in the proposed law, the House postponed further debate until the petition could be printed.[40] Pointing out that the bill as drafted would adversely affect many other vessels and merchants not engaged in the West Indian trade, the petition urged the elimination of the provision giving collectors the power to detain vessels on suspicion until the opinion of the President of the United States could be obtained.[41] The bill which passed the House on December 24 did not include the objectionable provision; furthermore, there were other indications that the Philadelphia merchants had influenced the shaping of the bill.[42] Immediately after the second reading of the bill in the Senate, Senator Mitchill presented a memorial from the Chamber of Commerce of New York "showing cause why merchantmen should be permitted to arm in certain cases, and respectfully stating the principles on which a bill on the subject should pass."[43] Although the Senate voted thirteen to twelve not to print the petition,[44] which filled fifteen pages in manuscript,[45] the petition was read in the Senate; and, since Senator Mitchill became chairman of the committee to whom the bill was referred, it may be assumed that the memorial received the committee's attention.

Whenever specific measures are closely examined, it becomes

[38] Brown, ed., *Plumer's Memorandum*, Feb. 6, 1805, p. 275.

[39] Giles to Madison, Thursday [Feb. 21, 1805], Madison Papers, Lib. Cong.

[40] *House Journal* (Dec. 10, 1804), v, 48; *Annals of Congress*, 8 Cong., 2 Sess. (Dec. 12, 1804), 808.

[41] A copy of the memorial is in Senate Records, RG 46, Natl. Archives.

[42] The bill as passed by the House is in Senate Records, Dec. 26, 1804, *ibid.*

[43] *Annals of Congress*, 8 Cong., 2 Sess., 27; the memorial dated Dec. 21, 1804, presented to the Senate Dec. 28, 1804, is in *ASP, Commerce and Navigation*, i, 582-583.

[44] Brown, ed., *Plumer's Memorandum*, Dec. 28, 1804, pp. 233-234.

[45] The original is in Senate Records, RG 46, Natl. Archives.

evident that the pressures on members of Congress were multiple and complex. It was tempting for presidential opponents to see congressmen as executive puppets, but a scrutiny of the record fails to give much credence to the charge. However, there is persuasive evidence that Jefferson exerted strong presidential leadership, both directly and through members of his Cabinet.

Department heads frequently acted as presidential spokesmen in their relations with Congress. "I send in the shape of a bill, the substance of what the President seems to think necessary in order to authorize him to occupy and temporarily govern Louisiana," Gallatin wrote to Senator Breckinridge in October 1803. "Will you consult with your friends and decide whether the authority be necessary, and if so, what form should be given to it."[46] The bill which Breckinridge presented to the Senate was essentially that drafted by Gallatin.[47] In a similar manner, Secretary of the Navy Smith in 1803 wrote to DeWitt Clinton, chairman of a Senate committee: "I am charged by the President to communicate to you his opinion that provision ought to be made for procuring eight gunboats, in addition to the four small vessels of war, at present contemplated by the Legislature. Should Congress concur in this opinion, it is presumed that an appropriation of 12000 Dollars, would enable the Executive to carry the measure into effect."[48] The final bill, after amendments made by the Senate, authorized the building of fifteen gunboats and appropriated fifteen thousand dollars for that purpose.[49]

Cabinet members provided a liaison between the President and members of Congress who shared the President's confidence. "I inclose a communication from Mr. Merry, which the P[resident] wishes to go to you," Madison wrote in a private note to Gallatin in 1804, "and from you to such member and ask such suggestions as may be proper; rather than make it the subject of a Message under present circumstances."[50] Gallatin in turn sent the communi-

[46] Gallatin to John Breckinridge [October 1803], Breckinridge Family Papers, Lib. Cong.

[47] The original draft of the bill in the Senate bill file is in Breckinridge's hand. Senate Records, Oct. 22, 1803, RG 46, Natl. Archives. Gallatin's draft is in the Breckinridge Family Papers, Lib. Cong.

[48] Smith to Clinton, Feb. 16, 1803, DeWitt Clinton Papers, Columbia Univ.; copy also in Letters from Sec. of Navy to Congress, RG 45, Natl. Archives.

[49] Act of Feb. 28, 1803, Annals of Congress, 7 Cong., 2 Sess., 100, 1566.

[50] Madison to [Gallatin], Mar. 24, 1803 [i.e., 1804], Nicholson Papers, Lib. Cong.

cation to Senator Breckinridge, suggesting a possible amendment and adding: "If any amendment shall be introduced in your house, have the goodness to communicate Mr. Merry's letter to Mr. Nicholson who was chairman of the committee which brought in the bill." The fact that both Madison's and Gallatin's letters were found in Nicholson's papers indicates that Breckinridge followed Gallatin's directions.[51] In matters of foreign affairs, where the President did not always want to reveal his intentions in public statements or messages, he relied on Cabinet members to assist in making the proper contacts in Congress. "Who are the members of the committee on Spanish affairs?" Gallatin asked Nicholson in December 1805, when Jefferson was seeking an appropriation of two million dollars for the Floridas. "If you are one, I am requested to communicate a paper to you; and it would be perhaps as well that you should see the president before the committee meet."[52]

The close working relationship that existed between the administration and certain members of Congress was further revealed in a letter Gallatin wrote to the President in 1807: "You gave two years ago to Col. Worthington the sketch of the Orleans bill with a request that I should, taking its provisions for a basis, draw one consistent with the general arrangements of our complex land laws. This was accordingly done; Mr. Worthington introduced the bill in the Senate, whence it was amended, passed to a third reading and then postponed." Gallatin went on to explain that he was forwarding a copy of the bill on which the President could make any desired changes, after which he would have a copy made and return it to the President "to be put in the hands of such member as you may think proper."[53]

In addition to helping the President put measures before Congress, members of the Cabinet in their individual roles as department heads participated regularly in the normal legislative process, working formally and informally with congressional committees. After the House appointed a committee in December 1801 "to inquire and report, whether moneys drawn from the Treasury have been faithfully applied to the objects for which they were appropriated, and whether the same have been regularly accounted for,"[54]

[51] Gallatin to Breckinridge, Mar. 24, 1804, enclosing the foregoing. *Ibid.*
[52] Gallatin to Nicholson, Dec. 7, 1805, Adams, ed., *Gallatin Writings*, I, 282.
[53] Gallatin to Jefferson, Nov. 25, 1807, Jefferson Papers, Lib. Cong.
[54] *Annals of Congress*, 7 Cong., 1 Sess. (Dec. 14, 1801), 319-324.

Nicholson, who had proposed the investigation and was appointed as chairman of the committee to conduct it, conferred with Gallatin. A cousin of Mrs. Gallatin and a regular caller at the Gallatin home on Capitol Hill, Nicholson had frequent opportunities to confer with the Secretary of the Treasury, and much that passed between them was left unrecorded. In regard to this particular investigation, however, the written records are sufficiently full to reveal the close working relationship between them. On January 19, 1802, Gallatin drew up a memorandum for Nicholson in which he outlined "the objects of inquiry for your committee" and suggested: "You may write me a letter asking generally information on those subjects, or if you prefer a less methodical arrangement and to put more pointed queries, I have written some on the next page, which, I believe, embrace all those objects."[55] On the accompanying sheet, Gallatin listed ten questions which he thought the committee should consider in its investigation. Two days later, Nicholson addressed a formal letter to the Secretary of the Treasury, saying: "I this morning submitted to the committee appointed to investigate the state of the Treasury Department, etc., a proposition that the committee should direct their enquiries to the several particular objects in the annexed statement. This proposition was agreed to, and I have been desired by the committee to enclose it to you for the purpose of obtaining from you such information as you may be able to furnish, in answer to these enquiries."[56] The proposition to which the committee had agreed was precisely the outline of major objectives specified in Gallatin's memorandum to Nicholson, and the list of questions submitted to Gallatin was the exact list that Gallatin had sent to Nicholson.

That the same sort of relationship continued throughout the investigation is suggested by the following note from Gallatin to Nicholson in April 1802:

> I will thank you to send me the papers transmitted by the Secretary of War or Accountant to the Committee of investigation. I want them only a few minutes in order to fill some blanks in my letter to you. I return herewith the account etc. of the accountant of the Navy. When I shall have finished my

[55] Gallatin to Nicholson, Jan. 19, 1802, Adams, ed., *Gallatin Writings*, I, 74-75.

[56] Nicholson to Gallatin, Jan. 21, 1802, *Communication from the Secretary of the Treasury, to the Chairman of the Committee, Appointed to Investigate the State of the Treasury*, p. 3.

letter to you, if you and Mr. Giles will meet me, we will consult on the best shape in which to throw your investigation and report."[57]

There is no evidence here of any barrier between legislative and executive branches. Gallatin himself referred to his "confidential intercourse with Republican members of Congress" and his "free communications of facts and opinions to Mr. Randolph," chairman of the House Ways and Means Committee.[58] A similar confidential relationship is indicated in the following note, marked *private*, which Madison sent to Nicholson in November 1803:

> Your request of the naval force of Morocco was sent you this morning. I now inclose a list of impressments. You will please to understand that this is not officially done, and in expectation that no official use will be made of either; the regular course requiring that information should be furnished by a call of [the House] on the President. I will take occasion to talk with you on this subject generally. At present I suggest only that it is particularly proper that the business of impressments should be too important to [be] managed in any subordinate or irregular way.[59]

The concept of the separation of executive and legislative powers which governed the actions of the President and the Congress, at least formally and officially, did not prevail in the same manner in the relations between members of the Cabinet and the Congress. While the President felt compelled to keep his role in the drafting of legislation confidential, there was little similar compulsion felt by Cabinet officers. Department heads were regularly called upon by congressional committees for assistance in the preparation of bills, and proposals under consideration were commonly submitted to them for review and recommendations. "The inclosed Bill has just been referred to a Select committee in the Senate," Abraham Baldwin wrote to Gallatin in 1802. "Will you have the goodness to note on the bill any amendments which you think proper to recommend to their consideration. They are desirous of making their report as soon as it can conveniently be done."[60] In another instance

[57] Gallatin to Nicholson, April 1802, Nicholson Papers, Lib. Cong.

[58] Gallatin to Jefferson, Oct. 13, 1806, Adams, ed., *Gallatin Writings*, I, 310.

[59] Madison to Joseph H. Nicholson, Nov. 19, 1803, Nicholson Papers, Lib. Cong.

[60] Baldwin to Gallatin, Mar. 24, 1802, Gallatin Papers, N.-Y. Hist. Soc.

Baldwin wrote to Attorney General Breckinridge in 1806: "Will you have the goodness to note in the margin of the inclosed Bill any thing that may occur to you as proper to be considered by the Committee?"[61] In 1803, Senator John Quincy Adams, chairman of a Senate committee on an appropriation bill, reported that the committee "postponed the report to consult the Secretary of the Treasury on a question occurring from the bill. . . . After the adjournment, I called upon the Secretary of the Treasury, and consulted with him on the Appropriation bill; upon which he gave me the information desired."[62] In the executive review of pending legislation, specific changes were commonly recommended.[63]

Both standing and select committees relied heavily on department heads and executive officers for facts and recommendations. When the House referred a matter to a committee, not uncommonly the first thing the committee did was to call on a department head for information. When portions of the President's annual message of 1803 were referred to the House Committee of Commerce and Manufactures, the chairman wrote immediately to the Secretary of State "to request the aid and information which he can afford, towards framing a proper Bill for restraining the Evils alluded to. I shall be glad to learn," he stated, "whatever the Secretary may think proper to lay before the Committee, and to receive all instructions on these subjects that he shall think proper to communicate."[64] Similar letters went regularly to the desk of the Secretary of the Treasury whenever Congress was in session. The letters asked not only for information but for opinions and recommendations. "I am directed by the Committee of Ways and Means," Chairman George W. Campbell wrote to Gallatin in December 1807, "to request that you will please to furnish them with such information relative to the subject of the enclosed resolutions as may be in possession of your Department—together with your opinion in regard to the propriety of continuing in force the law mentioned therein."[65] William B. Giles, the chairman of a Senate

[61] Baldwin to Breckinridge, Apr. 15, 1806, Breckinridge Family Papers, Lib. Cong.

[62] Adams, ed., *Memoirs of John Quincy Adams*, Nov. 7, 1803, I, 272.

[63] Gallatin to Uriah Tracy, Jan. 4, 1807, Treasury Dept., Letters and Reports to Congress, "E" Series, v, 6, RG 56, Natl. Archives.

[64] Samuel L. Mitchill to Madison, Oct. 20, 1803, Madison Papers, Lib. Cong.

[65] Campbell to Gallatin, Dec. 23, 1807, House Records, RG 233, Natl. Archives.

committee, called on Gallatin in November 1808 for help in regard to the critical issue of the embargo.

> I am instructed by the Committee appointed to consider the several embargo Laws, etc., to request you to lay before them with as little delay as possible, such information as your Department affords upon the following questions.
>
> First. What measures would be most effectual in preventing the violations or evasions of the several embargo Laws; and enforcing a due observance thereof?
>
> Second. Can any of the inconveniences of the present system be remedied by further modifications; and what modifications would effect that object?[66]

While the Secretary of the Treasury had the heaviest demands made on him, all other department heads received and responded to similar requests from congressional committees.[67] The data supplied by the departmental offices and the recommendations from executive officers frequently filled committee reports; in fact, these reports sometimes did little more than communicate the information received and propose that the recommendation of a department head be implemented. When the House instructed the Committee of Ways and Means to inquire into whether any alterations were needed in a tax law, the chairman of the committee took the question to the Secretary of the Treasury and submitted the Secretary's reply as part of the committee's report, explaining: "Your Committee conceive it unnecessary to offer any reasons in addition to those contained in the letter of the Secretary of the Treasury, hereto subjoined, tending to prove the inexpediency of any legislative provision in relation to this subject."[68] In other cases committee chairmen used the information or recommendations from a department head as the basis of the committee's report, sometimes incorporating excerpts from a department head's letter into the report.[69] These procedures were followed by standing and select com-

[66] Giles to Gallatin, Nov. 14, 1808, Senate Records, RG 46, Natl. Archives.

[67] Dearborn to Randolph, Dec. 15, 1806, Reports to Congress from the Secretary of War, microcopy M-220, Natl. Archives; Smith to Thomas Blount, chairman, Nov. 30, 1807, Original Reports of the Navy Department, House Records, RG 233, Natl. Archives.

[68] Report made Jan. 24, 1803, including letter of Albert Gallatin to John Randolph, Jan. 3, 1803, Reports of the Committee of Ways and Means, I, 403-404, House Records, RG 233, Natl. Archives.

[69] Jacob Crowninshield to Gallatin, Jan. 25, 1805; Gallatin to Crownin-

mittees and in both the House and the Senate. All committees expected the executive offices to do the staff work for them, since they had no staffs of their own. Because individual members of Congress had no staff assistance either, the departmental offices had to carry the full burden of such work for both the executive and legislative branches. Once, while he was chairman of the House Committee of Ways and Means, Randolph called for assistance from the Secretary of the Treasury in the mechanics of drafting the appropriations bill. "The labour of penmanship has hitherto deterred me from reporting the appropriation bill for the support of Government during the present year," he wrote to Gallatin. "Is there any Clerk in your department who has leisure on his hands sufficient to execute the mechanical part. The law of last session and the estimates for this year, will direct him with sufficient precision."[70] The dependence of congressional committees upon departments for staff services put executive officers in a position to exert considerable influence on legislative action.

Cabinet members did not appear on the floor of Congress, and most communications between congressional committees and executive officials were in writing; but department heads were called to testify before committees of both the House and the Senate. No minutes of such meetings were normally kept, but sufficient references survive to indicate the practice. The following note, dated February 12, 1802, from the chief clerk of the Navy Department to the chairman of a House select committee on naval affairs is revealing in regard to such procedures.

> I have the honor to acknowledge the receipt of your letter to the Secretary of the Navy this date, in which you request his personal attendance on the Committee on *Naval Affairs* on Saturday morning at 10 O'clock, and to inform you that he is now at Baltimore and that his return is not expected before Sunday or Monday next. In the meantime should the Committee require any information for which the Office affords the materials, the same shall be promptly furnished on your request.[71]

Secretary of the Treasury Gallatin was summoned to a hearing in November 1808 by Senator Giles, who wrote: "Under instruc-

---

shield, Jan. 26, 1805; Report of the Committee of Commerce and Manufactures, Dec. 16, 1806, House Records, RG 233, Natl. Archives.

[70] Randolph to Gallatin [1806], Gallatin Papers, microfilm edition.

[71] Abishai Thomas to Samuel L. Mitchill, Feb. 12, 1802, Letters from Sec. of Navy to Congress, RG 45, Natl. Archives.

tions from the Committee appointed to consider the several embargo laws, I have to request the favor of your attendance in the Committee Chamber of the Senate at 10 O'clock on Monday morning next, prepared to give such information to the Committee as your Department affords, respecting the subjects embraced by the enclosed resolution."[72] The resolution to which Giles referred directed the committee to examine whether further measures to enforce the embargo laws were required or whether any modifications were needed in the laws;[73] the hearing that followed was one of the most critical of Jefferson's administration.

Department heads did not always wait to be contacted by legislators; they kept track of measures before Congress affecting their departments and offered suggestions on their own initiative. "I take the liberty of laying before the Committee, who have under consideration the rules and articles for the government of the Army, the following propositions and remarks," the Secretary of War wrote in 1804, "with a hope that the subject will be considered of sufficient importance to deserve the attention of the Committee."[74] When the Secretary of the Navy was unhappy with the Navy appropriations bill passed by the House in 1802, he made his objections known to the chairman of the Senate committee to whom the measure was referred.[75] On another occasion when Smith was concerned about a pending bill, he wrote the President: "Having obtained a sight of the Bill now before the Senate . . . for a Naval Peace Establishment . . . I lose no time in informing you that under the restrictions of such an act of Congress, the Chesapeake as contemplated by you, cannot be sent to the Mediterranean."[76] Shortly after sending the President this letter detailing his objections and his proposed changes in the bill, the Secretary of the Navy received a request for his opinion on the measure from the chairman of the Senate committee considering the bill. In reply Smith sent a copy of the letter he had written the President, with the following note:

[72] Giles to Gallatin, Nov. 12, 1808, Senate Records, RG 46, Natl. Archives.

[73] *Annals of Congress*, 10 Cong., 2 Sess., 16-17.

[74] Henry Dearborn to Joseph B. Varnum, Jan. 23, 1804, Papers of Henry Dearborn, Lib. Cong.

[75] Robert Smith to Christopher Ellery, Apr. 22, 1802, Letters from Sec. of Navy to Congress, RG 45, Natl. Archives.

[76] Smith to Jefferson, Apr. 21, 1806, Original Reports of the Navy Dept., House Records, RG 233, Natl. Archives.

I have this moment received your letter of this morning, requesting my sentiments of the Navy Peace Establishment Bill now before the Senate, and proposing to me these Questions vizt.—"Is it correct? Are any alterations or amendments requisite? and if so, what?"

Without presuming to judge of the correctness of a bill sanctioned by the House of Representatives, I would only take the liberty of sending to you herewith a copy of a note this day transmitted by me to the President.[77]

In this case, the Senate committee waited for Smith's reply before reporting the bill with amendments.[78] Although the amended measure passed the Senate, the changes were not agreed to by the House, and the Senate receded from its amendments.[79]

In February 1809 Smith sent to Senator Giles "a hasty sketch of the ideas suggested to me in reading the Bill before the Senate . . . to amend the several acts for the establishment and regulation of the Treasury, War and Navy Departments." This "hasty sketch" with its enclosures filled forty-two pages and was communicated to the Senate by Giles on the same day he received it.[80] The direct involvement of Cabinet members in the legislative process is further confirmed by the Senate bill file for the Eighth Congress containing a Navy pension fund bill. The printed text has one change made in Smith's handwriting, and there is also in Smith's hand the draft of an additional section.[81] The proposed change and the new section were added to the bill as amendments in the Senate and appeared in the measure as enacted.[82]

Gallatin, whose numerous letters to chairmen of House and Senate committees attest to the frequency with which he was consulted on pending legislation, often took the initiative in seeking changes in bills under consideration. "I enclose the substance of a provision which seems necessary, and may be added to your Land Bill . . . ," he wrote to John Boyle, chairman of the House Committee on the Public Lands on one such occasion. "But observe that as the above

[77] Smith to James Turner, Apr. 21, 1806, *ibid.*

[78] Adams, ed., *Memoirs of John Quincy Adams*, Apr. 21, 1806, i, 436.

[79] *Annals of Congress*, 9 Cong., 1 Sess. (Apr. 21, 1806), 248-249.

[80] Smith to Giles, Feb. 25, 1809, Senate Records, RG 46, Natl. Archives; *ASP, Finance*, ii, 348-350.

[81] Bill introduced Jan. 17, 1804, Senate Records, RG 46, Natl. Archives.

[82] Act of Mar. 26, 1804, *Annals of Congress*, 8 Cong., 1 Sess., 1303; section 6 was drafted by Smith.

sketch of a Section is intended to convey a right, it ought to be drawn with great care."[83] In sending Jefferson a copy of an act in relation to the direct tax, Gallatin explained that "the last section of the act was introduced on my particular suggestion."[84] The original draft of a supplementary act relating to the convention of 1802 with Great Britain is entirely in Gallatin's hand.[85] Its presence in the Senate bill file with the usual endorsements of the Secretary of the Senate indicates that there was no effort made to conceal the authorship. There are other drafts of bills in Gallatin's handwriting in the private papers of members, such as a bill to extend the jurisdiction of territorial and state courts in the papers of Senator Breckinridge, who added marginal notes.[86] Gallatin's drafting of certain legislation was generally known and in some cases carried special weight—at least with some members. In recording the debate on a bill creating the stock for the payments required by the Louisiana Treaty, John Quincy Adams complained that Senator Robert Wright "was against every amendment that could possibly be proposed to the bill, because it was drawn up by the Secretary of the Treasury, who could better legislate for us on this subject than we can do congressionally."[87]

Gallatin devoted considerable time to legislative concerns. His comments on bills under consideration were often detailed, containing specific proposed amendments and modifications.[88] He was also the most active member of Jefferson's administration in the initiation of legislation.[89] Many of his legislative suggestions related to technical details, but he also found time to develop recommendations for broad policies. In sending his most famous proposal to Congress, he wrote to Senator Mitchill:

> I send this day to the Senate a report on the subject of roads and canals which I beg leave to recommend to your special patronage, not certainly on account of its intrinsic merit, but be-

[83] Gallatin to Boyle, Feb. 6, 1807, Treasury Dept., Letters and Reports to Congress, "E" Series, v, 29, RG 56, Natl. Archives.

[84] Gallatin to Jefferson, Apr. 8, 1802, Jefferson Papers, Lib. Cong.

[85] Bill, Mar. 1, 1805, Senate Records, RG 46, Natl. Archives.

[86] Breckinridge Family Papers, v. 25, p. 4410, Lib. Cong.

[87] Adams, ed., *Memoirs of John Quincy Adams*, Nov. 1, 1803, I, 270.

[88] For examples, see Gallatin to Thomas Worthington, Feb. 14, 25, 1807, Treasury Dept., Letters and Reports to Congress, "E" Series, v, 33, 37, RG 56, Natl. Archives; Gallatin to Joseph H. Nicholson, Apr. 27, 1802, Nicholson Papers, Lib. Cong.

[89] See Gallatin to Madison, Feb. 3, 1807, enclosing letter to Peter Early, Feb. 3, 1807, Gallatin Papers, Lib. Cong.

cause the subject itself deserves a much greater attention than has heretofore been paid to it by our Statesmen. I have availed myself of the order of the Senate to procure all the information which could be obtained not only on works already existing or undertaken, but also on those general Geographical features of the country and levels which must determine national lines of communication. And viewing a general system of improvements intended to connect the most distant parts of our extensive territory, as one of the strongest bonds of Union which can be superadded to those which already connect the several States, I have attempted to point out the great outlines of such system and the practicability of effecting it without impairing the revenue or breaking on any other national object of expenditures, plans of defence, etc.[90]

Gallatin's proposal was not to mature into legislation while Jefferson was President. Nevertheless, his report on internal improvements demonstrated the ability of Jefferson's Secretary of the Treasury to think beyond the pressing problems of the day and showed the innovative role of executive leadership.

Congress, of course, did not always follow the recommendations of executive officers. In November 1803 the House of Representatives referred to the Committee of Ways and Means a resolution to discontinue the offices of the commissioners of loans in the different states and to transfer the duties of those officers to the Secretary of the Treasury. Committee chairman Randolph sent a copy of the resolution to Gallatin, requesting "such information touching the practicability and expediency of carrying it into effect, as may be in the possession of the Department of the Treasury and which you may deem material."[91] In a long and detailed letter, Gallatin indicated that the proposal was practicable and estimated that the work of the thirteen commissioners and their twenty-one clerks could be handled by eight clerks in the Treasury at an annual saving of twenty thousand dollars.[92] Although Randolph agreed with Gallatin,[93] the Ways and Means Committee took a different stance. When the committee made its report, it recommended against discontinuing the offices, explaining that "the abolition of the loan

[90] Gallatin to Mitchill, Apr. 6, 1808, *ibid.*

[91] Randolph to Gallatin, Nov. 19, 1803, enclosing resolution of Nov. 17, 1803, Reports of the Committee of Ways and Means, II, 2-11, House Records, RG 233, Natl. Archives.

[92] Gallatin to Randolph, Nov. 28, 1803, *ibid.*

[93] Brown, ed., *Plumer's Memorandum*, Dec. 14, 1803, p. 88.

offices, by impeding the facility of transferring the debt, may tend, in some degree, to impair its value." The committee affirmed that it was "unwilling to advise a measure which may, in any manner, however remote, affect the public credit, or which may be construed into a breach of the public faith."[94]

In rejecting the Secretary of the Treasury's recommendation, which also had the support of the President,[95] the Ways and Means Committee was responding to the pressures from the various states to retain the offices. On the same day that the committee reported against the proposal to abolish the offices, Senator David Stone wrote to John Haywood, the treasurer of North Carolina, who had expressed his concern about the proposal: "There is not I think any reason to suppose that Congress will consent . . . to abolish the Loan Offices. Many propositions are made here as well as at other places *ad captandum* and I incline to think this one. The reasons stated in your Letter for keeping up the Office are with me conclusive and in my estimation they have peculiar force as applied to North Carolina, as in most other States the Banks would afford a facility for doing the business which in that State must be done by a Loan Officer or by a Person to be appointed and called by some other name."[96] The North Carolina senator's comments furnish an interesting example—often difficult to document—of pressures from constituents on their senators and representatives. In this case Haywood had likewise written to Representative Thomas Wynns, whose reply revealed congressional responsiveness to pressure from below:

Soon after the receipt of yours of the 28th ultimo I consulted several of our delegation on the resolution for doing away the loan offices in the several States and told them your reasons for believing our State benefited by the establishment. The resolution was introduced by Mr. Eppes and the Secretary of the Treasury is in favor of it and seems to contemplate a saving of 17 or 18,000 dollars by the adoption of it, but I do not think it will be carried into effect unless it can be clearly shewn that individuals will not be injured by it. North Carolina having no Bank will render it more inconvenient to those creditors who wish to draw their money there than most other States. It is

[94] Committee report, Dec. 8, 1803, Reports of the Committee of Ways and Means, II, 2-11, House Records, RG 233, Natl. Archives.

[95] Brown, ed., *Plumer's Memorandum*, Dec. 14, 1803, p. 88.

[96] Stone to John Haywood, Dec. 8, 1803, Earnest Haywood Collection, Univ. of N. C.

probable some of our members will be in favor of the measure, others will not unless such arrangements are made as will prevent its producing any injury to our State. There does however appear to be a number of advocates for the resolution, altho the Committee has reported against it.[97]

The House refused to accept the committee's view that it could not abolish the offices without impairing public credit and voted to disagree with the report of the committee, but it later refused to appoint a committee to bring in a bill to discontinue the offices.[98] Randolph, who joined the majority in voting to leave the offices undisturbed, explained that he did so out of respect for the opinions of members from several states, especially Massachusetts, New York, and North Carolina, and in deference "to that which at present appeared to be the public opinion."[99] Congress had thus allowed time for constituent sentiment to reach its members, and in this case constituent pressures were strong enough to overrule the recommendation from the executive branch. Senator Plumer, who reported that the "Administration is alarmed on the subject,"[100] may have overstated that concern, but the action indicated that the Republican majority did not blindly follow executive direction.

The weight of the executive branch in initiating legislation, supplying data for legislative decisionmaking, and shaping bills under congressional consideration was but one force operating on a legislature where House members stood for reelection every two years and senators were dependent upon the support of their state legislatures. Constituent pressures were exerted not only in the electoral process but also in the constant flow of petitions to the halls of Congress. The legislative process was shaped by multiple and diverse influences in which executive-congressional relationships were powerful, but not always determining, factors.

Informal social contacts between members of Congress and executive officers aided both legislative and executive functions. The idea that during Jefferson's presidency there were separate societies of legislators and executive officers[101] is not supported by the his-

[97] Thomas Wynns to Haywood, Dec. 12, 1803, *ibid.*

[98] Brown, ed., *Plumer's Memorandum*, Dec. 14, 1803, p. 88; *Annals of Congress*, 8 Cong., 1 Sess., 778, 958.

[99] *Ibid.*, 958.

[100] Brown, ed., *Plumer's Memorandum*, Jan. 30, 1804, p. 126.

[101] See James S. Young, *The Washington Community, 1800-1828* (New York, 1966), p. 78.

torical record. On this point the generally informative and reliable diary of Senator Plumer is misleading. Plumer recorded in March 1807:

> The Heads of Department visit few members of either House. Madison for this two or three years past has entirely omitted even the ceremony of leaving cards at their lodgings. He invites very few to dine with him.
>
> Mr. Gallatin leaves no cards, makes no visits—scarce ever invites a Member to dine—or even has tea parties—Mrs. Gallatin is a domestic wife and adverse to company. He is himself frugal and parsimonious. . . .
>
> General Dearborn leaves cards for all the members—invites few to dine—some to tea parties. He has taken care to avoid company by living in a remote part of George Town.
>
> Robert Smith leaves cards with all members—invites few to tea, and scarse any to dine.
>
> These gentlemen do not live in a style suited to the dignity of their offices.[102]

Whether Plumer's impressions resulted from the fact that he was a Federalist in a predominantly Republican society or whether they resulted from his own conception of the style in which a Cabinet officer should live, his statements are little supported by the testimony of other witnesses who were in better positions than he to observe the social contacts between the executive officers and members of Congress. Plumer may have been excluded from the social circle of the Cabinet, but other members of Congress were not. He may not have been invited to dine with the Secretary of State, but other members were. In November 1807, Senator Mitchill, reporting that he had recently dined with Madison, noted: "He goes on regularly in giving dinners to the Members of Congress and to reputable strangers." Mitchill, indeed, saw Madison's social invitations as an important political asset. Mrs. Madison, as he saw it, was "giving her husband powerful aid in his approaches towards the Presidency." "In these ways of conciliating good and extending acquaintance, he has no rival; for his competitor, our venerable Vice President . . . practices nothing of the kind."[103] In the same month that Mitchill reported dining with the Secretary of State, Senator John Quincy Adams also recorded in his diary:

[102] Brown, ed., *Plumer's Memorandum*, Mar. 1, 1807, p. 634.
[103] Mitchill to his wife, Nov. 25, 1807, Mitchill Papers, Museum C.N.Y.

"I dined at Mr. Madison's with a company consisting principally of heads of departments." Also present was the Speaker of the House of Representatives and two other members of Congress.[104] Neither Mitchill nor Adams was a stranger at Madison's home, nor were many other members of Congress. Mitchill had received periodic invitations since taking his seat in the House of Representatives in 1801; he had been among the guests at the Madisons' Christmas dinner in 1801, when Senators George Logan of Pennsylvania and James Jackson of Georgia were also guests.[105] Adams reported attending a party at Madison's in 1806 at which there were about seventy people present. "I had considerable conversation with Mr. Madison, on the subjects now most important to the public," Adams confided to his diary. "Mr. Madison expressed his entire approbation of the bill I have brought in respecting foreign Ministers; that is, of the principle. The bill itself he has not seen."[106] As Adams revealed, congressional business was discussed at Washington parties.

Plumer's remarks about other department heads are as misleading as his impressions of Madison. Madison and Gallatin may not have gone through the ritual of making calls and leaving cards, but they had more useful contacts with members of Congress. Gallatin, who lived on Capitol Hill, had almost daily contact with some Republican members of Congress who regularly dropped by his house and sometimes spent the evening. Frances Few, a niece of Mrs. Gallatin, visited the Gallatins during the winter of 1808-1809 and kept a diary of her visit in which she noted the daily routine at the Gallatins. In the evenings, she said, "as soon as we have risen from the table the members of Congress make their appearance, and tell us what has been going on in the house— usually four or five spend their evenings with us."[107] She named as the most constant visitors Senator Samuel Smith of Maryland and Representatives Nathaniel Macon of North Carolina, John Montgomery of Maryland, Wilson Cary Nicholas of Virginia, and George W. Campbell of Tennessee. Of this group, only Montgomery, who was Mrs. Gallatin's brother-in-law, was not a leading member of Congress. Campbell was chairman of the House Ways

[104] Adams, ed., *Memoirs of John Quincy Adams*, Nov. 13, 1807, I, 475.

[105] Mitchill to his wife, Jan. 2, 1802; Nov. 23, 1803, Mitchill Papers, Museum C.N.Y.

[106] Adams, ed., *Memoirs of John Quincy Adams*, Feb. 13, 1806, I, 408.

[107] Cunningham, ed., "The Diary of Frances Few, 1808-1809," *Jour. So. Hist.*, XXIX (1963), 354.

and Means Committee—the committee with which Gallatin had to work most closely. That they talked politics might be assumed, and Miss Few confirmed that such was the case. "Last night Mr. Macon was talking politics 'till 12 o'C[lock]," she wrote in January 1809, when the embargo was the main topic of conversation.[108] Contrary to Senator Plumer's assertion, Miss Few, who was in a position to know, also reported that the Gallatins had a dinner party once a week.[109]

Among those Gallatin invited in December 1808 was Senator Mitchill, whose papers also contain specific references to his dining with every other department head.[110] Mitchill was not exceptionable. At a dinner party at Robert Smith's in December 1802, Mitchill found among the guests many members of Congress, both Federalist and Republican. Among them were Nathaniel Macon, who was then Speaker of the House, John Randolph, then chairman of the House Ways and Means Committee, Representatives William Eustis of Massachusetts, John Rutledge of South Carolina, Samuel Hunt of New Hampshire, and Thomas Morris of New York, and Senators Gouverneur Morris of New York, Jonathan Dayton of New Jersey, Samuel White of Delaware, and Jonathan Mason of Massachusetts.[111] Adams, too, reported numerous social occasions where Cabinet members were present. At a ball at Navy Secretary Smith's, Adams played chess with Madison.[112] At a dinner with a company of some twenty gentlemen, including members of both houses of Congress and of both political parties, Adams "had some conversation with Mr. Madison" on a matter before Congress.[113]

Cabinet members and Republican members of Congress also mingled at the annual Republican celebrations on March 4. The *National Intelligencer* reported in 1802 that the "Fourth of March being the Anniversary of the National Government and of the present administration, the Vice President, members of both Houses of Congress, and the heads of Departments, to the number of

[108] Frances Few to Maria Nicholson, Jan. 29, 1809, Gallatin Papers, N.-Y. Hist. Soc.

[109] Cunningham, ed., "Diary of Frances Few," *Jour. So. Hist.*, xxix (1963), 355.

[110] Mitchill to his wife, Dec. 26, 1802; Feb. 3 and 11, 1803, Mitchill Papers, Museum C.N.Y.

[111] Mitchill to his wife, Dec. 26, 1802, *ibid.*

[112] Adams, ed., *Memoirs of John Quincy Adams*, Dec. 30, 1803, i, 281-282.

[113] *Ibid.*, Jan. 30, 1805, i, 341.

seventy, met at the Republican Hotel to dine."[114] The dinner was presided over by Senator Stephen R. Bradley, later to preside over the Republican nominating caucuses of 1804 and 1808. On January 27, 1804, the Republican members of Congress gave a feast in celebration of the accession of Louisiana, to which the President, the Vice-President, and heads of departments were invited.[115]

Since most members of Congress lived in boardinghouses or hotels, their entertaining was limited, though one invitation has been found in which three members invited Attorney General Breckinridge to dine with them at a boardinghouse.[116] But separate social circles of legislators and executive officers did not dominate Washington in Jefferson's day. The opportunities for informal contact between officials in the Cabinet and members of Congress existed, and such contacts played a part in the process of government.

[114] *National Intelligencer*, Mar. 8, 1802.
[115] Brown, ed., *Plumer's Memorandum*, Jan. 27, 1804, p. 123.
[116] Nathaniel Macon, John Boyle, and Thomas Worthington to John Breckinridge, Jan. 11, 1806, Breckinridge Family Papers, Lib. Cong.

X. The Anatomy of Congressional Committees

A MEMBER OF THE HOUSE OF REPRESENTATIVES observed in 1809 that "our practice is to send propositions to committees when they are not likely to pass."[1] Although they were used in this way, the committees had more important roles and performed much of the work of Congress. While rarely the initiators of legislation, committees provided the means by which proposals were shaped into laws. They were also the principal information-gathering agencies of the legislature; numerous committee records testify to the diligent efforts of committees to obtain information before acting. If to some casual visitors attending the debates in Congress a scene of confusion seemed to prevail, one should not be led to the conclusion that "chaotic conditions of procedures and organization" prevailed in Congress.[2] Though not always visible from the gallery, committee systems functioned effectively in both the Senate and the House.

The rules of the House of Representatives provided for the appointment of designated standing committees at the beginning of each session. At the outset of Jefferson's presidency there were five standing committees:[3]

Committee of Elections
Committee of Claims
Committee of Commerce and Manufactures
Committee of Ways and Means
Committee of Revisal and Unfinished Business

The Committee of Ways and Means had nine members in 1801 but was reduced to seven at the next session after a revision of the House rules.[4] Except for the Committee of Revisal and Unfinished

---

[1] Burwell Bassett to St. George Tucker, Jan. 7, [1809], Tucker-Coleman Collection, College of William and Mary.

[2] The quoted words are from Young, *Washington Community*, p. 304, who relied heavily on the accounts of foreign visitors.

[3] House rules, Jan. 7, 1802, *House Journal*, IV, 40.

[4] The Committee of Ways and Means appointed Dec. 8, 1801, before the revision of the rules, Jan. 7, 1802, had nine members; the committee appointed Dec. 14, 1802, had seven members. *Ibid.*, pp. 7, 249.

Business, which had three members, the other committees consisted of seven members each. In addition to the five standing committees, there was a joint standing Committee on Enrolled Bills composed of one member from the Senate and two from the House.[5] During the period of Jefferson's presidency, four new standing committees were created by the House:[6]

	Date Established
Committee of Accounts	December 27, 1803[7]
Committee on the Public Lands	December 17, 1805
Committee for the District of Columbia	January 27, 1808
Committee of the Post Office and Post Roads	November 9, 1808

The Committee of Accounts was composed of three members; the Committee on the Public Lands and the Committee for the District of Columbia each had seven members; the Committee of the Post Office and Post Roads contained one member from each state, a total of seventeen.[8] There was also a joint Committee on the Library of Congress, established in 1806, with three members from the House and three senators.[9]

The standing committees created by the House of Representatives during the period from 1801 to 1809 resulted partly from Republican theory but mostly from practical experience that demonstrated the need for additional committees. The Committee of Accounts reflected Republican emphasis on frugality, for its task was to apply to the expenditures of the House the same accountability demanded of executive officers. The duty of the committee as stated in 1803 was "to superintend and control the expenditure of the contingent fund of the House of Representatives, and to audit and settle all accounts which may be charged thereon."[10] In the House rules of 1805 it was further provided that the committee "audit the accounts of the members for their travel to and from the seat of government, and their attendance in the house."[11]

The standing committees concerned with public lands, the Dis-

---

[5] *Ibid.*, p. 42.   [6] *Ibid.*, IV, 503; V, 202; VI, 146, 345.

[7] The Committee of Accounts was established Dec. 27, 1803; it was designated a standing committee in the rules adopted Dec. 17, 1805. *Ibid.*, IV, 503; V, 202.

[8] *Ibid.*, IV, 503; V, 202; VI, 146, 345.   [9] *Ibid.*, V, 302, 306.

[10] *Ibid.*, IV, 503.   [11] House rules, Dec. 17, 1805, *ibid.*, V, 203.

trict of Columbia, and post offices and post roads evolved from select committees. Normally after a matter was referred to a select committee, subsequent questions on the same subject were referred to that committee. During the first session of the Ninth Congress, fifty petitions were referred to a select committee on post offices and post roads.[12] Thus, as more and more problems relating to a common subject were referred to one select committee, it in effect became a standing committee, and in time this was recognized by the creation of a new standing committee.

Of the nine standing committees of the House, the Committee of Ways and Means was the most important. When the committee was appointed in December 1801 at the opening of the Seventh Congress, its charge was "to take into consideration all such reports of the Treasury Department, and all such propositions, relative to the revenue, as may be referred to them by the House; to inquire into the state of the public debt, of the revenue, and of expenditures; and to report, from time to time, their opinion thereon."[13] This was the same language used when the initial standing Committee of Ways and Means had been created in December 1795.[14] When the House revised its rules in January 1802, it expanded the duties of the committee to include the responsibility "to examine into the state of the several public departments, and particularly into the laws making appropriations of moneys, and to report whether the moneys have been disbursed conformably with such laws; and, also, to report, from time to time, such provisions and arrangements, as may be necessary to add to the economy of the departments, and the accountability of their officers."[15] This change represented a major expansion of the functions of the committee, making it a watchdog committee charged with keeping an eye on all executive departments. The rules adopted in 1802 defining the duties and fixing the membership of the Ways and Means Committee at seven members remained unchanged throughout Jefferson's presidency.

[12] Petition Book, 7 Cong., 2 Sess.–10 Cong., 1 Sess., House Records, RG 233, Natl. Archives.

[13] *House Journal* (Dec. 8, 1801), iv, 7.

[14] *Ibid.* (Dec. 21, 1795), ii, 385. The origin of the House Committee of Ways and Means is well covered in Patrick J. Furlong, "The Evolution of Political Organization in the House of Representatives, 1789-1801" (Ph.D. Dissertation, Northwestern University, 1966), Chap. 5.

[15] House rules, Jan. 7, 1802, *House Journal*, iv, 40.

The broad responsibilities of the Committee of Ways and Means in relation to revenues and appropriations resulted in a large proportion of major legislation passing through that committee and necessitated extensive committee work. When at the beginning of each session the Secretary of the Treasury furnished Congress with detailed estimates of revenues and expenditures, the committee did not simply report legislation to implement the executive requests. Jealous of its power of the purse, the House demanded a review of the administration's requests by its own Committee of Ways and Means. With a Republican administration, a Republican majority in Congress, and Republican control of the committee, the process was less one of confrontation than of cooperation, but the Committee of Ways and Means made its own assessment of the state of finances before presenting its recommendations to the House.[16] The committee conferred with department heads and on occasion secured revised estimates from them. At the request of the Ways and Means Committee, both the Secretary of the Navy and the Secretary of War submitted revised estimates in 1802, reducing the proposed expenditures in their departments.[17]

Though in contact with all department heads, the Committee of Ways and Means consulted most closely with the Secretary of the Treasury, who had a strong influence on the committee's recommendations. Secretary of the Navy Smith complained in 1802 that he had not been sufficiently consulted. "If the Chairman of the Committee of Ways and Means had conceived it expedient to consult me upon the subject, I was prepared to shew him a classification that would have suited yours as well as my Department," he wrote the Secretary of the Treasury in a dispute over how warrants were to be issued by the Navy.[18] Smith's resentment of Randolph's neglect was not without foundation, for Randolph shared Gallatin's mistrust of the Navy and his discontent with Smith's management of the Navy Department. In a letter to Nicholson in February 1807 Randolph complained: "I called, some time since, at the Navy office, to ask an explanation of certain items of the estimate for this year. The Secretary called up his chief clerk, who knew

---

16 *ASP, Finance*, I, 734-735.

17 Dearborn to Randolph, Jan. 27, 1802, Reports of the Committee of Ways and Means, I, 336, House Records, RG 233, Natl. Archives; Dearborn to Gallatin, Mar. 27, 1802, Gallatin Papers, microfilm edition; Smith to Randolph, Jan. 30, 1802, Letters from Sec. of Navy to Congress, RG 45, Natl. Archives.

18 Smith to Gallatin, May 6, 1802, Gallatin Papers, microfilm edition.

very little more of the business than his master. I propounded a question to the head of the Department—he turned to the Clerk, like a boy who cannot say his lesson, and with imploring countenance beseeches aid. The Clerk with much assurance gabbled out some common place jargon, which I would not take for sterling. . . . There was not one single question, relating to the department, that the Secretary could answer."[19] Besides indicating Randolph's opinion of Smith, this letter is revealing of the procedures followed by the chairman of the Ways and Means Committee, showing that he called personally at department offices to seek explanations of items in the estimates.

Although the Committee of Ways and Means made minor revisions in departmental requests, the major changes in appropriations resulted from legislative actions, such as the reduction or expansion of military forces or adjustments in import duties and other revenue sources. There is no indication that departments asked for more money than they needed, expecting their requests to be cut, nor that legislators assumed that such practices were employed. It could be honestly assumed that if a department budget were cut, service would be curtailed and that if military and naval appropriations were reduced, men would be discharged from the Army and ships taken out of service. These matters were in Congress's power to decide. As Gallatin pointed out, and as Congress found to be true, there were not many clerkships that could be eliminated. Thus, the revisions that the Committee of Ways and Means could make in the administration's estimates were closely tied to the legislative program of Congress, and it is not surprising that the chairman of that committee was a key figure in most major actions of the House.

With the chairmanship of the Committee of Ways and Means providing the opportunity for leadership, Randolph established himself as the Republican majority leader in the House. When Randolph broke with the President and was removed from the committee, Gallatin objected that the move would increase the work of the Treasury, but the change indicated that the Republican majority in the House believed that control over the Committee of Ways and Means was important to party control of the House.

The Committee of Commerce and Manufactures was the second most influential House committee. As broadly stated in the rules, its duties were "to take into consideration all such petitions, and

19 Randolph to Nicholson, Feb. 17, 1807, Nicholson Papers, Lib. Cong.

matters or things touching the commerce and manufactures of the United States, as shall be presented, or shall or may come in question, and be referred to them by the House; and to report, from time to time, their opinion thereon."[20] The House might also order that the committee "be authorized to report by bill, or bills, or otherwise, on all such matters as shall from time to time be referred to them by the House."[21] Without such instructions a committee had to report its recommendations and then be instructed to bring in a bill; the broader authority to report by bill reduced the paperwork and speeded the legislative process. Similar authorization was given to the Committee of Ways and Means.[22]

Much of the work of the Committee of Commerce and Manufactures resulted from petitions referred to the committee. Unlike private petitions, such as those directed to the Committee of Claims, that rarely affected public policy, the petitions referred to the Committee of Commerce and Manufactures frequently related to major policy questions and were designed to influence broad legislative action. While there were many petitions from individuals seeking such private purposes as the remission of duties on a particular shipment of goods, many other petitions were from groups and were of a public nature. Generally they sought advantages for particular groups or areas—a lighthouse, a port of entry, or higher pay for workers at the port of New York—but the petitions also often related directly to major issues. Requests for higher import duties were frequent subjects.[23] Something of the scope of the matters that came before the committee is indicated in a letter written by Samuel L. Mitchill on December 8, 1803: "This Morning I met with the Committee of Commerce and Manufactures as their Chairman. We took into consideration the Manufacture of refined Sugar, the registering of Ships and vessels, and the violation of the rights of neutrality by belligerent Powers in our Ports, harbours, and acknowledged Territorial Limits."[24]

A few weeks earlier Mitchill had written: "I am burthened with as much business as ever, in my capacity of Chairman of the

---

[20] House rules, Jan. 7, 1802, *House Journal*, IV, 40.

[21] *Annals of Congress*, 7 Cong., 1 Sess. (Dec. 21, 1801), 343.

[22] *Ibid.* (Jan. 13, 1802), 420.

[23] These observations are based on an examination of the Reports of the Committee of Commerce and Manufactures, 7th-10th Congresses, House Records, RG 233, Natl. Archives.

[24] Mitchill to his wife, Dec. 8, 1803, Mitchill Papers, Museum C.N.Y.

Committee of Commerce and Manufactures. For to this Committee a great amount of business is referred, to be considered and reported upon."[25] In the course of the session to which Mitchill's comments pertain, sixty-five matters were referred to his committee, and committee records indicate that reports were made on all but thirteen of them before the end of the session. The subjects committed to the committee included a portion of the President's message at the beginning of the session, six resolutions from the House, two bills from the Senate, and fifty-six petitions.[26] The workload for this session appears to have been about average for the first sessions of the Congresses during the period. During the first session of the preceding Congress, the committee handled sixty-eight assignments.[27] In the shorter second sessions of each Congress, which had to adjourn by March 4 in the odd-numbered years, the workload was always lighter. In the second session of the Eighth Congress, fifty matters, including forty petitions, were referred to the committee.[28]

Under both Samuel Smith and Samuel L. Mitchill, the Committee of Commerce and Manufactures was a hard-working committee whose reports were often extensive. In reporting on a portion of the President's annual message of 1802 relating to discriminating and countervailing duties, the committee's detailed report of January 10, 1803, examined the options open to the United States and the anticipated consequences of different courses of action. The committee then recommended that discriminating and countervailing duties be repealed with respect to any power that levied no such duties against the United States.[29] While much of the factual data came from an accompanying letter from the Secretary of the Treasury, the report presented by Smith gave evidence of considerable effort by the committee itself in evaluating data and proposing policy. Similar effort was reflected in a report presented by Mitchill at the next Congress in December 1803 in response to a resolution of the House calling on the committee "to inquire and report by bill, or otherwise, whether a drawback of duties ought not to be allowed on sugar refined within the United States, and exported to foreign ports or places."[30] The report began by

[25] Mitchill to his wife, Oct. 22, 1803, *ibid.*

[26] Reports of the Committee of Commerce and Manufactures, I, 474-489, House Records, RG 233, Natl. Archives.

[27] *Ibid.*, pp. 240-257.   [28] *Ibid.*, pp. 474-489.

[29] *Ibid.*, pp. 273-297; *Annals of Congress*, 7 Cong., 2 Sess., 347-351.

[30] *House Journal*, IV, 439.

reviewing past legislation relating to the question, proceeded to present a detailed examination of sugar refining and sugar importations, called attention to the changes that the recent acquisition of Louisiana would bring, and concluded: "A good reason does not recur to the committee wherefore both the treasury of the nation and the pockets of individual citizens should be subjected to greater payments than at present. . . . In the case of sugar, the committee is inclined to think that the operation of refining has already been patronized to as great an extent by government as is consistent with political economy and public good." The committee thus recommended that "it would be improper at this time and under existing laws and regulations to allow a drawback upon the exportation of domestic refined sugar."[31] Not all committee reports were so thorough as these examples, and, like other committees, the Committee of Commerce and Manufactures depended heavily on data supplied by the departmental offices; nevertheless, there is much evidence that the real work of Congress was done in committees.

"The Business of Chairman of a standing committee is very arduous and attended with much labour," Senator Plumer observed in reference to practices in the House. "His duty is to call the Committee together, draw up the report in writing, which frequently is prolix and argumentative—And in the House he must support and defend the Report."[32] If a chairman were absent or refused to call a meeting, the committee was required to meet on the call of any two members of the committee.[33] Sometimes disputes arose over the proper committee to which a subject should be referred. In December 1801 Smith moved that the Committee of Commerce and Manufactures be directed to consider alterations in the acts levying import duties. This was objected to by Roger Griswold, a member of the Ways and Means Committee, who raised the issue, he said, because he did not see the chairman of that committee in his seat. Griswold, who had been chairman of the Ways and Means Committee before the Federalists lost control of Congress in 1801, contended that the subject "properly attached itself to the Committee of Ways and Means." Arguing that "any

[31] Reports of the Committee of Commerce and Manufactures, Dec. 20, 1803, I, 376, House Records, RG 233, Natl. Archives.

[32] Brown, ed., *Plumer's Memorandum*, Nov. 26, 1804, p. 206.

[33] *Supplement to the Standing Rules and Orders of the House of Representatives of the United States, 20th December, 1805* (Washington, D. C., 1805), Rare Book Division, Lib. Cong.

alteration whatever would either increase or diminish the revenue, and therefore belonged to the financial system, which the Committee of Ways and Means especially had in charge," Griswold moved that the matter be referred to that committee.[34] In the arguments advanced by Smith in the debate that ensued before the House voted to refer the matter to Smith's committee, a significant aspect of the Committee of Commerce and Manufactures was revealed. This was the fact that the committee was composed of commercial men. Smith argued that "it was usual and necessary for the subject to be discussed by commercial men, of whom alone the Committee of Commerce and Manufactures was composed." "By a reference to the commercial men," he said, the House might be informed of "how far certain articles would bear additional duties, or how far others admitted a diminution, proportional to the wants of the country." In contending that the issue should be referred to his committee, Smith suggested that "commercial men were practical men, and therefore, without disparaging the merits or talents of the gentlemen composing the other committee, whose express appointments did not so pointedly relate to commerce, but to revenue, he thought the original motion ought to be carried."[35] Whether for these or other reasons, a majority of the House rose in favor of sending the matter to the Committee of Commerce and Manufactures; and no one challenged Smith's assumption that the committee was, and should be, composed of commercial men.

The different duties of committees determined that the extent of their labors and the nature of their influence would vary considerably. The Committee of Elections—the first standing committee created by the House of Representatives in 1789—had the task of examining the certificates of election or other credentials of all members and of considering and reporting upon any petitions or other matters touching elections that might be referred to the committee.[36] The examination of certificates and credentials was largely routine and disposed of in the opening weeks of the session when the committee reported the names of those members whose credentials were "sufficient to entitle them to their seats in this House."[37]

[34] *Annals of Congress*, 7 Cong., 1 Sess. (Dec. 11, 1801), 317-318.
[35] *Ibid.*
[36] House rules, Jan. 7, 1802, Dec. 17, 1805, *House Journal*, iv, 40; v, 202.
[37] *Annals of Congress*, 7 Cong., 1 Sess. (Jan. 8, 1802), 415. Reports of Nov. 5, Dec. 7, 17, 1807, House Records, RG 233, Natl. Archives.

In cases of contested elections, the Committee of Elections had considerable responsibilities; it collected evidence by deposition and by testimony before the committee and recommended decisions to the House. During the four Congresses from 1801 to 1809, twelve contested elections or questions relating to a member's right to a seat in the House were referred to the committee, with from one to three cases at a session.[38] In each case the House confirmed the recommendation of the committee, although the vote on the floor was sometimes close.[39]

The standing committee with the most routine duties was the joint Committee on Enrolled Bills. After a bill was passed by both houses of Congress, it was enrolled, or copied, on parchment by the Clerk of the House or the Secretary of the Senate, depending upon which house had originated the bill. The enrolled bill was then examined by the joint committee, compared with the engrossed bills passed by the two houses, and any errors were corrected. After the report of this examination was made to the two houses, the bill was signed by the Speaker of the House and the President of the Senate, and the Committee on Enrolled Bills presented the bill to the President for his approval.[40] The work of this committee required no exercise of judgment, but it did require absolute accuracy, and the precision with which the committee discharged its task was of utmost importance.

Next to the joint Committee on Enrolled Bills, the committee with the most routine duties was the Committee of Revisal and Unfinished Business, which was charged with reporting expiring laws that required reenactment or extension and examining the journal of the preceding session to determine matters that were pending.[41] These included unfinished bills, reports, and petitions.

The Committee of Claims, to which were referred all petitions and matters relating to demands on the United States, had an unusually heavy workload. There were more petitions on private claims than on any other subject, and the committee was expected to examine each of these and propose any proper relief. Until the Committee on the Public Lands was created, land claims were

[38] Journal of Committee of Elections, 1789-1828, MSS vol., Duke University Library; M. St. Clair Clarke and David A. Hall, eds., *Cases of Contested Elections in Congress* (Washington, D. C., 1834), pp. 120-233.

[39] *Ibid.*, pp. 165, 233.

[40] House rules, Jan. 7, 1802, Dec. 17, 1805, *House Journal*, iv, 42; v, 204.

[41] *Ibid.*, iv, 40; v, 203.

referred to the Committee of Claims. At the first session of the Seventh Congress, sixty-six petitions were referred to the Committee of Claims; at the first session of the Eighth Congress, eighty-three; and at the first session of the Ninth Congress, ninety-five.[42] In each of these sessions, the number of petitions sent to the Committee of Claims was larger than that referred to any other committee.[43]

The Committee on the Public Lands also had a large workload. During the first session of the Ninth Congress, at least sixty matters were referred to this newly constituted standing committee, including four resolutions from the House, two bills from the Senate, a report of the Secretary of the Treasury, and fifty-three petitions.[44] In a period of fifteen weeks from January to April 1806 the chairman of the committee, Andrew Gregg of Pennsylvania, made at least twenty-five reports to the House.[45] As a select committee, its work had been largely confined to questions relating to the sale of public lands, but after becoming a standing committee, the Committee on the Public Lands also handled land claims.

A House committee on foreign affairs was not established until 1822. During the period of Jefferson's presidency, matters relating to foreign affairs were usually referred either to select committees or to one of two standing committees—the Committee of Ways and Means or the Committee of Commerce and Manufactures. It was not always clear on what basis the House made its decision on referrals to committee, and both standing committees were much engaged in matters of foreign relations.

In December 1805 the House referred to the Committee of Ways and Means that part of the President's annual message relating to the conduct of belligerent powers toward the United States, with instructions to inquire into the violations of neutral rights and the "legislative measures the true interest of the United States requires to counteract such violations."[46] A few days later,

[42] Petition Book, 4 Cong., 1 Sess.–7 Cong., 1 Sess.; Petition Book, 7 Cong., 2 Sess.–10 Cong., 1 Sess., *ibid*. Figures are for initial references of petitions only.

[43] See Table 16 below.

[44] Reports of the Committee on the Public Lands, I, 70-81, House Records, RG 233, Natl. Archives. The figure on petitions is not limited to petitions initially referred and thus is larger than that shown in Table 16.

[45] *Ibid.*

[46] *Annals of Congress*, 9 Cong., 1 Sess. (Dec. 4, 1805), 262.

from the committee room of the House, Randolph addressed the following note to the Secretary of State:

> The committee of ways and means have instructed me to request, that you will cause to be laid before them such information, on the subject of the enclosed resolution, as the Department of State can furnish.
>
> The more peculiar objects of our research are
>
> 1. what new principles, or constructions, of the laws of nations have been adopted by the belligerent powers of Europe, to the prejudice of neutral rights?
>
> 2. the governments asserting those principles and constructions?
>
> 3. the extent to which the commerce of the U. S. has been thereby injured?[47]

This letter is illustrative of the wide-ranging concern the Ways and Means Committee had with respect to the conduct of foreign relations. Concurrently the committee's chairman was also involved in another major matter of foreign affairs. Only a few days before, he had been appointed to head the select committee to which was referred the President's confidential message on Spanish affairs— a message designed to obtain from Congress an appropriation of two million dollars to be used in the purchase of Florida.[48]

At times, the Committee of Commerce and Manufactures was as immersed in the consideration of foreign affairs as the Committee of Ways and Means. Early in the Tenth Congress, which assembled in October 1807 to face the crisis precipitated by the British attack on the *Chesapeake*, Thomas Newton, the chairman of the Committee of Commerce and Manufactures, wrote to the Secretary of State raising questions similar to those asked by the chairman of Ways and Means two years before. Written from the committee room on November 5, 1807, Newton's note was even broader than Randolph's:

> So much of the Presidents message as relates to our maritime rights, and to impositions on and interdictions of our neutral trade has been referred to the Committee of Commerce and Manufactures. It is the desire of the Committee to procure all

[47] Randolph to Madison, Dec. 11, 1805, Original Reports of the Secretary of State, House Records, RG 233, Natl. Archives.

[48] Adams, *History*, III, 132; *Annals of Congress*, 9 Cong., 1 Sess., 1117.

the information necessary to place those interesting and important subjects in the proper point of view. I am therefore as their organ directed to request of you whatever facts or information may be in your possession touching those subjects.[49]

Madison's replies to these two requests suggest that he was not eager to encourage either committee to become active in foreign affairs. His reply to Randolph's request of December 11, 1805, was not sent until January 25, 1806, and consisted of the following communication:

> The Secretary of State presents his respects to Mr. Randolph, and has the honor to transmit him a copy of a report this day made to the President of the United States, respecting interpolations, by foreign powers, of new and injurious principles, in the law of nations. This report with the communications made by the President to Congress, particularly that of the 17th instant will, it is hoped, afford the information, requested for the Committee of Ways and Means by Mr. Randolph's letter of the 11th ultimo.[50]

Madison's reply to Newton two years later was similar:

> On a review of the interdictions by foreign powers of our maritime rights, authenticated to this Department, I do not find any within the presumed contemplation of the Committee of Commerce and Manufactures, other than those communicated by the President to the 2d Session of the 9th Congress, and the two acts, one of Great Britain, the other of Spain, which accompanied his message at the opening of the present session of Congress.[51]

Madison obviously gave a narrow reading to the committee's request. The wording of Newton's letter suggests that the intention of the committee was far broader than simply a request for the texts of interdictions by foreign powers.

While the Secretary of State attempted to limit the involvement of the House Committee of Commerce and Manufactures, the House itself directed to that committee an important share of responsibility in the area of foreign affairs. At the same time, nu-

---

[49] Newton to Madison, Nov. 5, 1807, Original Reports of the Secretary of State, House Records, RG 233, Natl. Archives.

[50] Madison to Randolph, Jan. 25, 1806, *ibid.*

[51] Madison to Newton, Nov. 11, 1807, *ibid.*

merous select committees appointed to deal with specific problems of foreign affairs shared with both the Committee of Ways and Means and the Committee of Commerce and Manufactures the assignments of the House. In regard to the *Chesapeake* incident, for example, the House appointed a select committee to consider those portions of the President's message relating to "aggressions committed within our ports and waters by foreign armed vessels."[52]

Although some House standing committees, particularly the Committee of Ways and Means and the Committee of Commerce and Manufactures, were active in drafting legislation, considerable legislative work was done in select committees. This can be seen in the legislative procedures relating to the President's annual message to Congress. Jefferson's first annual message was committed for consideration to the Committee of the Whole on the State of the Union;[53] in subsequent years major portions of the message were referred to various standing and select committees. The sections relating to finances were normally referred to the Committee of Ways and Means, and the portions concerned with commerce or related matters were usually referred to the Committee of Commerce and Manufactures. Most of the subjects presented by the President in his annual message, however, were referred to select committees. Since the President presented his major legislative proposals in his annual message, those select committees played a major role in the legislative process.

The members of all standing and select committees of the House were appointed by the Speaker. By the order in which he named the members to each committee, he designated the chairman and established the rank of each member on the committee. Initially it was simply understood that the person named first to a committee was the chairman, but in November 1804 an addition to the House rules specified that "the first named member of any committee appointed by the Speaker, or the House, shall be the Chairman, and in case of his absence, or being excused by the House, the next named member, and so on as often as the case shall happen, unless the committee shall, by a majority of their number, elect a Chairman."[54] The election of a chairman by a committee

[52] *Annals of Congress*, 10 Cong., 1 Sess. (Oct. 29, 1807), 795. See also Robert Smith to Thomas Blount, Nov. 12, 1807, House Records, RG 233, Natl. Archives.

[53] *Annals of Congress*, 7 Cong., 1 Sess., 313, 325-326.

[54] *House Journal* (Nov. 23, 1804), v, 22; Brown, ed., *Plumer's Memo-*

was unusual. One such instance led to the adoption of the above rule. In November 1804, John Cotton Smith of Connecticut asked to be excused from the Committee of Claims, of which he had been chairman since 1801 and to which he had been again named chairman. The House consented to Smith's request, and Samuel W. Dana, also from Connecticut, was appointed in his place. When the committee met, the members elected Dana as chairman, but Dana refused to accept on the ground that it had generally been understood that the person named second on a committee should succeed to the chairmanship if the chairman were absent or excused. After considering several proposed rules, the House adopted the rule quoted above; and the Committee of Claims again elected Dana as chairman. Dana then requested to be excused from the committee but was refused permission by the House. Only then did he accept the chairmanship.[55]

The most notable example of the election of a committee chairman during the period of Jefferson's presidency was the election of Randolph as chairman of the Committee of Ways and Means by that committee in December 1806. When the House ordered the appointment of standing committees on December 1, 1806, the first day of the session, Randolph, who had been chairman of the Ways and Means Committee since 1801, had not yet taken his seat and according to practice could not be named to the committee. Speaker Macon thus appointed a committee without Randolph. To a friend, Macon confided: "In the disagreeable seat of Speaker . . . I have been obliged to hear the journal read, in which the name of J. R. was not on the Committee of Ways and Means. Many may no doubt think my feelings were too nice on this occasion, but such was my sense of duty, that I could not act otherwise."[56] Macon's reference to his nicety apparently refers to the fact that Randolph took his seat twenty minutes after the motion to appoint the standing committee had been passed.[57] Since the practice was "to appoint no man on a Committee whose name was not previously on

---

randum, Nov. 26, 1804, p. 208. The rule was repassed at the next Congress. *Supplement to the Standing Rules and Orders of the House of Representatives of the United States*, 20th December, 1805.

[55] Brown, ed., *Plumer's Memorandum*, Nov. 26, 1804, pp. 206-208; *House Journal*, v, 5, 6.

[56] Macon to Nicholson, Dec. 2, 1806, William E. Dodd, ed., "Macon Papers," Randolph-Macon College, *John P. Branch Historical Papers*, III (1909), 49.

[57] Macon to Nicholson, Dec. 1, 1806, Nicholson Papers, Lib. Cong.

the Journals of the session in which he was appointed,"⁵⁸ Randolph
was not appointed, even though he was present on the day the committee was named. Four days after the Ways and Means Committee
was appointed, Randolph's close friend James M. Garnett of Virginia, who was serving his first term in the House, asked to be
excused from serving on the committee. Macon then appointed
Randolph in his place, and Joseph Clay, another Randolph supporter who had been named first on the committee, stepped aside,
and the committee elected Randolph as chairman.⁵⁹

The House rules provided that a member might excuse himself
from serving on any committee at the time of his appointment, if
at that time he was a member of two other committees.⁶⁰ However,
there was no effort to limit members to two committees. During
the first two months of the Seventh Congress, Representative
Samuel L. Mitchill was appointed to one standing committee and
seven select committees. Mitchill's description of his assignments
listed the following:

1. The Standing Committee of *Commerce and Manufactures.*
2. The Committee for *revising and amending the Naturalization-
   laws.*
3. The Committee for *protecting the American Commerce and
   Seamen against the Tripolitan Corsairs.*
4. The Committee on *the Naval Affairs* of the United States.
5. The Committee on the Memorials concerning *Perpetual Motion.*
6. The Committee on amending the Act *concerning Patent-
   rights.*
7. The Committee on repealing the Laws *concerning the Mint*
   of the U. S.
8. The Committee for considering the Memorials of the *American Merchants for relief against French Spoliations.*⁶¹

These committee assignments suggest that Mitchill, a scientist and
a member from the City of New York, was named to committees
for which he was presumed to have special competence. In a House
dominated by lawyers and farmers,⁶² Mitchill may not be considered

⁵⁸ Brown, ed., *Plumer's Memorandum*, Nov. 26, 1804, p. 205.
⁵⁹ *Annals of Congress*, 9 Cong., 2 Sess. (Dec. 5 and 9, 1806), 115,
130; Plumer to Bradbury Cilley, Dec. 9, 1806, Plumer Papers, Lib. Cong.
⁶⁰ *House Journal* (Dec. 17, 1805), v, 202.
⁶¹ Mitchill to his wife, Feb. 10, 1802, Mitchill Papers, Museum C.N.Y.
⁶² Long, "Jefferson and Congress," pp. 54-55.

as typical, but his assignments indicate that the Speaker sought to utilize the talents of members.

The majority party in the House maintained control of the standing committees through the Speaker. Table 3 shows the party composition of the standing committees appointed at the opening of the Seventh Congress in December 1801.[63] The Republicans had a majority on every committee. Federalists were chairmen of two of the five committees, but those required the most routine work

TABLE 3. PARTY COMPOSITION OF STANDING COMMITTEES, HOUSE OF REPRESENTATIVES, DECEMBER 1801

Committee	Republicans	Federalists	Chairman
Ways and Means	5	4	John Randolph (Republican)
Commerce and Manufactures	5	2	Samuel Smith (Republican)
Claims	4	3	John Cotton Smith (Federalist)
Elections	4	3	John Milledge (Republican)
Revisal and Unfinished Business	2	1	John Davenport (Federalist)
TOTAL	20	13	

and had the least concern with policy. In addition to party affiliation, legislative experience and geographical distribution were major criteria applied in making appointments to the standing committees. For example, none of the committees named in 1801 contained two members from the same state. Only two states, Kentucky and Rhode Island, were not represented. The states having the largest number of members on the standing committees, with members on four of the five committees, were Connecticut, Maryland, Pennsylvania, and Virginia. Massachusetts and New York members were on three committees. Thus, in general, the states with the largest delegations were given the most committee assignments. No member was named to more than one standing committee, although after the session had been under way for about a month, John Milledge, the chairman of the Committee of Elec-

[63] *Annals of Congress*, 7 Cong., 1 Sess., 312.

tions, was named to replace the ill William Dickson on the Committee of Ways and Means.[64] By this time, however, the major work of the Committee of Elections had been completed.

Of the thirty-three members composing the five standing committees in 1801, twenty-one had been members of the preceding House and two others had been in earlier Congresses. All chairmen except Milledge had been in the preceding House, and he had been a member of the House in three earlier Congresses. All committees had a majority of members who had been in the preceding Congress except the Committee of Commerce and Manufactures, where five of the seven members had never been in Congress before. However, Samuel Smith, the chairman of this committee, had been chairman of the same committee during the last Congress and was the only committee chairman to be reappointed. Even with the party turnover in 1801, eight of the thirty-three committee members had been on the same committee in the preceding session. On the Ways and Means Committee, Roger Griswold, the Connecticut Federalist who had been chairman of the committee during the previous session, was reappointed along with two Republicans, Joseph H. Nicholson and John Smilie, who had been on the committee during the preceding session. Three of the seven members of the Claims Committee had served on that committee during the previous session. The Committee of Elections was the only standing committee without at least one member who had been on the same committee in the Sixth Congress.

Table 4 shows that during the four Jeffersonian Congresses, the committee turnover varied from about one-half to three-fourths of the total committee membership, but that in most instances the committees retained a core of experienced members. The greatest continuity of membership occurred during the Eighth and Ninth Congresses, especially on those committees most involved in the legislative process. But at the opening of the Tenth Congress in October 1807 the turnover in committee membership was nearly as great as that following the advent of Republican control in 1801. The upheaval in 1807 was a product of Randolph's break with the Republican majority that led to the naming of an entirely new Ways and Means Committee by the new Speaker, Joseph B. Varnum.

It should be noted that the figures in Table 4 refer only to the first session of each Congress. At the second sessions far greater continuity in committee membership prevailed. At the second ses-

[64] *Ibid.* (Jan. 4, 1802), 361.

TABLE 4. MEMBERSHIP TURNOVER ON STANDING COMMITTEES OF
THE HOUSE OF REPRESENTATIVES, 1801-1809

Committee	7th Congress 1st Session (1801-1802)		8th Congress 1st Session (1803-1804)		9th Congress 1st Session (1805-1806)		10th Congress 1st Session (1807-1808)	
	Total Committee	Reappointed Members	Total Committee	Reappointed Members	Total Committee	Reappointed Members	Total Committee	Reappointed Members
Elections	7	0	7	0	7	3	7	1
Claims	7	3	7	5	7	4	7	2
Commerce and Manufactures	7	1	7	5	7	5	7	4
Ways and Means	9	3	7	3	7	4	7	0
Revisal and Unfinished Business	3	1	3	0	3	1	3	0
Accounts					3	0	3	0
Public Lands							7	4
	33	8	31	13	34	17	41	11

sion of the Seventh Congress, twenty-two of the thirty-one members on standing committees had served on the same committee during the first session.[65] At the second session of the Tenth Congress, thirty-five of the forty-one committee members were renamed to the same committee.[66] Though committee appointments were made at each session, they tended in effect to be for the term of Congress.

As shown in Table 5, there was no pattern of long tenure in committee chairmanship. Only two chairmen served continuously through three consecutive Congresses, and only Randolph, as chairman of the Committee of Ways and Means, retained a powerful chairmanship for six years. With both Smith and Mitchill

[65] *Ibid.*, 7 Cong., 2 Sess., 275, 278.

[66] *Ibid.*, 10 Cong., 2 Sess., 472. The total of forty-one committee members includes only those committees that existed throughout both sessions; the Committee for the District of Columbia and the Committee of the Post Office and Post Roads are not included.

Committee	7th Congress 1 Sess.	7th Congress 2 Sess.	8th Congress 1 Sess.	8th Congress 2 Sess.	9th Congress 1 Sess.	9th Congress 2 Sess.	10th Congress 1 Sess.	10th Congress 2 Sess.
Elections	John Milledge (R., Ga.)	John Bacon (R., Mass.)	William Findley (R., Pa.)					
Claims		John Cotton Smith (F., Conn.)		Samuel W. Dana (F., Conn.)	John Cotton Smith (F., Conn.)		David Holmes (R., Va.)	
Commerce and Manufactures		Samuel Smith (R., Md.)	Samuel L. Mitchill (R., N. Y.)		Jacob Crowninshield (R., Mass.)		Thomas Newton, Jr. (R., Va.)	
Ways and Means			John Randolph (R., Va.)				George W. Campbell (R., Tenn.)	
Revisal and Unfinished Business		John Davenport (F., Conn.)		Samuel Tenney (F., N. H.)			John Clopton (R., Va.)	
Accounts					Frederick Conrad (R., Pa.)		Nicholas R. Moore (R., Md.)	
Public Lands					Andrew Gregg (R., Pa.)	John Boyle (R., Ky.)		Jeremiah Morrow (R., Ohio)
District of Columbia							Philip B. Key (F., Md.)	Joseph Lewis, Jr. (F., Va.)
Post Office and Post Roads							John Rhea (R., Tenn.)	

advancing to the Senate, the Committee of Commerce and Manufactures had a new chairman in each Congress. Party control of
the chairmanships was consistently maintained. With declining
Federalist membership in the House, Federalist chairmanships
dropped from two to one in 1806, but the change was hardly
significant, for Republicans had kept the most powerful committees
under Republican chairmen. As in the total membership of standing
committees, the greatest turnover in committee chairmen came at
the beginning of the Tenth Congress in 1807 when a new Speaker
was elected—a clear demonstration of the power of the Speaker
in the organization of the House.

SENATE COMMITTEES

The Senate committee system differed substantially from that
of the House in the use of standing committees and in the method
of naming committees. The employment of standing committees
in the Senate was extremely limited. Other than the two joint committees of the House and Senate on Enrolled Bills and on the
Library of Congress, there were only two standing committees
created in the Senate, both of which were housekeeping committees. The Senate rules adopted in 1806 provided for a committee
on engrossed bills,[67] and in 1807 a committee was added "to
audit and control the contingent expenses of the Senate."[68] No
other standing committees were created in the Senate prior to
1816.[69]

Almost all of the committee work of the Senate was performed
by select committees. Bills from the House of Representatives, presidential messages, motions, resolutions, petitions, drafts of bills,
and nearly every matter assigned for consideration went to a committee specifically named for the purpose. In practice, similar subjects were referred to the same select committee; and in 1806 the
Senate recognized the procedure by adding to its rules the provision
that "when any subject or matter shall have been referred to a

[67] Rules adopted Mar. 26, 1806, *Senate Journal*, IV, 67.

[68] Adopted Nov. 4, 1807, *ibid.*, p. 191.

[69] *Statement of the rules and practices of the Senate of the United States,
in the appointment of its committees, from the commencement of the government under the Constitution, being from the 4th of March 1789, to the
14th of March, 1863* by W. Hickey, Chief Clerk of the Senate, *Senate
Miscellaneous Document*, No. 42, 37 Cong., 3 Sess., pp. 1-3.

select committee, any other subject or matter of a similar nature, may, on motion, be referred to such committee."[70]

Normally, Senate committees were composed of three members, but five-member committees were chosen for the most important matters, and occasionally a seven-member committee was named. Of 116 committees in the first session of the Eighth Congress, eleven were five-men committees; of 109 committees in the first session of the Tenth Congress, eighteen were composed of five members and three had seven. Conference committees with the House of Representatives and joint select committees, such as committees to call on the President, normally had two senators. Most committees did not contain two senators from the same state; but there was no rule against it and some did. Senators Abraham Baldwin and James Jackson, both from Georgia, sat together on no less than nine committees during the first session of the Eighth Congress.

In contrast to the House of Representatives where committees were appointed by the Speaker, committees in the Senate, where the Vice-President presided, were elected by the full membership. The Senate rules provided that "all committees shall be appointed by ballot, and a plurality of votes shall make a choice."[71] In electing committee members, each senator voted for as many members as places on the committee, though he might choose to throw away one or more of his votes. On some particularly important or controversial questions, every vote can be accounted for. Thus, in electing the committee of five to which the bill to repeal the judiciary act of 1801 was committed on January 27, 1802, the thirty members present cast 150 votes. On the other hand, on the following day on ballots for four different, less critical three-member committees, the total votes cast ranged from 73 to 78 out of a possible total of 90.[72] Unlike roll-call votes, which were recorded in the public record, ballots for committees were secret. During the debate over the repeal of the judiciary act of 1801, Federalist Senator Gouverneur Morris reported the comments of a Republican leader who privately expressed "Disappointment at the Ballot for a Committee on the judiciary Bill" and indicated that "if the Question on the

[70] Rules of the Senate adopted Mar. 26, 1806, *Annals of Congress*, 9 Cong., 1 Sess., 202.

[71] *Rules for Conducting Business in the Senate of the United States*, December 7th, 1801, Rare Book Division, Lib. Cong.

[72] Senate Records, RG 46, Natl. Archives.

Repeal were taken by Ballot they would certainly lose it but by calling for the Yeas and Nays they could hold every Man to the Point."[73] The suggestion that some members voted differently on the secret ballots for committees than they did on roll-call votes may well be surmised.

If two members had an equal number of votes on a ballot, the person first in alphabetical order on the Senate roster was chosen.[74] The senator with the highest number of votes served as chairman of the committee, and other members were listed in the *Senate Journal* in the order in which they stood in the balloting. The *Senate Journal* does not record the vote for each committee, but a large number of the original vote tallies for committees survive, though they do not appear to have been noticed by scholars. In recording the votes for committees, the Secretary of the Senate and his clerks wrote on the same printed tally forms used for recording the yeas and nays. Through the years the committee tallies have remained, apparently unused, among the tallies of yeas and nays in the National Archives.[75]

The survival of committee tallies thus provides an unusual opportunity to analyze the committee process in the Senate. For those sessions for which the records are essentially complete, the committee service of each member can be determined. By examining the tallies, the votes received by each member for every committee elected during a session can be discovered. These votes provide a key indication of leadership roles. Senator John Quincy Adams noted in his diary in 1805: "As our committees are all chosen by ballot, the influence and weight of a member can be very well measured by the number and importance of those upon which he is placed."[76] In order to analyze this mass of unexplored data, all tallies for committees for one session of each of the four Jeffersonian Congresses have been employed.[77] Tables 6 through 9,

[73] Morris to Nicholas Low, Feb. 12, 1802, Letter Book, Papers of Gouverneur Morris, Lib. Cong.

[74] This was not in the rules but was followed in practice. See Adams, ed., *Memoirs of John Quincy Adams*, Mar. 3, 1805, I, 369.

[75] For the 7th Congress there are some committee tally sheets for both sessions, but they are incomplete; for the 8th Congress the tallies are essentially complete for the first session, but are incomplete for the second session; for the 9th and 10th Congresses the tallies are largely complete for all sessions. Senate Records, RG 46, Natl. Archives.

[76] Adams, ed., *Memoirs of John Quincy Adams*, Jan. 4, 1805, I, 329.

[77] These data have been recorded in machine-readable form and analyzed with computer assistance.

based upon these data, show the leadership role and committee activity of members of the Senate during the first sessions of the Seventh, Eighth, Ninth, and Tenth Congresses.

Committee memberships, committee chairmanships, and the number of votes individual senators received for committees reveal much about Senate leadership. Election to committees showed not only the activity of a senator in handling matters that came to the Senate from the President or the House of Representatives, but also indicated his role in initiating action in the Senate. Generally, a senator who introduced a matter was elected to the committee to which the subject was referred, and he was usually named chairman. During the first session of the Eighth Congress, thirty committees can be identified as resulting from the initiative of a particular member; of these, twenty-two were chaired by the originating senator, and on only one such committee was that member not included.[78] Election to committees also indicated attendance in the Senate, though attendance alone did not insure committee duty. Occasionally a vote was recorded for a member who was not present, but it was so unusual as to indicate that the practice was to vote only for members attending on the day a committee was named. This is confirmed by a comparison of roll-call votes and committee ballots taken on the same day. An analysis of the following tables, together with an examination of the composition of each committee, yields useful insights into the operation of the Senate.

The most striking observation is the extent to which the Senate committee work was done by a group of leading senators. In order to provide a systematic basis for examining this leadership role throughout the period of Jefferson's administration, the role of the eight leading senators in terms of committee service has been examined in each of four sessions. In a Senate consisting of thirty-two members from 1801 to 1803 and of thirty-four members from 1803 to 1809, this leadership group of eight represents one-fourth of the Senate membership and tends to include most of the active Senate leaders in any one session.

The extent to which the eight leading senators dominated the committee structure in each of the four sessions examined is demonstrated by Table 10. In the session of 1801-1802 these eight senators filled 53 percent of the committee seats, held 67 percent

[78] These figures are based on a study of the *Senate Journal* and the *Annals of Congress*.

TABLE 6. MEMBERSHIP ON SENATE COMMITTEES, SEVENTH
CONGRESS, FIRST SESSION, 1801-1802[a]

Member's Name (in order of number of committees elected to)	State	Party	Votes on 20 Extant Ballots[b]	Number of Committees Elected to	Number of Committees Chaired
Tracy, U.	Conn.	F	135	35	11
Baldwin, A.	Ga.	R	92	26	10
Bradley, S.	Vt.	R	15	25	12
Nicholas, W.	Va.	R	74	20	6
Anderson, J.	Tenn.	R	89	18	8
Brown, J.	Ky.	R	41	15	4
Jackson, J.	Ga.	R	83	14	6
Breckinridge, J.	Ky.	R	70	14	3
Logan, G.	Pa.	R	66	12	2
Clinton, D.	N. Y.	R	0	12	2
Ellery, C.	R. I.	R	61	11	2
Dayton, J.	N. J.	F	49	11	1
Mason, S.	Va.	R	40	10	4
Foster, D.	Mass.	F	31	10	1
Mason, J.	Mass.	F	49	9	4
Franklin, J.	N. C.	R	6	8	4
Ogden, A.	N. J.	F	25	8	1
Morris, G.	N. Y.	F	52	7	2
Wright, R.	Md.	R	27	7	1
Howard, J.	Md.	F	41	6	0
Stone, D.	N. C.	R	34	6	0
Cocke, W.	Tenn.	R	50	4	2
Colhoun, J.	S. C.	R	36	3	1
Foster, T.	R. I.	R	22	3	1
Sheafe, J.	N. H.	F	37	3	0
Hillhouse, J.	Conn.	F	35	3	0
Sumter, T.	S. C.	R	20	3	0
Wells, W.	Del.	F	15	3	0
Olcott, S.	N. H.	F	19	2	1
Ross, J.	Pa.	F	13	2	0
Chipman, N.	Vt.	F	45	1	1
White, S.	Del.	F	32	0	0

[a] Committee membership has been compiled from the Senate manuscript roster "Committees, 1st Session, 7th Congress," Senate Records, RG 46, Natl. Archives; the roster has been collated with the Senate Journal.

[b] Only twenty ballots have been found for Senate committees during the first session of the Seventh Congress. This figure therefore has very restricted value, but the fact that each of the eight senators in the highest quartile in total votes ranked within the highest eleven in number of committee assignments for the entire session suggests that the twenty ballots are useful.

TABLE 7. MEMBERSHIP ON SENATE COMMITTEES, EIGHTH CONGRESS, FIRST SESSION, 1803-1804

Member's Name (in order of number of committees elected to)	State	Party	Total Votes[a]	Number of Committees Elected to	Number of Committees Chaired
Baldwin, A.	Ga.	R	474	41	7
Smith, S.	Md.	R	488	32	14
Tracy, U.	Conn.	F	485	31	16
Breckinridge, J.	Ky.	R	438	28	8
Bradley, S.	Vt.	R	454	25	11
Jackson, J.	Ga.	R	422	25	7
Anderson, J.	Tenn.	R	306	25	4
Dayton, J.	N. J.	F	336	15	1
Franklin, J.	N. C.	R	278	15	5
Nicholas, W.	Va.	R	202	14	5
Stone, D.	N. C.	R	240	13	0
Venable, A.	Va.	R	213	11	2
Armstrong, J.	N. Y.	R	175	11	1
Adams, J. Q.	Mass.	F	193	10	3
Wright, R.	Md.	R	174	10	4
Worthington, T.	Ohio	R	192	8	5
Ellery, C.	R. I.	R	152	8	1
Smith, I.	Vt.	R	211	7	1
Cocke, W.	Tenn.	R	137	5	2
Brown, J.	Ky.	R	115	5	0
Logan, G.	Pa.	R	137	4	0
Pickering, T.	Mass.	F	138	3	1
Smith, J.	Ohio	R	112	3	2
Maclay, S.	Pa.	R	107	2	0
Wells, W.	Del.	F	84	2	0
Butler, P.	S. C.	R	82	2	2
Clinton, D.	N. Y.	R	38	2	0
Smith, J.	N. Y.	R	27	2	0
White, S.	Del.	F	84	1	0
Potter, S.	R. I.	R	57	1	1
Sumter, T.	S. C.	R	48	1	1
Hillhouse, J.	Conn.	F	124	0	0
Plumer, W.	N. H.	F	89	0	0
Condit, J.	N. J.	R	58	0	0
Taylor, J.	Va.	R	41	0	0
Bailey, T.	N. Y.	R	38	0	0
Olcott, S.	N. H.	F	35	0	0

[a] This figure does not include three committees reported in the *Senate Journal* for which ballots have not been located.

TABLE 8. MEMBERSHIP ON SENATE COMMITTEES, NINTH CONGRESS,
FIRST SESSION, 1805-1806

Member's Name (in order of number of committees elected to)	State	Party	Total Votes[a]	Number of Committees Elected to	Number of Committees Chaired
Baldwin, A.	Ga.	R	746	70	9
Tracy, U.	Conn.	F	786	60	11
Anderson, J.	Tenn.	R	606	39	15
Mitchill, S.	N. Y.	R	553	38	15
Bradley, S.	Vt.	R	595	36	12
Smith, S.[b]	Md.	R	464	30	12
Adams, J. Q.	Mass.	F	468	28	3
Worthington, T.	Ohio	R	331	23	10
Wright, R.	Md.	R	320	16	4
Logan, G.	Pa.	R	312	12	5
Sumter, T.	S. C.	R	344	11	2
Stone, D.	N. C.	R	242	11	2
Smith, J.	Ohio	R	161	8	4
Bayard, J.	Del.	F	145	7	4
Adair, J.	Ky.	R	179	6	1
Smith, I.	Vt.	R	263	5	2
Moore, A.	Va.	R	201	5	0
Maclay, S.	Pa.	R	225	4	2
Turner, J.	N. C.	R	209	4	2
White, S.	Del.	F	206	4	1
Kitchell, A.	N. J.	R	196	4	1
Hillhouse, J.	Conn.	F	134	4	1
Pickering, T.	Mass.	F	138	3	0
Jackson, J.[c]	Ga.	R	61	3	0
Gilman, N.	N. H.	R	171	2	0
Thruston, B.	Ky.	R	158	2	1
Smith, J.	N. Y.	R	129	2	0
Smith, D.	Tenn.	R	103	2	0
Condit, J.	N. J.	R	157	1	0
Gaillard, J.	S. C.	R	123	1	1
Plumer, W.	N. H.	F	80	0	0
Howland, B.	R. I.	R	76	0	0
Fenner, J.	R. I.	R	44	0	0
Giles, W.	Va.	R	absent		

[a] This figure does not include two committees reported in the *Senate Journal* for which ballots have not been located.

[b] Samuel Smith presided over the Senate as president pro tempore from Dec. 2 to Dec. 16, 1805, and from Mar. 18 to Apr. 21, 1806, in the absence of Vice-President Clinton. Since Smith did not serve on committees during those periods, his leadership role was thus higher than this record indicates.

[c] Jackson was ill during much of the session and died Mar. 19, 1806, before the session ended.

TABLE 9. MEMBERSHIP ON SENATE COMMITTEES, TENTH CONGRESS, FIRST SESSION, 1807-1808

Member's Name (in order of number of committees elected to)	State	Party	Total Votes	Number of Committees Elected to	Number of Committees Chaired
Adams, J. Q.	Mass.	F	699	54	11
Bradley, S.	Vt.	R	510	48	6
Anderson, J.	Tenn.	R	564	46	17
Smith, S.	Md.	R	454	28	16
Gregg, A.	Pa.	R	380	23	5
Mitchill, S.	N. Y.	R	348	19	12
Franklin, J.	N. C.	R	293	17	3
Tiffin, E.	Ohio	R	274	15	3
Sumter, T.	S. C.	R	272	15	1
Giles, W.[a]	Va.	R	257	13	6
White, S.	Del.	F	229	11	3
Reed, P.	Md.	R	157	10	6
Pope, J.	Ky.	R	240	9	3
Crawford, W.	Ga.	R	234	9	2
Gilman, N.	N. H.	R	213	9	1
Milledge, J.	Ga.	R	197	7	2
Thruston, B.	Ky.	R	167	6	0
Robinson, J.	Vt.	R	106	6	1
Maclay, S.	Pa.	R	173	4	1
Turner, J.	N. C.	R	189	3	1
Hillhouse, J.	Conn.	F	143	3	1
Gaillard, J.	S. C.	R	139	3	0
Kitchell, A.	N. J.	R	135	3	0
Condit, J.	N. J.	R	115	3	0
Bayard, J.	Del.	F	79	3	0
Mathewson, E.	R. I.	R	66	3	1
Moore, A.	Va.	R	129	2	1
Smith, D.	Tenn.	R	127	2	1
Smith, J.	N. Y.	R	110	2	0
Pickering, T.	Mass.	F	104	2	0
Goodrich, C.	Conn.	F	93	2	1
Howland, B.	R. I.	R	68	1	0
Jones, G.	Ga.	R	24	1	0
Parker, N.	N. H.	R	81	0	0
Smith, J.	Ohio	R	1	0	0

[a] Giles did not take his seat until Jan. 7, 1808; the session had begun Oct. 26, 1807. Had he been present from the beginning of the session, his place on the list undoubtedly would have been higher.

TABLE 10. THE LEADERSHIP GROUP AND SENATE COMMITTEES, 1801-1808

Congress and Session	Total Number of Committees Elected	Committees Controlled by Majority of Leading Eight Senators		Committees Without a Leading Eight Member		Total Number of Committee Seats	Committee Seats Filled by Leading Eight Senators		Total Number of Committee Chairmanships	Chairmanships Filled by Leading Eight Senators	
	No.	No.	Percent	No.	Percent		No.	Percent		No.	Percent
7th Cong., 1st Sess., 1801-1802	97	50	52	12	12	311	167	53	90	60	67
8th Cong., 1st Sess., 1803-1804	116	76	66	14	12	362	222	61	104	68	65
9th Cong., 1st Sess., 1805-1806	133	102	77	3	2	442	325	76	120	87	72
10th Cong., 1st Sess., 1807-1808	109	83	76	4	4	382	250	65	105	73	70

of the committee chairmanships, and composed a majority on 52 percent of the committees elected. In the 1803-1804 session this group held 61 percent of the committee places, 65 percent of the chairmanships, and composed a majority on 66 percent of the committees. The increasing influence of this group was especially marked in the 1805-1806 session when the leading eight senators filled 76 percent of the committee seats, 72 percent of the chairmanships, and formed a majority on 77 percent of the committees. Their role was slightly less in the 1807-1808 session with 65 percent of the committee seats, but they chaired 70 percent of the committees and had a majority on 76 percent of the committees.

The leadership group was a highly stable group in the Jeffersonian Senate. In each of the sessions examined in the Eighth, Ninth, and Tenth Congresses, at least five of the eight leading senators had been among the eight leaders in the preceding Congress. The continuity of Senate leadership can be seen in Table 11, which shows the eight most active Senate leaders, as identified by committee service, during the first session of each of the four Congresses. Sixteen senators filled the thirty-two places of leadership. Anderson and Bradley were key leaders throughout all eight years; Baldwin, Smith, and Tracy were leading members in three consecutive Congresses; and Adams, Breckinridge, Jackson, and Mitchill appear in leadership roles in two consecutive Congresses. Only six senators are found as leaders in a single session, and three of these were in the last Congress. Furthermore, if the lowest-ranked senator in each list were dropped, three of the six single-session leaders would be eliminated.

Because only first sessions are analyzed, a few Senate leaders are not adequately recognized. The most noticeable example is William Branch Giles of Virginia, who took his seat in the second session of the Eighth Congress but was absent because of illness during the first session of the Ninth Congress. Giles's late arrival for the first session of the Tenth Congress also kept his name from appearing higher on the roster based on committee service. In general, however, the lists are an appropriate means of identifying leaders and showing continuity of leadership. Part of the continuity of Senate leadership resulted from the six-year term of senators. At the same time, during the eight-year period under study, six of the sixteen senators listed in Table 11 were reelected.[79] Deaths and resignations changed Senate leadership more than the election process.

[79] Tracy, Baldwin, Bradley, Anderson, Smith, and Franklin.

TABLE 11. LEADING SENATORS IN COMMITTEE SERVICE, 1801-1808

7th Congress, 1st Session (1801-1802)	8th Congress, 1st Session (1803-1804)	9th Congress, 1st Session (1805-1806)	10th Congress, 1st Session (1807-1808)
Uriah Tracy (1)* (F., Conn.)	Tracy (3)	Tracy (2)	(died 1807)
Abraham Baldwin (2) (R., Ga.)	Baldwin (1)	Baldwin (1)	(died 1807)
Stephen R. Bradley (3) (R., Vt.)	Bradley (5)	Bradley (5)	Bradley (2)
Wilson C. Nicholas (4) (R., Va.)	(resigned 1804)		
Joseph Anderson (5) (R., Tenn.)	Anderson (7)	Anderson (3)	Anderson (3)
John Brown (6) (R., Ky.)			
James Jackson (7) (R., Ga.)	Jackson (6)	(died 1806)	
John Breckinridge (8) (R., Ky.)	Breckinridge (4)	(appointed Attorney General, 1805)	
	Samuel Smith (2) (R., Md.)	Smith (6)	Smith (4)
	Jonathan Dayton (8) (F., N.J.)		
		Samuel L. Mitchill (4) (R., N.Y.)	Mitchill (6)
		John Quincy Adams (7) (F., Mass.)	Adams (1)
		Thomas Worthington (8) (R., Ohio)	
			Andrew Gregg (5) (R., Pa.)
			Jesse Franklin (7) (R., N.C.)
			Edward Tiffin (8) (R., Ohio)

* (Numbers) indicate ranking by number of committees elected to.

The Republican party domination of the Senate leadership is clear; never did more than two Federalists appear among the top eight leaders. However, Federalist Senator Tracy led all senators in committee posts during the first session of the Seventh Congress, chaired more committees than any Republican during the first session of the Eighth Congress, and remained among the top three Senate leaders until his death in 1807.

During much of the period of Jefferson's presidency, Senate leadership was disproportionately in the hands of members from the less populous states. In the sessions of 1801-1802 and 1803-1804 senators from Georgia, Kentucky, Tennessee, and Vermont were especially prominent, and Senators Anderson of Tennessee and Bradley of Vermont were among the leading members from 1801 to 1809. On the other hand, Nicholas of Virginia was a leading figure in the 1801-1802 session, and Smith of Maryland was a key Republican leader from 1803 on, while Mitchill of New York joined the leaders soon after he was transferred from the House in 1804.

The first session of the Ninth Congress, 1805-1806, represents the highest level of domination of the Senate committee system by a group of eight leading senators, and it seems appropriate to single out this session for scrutiny. Eight senators filled 325 of the 442 committee places assigned during the session and held 87 of the 120 committee chairmanships.[80] Thus, one-fourth of the senators filled three-fourths of the committee assignments and nearly the same proportion of committee chairmanships. Senator Baldwin of Georgia served on over half of all the committees named during the session, and Senator Tracy of Connecticut was not far behind with membership on 45 percent of the committees. When the composition of all Senate committees during the session is examined, the domination of the Senate by the group of eight senators with the highest committee-service scores appears extraordinary. The Senate practice of naming five-member committees (and in a few cases seven-member committees) to consider major subjects provides a reliable basis for determining which committees were most important. Twenty-four such committees were chosen during the session; seven of these were composed entirely from the leadership group, and on all but three of the twenty-four

[80] Committees to call on the President, joint committees, and conference committees are not included as chaired committees. The number of committees elected totaled 133. See Table 8 above.

committees the eight leaders had a majority. Of the 126 seats on these committees, the eight senators occupied 96. Since the leadership group dominated the committees that considered the major business before the Senate, it might be suspected that the leaders left lesser matters to be dealt with by other members. But the records do not show this to be the case. Instead, they reveal that these eight men dominated the routine committee assignments also. Of the 133 committees elected during the first session of the Ninth Congress, 102 were controlled by a majority of members who were among the top eight leaders. Moreover, at least one of the eight leading senators was on virtually every committee chosen during the session. The Senate place on the joint Committee on Enrolled Bills, a laborious assignment, went to a low-ranking member, Senator Gilman of New Hampshire, who was serving his first session in the upper house. Other than this, there were only two committees which did not include at least one of the eight leading senators.

If one adds to the top eight committeemen the four next most active senators, these twelve senators did most of the work for the thirty-three members in attendance. Not only did John Quincy Adams recognize the influence of members who dominated the Senate's committees, he also understood the work involved. "As much of the labor of business is transacted in committees," he observed, "an exemption from those which are important is also an exemption from toil, and leaves proportionable leisure."[81] The prominence of Adams's distinctive handwriting in the manuscript papers of Senate committee records indicates that he knew from experience what he was saying.

There was some recognition of expertise within the leading group. Thus Senators Mitchill (New York), Adams (Massachusetts), Baldwin (Georgia), Smith (Maryland), and Tracy (Connecticut) were prominent on committees to which matters relating to commerce and manufactures were referred, while Worthington (Ohio) and Anderson (Tennessee) were not likely to be found on such committees. On the other hand, committees dealing with public lands and the territories were led by Baldwin (Georgia), Tracy (Connecticut), Worthington (Ohio), Bradley (Vermont), and Anderson (Tennessee), while Mitchill, Adams, and Smith were rarely elected to such committees. Committees dealing with foreign relations were dominated by Baldwin, Smith, Tracy, Adams, and Mitchill.[82] With a small group of leading men,

[81] Adams, ed., *Memoirs of John Quincy Adams*, Jan. 4, 1805, I, 329-330.
[82] See also Ralston Hayden, *The Senate and Treaties, 1789-1817: The*

each was likely to be found on committees in several areas, but, despite overlapping, the groupings indicate that certain persons tended to be elected to committees in particular areas.

The role of Tracy in the Senate leadership is of peculiar interest because he was a Federalist in a strongly Republican Senate. Toward the end of the 1805-1806 session, Jefferson noted that the absence of Giles of Virginia, who had been a Republican leader in the Senate during the preceding session, had been "a most serious misfortune," explaining: "A majority of the Senate means well. But Tracy and Bayard are too dexterous for them, and have very much influenced their proceedings. Tracy has been of nearly every committee during the session, and for the most part the chairman, and of course drawer of the reports. Seven federalists voting always in phalanx, and joined by some discontented republicans, some oblique ones, some capricious, have so often made a majority, as to produce very serious embarrassment to the public operations."[83] While Jefferson's comments exaggerated Tracy's role, the figures in Table 8 show the basis for his observation. That Tracy's influential leadership position resulted from a combination of Federalist and discontented Republicans votes cannot be verified, since there are no records which show how each member voted in the balloting for committees—only the final tallies survive. However, Senator Adams saw Tracy's talents as a legislator as the major source of his influence. "Mr. Tracy shows in all his public conduct great experience, and a thorough familiarity with the *order* and course of legislative proceedings," Adams observed. "His manner is peculiarly accommodating and conciliatory; his command of temper exemplary. In public affairs, it appears to me, there is no quality more useful and important than good humor, because it operates continually to soften the asperities which are continually rising in collisions of adverse interests and opinions; and this quality Tracy possesses in a high degree."[84]

The qualities that Adams observed may well explain why Tracy was so frequently a member of conference committees. Of the eight conference committees elected by the Senate during the first session of the Ninth Congress, Tracy was on seven. (The only one on which he did not serve related to a private claim.) While all

Development of the Treaty-Making Functions of the United States Senate during Their Formative Period (New York, 1920), p. 181.

[83] Jefferson to Wilson Cary Nicholas, Apr. 13, 1806, Ford, ed., *Jefferson Writings*, VIII, 435.

[84] Adams, ed., *Memoirs of John Quincy Adams*, Dec. 7, 1805, I, 377.

of the other conference-committee members were among the top group of active committee members, no other senator served on more than two conference committees. Jefferson may have been correct in suggesting that Tracy attracted the votes of all Federalists and discontented Republicans, but Tracy often showed broader support. On a ballot for a conference committee of two members on April 18, 1806, on which forty-eight votes were cast —indicating that at least twenty-four senators voted—Tracy received nineteen votes. On a similar ballot, in which at least twenty senators voted, Tracy received eighteen votes.

While the tabulations of ballots for committees are revealing of the sources of leadership, they are equally revealing of the lack of participation in Senate business by some members. During the first session of the Ninth Congress, three of the thirty-three senators attending never were elected to any committee, and two were on only one committee. Ten of the thirty-three members never chaired a committee during the session. While some of these low-service members were high absentees, others like Senator Plumer were regular in attendance.[85] Plumer, in fact, received at least one vote on 60 out of the 133 ballots recorded during the session, but he never received more than three votes and that only on three ballots. While in an unusual instance a member might win a committee assignment with three votes, Plumer never came close. He rarely participated in the debates on the floor, and this silence on the floor more than his Federalism may explain his absence from committees. Lack of talent may well account for the low committee service of some members. Reporting on the Ninth Congress, George Hoadley, the Washington correspondent of the *United States Gazette*, found a "great dearth of talents" in the House of Representatives, but observed that "the Senate is very respectable in point of talents. The New Jersey and Rhode Island senators are miserable creatures," he wrote, "but there is a large portion of talents in that body."[86] It is interesting to note that in committee assignments in the Ninth Congress, the Rhode Island and New Jersey senators are low on the list. Indeed, the two senators from Rhode Island are the two lowest members—neither was elected to a single committee during the session examined. One New Jersey senator was

[85] Plumer's biographer writes that "no senator was more punctual and constant in his attendance than Plumer." Lynn W. Turner, *William Plumer of New Hampshire, 1759-1850* (Chapel Hill, N. C., 1962), p. 100.

[86] George Hoadley to Jeremiah Evarts, Feb. 5, 1807, Photostat File E.E.E., Va. Hist. Soc.

named to four committees, while his colleague served on only one committee.

The most active senators in the Ninth Congress were among the most experienced members of that body. Baldwin had ten years' service in the House and six in the Senate; Tracy had been in the House three years and in the Senate for nine; Bradley had eight years in the Senate. Although Smith had only two years in the Senate, he had served ten years in the House. Mitchill with one year in the Senate had served three years in the House. Adams and Worthington, the two members with the lowest scores in the top group, each had served two years in the Senate. Previous experience in the national legislature did not insure a leadership role. Hillhouse, a Connecticut Federalist, had served five years in the House and nine in the Senate but won election to only four committees, and the only committee he chaired was on a private claim. On the other hand, most of the members in the lowest quarter of the list of committee assignments were among the senators with the least experience in Congress.

While committee posts were heavily concentrated in a few hands, there was a high level of participation in the balloting for committees and a wide distribution of votes. Votes for committee membership were never confined to the members winning election. Sometimes one person would receive a large vote and the remainder would be scattered; on other ballots votes would be concentrated on three or five members with some scattered votes. At times the votes were so widely distributed that a member might become a committee chairman with as few as five or six votes, and on one ballot, for example, the three committee members received four votes each.[87] There were many ballots on which numerous members received one or two votes. Yet, whatever the voting pattern, the process resulted in the repeated election of the same men.

How many committees were arranged informally prior to balloting is impossible to discover, but there is some evidence to suggest that at times this must have been done. Senator Adams noted in 1806: "When the New York memorial was presented, Wright wanted it to lie over till the next day, for the purpose of having the committee men agreed upon out of doors, by the *party*."[88] In this case the motion did not carry, but it may be supposed that in

[87] Committee on a bill concerning the sale of public lands, Mar. 11, 1808, 10 Cong., 1 Sess., Senate Records, RG 46, Natl. Archives.

[88] Adams, ed., *Memoirs of John Quincy Adams*, Jan. 15, 1806, I, 385.

other instances matters were delayed to allow time for consultations before committees were elected.

The role of party in the election of committees is indicated by a comparison of party strength in the Senate with the proportion of votes received by members of each party in the balloting. Table 12 shows that both parties won votes roughly proportionate to their strength in the Senate. The proportion of the total vote received by each party in most cases was also closer to the relative strength of the two parties than was the proportion of committee seats held by members of the two parties. The figures indicate that the dominant Republican party allowed Federalists their full proportion of committee seats only when the Federalist strength in the Senate was the weakest, which also was when Republican party unity was weakest. In the 1801-1802 session when the Federalists held 44 percent of the Senate seats, they won only 32 percent of the committee seats; in the 1807-1808 session when the Federalists had 18 percent of the Senate seats, they had 20 percent of the committee places.

In analyzing the role of party, it is useful to look at the party composition of individual committees. These data are summarized in Table 13.

Together Tables 12 and 13 display the extent of the Republican domination of the Senate committee system. Only in the Seventh Congress, when the Republican majority in the Senate was 56 percent, did the Federalists control any significant number of committees. By the Eighth Congress the Republican majority had risen to 74 percent, and the Republicans controlled nearly all of the committees and totally excluded Federalists from over half of the committees. The Eighth Congress represents the highest level of Republican domination of the committee system; and it came during a period when the Republican party enjoyed a high degree of unity. Although the Republican majority in the Senate increased to 79 percent in the first session of the Ninth Congress and reached 82 percent in the Tenth Congress, internal Republican divisions during Jefferson's second term contributed to greater Federalist participation in committees. This increase, however, did not significantly alter the overwhelming control of most Senate committees by Republicans.

The Senate system of electing select committees by ballot was unchallenged during the period from 1801 to 1809;[89] and, though

[89] The first departure from the practice of electing committees in the

TABLE 12. PARTY DIVISIONS IN SENATE COMMITTEE ELECTIONS, 1801-1808

Senate Session and Date	Party Strength		Total Votes Cast	Votes for Repub.	Votes for Fed.	Committee Seats Filled		
	Repub.	Fed.				Total Number	Won by Repubs.	Won by Feds.
7th Cong. 1st Sess., 1801-1802	18 (56%)	14 (44%)	1,404[a]	839 (60%)	565 (40%)	311	213 (68%)	98 (32%)
8th Cong. 1st Sess., 1803-1804	25 (74%)	9 (26%)	6,984	5,416 (78%)	1,568 (22%)	362	300 (83%)	62 (17%)
9th Cong. 1st Sess., 1805-1806	26[b] (79%)	7 (21%)	8,926	6,969 (78%)	1,957 (22%)	442	336 (76%)	106 (24%)
10th Cong. 1st Sess., 1807-1808	28 (82%)	6 (18%)	7,370	6,023 (82%)	1,347 (18%)	382	307 (80%)	75 (20%)

[a] Total is on 20 extant ballots for this session.
[b] Elected strength was 27 Republicans, but one Republican senator was absent during the entire session.

TABLE 13. PARTY COMPOSITION OF SENATE COMMITTEES, 1801-1808

Senate Session and Date	Committees Having a Republican Majority	Committees Having a Federalist Majority	Committees Evenly Divided	Total Committees	Committees With No Federalists	Committees With No Republicans
7th Cong., 1st Sess., 1801-1802	70	23	4	97	20	1
8th Cong., 1st Sess., 1803-1804	106	4	6	116	60	0
9th Cong., 1st Sess., 1805-1806	118	8	7	133	49	1
10th Cong., 1st Sess., 1807-1808	102	7	0	109	47	1

some differentiation of functions among select committees was developing, no standing committees of a legislative character were created. The smaller membership of the Senate and less pressing calendar of business permitted the election of committees that the larger House with a fuller calendar would have found excessively time-consuming. The expanding structure of standing committees in the House became more firmly established during the Jeffersonian years, setting the pattern that the Senate would later follow. Although different procedures prevailed in the House of Representatives and the Senate, a committee system occupied a central place in the legislative apparatus of each house, providing an orderly and workable structure for managing the legislative business and playing a crucial role in the process of government.

Senate came in 1823. See George H. Haynes, *The Senate of the United States: Its History and Practice*, 2 vols. (Boston, 1938), I, 273-274.

XI. A Deliberative Body

THE HOUSE OF REPRESENTATIVES IN 1801 WAS composed of 106 members; in 1803, following the new apportionment under the second census and the admission of Ohio as a state, the membership increased to 142. No further additions were made during Jefferson's presidency. After the admission of Ohio, the Union embraced seventeen states, of which the most populous was Virginia with twenty-two members in the House of Representatives, followed by Pennsylvania with eighteen, and Massachusetts and New York, each with seventeen members. Each of the four Congresses under Jefferson contained a sizable number of new members, though the proportion was greatest in the two Congresses of Jefferson's first term. In the Seventh Congress, which met in 1801 following the Republican sweep in the elections of 1800, 52 of the 106 House members had not been in the preceding Congress. In the newly apportioned Eighth Congress in 1803, 72 of the 142 House members had not been in the preceding Congress. With the membership of the House remaining at 142, the Ninth Congress had 50 new members in 1805 and the Tenth Congress, 48 in 1807.[1]

Most members of the House of Representatives, whether newly elected or returning members, had had legislative experience at the state level. In the Seventh Congress 74 percent of the members had previously served in a state legislature, the average period of service being just under five years. Fifty-seven percent of the representatives had previously been in Congress, almost all of them serving in the House. Only one member had served in the Senate. The number of years of congressional service ranged from one to ten years, with the average slightly over four years. Three members of the House in 1801 had been in the First Congress, but none had served continuously since 1789. Only 11 percent of the members had had no previous legislative experience. The age of the representatives ranged from twenty-five to sixty-seven, with

---

[1] Membership in each Congress is that at the opening session. If an elected member resigned or died before taking his seat, he is not considered as a member. *Biographical Directory of the American Congress, 1774-1971* (Washington, D. C., 1971).

the average age of members of the House in 1801 being forty-four years. Seventy-three percent of the House membership was under fifty years of age.[2]

Since the membership in the Senate increased only upon the addition of new states, the only change during Jefferson's presidency came after the admission of Ohio in 1803, when the Senate increased from thirty-two to thirty-four members. The provisions of the Constitution made the Senate a continuing body, where at least two-thirds of the membership had normally served in the previous session. Although long service in the Senate was not yet common, the Senate consisted of experienced legislators, and the level of experience tended to increase with each session. In 1801 71 percent of the senators could record previous service in one of the two houses of Congress, and 65 percent had served in the legislature of one of the states. Only 13 percent had had no previous legislative experience. The years of previous congressional service of individual members ranged from one to twelve—the maximum that anyone could have served since the organization of Congress in 1789. The average length of prior congressional service by senators who had been in the House or the Senate was slightly over six years.

In each of the subsequent Congresses that assembled under Jefferson, the experience level in the Senate was even higher. The percentage of senators who had previously served in Congress increased from 71 percent in 1801 to 81 percent in 1803 and soared to 88 percent in 1805 before dropping back to 80 percent in 1807. The number of senators with no previous legislative experience dropped from four (13 percent) in 1801 to two in 1803, and there was only one unexperienced member in 1805 and in 1807.

The Senate was not an assemblage of old men in the Jeffersonian years. In 1801, 87 percent of the Senate membership was under fifty years of age and only 6 percent (two senators) was above fifty-five. The average age drifted upward from forty-five in 1801 to forty-nine in 1807, but 51 percent of the Senate was under fifty in 1807 and 86 percent was under sixty. The oldest man in the Senate in 1801 was Thomas Sumter at sixty-seven, and at seventy-three he remained the oldest member in 1807; in the intervening years only one other senator passed the age of seventy.

[2] This summary is based on data in Long, "Jefferson and Congress," pp. 50-52, 405-408.

Both the Senate and the House of Representatives normally convened at eleven each morning, Monday through Friday, and usually adjourned by three in the afternoon, though at times debates continued into the evening. Senate meetings were generally shorter than those of the House and frequently adjourned by two.[3] Near the close of sessions, longer daily meetings became necessary, especially in the House. A month before the end of the second session of the Eighth Congress, the House began meeting at ten each morning and on Saturdays; during the last week of the session, evening meetings were also held, and the final meeting—convening at nine on Sunday morning, March 3, 1805—reassembled at five P.M. to conclude the business of the session.[4]

The roll calls recorded in the journals of the House of Representatives and the Senate indicate a high level of participation in voting in Congress; this in turn suggests similar levels of attendance. When members were present to vote, they were likely to have been present during debates, for they had no offices to which to retreat between roll calls. Tables 14 and 15 show the levels of voting participation in both houses during the Congresses of Jefferson's presidency. In the four Congresses from 1801 to 1809 a level of participation in voting of 70 percent or better prevailed in the House of Representatives on 67 percent of the roll calls in the Seventh Congress, on 83 percent in the Eighth Congress, on 75 percent in the Ninth Congress, and on 74 percent in the Tenth Congress. In the Senate a 70 percent participation level was maintained or surpassed on 76 percent of the roll calls in the Seventh Congress, on 88 percent in the Eighth Congress, on 99 percent in the Ninth Congress, and on 94 percent in the Tenth Congress. The voting record of senators as a group was thus better than that of representatives, but in neither house did the average participation rate for a Congress fall below 75 percent. During the Tenth Congress, the average reached 84 percent in the Senate.[5]

Although members were not always attentive while debates were in progress and left their seats to gather around the fireplaces, they did attend the debates; and conscientious members regularly put in a full day's work at the Capitol. Explaining the difficulty of keeping up with his correspondence, Delaware's Representative Bayard

[3] Adams, ed., *Memoirs of John Quincy Adams*, I, 269-272.
[4] *House Journal*, v, 116, 119, 130, 150, 169, 173.
[5] Based on roll-call data made available by the Inter-university Consortium for Political Research, Ann Arbor, Michigan.

TABLE 14. VOTING PARTICIPATION IN THE HOUSE OF
REPRESENTATIVES ON RECORD ROLL CALLS
(Seventh Through Tenth Congresses, 1801-1809)[a]

Percentage of Members Voting	7th Congress No. of Roll Calls	Percent	8th Congress No. of Roll Calls	Percent	9th Congress No. of Roll Calls	Percent	10th Congress No. of Roll Calls	Percent
30 to 39.9							1⎫	2
40 to 49.9	1	1					4⎭	
50 to 59.9	11	8	5	4	12	8	15	6
60 to 69.9	34	24	18	13	27	17	43	18
70 to 79.9	42	30	67	51	49	31	72	31
80 to 89.9	49	34	41	31	57	36	95	40
90 to 100	5	3	1	1	13	8	7	3
Total No. of Roll Calls	142		132		158		237	
Average Level of Participation	75%		76%		77%		76%	

TABLE 15. VOTING PARTICIPATION IN THE SENATE ON RECORD ROLL CALLS
(Seventh Through Tenth Congresses, 1801-1809)[a]

Percentage of Members Voting	7th Congress No. of Roll Calls	Percent	8th Congress No. of Roll Calls	Percent	9th Congress No. of Roll Calls	Percent	10th Congress No. of Roll Calls	Percent
50 to 59.9	2	2	2	1				
60 to 69.9	19	22	17	11	1	1	5	6
70 to 79.9	27	31	36	24	21	24	19	21
80 to 89.9	31	35	49	33	47	53	33	36
90 to 100	9	10	46	31	19	22	34	37
Total No. of Roll Calls	88		150		88		91	
Average Level of Participation	76%		81%		83%		84%	

[a] Based on roll-call data made available by the Inter-university Consortium for Political Research, Ann Arbor, Michigan.

said: "The morning is spent on Committees, the day in the House, and the evening generally finds me without much disposition to have recourse to my pen."[6] Before the end-of-the-session rush, mornings and Saturdays were regularly used for committee meetings, ten A.M. being the most common assembling hour.[7] Representative Mitchill indicated that considerable committee business was done on Saturdays. "It is very much a custom for Congress to adjourn its Sessions from Friday untill Monday," he explained. "This is done not thro idleness, but that the Committees to whom business is intrusted may have time for their various employments and mature their Reports. This kind of business cannot be so well done on the other days of the week, because it is the duty of the Members to attend the House."[8] House rules provided that no committee could meet during the sitting of the House, unless by special permission.[9] Many members went to the Capitol on Saturdays even if they had no committee business requiring their attendance. The lack of offices—and in some cases a lack of adequate private quarters—forced the members to use their desks in the legislative chambers for writing letters and other paperwork. The Capitol on Saturdays also became a place to confer and to visit with colleagues. "I am now at my seat in the Representative Chamber and have been already several times interrupted by Members coming up to speak to me," wrote Congressman Mitchill. "This is Saturday, and no business being done in the Hall, the Gentlemen frequent it as they would a Coffee-House or other public room."[10]

Senators and representatives were paid six dollars for each day of attendance while Congress was in session. In addition, members received an allowance of thirty cents per mile for travel to and from Washington for one trip each session. The pay voucher of Senator Bradley of Vermont for the first session of the Seventh Congress showed:[11]

[6] James A. Bayard to Andrew Bayard, Jan. 9, 1802, Elizabeth Donnan, ed., *Papers of James A. Bayard, 1796-1815*, American Historical Association, *Annual Report, 1913* (Washington, D. C., 1915), II, 145.

[7] Abishai Thomas to Samuel Mitchill, Feb. 12, 1802, Letters from Sec. of Navy to Congress, RG 45; William B. Giles to Albert Gallatin, Nov. 12, 1808, Senate Records, RG 46, Natl. Archives; Adams, ed., *Memoirs of John Quincy Adams*, I, 274, 278.

[8] Mitchill to his wife, Jan. 17, 1802, Mitchill Papers, Museum C.N.Y.

[9] *House Journal* (Dec. 17, 1805), v, 203.

[10] Mitchill to his wife, Jan. 28, 1803, Mitchill Papers, Museum C.N.Y.

[11] Senate Records, RG 46, Natl. Archives.

Travel to Congress 490 miles	$ 147.00
Attendance in Congress 133 days	798.00
Travel from Congress returning 490 miles	147.00
	$1,092.00

A few minor emoluments went with the office. Members had the privilege of franking letters and packages not heavier than two ounces.[12] They were promptly supplied with stationery and writing materials upon their arrival in the capital. As a new member in 1801, Representative Mitchill provided a detailed description of the practice, explaining: "Immediately after getting into Lodgings, the Messenger waits upon them with a bundle of *common* letter-paper, *gilt* letter-paper, and *ordinary* drafting paper tied nicely into a bundle with Stationers Tape; he furnishes them also with a parcel of pens ready made and of quills to make more; and with an ink-stand, sand-box, a phial of Ink, a packet of Sand; a Box of Wafers and two Sticks of Sealing Wax."[13] New members were also given sets of the laws of the United States.[14]

Both the House of Representatives and the Senate provided each of its members with subscriptions to three daily newspapers or as many copies of three nondaily papers as equaled three dailies, if a member so selected.[15] Extra copies could be sent to constituents. For some sessions the records kept by the Secretary of the Senate of the newspapers to which each senator subscribed have survived.[16] These rosters provide an unusual opportunity to define one principal source of information for members of Congress and of their constituents. An analysis of the subscription list for the first session of the Eighth Congress shows that thirty-four senators received ninety-five subscriptions to twenty-three different newspapers. The largest group of senators, twenty-two, subscribed to the Washington *National Intelligencer*—a Republican paper whose editor, Samuel Harrison Smith, not only had close access to the administration

[12] Mitchill to his wife, Dec. 9, 1801, Jan. 13, 1802, Mitchill Papers, Museum C.N.Y.

[13] Mitchill to his wife, Dec. 9, 1801, *ibid.*

[14] Jacob Wagner to Samuel A. Otis, Dec. 16 and 17, 1801, Senate Records, RG 46, Natl. Archives.

[15] *Annals of Congress*, 7 Cong., 2 Sess., 275, 282-285; *Senate Journal*, III, 156; IV, 106.

[16] There are rosters for the 1st and 2nd sessions of the 7th Congress and the 1st session of the 8th Congress in Senate Records, RG 46, Natl. Archives. No rosters for the 9th and 10th Congresses have been found.

but also published the fullest record of congressional debates. At first only three of the subscribers were Federalists, but another Federalist, Timothy Pickering, joined the group explaining that "as the National Intelligencer is, unfortunately, the only paper here in which debates in Congress are detailed, I find myself under the necessity of taking it."[17] Five Federalist senators managed without the *National Intelligencer*; all of them subscribed to the *Washington Federalist*, which attracted only three Republican subscribers. Next to the *National Intelligencer* the most widely received newspaper was the Philadelphia *Aurora*, which rivaled Smith's paper as the leading Republican organ in the nation. Eighteen senators, all Republicans, took the *Aurora*. Four senators, all Federalists, subscribed to the competing Philadelphia *Gazette of the United States*, a major Federalist paper. The leading New York Republican print, the *American Citizen*, went to nine senators, all Republicans, while the rival Federalist *New-York Evening Post* attracted two Federalists and one Republican. Only eleven of the thirty-four senators included among their Senate subscriptions a paper from their home state, although Senator Samuel Maclay of Pennsylvania limited his choices to three Pennsylvania papers. Three senators signed up for two subscriptions to the *National Intelligencer*, and one member confined his three subscriptions to it. Although the ninety-five subscriptions listed in the Senate records were divided among twenty-three newspapers, four leading papers—the *National Intelligencer*, the *Aurora*, the *American Citizen*, and the *Washington Federalist*—with sixty-two subscriptions accounted for two-thirds of the Senate total.[18]

As the popularly elected chamber, the House of Representatives attracted wider public attention than the Senate, whose members were chosen by the legislatures of the states. The debates in the House were more extended and received fuller coverage by the press than those of the Senate.[19] Harder-working House members originated more bills and demanded more roll calls. The constitutional provision providing that all revenue bills originate in the House increased both the labor and the power of its members. When Mitchill resigned his seat in the House to enter the Senate in 1804, he wrote to his wife: "Henceforward you will read little

[17] Pickering to William Coleman, Oct. 28, 1803, Pickering Papers, Mass. Hist. Soc.
[18] Lists of newspaper subscriptions in Senate Records, RG 46, Natl. Archives.
[19] Brown, ed., *Plumer's Memorandum*, Mar. 12, 1806, pp. 449-450.

of me in the Gazettes. Senators are less exposed to public view than Representatives. Nor have they near so much hard work and drudgery to perform."[20]

At the same time, there was greater prestige associated with the upper house. The Constitution set a minimum age of thirty for senators and twenty-five for representatives. The role of the Senate in confirming presidential appointments and ratifying treaties gave that body an executive role that the lower house did not have. When Mitchill entered the Senate, he spoke of becoming a member of "the supreme executive Council of the Nation." He saw himself as resigning as one of "the Representatives of the People" and becoming one of "the Senators of the Nation" with "a share of the *Executive* Power." "For," he explained, "besides the performance of Legislative functions, the Senate are the Presidents Council in ratifying Treaties with foreign Nations and in making appointments to office at home."[21] This role of the Senate led foreign ministers to the United States to pay first calls on all senators but to wait for visits from representatives. Senators outranked representatives; their names appeared first in congressional rosters. They sat in *"superb scarlet Chairs* lined with Moroquin leather"; the inkstand and the sandbox that each new senator received as part of his stationery supply were of superior quality to those furnished to members of the House of Representatives.[22] If there was more power in the House, there was more prestige in the Senate; most members who moved from one chamber to the other moved from the House to the Senate. In the Seventh Congress, which met in 1801, only 1 of the 106 members of the House had previously served in the Senate, while 11 of the 32 senators had previously served in the House. During the period of Jefferson's presidency, the upward movement of members from the House to the Senate continued, with nine members leaving the House to enter the Senate and no senator resigning from the Senate to take a seat in the House. The transferees to the Senate included several active House leaders, among them Smith of Maryland, Giles of Virginia, and Mitchill of New York.

While each House acted independently in the consideration of legislation, both representatives and senators kept in close touch with what was happening in the other chamber. Aside from the

[20] Mitchill to his wife, Nov. 26, 1804, Mitchill Papers, Museum C.N.Y.
[21] Mitchill to his wife, Nov. 17 and 26, 1804, *ibid.*
[22] Mitchill to his wife, Nov. 26 and 31, 1804; Jan. 1 and 19, 1805, *ibid.*

formal contact between the House and the Senate in the enactment of legislation, as in conference committees, there was considerable informal contact among senators and representatives who lived in the same boardinghouses, dined at the same tables, and learned daily what had transpired in the other chamber. Most exchanges between senators and representatives regarding pending legislation took place in conversations of which no record was ever made. Only an occasional note or letter indicates the kind of relationship that existed among some members, as when Senator Breckinridge wrote to Representative Nicholson in 1804: "I believe you introduced the inclosed Bill into the House of Representatives. It is opposed here—suggest to me the necessity for it; and referring to the existing laws, whose defects the several sections are intended to remedy. This will save me time I cannot well spare to devote to it by tomorrow, when the Bill will be on its passage."[23] In another instance Representative Mathew Lyon, concerned about the effect on his Kentucky constituents of certain provisions in a bill that had passed the House, wrote to Senator Breckinridge, also from Kentucky, calling attention to what he regarded as objectionable provisions of the bill. Reporting his unsuccessful efforts to get changes made in the House, Lyon put the matter in Breckinridge's hands.[24] It is impossible to trace Breckinridge's role in the changes made in the bill by the Senate, but he was a member of the committee to whom the bill was committed and chairman of the committee to whom it was recommitted; and the final bill did not contain the provisions that Lyon found most objectionable.[25]

The legislative function could no doubt have been speeded up, as some members and executive officers suggested, but the records of Congress reveal a careful process of deliberation. Anyone who examines the working papers of the two houses during this period cannot but be impressed with the methodical procedures employed.

[23] Breckinridge to Nicholson, Mar. 13, 1804, Nicholson Papers, Lib. Cong.

[24] Lyon to Breckinridge, Dec. 20, 1803, Breckinridge Family Papers, Lib. Cong. The spelling *Mathew* Lyon is documented by its use in a circular letter, Apr. 26, 1808, published by Lyon (Essex Institute, Salem, Mass.) and by its use in a magazine published by his son James Lyon. *A Republican Magazine: or Repository of Political Truths*, I (Oct. 1, 1798), 14.

[25] *Annals of Congress*, 8 Cong., 1 Sess., 220, 227, 1253-1258. Reference is to "A bill giving effect to the laws of the U. S. within the territories ceded to the U. S. by the treaty of the 30th of April 1803 between the U. S. and the French Republic, and for other purposes," which passed the Senate with amendments Jan. 14, 1804.

The Senate records are the most revealing in this respect, since the Secretary of the Senate appears to have preserved most of the papers that came into his hands. In cases where the original manuscript drafts of bills have been preserved along with the printed copies, committee reports, and amendments, the painstaking legislative methods are most evident. Senate rules provided that all bills were to be printed after the first reading;[26] the printed drafts of bills were then gone over closely. Printed copies in the Senate files show numerous changes, and when the revisions became extensive, the bill was sent to the printer again for a new printing. Attention was paid not only to the substance of each bill but also to the language, revealing an awareness that in the process of legislating, Congress was preparing a legal document. Most of the work reflected in the records was done in committees, but before decisions were made, all members ordinarily had in their hands printed copies of bills together with printed copies of amendments and other relevent documents. While some members may never have read the documents placed on their desks, as Senator Plumer suggested,[27] the mechanisms for participation were available. The legislative journals and the notations by the Secretary of the Senate on the bills that passed through that house show that there was no routine endorsement of committee recommendations by the full Senate. Many bills after being reported upon by one committee were recommitted to another. Enough members took their responsibilities seriously to ensure a faithful process of legislation, though less deliberation took place toward the end of sessions. "As the close of the session approaches," Senator Adams complained in 1804, "very little attention is paid to the business, and almost everything passes without discussion."[28]

Most nominations submitted to the Senate by the President were acted upon without hearings and without being referred to a committee, but occasionally such procedures were employed. A rare document in the Senate records for the Tenth Congress reports the minutes of the proceedings of a committee considering the nomination of Robert Williams for reappointment as governor of the Mississippi territory. The minutes show that the committee held a full-scale hearing and made a thorough inquiry. In three meetings during a twelve-day period, the committee heard testimony from

[26] *Rules for Conducting the Business of the Senate of the United States*, Dec. 7, 1801, p. 7.
[27] See p. 269 below.
[28] Adams, ed., *Memoirs of John Quincy Adams*, Mar. 23, 1804, I, 311.

the territorial delegate to Congress and several other witnesses, and reviewed at least sixteen letters and other documents from the Mississippi territory before reporting in favor of the nomination.[29] In the case of Secretary of War Dearborn, nominated by Jefferson to be collector of the port of Boston in the closing weeks of his administration, Dearborn was called to testify personally before a Senate committee before his nomination was confirmed.[30]

Although the working papers of the House in the drafting and the enactment of legislation are less full than those of the Senate, the records that survive indicate a systematic process of deliberation. The rules of the House specified procedures to promote the careful examination of all pending legislation. For every bill committed to a Committee of the Whole, where the major consideration of bills took place, the rules provided that the bill be first read throughout and "then again read and debated by clauses." After the bill was reported to the House from the Committee of the Whole, the rules provided that "the bill shall again be subject to be debated and amended by clauses, before a question to engross it be taken."[31] House bills appear to have been regularly printed after the second reading, although there was no such requirement in the rules. As in the Senate, bills that were extensively amended were reprinted before final passage.[32]

In both the House of Representatives and the Senate the principal discussion of matters before Congress took place in a Committee of the Whole. The Senate rules specified that, unless otherwise ordered, all bills on a second reading were to be considered as if the Senate were in a Committee of the Whole before they were to be taken up by the Senate.[33] Unlike the journals of the House

[29] Minutes of the proceedings of the Committee to whom were referred the nominations of Robert Williams and others, Feb. 27–March 10, 1808, Senate Records, RG 26, Natl. Archives; *Senate Executive Journal*, II, 69, 72.

[30] Senate Records, RG 46, Natl. Archives; *Senate Executive Journal*, II, 109.

[31] House rules, Dec. 17, 1805, *House Journal*, V, 203-204.

[32] Few printed bills are found in the House Records for the period in the National Archives, although some bills printed by the House are in the Senate Records. The most useful source for House bills is the microfilm edition of House Bills, 7th-10th Congresses, prepared by the Library of Congress (1965), which also prepared a similar edition of Senate Bills, 7th-10th Congresses.

[33] *Rules for Conducting Business in the Senate of the United States*, Dec. 7, 1801; Rules of the Senate, Mar. 26, 1806, *Annals of Congress*, 9 Cong., 1 Sess., 202.

which regularly indicated the reference of matters to the Committee of the Whole, the Senate journals only occasionally mention a Committee of the Whole; but, as the rules prescribed, every bill was discussed in a Committee of the Whole unless the Senate directed otherwise.

The House regularly referred pending bills and resolutions to a Committee of the Whole for consideration, at which time the Speaker left the chair and appointed a chairman to preside. This procedure provided more opportunity for debate than in the House itself. The House rules provided that no member could speak more than twice on the same subject without permission, nor more than once until every member choosing to speak had spoken, but the rule did not apply to a Committee of the Whole. Until 1805 there was no limitation upon speaking in committee. The revised rules of 1805 provided that no member could speak twice until every member choosing to speak had spoken; after that, members could speak as often as they wished.[34] A Committee of the Whole provided more flexibility in making changes in bills under consideration. All amendments were incorporated into a motion when it was reported to the House,[35] thus simplifying the revision of bills. Since no votes were recorded, the mechanism also offered freedom from roll calls.

The Committee of the Whole had been regularly used during the Federalist-controlled Congresses,[36] but the Republicans made greater use of the procedure after gaining control in 1801. Comments by members and actions recorded in the journals confirm the change.[37] On December 29, 1801, John Randolph moved the adoption of a resolution declaring that it was expedient to reduce the military establishment of the United States. Announcing that he did not wish to precipitate a decision on the subject, he indicated his willingness that the motion be tabled for future consideration, and this was done. On the following day, Randolph moved that the House go into a Committee of the Whole; when this was

[34] House rules, Jan. 7, 1802, *House Journal*, IV, 38-42; *Report of the Committee, Appointed on the Seventeenth Instant to Prepare and Report Such Standing Rules and Orders of Proceeding, As Are Proper to be Observed in this House*, Oct. 20, 1803, p. 15, Rare Book Division, Lib. Cong.; House rules, Dec. 17, 1805, *House Journal*, V, 204.

[35] *Ibid.*, pp. 203-204.

[36] Furlong, "Organization in the House of Representatives, 1789-1801," p. 35.

[37] See Joseph Cooper, *The Origins of the Standing Committees and the Development of the Modern House*, Rice University, *Studies*, LVI, No. 3 (1970), 12.

formed, he submitted the motion that he had made in the House on the preceding day, explaining that "he made the motion in Committee of the Whole as it appeared to be more consonant to the proceedings of the House."[38] The Committee of the Whole agreed to Randolph's resolution and reported it to the House, which concurred and appointed a committee to bring in a bill.

The House, however, did not follow Randolph's model of procedure the next day when Thomas Davis moved for the appointment of a committee to inquire into the expediency of repealing the internal taxes. Davis said that his object in making the motion was that the House should accomplish directly what "had been this session attempted in so circuitous a way as to embarrass and delay its proceedings. He saw no reason for going into a Committee of the Whole, in order to arrive at decisions that might better be made directly by the House itself."[39] After a lengthy debate on whether the subject should be referred to a select committee or a Committee of the Whole, Davis's motion was tabled. The next speaker to rise was Samuel L. Mitchill, who indicated that he wished to offer a resolution proposing that a committee be formed to inquire into the expediency of applying the proceeds of the sale of public vessels to naval purposes. On the suggestion of Speaker Macon, Mitchill moved that the House go into a Committee of the Whole in which he would make his proposed motion. Debate followed on this motion, during which Davis declared that it was "time to determine the propriety of that circuitous mode of procedure, which had been practiced this session."[40] The House then voted to go into a Committee of the Whole, where Mitchill made his motion and it was agreed to and reported to the House. A committee was then appointed. Davis thus was answered that the House wished to follow the circuitous route via a Committee of the Whole.

Although the principal purpose of a Committee of the Whole was to provide for freer discussion and less parliamentary entanglements while measures were being worked out, reference to a Committee of the Whole could also serve as a means of indefinite postponement. A motion might be referred to a Committee of the Whole on Monday next and never taken up at that time, or, if so, it might be postponed for further consideration to a later date and never taken up at that time.[41] Similar postponements could also be achieved without the use of a Committee of the Whole.

[38] *Annals of Congress*, 7 Cong., 1 Sess., 352, 354.
[39] *Ibid.*, 354.   [40] *Ibid.*, 355.
[41] For an example see *House Journal*, v, 104, 110, 111.

The procedures of the early Congresses worked against the introduction of bills which would never be seriously considered. In the House, most matters came before it in the form of resolutions proposing a specific legislative purpose; only after a resolution was debated and adopted was the matter referred to a committee to bring in a bill. It was resolved, for example, "that the laws respecting naturalization ought to be revised and amended," and then a committee was appointed to bring in a bill or bills.[42] In the House a member who wished to initiate legislation proposed a resolution rather than a bill. If the resolution passed, he might be named to the committee to bring in a bill. House rules required a member to obtain permission to bring in a bill,[43] but the rules did not prevent any member from introducing a resolution proposing legislative action.

In the Senate the most common practice in the initiation of a bill was the introduction of a motion that a committee be appointed to inquire into a specific subject and to report by bill or otherwise.[44] It was also a practice in the Senate for members to ask leave to bring in a bill; if granted, which was generally the case, a bill was presented, and then the matter was referred to a committee.[45] The number of bills introduced in the Senate was smaller than the number presented in the House. During the Tenth Congress, for example, 173 bills originated in the House, and 81 of these were passed by the House and sent to the Senate. In comparison, the Senate sent 54 bills which had originated there to the House.[46]

The rules of the House of Representatives provided that five members could demand the previous question, which was to be put in the form "Shall the main question be now put?" Until this was decided, all amendments and further debate on the main question were precluded. Until 1805, no member could speak on a previous question more than once without leave; in the rules modification of 1805, all debate on a previous question was prohibited.[47] While in present-day practice a motion for the previous question is a motion to close debate, the rule was not generally used in this manner in the Jeffersonian Congresses. In his *Manual of Parlia-*

[42] *Annals of Congress*, 7 Cong., 1 Sess. (Dec. 15, 1801), 326.

[43] House rules, Dec. 17, 1805, *House Journal*, v, 203.

[44] The Senate records for the 9th Congress contain numerous such motions on small slips of paper, generally in the handwriting of the person introducing the motion. Senate Records, RG 46, Natl. Archives.

[45] For an example see *Senate Journal*, iii, 427, 429.

[46] *House Journal*, vi, 612-625.

[47] See House rules, Dec. 17, 1805, *ibid.*, v, 201.

mentary Practice, prepared while presiding over the Senate as Vice-President, Jefferson explained the contemporary usage of the rule:

> The proper occasion for the previous question is when a subject is brought forward of a delicate nature as to high personages, etc., or the discussion of which may call forth observations which might be of injurious consequences. Then the previous question is proposed, and in the modern usage the discussion of the main question is suspended and the debate confined to the previous question. The use of it has been extended abusively to other cases, but in these it has been an embarrassing procedure. Its uses would be well answered by other more simple parliamentary forms, and therefore it should not be favored, but restricted within as narrow limits as possible.[48]

In the Tenth Congress, however, Randolph protested that the previous question was being used to prevent debate on resolutions by employing the device to demand a vote on the question of considering a resolution. According to the House rules, when a member made a motion, it was the right of any member to require that it be reduced to writing. Then, according to the Speaker's interpretation of the rules, a previous question became necessary on whether the House would consider the motion or not. Randolph referred to the procedure in April 1808 as having been lately introduced into the House and as a "novel construction of the old rule." He denounced it as "at war with the Constitution itself; it is the engine by which a majority of this House may be enabled at any time to prevent any question from being deliberated within these walls, unless it shall have received their previous sanction. . . . The majority being once fixed, it is utterly impossible for any member, not of that majority, to have any question he may choose to raise, discussed."[49]

Randolph acknowledged that there were superfluous speeches in the House, but he argued that if the purpose were to curtail that abuse, it could be done by preventing a member from speaking more than twice in the Committee of the Whole or more than once in the House on the same question. "Whatever method we take to cure it, for Heaven's sake let us not be excluding one part of the Assembly from having their motions deliberated upon and discussed at all," he exclaimed.[50] Richard Stanford, supporting

[48] Jefferson, *Manual of Parliamentary Practice*, Section xxxiv.
[49] *Annals of Congress*, 10 Cong., 1 Sess. (Apr. 1, 1808), 1889.
[50] *Ibid.*, 1889-1890.

Randolph's position, said he was "well acquainted with the history of this padlock upon debate; it was in fact an innovation."[51] John Smilie, replying to Randolph, argued that the member making a motion was at liberty to speak at length in introducing the motion; other members of the House were then "capable of judging for themselves, after so long a preface, whether the motion is of such a nature that it will be proper to consider it."[52] Following the debate on the issue, the House refused to take up two resolutions introduced by Randolph to lift injunctions of secrecy, thus supporting the Speaker's ruling that debate could not be held on the question of whether a resolution was to be considered.[53] The House could, and did, then refuse to debate matters by refusing to agree to consider resolutions presented.

Senate rules until 1806 provided that the previous question should be put when moved and seconded,[54] but the rule was rarely used. In his farewell address to the Senate in March 1805, Vice-President Burr recommended that the rule be eliminated, noting that it had been used only once during his four years as presiding officer and then upon an amendment. He suggested that its purposes were much better answered by the question of indefinite postponement.[55] When the Senate revised its rules in 1806, Burr's advice was followed; the rule was dropped, and no means for cloture was provided.[56]

The role of debates in the legislative process was commonly viewed by participants as of less importance than the operation of committees, and the arguments of debates were generally regarded as less persuasive than the influences of the administration and the pressures of political parties. Some members believed that no votes were ever changed as a result of debates. "The House of Representatives are now engaged in a very interesting debate on the bill from the Senate for repealing the judiciary system of the last session, which is expected to last for many days," Connecticut's Federalist Senator Hillhouse wrote in February 1802, "but I have not the smallest expectation or hope that the vote of a single member will be changed by the most impressive eloquence, or arguments

[51] *Ibid.*, 1890.   [52] *Ibid.*, 1892.   [53] *Ibid.*, 1895-1896.

[54] *Rules for Conducting Business in the Senate of the United States,* Dec. 7, 1801.

[55] Adams, ed., *Memoirs of John Quincy Adams,* Mar. 2, 1805, I, 365.

[56] Rules of the Senate, Mar. 26, 1806, *Annals of Congress,* 9 Cong., 1 Sess., 201. The previous question rule was never restored in the Senate. Haynes, *The Senate of the United States,* I, 394.

the most conclusive. All questions are settled in private meetings, and every member composing the majority of both houses comes pledged to support the measures so agreed on." Writing during the first session after the party turnover in 1801, Hillhouse saw party as the dominant influence. "In the conflict of party," he concluded, "reason and argument are altogether unavailing, and have not the smallest influence in the decision of any question or measure that is taken up in Congress."[57]

Senator Plumer, a New Hampshire Federalist, wrote in 1806:

> The business of speaking in the Senate has become, on most subjects of little importance—and very seldom changes a single vote. This is owing to various causes. I will enumerate a few. All our bills, amendments, the Presidents messages, reports from heads of Departments, committees, and all documents are printed and laid on our tables daily. These we read, and those who are industrious and independent form their own opinions on each subject. Some give themselves little trouble, seldom read the documents or even the bills. These have a file leader—a senator—whose opinion is to them oracular and whose vote they implicitly follow. On a few intricate or important subjects, debates are useful and interesting. But in general by the time a senator has been speaking ten minutes it is rare that there is a quorum within the Bar—and many of those that are there, are either writing letters or reading newspapers. At the fire side a majority is seated, and often in a private conversation the question under debate is there settled by a free interchange of opinions. I have done more at one of these private circles in carrying a question than the animation of a Tracy or the eloquent reasoning of an Adams has been able to effect in public discussion.[58]

Plumer's observations must be read in light of the fact that he lacked the self-confidence to participate in Senate debates and rarely spoke on the floor.[59] Plumer might also have added that the tendency of senators to gather around the fireplaces was promoted by the coldness of the chamber. During periods of wintery weather, Senator Mitchill found "little comfort in our grand Senatorial Hall.

[57] Hillhouse to Simeon Baldwin, Feb. 18, 1802, Baldwin Family Papers, Yale Univ.

[58] William Plumer to William Plumer, Jr., Mar. 15, 1806, William Plumer Papers, Lib. Cong.

[59] Turner, *William Plumer*, p. 98.

The room is so spacious and the fire-places so inconveniently placed that it is almost as cold as a barn."[60]

Plumer attributed part of the lack of attention during Senate debates to the absence of listeners in the galleries and stenographers on the floor; if a senator wanted to see one of his speeches printed in the newspapers he had to write it out himself. Plumer noted that "in the other House it is different—galleries are usually attended, frequently crouded, with spectators—Always one, often two, stenographers attend, and their speeches are reported in the gazettes. The house is more numerous—several of them absolutely depend upon their file leaders to direct their vote—Yet I believe even in that House there are few votes changed by the public arguments of the members." But Plumer admitted that "there are indeed a few subjects where discussions, in each house, are useful —where they not only influence the decision but absolutely govern the vote."[61]

Having no offices to which to escape, members tended to remain in the chamber while debates were in progress, even if they gathered around the fireplaces. However, some senators did steal away when there was a lively debate in the House; and when the Senate finished its daily business, some senators stopped by to hear the House debates. Senator Morris recorded in his diary that he attended House debates after the adjournment of the Senate and on a Saturday when the Senate was not in session.[62] Senator Adams indicated that it was his habit to attend the House debates whenever the Senate adjourned early, and numerous entries in his diary testify that he did so with regularity.[63]

In both the House and the Senate, many members thought that there was too much talking. "No important vote can be had but by wading into the night for it," complained Representative Burwell Bassett. "On Thursday they kept us untill daybrake."[64] While such sessions were unusual, Congressman Mitchill reported the House staying in session until nine o'clock in the evening, without any recess for dinner.[65] In April 1808, after Congress had been in ses-

[60] Mitchill to his wife, Jan. 23, 1805, Mitchill Papers, Museum C.N.Y.

[61] Brown, ed., *Plumer's Memorandum*, Mar. 12, 1806, pp. 449-450.

[62] Diary of Gouverneur Morris, Feb. 20 and 27, Mar. 1, 1802, Papers of Gouverneur Morris, Lib. Cong.

[63] Adams, ed., *Memoirs of John Quincy Adams*, I, 267, 277, 279, 284, 317.

[64] Bassett to [St. George Tucker], Jan. 7, 1808 [i.e., 1809], Tucker-Coleman Collection, College of William and Mary.

[65] Mitchill to his wife, Dec. 8, 1803, Mitchill Papers, Museum C.N.Y.

sion since October, Representative William Findley reported: "We are nearing the end of a tedious session. . . . We have postponed 33 bills and several reports most of which might and ought to have been passed had we not talked so much and done so little."[66]

Many persons complained of the slowness of legislative proceedings. "God knows when Congress will rise. I never saw business proceed so slowly," Attorney General Breckinridge wrote to his wife in 1806.[67] More resignedly, Representative Richard Stanford explained: "Large bodies like Congress move slow!"[68] Speaker Macon thought that all the national business could be disposed of in two months instead of the normal three-to-five-month sessions.[69] President Jefferson was convinced that with better floor leadership Congress could shorten its sessions by one month each year, and save thereby thirty thousand dollars per year.[70] But sessions grew no shorter during Jefferson's presidency; in 1807 Macon was still complaining that "Congress seem to be going on in the old way, postponing from day to day."[71]

Many a letter was written from the halls of Congress while an uninspiring debate or lengthy speech was in progress. Mitchill started one such letter "while a Member from Vermont is holding forth in a dull, pedantic and stupifying speech," but before he finished the letter, he was reporting that "the debate is now going on with great zeal and animation."[72] Writing to Nicholson, Randolph explained that his letter was being "written whilst Col. Talmadge of Connecticut is making a long and elaborate Exchequer Speech—or rather trying to read one which he (or some one for him) had previously made."[73] Randolph was one of the few members who could justly complain about dull speeches, for no one accused Randolph of being dull. When he was speaking, both the floor and the gallery were likely to be filled. Listening to a debate

[66] Findley to Joseph Hiester, Apr. 9, 1808, Papers of Joseph Hiester, Gregg Collection, Lib. Cong.

[67] Breckinridge to his wife, Feb. 14, 1806, Breckinridge Family Papers, Lib. Cong.

[68] Stanford to his wife, Feb. 6, 1804, Richard Stanford Personal Papers, Miscellaneous, Lib. Cong.

[69] Nathaniel Macon to Joseph H. Nicholson, Sept. 3, 1803, Nicholson Papers, Lib. Cong.

[70] Jefferson to Caesar A. Rodney, Dec. 31, 1802, Jefferson Papers, Lib. Cong.

[71] Macon to Nicholson, Jan. 6, 1807, Nicholson Papers, Lib. Cong.

[72] Mitchill to his wife, Oct. 25, 1803, Mitchill Papers, Museum C.N.Y.

[73] Randolph to Nicholson, Apr. 17, 1806, Nicholson Papers, Lib. Cong.

dominated by Randolph, a reporter for the *United States Gazette* wrote in 1807: "I never heard a debate so interesting and I should be very willing to come from Connecticut only to attend that debate. . . . Mr. Randolph is by far the most interesting speaker I ever heard. I have often heard good speakers whom I could listen to with pleasure for any length of time, but compared with Mr. Randolph they all dwindle into insignificance."[74] This was praise that was not lightly given by the Connecticut Federalist who otherwise found "a great dearth of talents" in the House of Representatives, particularly in Republican ranks, among whom he found "several who would disgrace any state legislature in the union" and "some dunces who are and I hope ever will be without parallel in Connecticut."[75]

However much visitors and members alike complained of dull speakers and tedious debates, and however much their accounts of congressional proceedings were shaped by partisan attachments, the debates in Congress were regarded as an essential part of the legislative process. Debates on major questions did deal with leading issues. Visitors who filled the galleries when important subjects were before Congress expected to hear the issues debated; and, while few listeners may have evaluated what they heard in an impartial light, they certainly heard opposing viewpoints expressed and public issues subjected to vigorous discussion. Members and informed visitors were well aware that congressional debates did not constitute the legislative process, but few, if any, could have conceived of that function succeeding without those debates.

[74] George Hoadley to Jeremiah Evarts, Feb. 5, 1807, Photostat, File E.E.E., Va. Hist. Soc.

[75] *Ibid.*

XII. Parties and Pressures in Congress

NEITHER THE CONSTITUTION NOR THE RULES OF either chamber of Congress recognized the existence of political parties, but by the time of Jefferson's presidency, parties were actualities of political life and clearly visible in the operations of the national legislature. Following the Republican victories in the state and congressional elections of 1800 and 1801, control of both houses of Congress passed from Federalist to Republican hands at the opening of the Seventh Congress in December 1801. "We have a very commanding majority in the house of Representatives, and a safe majority in the Senate," Jefferson observed in counting sixty-six Republicans and thirty-seven Federalists present in the House with two Republicans absent and one seat vacant. "I believe therefore all things will go on smoothly, except a little ill-temper to be expected from the minority, who are bitterly mortified."[1] In the Senate the party division was eighteen Republicans and fourteen Federalists.[2]

The Federalist minority was stronger in the Seventh Congress than it would be in any other Congress under Jefferson, and in this Congress the Federalists constituted an effective opposition. Despite their defeat in the election of 1800, Federalists still controlled most of New England and had substantial support in the Middle Atlantic States. Though shaken by defeat, the party had not collapsed. Neither Republicans nor Federalists could know in 1801 that Federalists would never return to power in the national government. The contest of parties which had dominated the two Congresses under Adams thus continued after the party turnover in 1801. "There is in fact two real parties in Congress," wrote Senator Plumer in 1802; "and tis as easy and as natural for day and night to become one, as these parties to coalesce in the great measures of government."[3]

From the outset, the Federalists anticipated the possibility of Republican disunity. "The very magnitude . . . of the majority

[1] Jefferson to Maria Jefferson Eppes, Dec. 14, 1801; Jefferson to T. M. Randolph, Jr., Jan. 1, 1802, Jefferson Papers, Lib. Cong.

[2] Jefferson to T. M. Randolph, Jr., Jan. 1, 1802, *ibid.*

[3] Plumer to Oliver Peabody, Dec. 22, 1802, Plumer Papers, Letter Book, Lib. Cong.

furnishes us some hopes," Representative James A. Bayard, a Federalist leader in the House, pointed out to a Federalist colleague who had not yet taken his seat. "You well remember how much more manageable be found a small than a large majority. Every Party is made up of jarring elements, which can be kept together only by a certain external pressure. A Party too powerful to fear an opposition is ever in danger of self division." Bayard went on to explain Federalist strategy in the House at the opening of the Seventh Congress. "We have cautiously abstained from declamation on Party topicks," he noted. "Suffered them to adopt their own *forms* of doing business and have avoided with great care taking any ground likely to concentrate their forces by inflaming Party feelings. If we can persevere in the course we have begun it will be impossible for them to preserve union among themselves."[4] Bayard's letter thus makes it quite clear that the Federalist minority in Congress gave attention to party strategy. Comments by other Federalists in the course of the Seventh Congress also reveal that Federalists in Congress were adjusting their tactics to their new role as the minority party and developing some party *esprit*.[5] In March 1802 Senator Morris reported to Hamilton: "As to the state of parties, the Federalists are become a column of steel and have such a sense of their strength that there is now no danger of desertion. The Demos feel their weakness."[6] At the opening of the second session of the Seventh Congress in December 1802, Senator Plumer insisted: "The federalists are a minority; but have much talents and respectability. The southern democrats fear New England federalism. Tho' our numbers are small, we are feared and respected. We can seldom carry any measure; but we prevent the ruling party from doing much mischief."[7]

As the Federalists' strength and numbers dwindled in the succeeding Congresses under Jefferson, so also did their spirits. In the Eighth Congress, following the new apportionment under the census of 1800 and the admission of Ohio as a state, the party division in the House of Representatives was 103 Republicans and 39 Federalists. In the Senate there were twenty-five Republicans

---

[4] Bayard to John Rutledge, Dec. 20, 1801, John Rutledge Papers, Univ. of N. C.

[5] Smith to Tapping Reeve, Mar. 8, 1802, Park Family Papers, Yale Univ.

[6] Morris to Hamilton, Mar. 11, 1802, Private Correspondence Letter Book, Papers of Gouverneur Morris, Lib. Cong.

[7] Plumer to David Lawrence, Dec. 27, 1802, Plumer Papers, Lib. Cong.

and nine Federalists.[8] "The favorite measures of the present administration will be carried against all opposition, by the weight of numbers," Representative Simeon Baldwin concluded. "Our opposition to such measures is never with a prospect of success."[9] By the end of the session, Baldwin was thoroughly discouraged. "Federal men have in some instances been serviceable, where the measures have been so gross as to divide the less thorough Democrats from their leaders," he wrote. "In such cases they have been able to feel their importance by adding their weight to the democratic minority—but even this field for usefulness seems to be lost by their alarm at its success. We are now indeed a degraded minority, with no hope of success, but from silence and seldom even by that."[10]

Following the sweeping Republican victory in the election of 1804, Federalist strength in the House at the opening of the Ninth Congress fell to twenty-seven—"not quite one 5th of the house—not a sufficient number to demand the yeas and nays to be entered on the journals," Senator Plumer pointed out.[11] In the Senate the Federalist minority dropped to seven out of the thirty-four members, and this decline was reflected in the increasing signs of Republican disunity. "You ask what is the matter with the Republicans here that they quarrel so?" Senator Mitchill wrote at the beginning of 1806. "The principal cause is that the majority is too great. The minority is too inconsiderable to keep them in order. And as is usual with men (who are disputing animals), if they overcome their present opponents, they will very soon break out into new controversies among themselves. This is the case with the present republican majority. Having subjected their old opponents the federalists, they have nobody but their own side to contend with."[12] While problems of Republican unity increased as Federalist opposition diminished, there was little decline in party identification. Party affiliation remained the most prominent fact of political life. Dissident Republicans insisted that they were the real Republicans or that they spoke for the "old Republican party." Although Republicans argued among themselves over who was to

[8] *National Intelligencer*, Oct. 19, 1803; William Plumer to Daniel Plumer, Nov. 15, 1803, Plumer Papers, Lib. Cong.

[9] Baldwin to his wife, Dec. 27, 1803, Baldwin Family Papers, Yale Univ.

[10] Baldwin to his wife, Mar. 16, 1804, *ibid.*

[11] Brown, ed., *Plumer's Memorandum*, Dec. 1, 1805, p. 337.

[12] Mitchill to his wife, Jan. 29, 1806, Mitchill Papers, Museum C.N.Y.

give direction to their party and over who was to succeed Jefferson as President, all sides continued to regard themselves as Republicans.

The period of Jefferson's presidency was one of party government in the administration and in the Congress. Party control of the House of Representatives gave Republicans the power to elect the Speaker, who in turn had the authority to appoint all standing committees and all other committees unless otherwise directed by the House.[13] On occasion the House elected a committee by ballot, but this was an unusual procedure.[14] By the order in which the Speaker named members to committees, he designated the chairman of each committee, thereby greatly influencing the course of legislative proceedings. Barnabas Bidwell, a Republican member from Massachusetts, observed in 1806: "In every legislature, the introduction, progress and conclusion of business depend much upon committees; and, in the House of Representatives of the U. S., more than in any other legislative body within my knowledge, the business referred to Committees, and reported on by them, is, by usage and common consent, controlled by their chairman. As the Speaker, according to the standing rules of the House, has the appointment of Committees, he has it in his power to place whom he pleases in the foreground, and whom he pleases in the background, and thus, in some measures, affect their agency in the transactions of the House."[15]

In electing Nathaniel Macon as Speaker of the House in 1801, the majority chose a staunch Republican who had the support of all segments of the party. There is no evidence that Jefferson exerted any influence in the election of the Speaker or in regard to the appointments which Macon made to committees. The posture of key committee members in regard to the administration did, however, affect the attitude of House Republicans toward the Speaker and led ultimately to a decline of confidence in Macon. At the beginning of the Ninth Congress in 1805, three ballots were required to give Macon the necessary majority for election to his third term as Speaker.[16] In the course of the session, John Randolph, chairman of the Committee of Ways and Means, broke

[13] House rules, Dec. 17, 1805, *House Journal*, v, 200.
[14] Mitchill to his wife, Jan. 26, 1803, Mitchill Papers, Museum C.N.Y.
[15] Bidwell to Jefferson, July 28, 1806, Jefferson Papers, Lib. Cong.
[16] Samuel Smith, Letter Book, Dec. 2, 1805, Samuel Smith Papers, Lib. Cong.

with the President, precipitating a movement in the House to strip the Speaker of his power to appoint standing committees, since Macon, a close friend of Randolph, had named him chairman of the influential committee in 1801. On April 21, 1806, a resolution was introduced to require the appointment of all standing committees by ballot.[17] Since this was the final day of the session, the motion was postponed until the next session, when a similar resolution was introduced on the opening day and narrowly defeated.[18] At the next Congress in October 1807, the Republican majority replaced Macon as Speaker, electing Joseph B. Varnum of Massachusetts to the post. The power of the Speaker to appoint committees was not altered, but the control of the party majority over that power had been demonstrated. In a display of the partisan application of the Speaker's power, Varnum changed the entire membership of the Committee of Ways and Means.

During the period when Randolph had headed the Ways and Means Committee, he had emerged as the majority party leader in the House. While there was no formal designation of any leadership post, Randolph clearly performed the role of Republican floor leader and was so recognized by the President. Some Federalists were critical of Randolph's methods and found his role offensive. Sitting in on debates in the House in 1803, Senator Plumer described Randolph as "profuse in censuring the *motives* of his opponents—artful in evading their arguments, and peremptory in demanding the vote—sitting on his seat insolently and frequently exclaiming *I hope this motion will not prevail*—or when it suited his view, *I hope this will be adopted*."[19] Some Republicans also found Randolph's manner grating, but Randolph was resourceful in debate; and, as Plumer observed: "Many of the party dislike him—and on trifling measures they quarrel with him, but on all measures that are really important to the party they unite with him."[20]

When Randolph openly attacked the administration, he lost the chairmanship of the Ways and Means Committee. While party leadership in Congress was not a product of presidential directive, the maintenance of leadership posts depended on continuing support of the administration. In breaking with the President, Ran-

[17] *Annals of Congress*, 9 Cong., 1 Sess., 1115; Macon to Joseph H. Nicholson, Apr. 21, 1806, Nicholson Papers, Lib. Cong.

[18] *Annals of Congress*, 9 Cong., 2 Sess. (Dec. 1, 1806), 111; Brown, ed., *Plumer's Memorandum*, Dec. 1, 1806, p. 519.

[19] *Ibid.*, Oct. 24, 1803, p. 25.   [20] *Ibid.*, Jan. 26, 1804, p. 123.

dolph carried into opposition with him only a handful of members. "The defection of so prominent a leader, threw them into dismay and confusion for a moment," Jefferson reported; "but they soon rallied to their own principles, and let him go off with 5 or 6 followers only." He believed that "the alarm the House has had from this schism, has produced a rallying together and a harmony, which carelessness and security had begun to endanger."[21] Jefferson himself had taken steps to isolate Randolph, and the collapse of Randolph's revolt provided impressive evidence of Jefferson's success as a party leader.

Formal party machinery within Congress was found only in the Republican nominating caucus, which was the key party mechanism in the national organization of the Republican party and gave the Republican members of Congress control over the selection of the party's candidates for President and Vice-President. Although the nominating caucus did not play a direct role in the legislative process, it was indicative of the importance of party in Congress and demonstrated the ability of the congressional Republicans to make major party decisions.

One hundred and eight members attended "the grand Caucus of the Republican Members of Congress,"[22] which met in the Senate Chamber on February 25, 1804. Unanimously agreeing *viva voce* to nominate Jefferson for reelection, they balloted for Vice-President and nominated George Clinton on the first ballot. The caucus also appointed a committee of thirteen members from different states "for the purpose of devising measures to promote the success of the republican nominations."[23] "The Business was conducted with remarkable decorum and harmony; and was dispatched at an early hour in the Evening," reported Senator Mitchill, who attended and was named to the committee.[24] Considering that the caucus had agreed to drop the incumbent Vice-President, Aaron Burr, from the ticket, the caucus action demonstrated the ability of the Republican party to resolve conflict and make decisions.[25]

[21] Jefferson to Wilson Cary Nicholas, Apr. 13, 1806, Ford, ed., *Jefferson Writings*, VIII, 435n.

[22] Mitchill to his wife, Feb. 26, 1804, Mitchill Papers, Museum C.N.Y.

[23] *Aurora* (Philadelphia), Mar. 6, 1804.

[24] Mitchill to his wife, Feb. 26, 1804, Mitchill Papers, Museum C.N.Y.

[25] This action seems a sounder basis for judging the party's capacity for action than the party's failure to agree on a single candidate for the speakership in the House of Representatives. The latter argument has been advanced by Young (*Washington Community*, pp. 117-119) to show the

The caucus also showed that Republican members of Congress formed the principal organization of the Republican party on the national level. The committee named by the caucus in 1804—the first caucus to name such a committee—served as something of a national committee. With the Twelfth Amendment not yet ratified, this committee was charged with preventing another tie vote between the Republican presidential and vice-presidential candidates such as had occurred in 1800. In carrying out its charge, the committee appointed a subcommittee "to digest the votes which might be expected for them in the different States, and to calculate in what manner they should be disposed of next Autumn to secure the Election of the two Candidates."[26] With Republican members of Congress so deeply enmeshed in party procedure, it was not to be expected that the legislative function would remain unaffected or that the party role of members would be separable from their legislative role. This became even clearer as the presidential election of 1808 approached and a contest developed for the Republican nomination for President. As early as 1806, Randolph charged in a debate on nonimportation that all eyes were fixed on the presidential mansion, that "the question was not what we should do with France, or Spain, or England, but who should be the next President. And at this moment, every motion that is made . . . is made with a view to the occupation of that House."[27] Randolph, a supporter of Monroe for the presidency, and others who shared his views refused to attend the nominating caucus of 1808, along with the New York members who favored George Clinton. "It was a pretty general understanding among those who did not wish to support Madison not to attend the meeting," one member of the House reported.[28] A majority of the Republican members of the House and Senate, however, did attend the caucus of 1808 and nominated Madison for President and Clinton for Vice-President.[29]

Even after the caucus made its decision, the presidential contest

---

inability of the party to act. The large Republican majority in the House, however, did not require unanimity to prevent a Federalist from being chosen as Speaker.

[26] Mitchill to his wife, Feb. 29, 1804, Mitchill Papers, Museum C.N.Y.

[27] *Annals of Congress*, 9 Cong., 1 Sess. (Mar. 13, 1806), 775.

[28] Samuel Taggart to Rev. John Taylor, Jan. 27, 1808, Haynes, ed., "Letters of Samuel Taggart," Amer. Antiq. Soc., *Proceedings*, New Ser., 33 (1923), p. 303.

[29] See Cunningham, *Jeffersonian Republicans in Power*, pp. 108-118.

continued to affect the business of Congress. "As the greater part of the Senators attended the Madisonian Caucus," Senator Mitchill noticed, "the Vice President is secretly irritated at almost all the members of the body over which he presides. He is so censorious that they almost all wish he was snug at home."[30] In view of the unresolved crisis with Great Britain that had led to the enactment of the embargo in December 1807, some members were concerned about the preoccupation of Congress with the presidential contest. "The election for the next President seems to have engrossed the thoughts of many more than the critical situation in which we are placed by the wicked acts of other governments," Macon wrote in March 1808. "That the election is of great importance cannot be denied, but that at this moment it ought not to concern us so much as our situation seems to be equally evident, especially as all parties appear to have selected their candidates."[31]

While the Republican nominating caucus provided the means for selecting presidential and vice-presidential candidates, formal party mechanisms for influencing the legislative process did not exist. Since the machinery of Congress was under the control of the majority party, the Republicans were in less need of other devices than the Federalists; and the Federalists—always less innovative than Republicans in such matters—devised no machinery other than informal party caucuses. Many caucuses, both Federalist and Republican, were not acknowledged publicly, making it impossible to determine the extent to which the device was employed. Nevertheless, the evidence shows that various informal party caucuses were held for legislative purposes by both Federalists and Republicans. Federalist Senator Gouverneur Morris recorded in his diary for April 3, 1802: "In the Evening attend at a Consultation on the proper steps to be taken respecting the Repeal of the Judiciary."[32] Another entry reads: "In the Evening a Meeting at my Chamber to consider of what may be most proper in Regard to the Judiciary."[33] Neither of these meetings was a gathering of all Federalist members of Congress, but both were informal caucuses for legislative purposes. In December 1805, Senator Plumer reported another Federalist caucus: "In the evening the

[30] Mitchill to his wife, Feb. 20, 1808, Mitchill Papers, Museum C.N.Y.

[31] Macon to ——, Mar. 26, 1808, Nathaniel Macon Papers, N. C. Dept. of Archives and History.

[32] Diary of Gouverneur Morris, Apr. 3, 1802, Papers of Gouverneur Morris, Lib. Cong.

[33] Entry of Apr. 24, 1802, *ibid.*

federal Members of the House to the number of twelve met at Coyle's in a Caucus to decide for whom they should vote as Speaker. Macon and Varnum are the democratic candidates—the caucus resolved they would vote for neither, but would sit up and support John Cotton Smith, a member from Connecticut." As a senator, Plumer did not participate, but he recorded that he "was present in the room where the Caucus met."[34]

Federalists charged that Republicans decided measures pending before Congress in "consultations out of doors"[35] and in "out-door arrangements."[36] Senator Hillhouse insisted that "all questions are settled in private meetings, and every member composing the Majority of both houses comes pledged to support the measures so agreed on."[37] In regard to a bill on upper Louisiana, Plumer reported: "The democratic senators held a Caucus last evening in which they settled the principles of the bill—and agreed to the same in the Senate without any debate."[38] Despite the Federalist suspicions, there is no evidence of regular caucusing by Republican members, but informal caucuses were held from time to time. Most of the meetings were so informal that even those who attended were reluctant to call them caucuses. "I do not recollect what is called a caucus, or any other meeting, to determine what should come before the Senate; or to consider any depending political subject or question, in a single case," John Taylor wrote of a two-month period of service in the Senate in 1803, "except what I shall relate should be considered in that light." Taylor then described a meeting of several members who consulted about a person to be supported for president pro tempore of the Senate and another meeting regarding the choice of the secretary of the Senate. "And there was a general meeting of the friends to the discriminating amendment (with a few exceptions) an evening or two before its passage. . . . This meeting was made no secret of, and the subject was discussed with great talents."[39] Reporting on the second of the meetings described by Taylor, Plumer noted that "the democratic senators met in caucus, to determine who should succeed

[34] Brown, ed., *Plumer's Memorandum*, Dec. 1, 1805, p. 337.

[35] Adams, ed., *Memoirs of John Quincy Adams*, Feb. 5, 1805, i, 346.

[36] Speech of John Rutledge, Jan. 25, 1802, *Annals of Congress*, 7 Cong., 1 Sess., 455.

[37] Hillhouse to Simeon Baldwin, Feb. 18, 1802, Baldwin Family Papers, Yale Univ.

[38] Brown, ed., *Plumer's Memorandum*, Feb. 8, 1804, p. 141.

[39] Taylor to Wilson C. Nicholas, June 23, 1804, Edgehill-Randolph Papers, Univ. of Va.

Otis as Secretary."[40] Plumer thus readily labeled as a caucus a meeting that Tayor had been hesitant to so designate. Whatever such meetings were called, they were informal caucuses, though no regularized procedures were developed and members who participated were not bound by the decisions.

In a day when travel was difficult and living accommodations in the new capital on the Potomac were uninviting, few wives accompanied members of Congress to Washington. While Congress was in session, most members lived in boardinghouses or hotels, sharing rooms and taking their meals in congressional messes provided by their landlords. Most of the boardinghouses were located on Capitol Hill, and in 1801 only a few members ventured to live as far away as Georgetown. But in 1804, Senator Breckinridge reported that "the boarding Houses on the Capitol Hill have raised in their prices to such a pitch of extravagance, that a great number of members have taken Lodgings in George Town."[41] Representative Mitchill, joining the exodus to Georgetown, explained:

> The reasons for moving from Washington were various. I had wintered three sessions on the Capitol-Hill and become so well acquainted with most things in that neighbourhood that very little of anything new was to be seen. The demand for lodgings thereabout was exorbitantly dear. The Society was less than it used to be. In addition to all these considerations I felt a desire to reside awhile at Georgetown, and take a nearer view of some things there. And the inducement was the stronger as I found a number of gentlemen of my former acquaintance were fixed there before me, forming a pleasant mess. . . .
> At present our Society at McLachlan's consists of Messrs. Moore and Thompson of Virginia, Messrs. Campbell, Rhea and Dickson of Tennessee, Messrs. Stanford and Alston of North Carolina, Messrs. Meriwether and Baldwin of Georgia, Genl. Sumpter of South Carolina and Mr. Thomas of New York. My Colleague Thomas and myself have agreed to take a Room together, and be chums for the Session. A very nice front Parlour on the second Story of a private House adjoining the Inn

[40] Brown, ed., *Plumer's Memorandum*, Oct. 27, 1803, p. 28.
[41] John Breckinridge to his wife, Nov. 29, 1804, Breckinridge Family Papers, Lib. Cong.

is preparing for us and I expect to be put in possession of it this Day.[42]

Some members arranged their quarters in advance; others did so after they arrived in the capital or counted on a friend to secure accommodations.[43] As might be expected, most members sought to live in houses with their friends and to dine with congenial colleagues; thus they formed themselves into informal club-like groups. "I removed to McLauchlins, where there is a Club of 17 Members, most of them my old acquaintances, six of them Senators," Senator Breckinridge explained to his wife in December 1804. "We live in high stile; have a separate table, and are sent to the Capitol every day in Hacks."[44] The group which Breckinridge joined was that described by Mitchill at the beginning of the session when it was composed of twelve members. Senators and representatives mingled freely in these groups.

In their search for congenial messmates, members tended to seek out colleagues from their own state and join similar groups from states in the same section of the country. Most boardinghouses had a concentration of members from a particular section—the South, New England, or the Middle Atlantic States—with westerners usually found with southern groups. A list of members showing their local addresses has survived for the first session of the Seventh Congress, which met in December 1801. Printed by Congress, the directory listed the members of the House and the Senate under the names of the boardinghouses, hotels, and private homes in which they lived.[45] The sectional pattern of this list is striking. Mrs. Wilson's, north of the Capitol, housed three members from Virginia, three from North Carolina, and one member each from Georgia, Maryland, Rhode Island, and Pennsylvania. At Mr. King's, east of the Capitol, were four members from Connecticut and four from Massachusetts. Mr. Birch's, also east of the Capitol, accommodated

[42] Mitchill to his wife, Nov. 10, 1804, Mitchill Papers, Museum C.N.Y.

[43] Breckinridge to his wife, Nov. 29, 1804, Breckinridge Family Papers, Lib. Cong.; Randolph to Nicholson, July 18, 1801, Nicholson Papers, Lib. Cong.

[44] Breckinridge to his wife, Dec. 19, 1804, Breckinridge Family Papers, Lib. Cong.

[45] *List of Members of the Senate and House of Representatives, with Their Places of Abode* [December 1801], Rare Book Division, Lib. Cong. This list has been reprinted in Perry M. Goldman and James S. Young, eds., *The United States Congressional Directories, 1789-1840* (New York, 1973), pp. 38-40.

four members from Pennsylvania and two from New Jersey. At Miss Finigan's, north of the Capitol, were four members from New York, two from New Jersey, two from Delaware, two from Maryland, and one from Vermont. Most groups at other places were similarly composed. Even more striking than the sectional composition of boardinghouse groups was their partisan character. All of the members living at Mrs. Wilson's and Mr. Birch's were Republicans; all of those at Mr. King's and Miss Finigan's were Federalists. Of the eleven boardinghouse groups of from six to twelve members, seven were Republican and four were Federalist —not one of them included members of opposite parties. When the smaller groups of two to four members, of which there were five, are included, in only one house were there members of opposite parties. In this instance a Federalist member from Connecticut and a Republican from Virginia lived at the same address. Eight members lived alone.

Regional affinities exerted a powerful pull in boardinghouse groupings, but regional identification yielded to party affiliation when the two did not coincide. The only southerner in a Federalist group at Stell's Hotel was a Federalist member from North Carolina. Two other North Carolina Federalists were the only southerners in a group of twelve Federalists at Mr. Frost's on Jersey Avenue, where the others came from New England and Pennsylvania. On the other hand, a Rhode Island Republican and a Pennsylvania Republican joined a group of southerners at Mrs. Wilson's. Of the eleven boardinghouse groups containing from six to twelve members, only two were exclusively restricted to members from one region. Although most had a majority from one section, an occasional group consisted of a geographical cross section.[46]

The partisan composition of the boardinghouse groups shown by an analysis of the congressional directory is supported by the observations of contemporaries. "The two parties board separately, and visit each other but seldom," wrote Senator Plumer in 1802.[47] "No Tavern or boarding house contains two members of opposite sentiments," another observer wrote in 1803.[48] In the same year,

[46] List of Members of the Senate and House of Representatives, with Their Places of Abode [December 1801].

[47] William Plumer to Oliver Peabody, Dec. 22, 1802, Plumer Papers, Lib. Cong.

[48] Benjamin G. Orr to John Steele, Feb. 13, 1803, Henry M. Wagstaff, ed., The Papers of John Steele, 2 vols. (Raleigh, N. C., 1924), I, 361.

Representative Simeon Baldwin, a Connecticut Federalist, wrote from Washington that "the men of different parties do not associate intimately. Federalists live mostly by themselves, there are about 50 in both Houses, of these we have 13 at our own Table. But we make ourselves some sport at the expence of the blunders as we conceive them, of the great folks in power."[49]

Gallatin, who as a representative from Pennsylvania lived in a Washington boardinghouse before his appointment as Secretary of the Treasury, wrote early in 1801: "You may suppose that being all thrown together in a few boarding-houses, without hardly any other society than ourselves, we are not likely to be either very moderate politicians or to think of anything but politics."[50] Five years later, Plumer felt much the same way, recording in his diary:

> At Capt. Coyle's where I now board there are 16 of us. This is too many—We have too much noise. . . . But there is another evil which to me is much more serious. The Gentlemen are all rigid federalists—Pickering, Tracy, Davenport are violent—and I dare not invite a gentleman to call upon me whose politic's are different, lest these violent inmates should treat him with rudeness and insult. The consequence is I am necessarily restrained from visiting many of the Gentlemen with whom I wish to cultivate an acquaintance. An interchange of sentiments tends to correct one's own errors—and leads us to think more favorably of others. The few federalists in Congress seldom, if ever, visit and of course do not receive visits, but only from each other. They therefore not only strengthen each others prejudices —but they encrease them—and remain ignorant of many things important to know.[51]

Plumer, whose views of Republicans were beginning to moderate by this date, found a new group of six associates at the next session; they were quiet and sober, but all were still federalists.[52] Plumer was pleased when Henry Clay and his uncle Matthew Clay joined his lodgings. "They are republicans and I am glad they have come," he said. "I dislike this practise of setting up such a partition wall against members of Congress, because one party are federalists and the other Republicans. The more we associate together the

[49] Baldwin to his wife, Dec. 20, 1803, Baldwin Family Papers, Yale Univ.

[50] Gallatin to his wife, Jan. 22, 1801, Adams, *Gallatin*, p. 255.

[51] Brown, ed., *Plumer's Memorandum*, Mar. 18, 1806, p. 458.

[52] *Ibid.*, Dec. 7, 1806, p. 523.

more favorable shall we think of each other."[53] Henry Clay, who
had been elected to fill the unexpired Senate term of John Adair,
had arrived after the session was under way when the choice of
boarding places was limited. As Plumer's remarks indicate, his
joining a group of Federalist boarders was exceptional.

Another congressional directory issued after the first session of
the Tenth Congress convened in October 1807 shows patterns
similar to those in 1801.[54] There were fourteen boardinghouses
with groups of six to sixteen members and a scattering of members living in smaller groups or alone. In most of the boardinghouses there was a majority from one region and more concentration of state delegations in 1807 than in 1801. The separation by
parties in 1807 was nearly as pronounced as in 1801. There were
fewer Federalists in Congress in 1807 and hence only two Federalist boardinghouses, but of the twenty-eight Federalists in
Congress,[55] twenty-one lived in one of these two houses. A few Federalists lived alone, and only three Federalists boarded with Republicans.[56]

The evidence is indisputable that the most important single
determinant of boardinghouse grouping was party affiliation.[57]
While camaraderie and a sense of group identity developed among
the boardinghouse units, such group identity was generally within
and subordinate to party association. "Our lodging-house has

[53] *Ibid.*, Jan. 12, 1807, p. 570.

[54] *Places of Abode of the Members of Both Houses of Congress* [1807],
Rare Book Division, Lib. Cong. This list has been reprinted in Goldman
and Young, eds., *United States Congressional Directories*, pp. 44-46.

[55] *Enquirer* (Richmond), Jan. 30, 1808.

[56] *Places of Abode of the Members of Both Houses of Congress* [1807].

[57] This evidence was missed by James Sterling Young, whose *The Washington Community, 1800-1828* offers the most extensive examination of
boardinghouse groups previously attempted. Young did not use the directory of members for the 7th Congress in 1801 and drew his earliest data
from the 1807 list. More serious, he did not attempt to identify the party
affiliations of members. Arguing that since the congressional roster did not
contain party designations, there was something less than a strong sense
of party identification among the legislators (p. 111), and concluding that
the research involved in identifying the party affiliations of members "stag-
gers the imagination and offers no assurance of yielding complete party
rosters for any one Congress" (p. 271, n. 4), Young did not attempt to
establish the party composition of boardinghouses. Instead, he concluded:
"On the question of whether boardinghouse groups were one-party or two-
party in composition, fragmentary evidence exists to indicate both" (p.
275, n. 35). The evidence presented above demonstrates that Young's
conclusions are not valid for the period of Jefferson's presidency.

become what is called here a very *strong* house," Representative Mitchill wrote in 1803; "that is to say, it contains a considerable number of important men, friendly to the administration."[58] As the Federalist minority in Congress diminished and divisions within Republican ranks developed, there was some grouping of Republican factions at the boardinghouses. One Republican representative from Pennsylvania in 1808 complained of a "flying squad who called themselves republicans but on whom we could not depend" consisting of four Pennsylvania representatives who lodged with Senator Samuel Maclay of Pennsylvania.[59] John Randolph boarded with James M. Garnett and Joseph Clay, two of his closest supporters, at Mr. Crawford's in Georgetown during the 1807-1808 session.[60] The New York supporters of George Clinton for President in 1808 were concentrated in one boardinghouse. But, despite factional groupings, there was not in the 1807-1808 session any one house which was exclusively composed of one faction of Republicans. A comparison of the list of those present at the Republican caucus of 1808[61] which nominated Madison for President with the directory of members shows that the only two boardinghouses not represented at the caucus were the two houses exclusively occupied by Federalists and that only two boardinghouses had all of their members present at the caucus. Nor did any boardinghouse stand as a bloc in signing the Randolph-led protest against the caucus.[62] Preference for Madison, Clinton, or Monroe rather than loyalty to a boardinghouse group determined whether a member attended the Republican caucus of 1808 and supported its decision. No instance has been found of a boardinghouse bloc which commanded a member's highest loyalty.

The efforts of state legislatures to instruct their senators and influence their representatives constituted an important influence on Congress, but the activity varied from state to state and from year to year according to the composition of the respective state assemblies. The Senate Journals contain numerous examples of senators stating on the Senate floor that they had been instructed to obtain specific legislation or constitutional amendments.[63] Whether

58 Mitchill to his wife, Jan. 8, 1803, Mitchill Papers, Museum C.N.Y.
59 William Findley to Joseph Hiester, Apr. 9, 1808, Gregg Collection, Lib. Cong.
60 *Places of Abode of the Members of Both Houses of Congress* [1807].
61 *National Intelligencer*, Mar. 16, 1808.
62 The protest, dated Feb. 27, 1808, was published in *ibid.*, Mar. 7, 1808.
63 *Senate Journal*, IV, 25, 76, 234, 235, 263, 265.

a senator accepted instructions from his state legislature as binding depended upon the individual senator, for the question of the
authority of a state legislature to issue binding instructions to its
senators was as unsettled during the Republican era as it had been
during the earlier Federalist period.[64]

Directives relating to proposals for constitutional amendments
were the most common type of instructions passed by state legislatures. After the 1800 presidential election, a number of states
instructed their senators to seek a constitutional amendment to
provide for separate balloting for President and Vice-President in
the electoral college.[65] Early in 1808 the Virginia General Assembly instructed its senators and requested its representatives in Congress to endeavor to obtain an amendment to the Constitution to
provide that senators might be removed from office by the vote of
a majority of the members of their respective state legislatures.[66]
After copies of the Virginia resolution were sent to the governors
of the other states, the Maryland legislature passed a resolution
declaring that the proposed alteration "is hereby disapproved by
the legislature of this state, and that the senators and representatives in the congress of the United States from this state be and
they are hereby requested to oppose the said alteration."[67] Actions
of one state often prompted similar moves or counteractions from
other states.

Most state legislatures worded their instructions to specify that
senators were *instructed* and representatives were *requested* to
endeavor to promote particular objects; but some, such as in the
Maryland resolution above, did not use the term "instruct." The
General Assembly of Vermont in passing resolutions in 1801 in
support of district election of presidential electors requested the
governor to "inform our Senators that it is our wish that they

[64] On the instruction of senators during the Federalist period, see Roy
Swanstrom, *The United States Senate, 1787-1801*, Senate Document No.
64, 87th Congress (Washington, D. C., 1962), pp. 159-172.

[65] Resolutions of North Carolina legislature, December 1801, *Journal of
the Senate of North Carolina*, Dec. 11, 1801, William S. Jenkins, ed.,
Records of the States of the United States of America: A Microfilm Compilation; Resolutions of New York legislature, Jan. 30, Feb. 1, 1802; Resolutions of Ohio legislature, Apr. 16, 1803; Resolutions of Vermont, Oct.
22, 24, 1803, Senate Records, RG 46, Natl. Archives.

[66] Resolutions of Virginia General Assembly, Jan. 13, 1808, read and
tabled by the Senate, Apr. 11, 1808, Senate Records, RG 46, Natl. Archives.

[67] Resolutions of Maryland General Assembly, Dec. 9, 22, 1808, addressed to Senator Philip Read, read in the Senate, Jan. 4, 1809, *ibid.*

should esteem themselves instructed, and the Representatives that they should esteem themselves requested, to afford their aid in carrying such concurrence into effect."[68] A resolution passed by the legislature of Tennessee stated that "it is the desire of this Legislature that the senators and representatives from this state in the Congress of the United States . . . use their best endeavours to effect a compromise between this state and the United States" relative to certain lands in Tennessee.[69]

Whether or not a legislature used the term "instruct," individual senators decided for themselves whether to consider such instructions binding. No senator resigned during the period rather than obey instructions, as later happened in some cases; on the contrary, some members did not follow their instructions. On February 2, 1802, the president of the New York Senate and the speaker of the Assembly transmitted to Senator Morris the resolutions of the New York legislature in support of district election of presidential electors and separate balloting for President and Vice-President. "We earnestly request that you will use your best exertions in carrying the same into effect," they wrote, pointing out that the resolutions had passed both houses without a dissenting voice.[70] Morris responded that the subject of the resolutions "shall meet the respectful attention due to that high authority by which it is recommended."[71] However, in a private letter to Hamilton, Morris said: "I believe I shall do little for or against them. My present impression is not I confess favorable and but for the approbation you express it would be decidedly hostile."[72] When the proposal for separate balloting for President and Vice-President came to a vote, Morris voted against it.[73]

In another case, the legislature of North Carolina resolved to "instruct the Senators of this State, and recommend to the Representatives thereof in Congress, to use their utmost endeavours

[68] Resolution of Nov. 5, 1801, enclosed in Governor Isaac Tichenor to Senator Stephen R. Bradley, Dec. 24, 1801, *ibid*.

[69] Undated resolution in Senate Records, 9th Congress, *ibid*.

[70] Jeremiah Van Rensselaer and Thomas Storm to Gouverneur Morris, Feb. 2, 1802, *ibid*.

[71] Morris to President of the Senate and Speaker of the Assembly of New York, Feb. 12, 1802, Private Correspondence Letter Book, Papers of Gouverneur Morris, Lib. Cong.

[72] Morris to Hamilton, Mar. 11, 1802, *ibid*.

[73] Morris to President of the Senate and Speaker of the Assembly of New York, Dec. 25, 1802, Jared Sparks, *The Life of Gouverneur Morris, with Selections from His Correspondence and Miscellaneous Papers*, 3 vols. (Boston, 1832), iii, 173-174.

to procure a repeal" of the judiciary act of 1801.[74] When the issue came to a vote in Congress, the state delegation split strictly along party lines. The North Carolina senators, both Republicans, voted for the repeal; but in the House all Republican members from the state supported the repeal while all Federalist members voted against it.[75] In a speech against the repeal of the act, Federalist Representative John Stanly denied the right of the legislature to control or influence his conduct, for which he was responsible only to his constituents;[76] and in a circular letter to his constituents he defended at length his vote against the repeal of the judiciary act.[77] The influence of party was far stronger than the pressure of the state legislature.

The instructions, requests, and resolutions of state legislatures were, nevertheless, important influences upon members of both houses of Congress. Some resolutions, such as many relating to the embargo, were designed to sway Congress in general; others concerned with special interests were directed largely to the members from a particular state. In many instances the views of senators and representatives coincided with those of their state legislature; in cases of conflict, members tended to follow their own judgments and their own assessments of the will of their constituents. In every case that has been found where party differences were basic to the conflict, the influence of party prevailed over that of a state legislature. Members gave due attention to the actions of their state legislatures, but they regarded such recommendations as but one expression of constituent opinion. While some state legislatures insisted upon the right to instruct the senators they elected, that right was never firmly established.

Petitions from groups of constituents were the most open pressures put on members of Congress, but individuals, both known and unknown to members, also wrote directly to representatives

---

[74] *Journal of the Senate of North Carolina*, Dec. 17, 1801; *Journal of the House of Commons of North Carolina*, Dec. 19, 1801; Benjamin Williams to senators and representatives from North Carolina in Congress, Dec. 23, 1801, Governor's Letter Book, Jenkins, ed., Records of the States: Microfilm Compilation.

[75] Delbert H. Gilpatrick, *Jeffersonian Democracy in North Carolina, 1789-1816* (New York, 1931), pp. 154-155.

[76] *Annals of Congress*, 7 Cong., 1 Sess., 569-579.

[77] John Stanly to his constituents, May 1, 1802, Noble E. Cunningham, Jr., ed., *Circular Letters of Congressmen to Their Constituents, 1789-1829*, 3 vols. (Chapel Hill, N.C., 1978), I, 288-293.

and senators seeking to influence public policy and promote private interests. "As one of your Constituents I avail myself of a liberty we claim of addressing our Representatives," a Kentucky citizen concerned about Revolutionary benefits began a letter to Senator Breckinridge.[78] From Virginia, where Breckinridge had once lived, James Marshel wrote: "In a Republican government like ours I hold it as a first principle that any individual member of the community or any number of individuals have a right to express their sentiment to the legislature or to any member thereof on subjects of a publick nature. Let this then be my apology for addressing you to whom I am perhaps scarcely known."[79] He wrote regarding the plans for the projected national road from Washington to the Ohio River, which were before a Senate committee of which Breckinridge was a member. "Perceiving you are a member of the committee respecting the road proposed to be opened from the Potomack to the Ohio, I take the liberty to drop you a few lines of that subject," another correspondent explained in urging that the road cross the Ohio River below Wheeling.[80]

While few members of Congress preserved so carefully as Breckinridge the mail from constituents, similar examples can be found in the papers of other members.[81] Committee members, especially chairmen, commonly received letters from persons interested in matters before their committees. "Understanding that the committee of ways and means have before them, for decision, the laws relative to the compensations of collectors of the revenue," Alexander Wolcott wrote to John Randolph in March 1806, "I beg leave to state to them a few facts for their consideration which relate to the collector of the district of Middletown in Connecticut."[82] Wolcott, who was himself the collector of Middletown and also the Republican state manager in Connecticut, was in Washington when he wrote the letter, and he was still there a week later when he sent another communication to the Ways and Means Committee.[83] Another collector, Allen McLane, the Federalist collector of Wilmington, wrote to Representative Michael Leib giving his

[78] John Coburn to Breckinridge, Dec. 23, 1803, Breckinridge Family Papers, Lib. Cong.

[79] Marshel to Breckinridge, Nov. 20, 1804, *ibid.*

[80] Archibald Woods to Breckinridge, Dec. 28, 1804, *ibid.*

[81] J. Prince to Eustis, Jan. 25, 1803; J. Hall to Eustis, Feb. 10, 1803, William Eustis Papers, Lib. Cong.

[82] Wolcott to Randolph, Mar. 16, 1806, *House Records*, RG 233, Natl. Archives.

[83] Wolcott to Randolph, Mar. 24, 1806, *ibid.*

account of a case that was expected to be discussed in committee, "observing that you are one of the Committee of Commerce and Manufactures, and concluding that in the course of your deliberations you would hear the case of the Ship Favorite mentioned."[84]

Most of the requests, appeals, and recommendations regarding legislative matters were sent to members of Congress in the form of letters or written petitions, but some persons went to Washington to plead in person. The mayor of nearby Alexandria, Virginia, went to the Capitol while the House was considering an alteration in the charter of incorporation of the town. "I remained in hopes during the whole of the day I was in the lobby of the house of representatives, notwithstanding appearances, that the Bill would be finally rejected," he explained in a rare contemporary confirmation of interested parties being present in the lobby of the House while measures were under consideration. After the measure passed the House, he wrote to Senator Mitchill, taking "the liberty of calling your attention to this subject, merely with a view of making a brief statement of circumstances, which if known to the Senate of the United States, I trust will defeat the further progress of the Bill before that house."[85] Whether because of these efforts or for other reasons, the bill was postponed to the next session of Congress.[86]

Some groups hired agents to present their cases to Congress. George Read, a prominent Delaware lawyer, spent six weeks in Washington attempting to counteract a report of a House committee that had reported unfavorably on a claim of his clients.[87] The New England Mississippi Company, a Yazoo land claimant, employed Postmaster General Granger to represent its interests before Congress.[88] Some persons with private claims appeared in Washington to promote their own causes, bringing with them letters of introduction such as that furnished to William Cutting by DeWitt Clinton, who wrote to Joseph H. Nicholson: "Mr. Cutting who will hand you this has some business at Washington which will probably come before Congress. Any facility you afford him

[84] McLane to Leib, Dec. 10, 1805, *ibid*.

[85] Elisha C. Dick to Samuel L. Mitchill, Jan. 2, 1805, Senate Records, RG 46, Natl. Archives.

[86] Above letter endorsed, Feb. 27, 1805, postponed to Dec. next; *Senate Journal*, III, 461.

[87] Read to Caesar A. Rodney, Nov. 29, 1807, Rodney Collection, Hist. Soc. Del.

[88] Abernethy, *The South in the New Nation*, p. 162.

will be highly gratifying to me. He is a gentleman of respectable connexions and standing and a good republican."[89]

Interested persons testified before House and Senate committees. Alexander McDonald, a messenger in one of the departmental offices, appeared before the House Ways and Means Committee in 1808 to plead the cause of higher salaries for government messengers and followed with a letter to the chairman.[90] John Mason of Georgetown, having heard that a committee on post roads was considering a petition to make certain alterations in routes to Virginia, wrote the chairman of the committee in 1807: "I take the liberty to solicit in behalf of myself, and sundry individuals deeply interested in this question, that I may be permitted to appear before your honorable Committee to shew cause why this alteration should not be made, and I am the more anxious to be heard on this subject, because I have reason to believe that some information, far from correct . . . has been conveyed to the Committee. Should my request be granted—be pleased Sir, to signify when I may attend."[91]

Constituent pressures on members of Congress found expression through the electoral process, through political parties, and through the direct pressures of petitions, private letters, and even personal appearances. The influence of such pressures can never be precisely measured, but the evidence of the operation of these influences is abundant. The most pervasive influence in the Jeffersonian Congresses was that of party. Few members were willing to acknowledge the legitimacy of an opposing party, but it was normal to accept the legitimacy of the party to which one gave allegiance. While regularly denying blind obedience to party, most members accepted party influence upon their legislative conduct. With the national party organization depending largely on the members of Congress, with the machinery of Congress under Republican control, and with the President the head of the Republican party and his Cabinet exclusively Republican, party was inseparable from the legislative process.

[89] Clinton to Nicholson, Jan. 1, 1804, Nicholson Papers, Lib. Cong.

[90] Alexander McDonald to George W. Campbell, Jan. 21, 1808, House Records, RG 233, Natl. Archives.

[91] John Mason to Joseph B. Varnum, Jan. 23, 1807, *ibid.*

XIII. The Process of Petition

THE ROLE OF PETITIONS, OFTEN LITTLE RECOG-
nized by historians, was an important element in the legislative process of the early Congresses. In the Jeffersonian Congresses much of the work of the standing committees of the House
of Representatives resulted from petitions addressed to Congress
and referred to committees for consideration and reports. The
principal standing committees of a legislative character were, to
a large extent, established as a result of the growing volume of
petitions. The Committee of Claims originated entirely as a mechanism to handle petitions;[1] and this continued to be its function.
An increasing number of petitions also led to the establishment of
the Committees of Commerce and Manufactures, Public Lands,
and the Post Office and Post Roads. Although these committees
had wider duties than responding to petitions, much of their time
and attention was directed to those appeals.

Petitions came in many forms. Some were handwritten; others
were printed; sometimes both handwritten and printed copies of
the same petition were presented by different petitioners. Some
petitions had long sheets of signatures attached. A memorial from
aliens in Philadelphia was signed in four columns across a sheet
of paper eight feet in length.[2] Many petitions had multiple pages
of signatures annexed. Petitions from large numbers of signers
tended to be in printed form with signatures attached to each copy.
A memorial of the people of the Mississippi territory regarding
lands came to the House of Representatives in seven copies, five
of which were printed and two handwritten. All copies contained
signatures, ranging in number from 58 to 136 and totaling 561
names on the seven petitions. Five of the seven petitions had at least
one name signed with an "X," ten of the 561 names being so subscribed.[3]

Usually addressed jointly to the Senate and the House, most
petitions were introduced in both chambers. Although the Senate

---

[1] Furlong, "Organization in the House of Representatives, 1789-1801,"
pp. 55-57.

[2] Memorial referred to a committee on naturalization laws Jan. 5, 1802,
House Records, RG 233, Natl. Archives.

[3] Memorial presented Nov. 25, 1803, *ibid*.

Journals did not ordinarily record the presentation of petitions, copies of many of the same petitions are in both the House and Senate records. Petitions were usually sent to a member for presentation. "You being the Representative of this City we have taken the liberty to transmit the inclosed Memorial to you requesting it may be presented to the House and flatter ourselves it will meet with your support," a glass manufacturer of Philadelphia wrote to Representative William Jones in 1802.[4] In sending a petition to their representative or senator, petitioners sometimes elaborated on the circumstances producing the petition and generally asked for support. When the umbrella manufacturers of Philadelphia forwarded a petition to Jónes, they accompanied it with a letter containing a detailed explanation regarding the manufacture of umbrellas in Philadelphia and in other parts of the country.[5] A Kentucky constituent wrote to Senator Breckinridge in 1802:

> I take the liberty of enclosing to you a Petition with 107 Signatures. I do so thus early in the business in order that you may be apprized of the objects contemplated therein. There are a number of those papers scattered throughout the state. And as there exists no doubt of their meeting very general patronage you may shortly expect a number of them to be forwarded.
>
> I am assured you will concur with the subscribers in opinion —that the Impost prayed for would operate greatly to the advantage of the Western states—And that you will take such measures for its accomplishment as may appear to you most proper and just.[6]

Some petitioners sent their applications by a special envoy charged with making further explanations to the member expected to introduce the petition.[7] Petitioners generally forwarded their petitions for presentation to Congress to members expected to be sympathetic; but, whatever their views, members regarded themselves as obligated to see that petitions sent to them were laid before Congress. When Senator Adams received two petitions from

[4] James Butland and Co. to William Jones, Feb. 4, 1802, accompanying memorial of glass manufacturers, *ibid.*

[5] Philip Jones to William Jones, Feb. 9, 1802, *ibid.*

[6] Thomas January to Breckinridge, Jan. 20, 1802, Breckinridge Family Papers, Lib. Cong.

[7] William Ward to Jeremiah Morrow, Nov. 21, 1808, accompanying petitions from inhabitants of Ohio presented Dec. 12, 1808, House Records, RG 233, Natl. Archives.

Massachusetts Yazoo land claimants, he introduced them and took the responsibility of seeing that they were considered, although he felt "very reluctant at being thus engaged in an affair which has already occasioned so many unpleasant altercations; but, as the agent of the petitioners has chosen to make his application to me, I could no more avoid it than any other part of my duty."[8] Adams also showed some irritation over the fact that Senator Thomas Sumter of South Carolina had carried a similar petition in his pocket for a week without presenting it. Sumter persuaded Adams to introduce his petitions first and immediately afterwards presented a petition from South Carolina claimants.

The rules of the House of Representatives provided that "petitions, memorials, and other papers, addressed to the house, shall be presented by the Speaker, or by a member in his place; a brief statement of the contents thereof shall verbally be made by the introducer, and shall not be debated or decided on the day of their being first read, unless where the House shall direct otherwise; but shall lie on the table, to be taken up in the order they were read."[9] In 1802 Randolph proposed to amend the rules to provide that if any petition or memorial contained matter in the opinion of any member "insulting to the dignity, or derogatory from the honor of the House, the reading of such paper, if objected to, shall be determined by a vote of the House."[10] Randolph argued that without this addition to the rules "any communication, however voluminous; any petition, however frivolous; any memorial, however foreign to their jurisdiction; any paper, however it might insult the dignity, however it might derogate from the honor of the House, must, of necessity, be read"; but he insisted that he had drafted his proposed amendment in such terms as "to leave untouched the sacred right of petition—a right which no one prized more dearly, and no one was more disposed to cherish and defend, than himself."[11] Randolph's proposal was referred to a select committee, and references to it disappear from the records, but the change was not made in the rules.[12] House rules were amended in 1806 to make the introducer of a petition a matter of record by providing that the

[8] Adams, ed., *Memoirs of John Quincy Adams*, Jan. 7, 1806, I, 381.

[9] *House Journal*, Jan. 7, 1802, IV, 39.

[10] *Ibid.*, Dec. 29, 1802, IV, 262; *Annals of Congress*, 7 Cong., 2 Sess., 297.

[11] *Ibid.*

[12] *Standing Rules and Orders of the House of Representatives of the United States; Established at the First Session of the Ninth Congress* (Washington, D. C., 1805), p. 8, Rare Book Division, Lib. Cong.

name of the member presenting a petition or memorial be recorded in the Journal.[13]

Some memorials were addressed jointly to the President and the Congress. In forwarding such petitions to Congress, Jefferson on occasion injected them into major policy deliberations. In January 1806 in a special message to Congress he called attention to "the oppression of our commerce and navigation by the irregular practices of armed vessels, public and private, and by the introduction of new principles, derogatory of the rights of neutrals, and unacknowledged by the usage of nations." He also communicated memorials from several bodies of merchants which, he said, "will develop these principles and practices, which are producing the most ruinous effects on our lawful commerce and navigation."[14] Since these memorials from the merchants of New York and Philadelphia had been addressed jointly to the President and Congress and had already been laid before the legislature,[15] the President's communication suggests an effort to prod Congress into action— especially in light of the fact that the Ways and Means Committee, to whom the subject had been referred after his annual message in early December, had not yet reported. In this instance the petitions were directly a part of the legislative process respecting major national policy.

Petitions more often resulted from problems of concern to a particular locality or a special-interest group that took the initiative in bringing a matter to the attention of Congress. The Philadelphia Chamber of Commerce petitioned Congress concerning the upkeep of the piers in the Delaware River.[16] Seventy shipmasters and owners petitioned for the erection of a lighthouse at the entrance of Penobscot Bay.[17] Ohio petitioners sought extension of the time for completing land payments because of economic distress resulting from the embargo of 1807.[18] The Journals of the House of Rep-

[13] *House Journal*, Mar. 22, 1806, v, 333.

[14] *Ibid.*, Jan. 17, 1806, v, 237.

[15] The petitions accompanying Jefferson's message of Jan. 17, 1806, are in Senate Records, RG 46, Natl. Archives. The memorial of the merchants of New York had been presented to the House on Jan. 6, 1806; the memorial of the merchants and traders of Philadelphia had been presented on Jan. 16, 1806; *House Journal*, v, 228, 236.

[16] Petition, Jan. 19, 1802, presented to Senate Jan. 25, 1802, and to the House Jan. 27, 1802, Senate Records, RG 46; House Records, RG 233, Natl. Archives.

[17] Petition presented Jan. 10, 1803, *ibid.*

[18] Petition presented Nov. 23, 1808, *ibid.*

resentatives are filled with references to the introduction of such petitions.

Other petitions attacked problems of broader significance. "The American convention for promoting the abolition of slavery and improving the condition of the African race" urged Congress to consider "the utility and propriety of passing such laws as shall prohibit the importation of slaves into the Territory of Louisiana."[19] A memorial from a meeting of Pennsylvania and New Jersey Quakers held in Philadelphia, December 25, 1804, declared that "as the representatives of a large body of citizens, we apprehend we have a right, by the Constitution, to address you in terms of respect, and to claim your attention upon subjects of importance, and interesting, to the welfare and happiness of our country." The petitioners sought to "again come forward to plead the cause of our oppressed and degraded fellow-men of the African race."[20]

Petitions were often the product of well-organized campaigns of special-interest groups. The hatters were one of the best organized of such groups. Between January and March 1802, no less than twenty-seven petitions came to Congress from hat manufacturers in twenty-seven different localities. A one-page printed petition had been prepared—probably by the Philadelphia hatters, since it was the first to reach Congress—providing a space for adding the name of the town of each group of petitioners. Hatters in at least fifteen places besides Philadelphia used this form. In signing the petition, the hatters of Dauphin County, Pennsylvania, listed next to their names the number of hats (ranging from 200 to 1,560) they manufactured in one year. Several handwritten copies of the same petition were also forwarded. At the same time, the hatters in several large cities, including New York and Baltimore, prepared original petitions of their own.[21] The common prayer of the petitions was that additional import duties be levied against hats.

Certain petitions reflected mass popular concern in the areas from which they came. The records of the House of Representatives for 1803 contain fifty printed copies, each with signatures, of a "Remonstrance and Petition of sundry persons, inhabitants of the State of Pennsylvania, West of the Allegheny Mountain," showing "that your Petitioners labour under a very serious grievance, by

[19] Petition, Jan. 13, 1804, *ASP, Misc.*, I, 386.

[20] Memorial presented to the Senate Jan. 21, 1805, Senate Records, RG 46, Natl. Archives.

[21] These petitions are in House Records, RG 233, Natl. Archives.

reason of the shutting of the Port of New-Orleans, without having an equivalent establishment assigned them on the Mississippi: That the Trade and Commerce of this Country are entirely checked, and will be destroyed, unless we are secured in the enjoyment of those privileges, which we vainly thought were guaranteed to us by the Treaty with Spain, made in 1795." The petitioners pledged support for whatever measures Congress might take to restore free navigation of the Mississippi River.[22] Notations on some of the copies of this petition indicate that printed copies were scattered through western Pennsylvania with various persons collecting signatures. Notes on several copies named the persons to whom the signed petitions were to be returned.

Concern about the defense of the harbor of New York precipitated an extensive petitioning effort in 1806. In March public meetings were held in the different wards of the city where a memorial was read and approved, and each of the nine wards sent Congress a copy of the petition, signed by a ward committee.[23] When Congress adjourned without taking action, the New York plea was renewed at the next session. A memorial, dated December 8, 1806, sought "to represent the defenceless condition of the Port of New-York, and to reiterate those claims for its efficient protection, which are enforced by every consideration of individual and national Interest and Honour." Signed by inhabitants of the City of New York, thirty printed copies of this petition, with varying numbers of signatures, were presented on December 22, 1806; sixteen additional copies of the same petition were presented on December 31, and seven copies, on January 5, 1807.[24] In addition to this massive appeal, a petition signed by twenty-seven subscribers who constituted "a general Committee appointed by the Republicans of the City and County of New York" also stressed that "the exposed and defenceless situation of this City has been long the occasion of a great anxiety and solicitude."[25] Meanwhile, the President in his annual message, December 2, 1806, recommended measures to improve the fortifications of seaports, though not specifically mentioning New York; and in the Senate, Mitchill

[22] Forty copies of the petition were referred to the Committee of the Whole House on the State of the Union Feb. 3, 1803, and ten additional copies were similarly referred Feb. 17, 1803, *ibid.*

[23] Copies of the petitions are in *ibid.*

[24] Copies are in *ibid.*

[25] Petition signed by John H. Sickels and others, Dec. 18, 1806, presented Dec. 24, 1806, *ibid.*

of New York was chosen chairman of the committee to whom that part of the President's message was referred. In his report Mitchill made special mention of New York; "and actually presented my Bill and got it in print before the Senate, a day or two before the Memorials from my Townsmen reached Washington," he wrote his wife.[26] Although massive petitioning got the attention of Congress, it did not always win legislative support. Despite the pressure from New York, Congress did not pass the major appropriation for fortifying New York harbor which New Yorkers sought, although a general appropriation to improve harbor fortifications was enacted.[27]

The volume of petitions and their major areas of concern are shown in Table 16 which lists the petitions presented to the House of Representatives during the first sessions of the Seventh, Eighth, and Ninth Congresses. Since select committees dealt with a variety of matters, all areas of concern have not been identified, but the most common subjects of petitions are indicated. Claims, commerce, manufactures, post offices, post roads, and public lands were the matters most frequently the subject of petitions. The second session of each Congress, being shorter, normally handled fewer petitions.

The number of petitions presented to Congress contradicts the arguments that the legislators in Washington were isolated from the people they governed and that the people themselves were indifferent to what the national government did.[28] Various groups constantly watched the proceedings of Congress and reacted to any proposed change that affected their interests. In a predominantly rural society with a widely scattered population, there was not equal access to information about congressional proceedings, but newspapers in the cities carried reports of debates that pro-

[26] Mitchill to his wife, Dec. 8 and 17, 1806, Mitchill Papers, Museum C.N.Y.

[27] *House Journal*, v, 571, 587, 605, 648; *Annals of Congress*, 9 Cong. 2 Sess., 1286; Adams, *History*, iii, 350-353.

[28] Young, *Washington Community*, concluded that a major factor in Jeffersonian government was "remoteness of the rulers from the citizenry and remoteness of the citizenry from the rulers." He saw a "negligibility of public response to the presence and the work of the early government," "indifference among citizens toward the national government itself," and the government "isolated beside the Potomac, virtually unwatched by the citizenry." He concluded that "government was conducted as nearly in a vacuum as it ever has been" (pp. 34-37).

TABLE 16. PETITIONS PRESENTED TO THE HOUSE OF REPRESENTATIVES, 1801-1806[a]

Committee or Department to which Petition was Initially Referred[b]	7th Congress 1st Session 1801-1802	8th Congress 1st Session 1803-1804	9th Congress 1st Session 1805-1806
Standing Committees			
Claims	66	83	95
Commerce and Manufactures	58	54	60
Ways and Means	7	8	18
Elections		3	2
Accounts			1
Public Lands			40
Committee of the Whole House on the State of the Union	2		9
Committee of the Whole House	35	14	13
Select Committees			
Post Roads and Post Offices	23	25	50
Sale of Public Lands		12	
Naturalization	8		
Government and Laws of Distrct of Columbia	24		
Bridge over the Potomac		5	
Spoliations	15		
Judicial Establishment	3		
Military Land Warrants		3	
Other Select Committees	32	49	50
Departments			
State	3		4
Treasury	6		5
War	1		2
Navy			2
Postmaster General			2
Other Agency			2
Tabled			10
TOTAL	283	256	365

[a] As recorded in Petition Book, 4 Cong., 1 Sess.—7 Cong., 1 Sess.; Petition Book, 7 Cong., 2 Sess.—10 Cong., 1 Sess., House Records, RG 233, Natl. Archives.
[b] Petitions not uncommonly were referred subsequently to another committee, and petitions directed to a department head were later referred to a committee.

vided more information than the House and Senate Journals. The chambers of commerce of Philadelphia and New York were frequent petitioners, often while legislation was pending. "Your memorialists view with much alarm the renewal of an attempt to repeal the acts making discrimination between American and foreign duties on Imports and Tonnage," the New York Chamber of Commerce declared in petitioning Congress in January 1803 not to repeal the discriminating duties.[29] A petition making a similar plea had been sent by the Philadelphia Chamber of Commerce two weeks earlier.[30] Other groups reacted equally promptly when matters of special concern were before Congress. "Your memorialists have seen with deep and affecting concern, a Resolution to exempt from impost duties, Arms manufactured in foreign Countries, pass in the house of Representatives of the United States," the gun manufacturers of Lancaster, Pennsylvania, prefaced their petition urging that the duty on arms not be removed.[31] The great volume of petitions relating to import duties attests to the close watch interested groups kept over legislation in that area. A chamber of commerce or a group of manufacturers were more likely to have the means of petitioning readily at hand than unorganized groups of the citizenry. Nevertheless, when their immediate interests were affected, citizen groups found ways to make their concerns known to Congress. The process of petition provided access to government by people of all circumstances, and Congress was ready to listen to grievances from anyone who claimed to be suffering under its laws.[32]

Rarely could petitioners expect a speedy decision. The endorsements made by House clerks on petitions reveal the often long and circuitous route of a petition as successive Congresses delayed action. A petition from the inspectors of the customs of the City of New York has the following endorsements:

5th December, 1805.
Referred to the Secretary of the Treasury.

[29] Petition signed by John Murray, Jan. 15, 1803, presented Jan. 24, 1803, Senate Records, RG 46, Natl. Archives.

[30] Petition signed by Thomas Fitzsimons, Dec. 31, 1802, presented Jan. 5, 1803, ibid.

[31] Petition, Jan. 28, 1803, presented Feb. 4, 1803, House Records, RG 233, Natl. Archives.

[32] See petition of settlers and purchasers of public lands Northwest of the Ohio, referred to the Committee on the Public Lands, Dec. 31, 1805; report, Apr. 2, 1806, ibid.

16th January, 1806.
report made, read and referred to the
Committee of Ways and Means.

12th December, 1806.
Referred to the Committee of Ways and Means.

13th November, 1807.
Referred to Committee of Ways and Means.

23d November, 1807.
report made and referred to Committee of
Whole House.

5th December, 1808.
Referred to the Committee of Commerce and
Manufactures.[33]

The petitioners sought an increase in pay, a request also made by inspectors in other ports, including Philadelphia, Baltimore, Boston, and Charleston, whose petitions were similarly referred.[34] The inspectors' salaries were not increased, but their case was carefully considered, and a report of the Committee of Ways and Means in 1807 gave a full explanation for the refusal.[35] Indeed, the endorsements on the numerous petitions that came before Congress show that whether granted or rejected, petitions received respectful attention. The Committee of Commerce and Manufactures in January 1808, for example, wrote a twelve-page report explaining why a petition from merchants and traders of Philadelphia for an exception to the general embargo ought not to be granted.[36]

The volume of petitions indicates little reluctance on the part of petitioners to address Congress directly. There is no evidence in the records of the petitioning process of the Jeffersonian era to suggest a feeling that the national government was distant and unapproachable. Instead, there are strong indications of a feeling that government was responsive to its citizens. And not only citizens petitioned Congress, but aliens as well. A number of petitions from aliens sought changes in the naturalization laws. A petition with

[33] Petition of the Inspectors of the Customs of the City of New York, *ibid*.
[34] Petitions from the inspectors in these cities are in *ibid*.
[35] Report of Committee of Ways and Means, Nov. 23, 1807, *ibid*.
[36] Report, Jan. 11, 1808, *ibid*.

some four feet of signatures of aliens living in Baltimore in 1803 commended Congress for the modification of the naturalization laws in 1802 but appealed for further changes.[37] While the act of 1802 had reduced the residence requirements from fourteen to five years, the Baltimore petitioners sought a two-year residence requirement. They were joined in their appeal by large numbers of aliens in other places, particularly in Pennsylvania, who sent similar petitions to Congress.[38]

The proposed repeal of the judiciary act of 1801 produced petitions on both sides of the issue. After Vice-President Burr cast the deciding vote in the Senate on January 27, 1802, to recommit the judiciary bill to a select committee,[39] public meetings to put pressure on Congress were organized by Philadelphia Republicans under the leadership of William Duane, editor of the *Aurora*. At public meetings in Philadelphia on January 30 and February 2, a memorial to Congress was prepared,[40] and printed copies were circulated for signatures. The first of these petitions, with seventy-three signatures, was presented to Congress on February 8, while the bill was under consideration in the House. Two additional copies with 125 signatures arrived the following day, and during the next ten days, nine more copies of the petition were presented. The twelve petitions contained a total of 466 signatures.[41] The brief text expressed approval of the arguments made in favor of the repeal of the act by Republican senators and urged action. The aim of the petition was not to present new arguments but to demonstrate popular support for Republican policy. None of these petitions had arrived in time to influence the Senate decision on the passage of the bill, although on February 2 Federalist Senator James Ross of Pennsylvania had presented a memorial from the Philadelphia bar against repeal.[42] On the same day, as a result of

[37] Memorial of the Aliens, Inhabitants of the City of Baltimore, presented Feb. 17, 1803, *ibid.*

[38] Printed petitions, with the name of the town or county inserted by hand, came from aliens in Lancaster, Carlisle, Dauphin County, Cumberland County, Montgomery County, and Pittsburgh during February 1803. House Records, RG 233; Senate Records, RG 46, Natl. Archives.

[39] *Annals of Congress*, 7 Cong., 1 Sess., 150.

[40] Sanford W. Higginbotham, *The Keystone in the Democratic Arch: Pennsylvania Politics, 1800-1816* (Harrisburg, Pa., 1952), p. 42.

[41] The Memorial of the Subscribers, Inhabitants of the City and County of Philadelphia, Feb. 2, 1802, House Records, RG 233, Natl. Archives.

[42] *Annals of Congress*, 7 Cong., 1 Sess., 152-153. See also Richard E. Ellis, *The Jeffersonian Crisis: Courts and Politics in the Young Republic* (New York, 1971), p. 48.

an absent Republican senator having taken his seat, the select committee to which the bill had earlier been referred by the casting vote of the Vice-President was discharged. With this change in the party alignment in the Senate, Burr predicted that the bill would pass the Senate on the following day by a vote of 16 to 15. "Nothing short of the death of a Democratic Senator can prevent the immediate passage of the Bill," he concluded.[43] His prediction was confirmed when the Senate on February 3 passed the bill by a vote of 16 to 15.[44]

The closeness of the vote in the Senate provoked additional petitions aimed at influencing the final outcome. A petition signed by 225 merchants of Philadelphia was presented to the House on February 16 opposing the repeal.[45] The New York Chamber of Commerce also petitioned against the repeal,[46] as did "sundry counsellors at law practicing in New Jersey."[47] By the time the House of Representatives voted on the bill's passage on March 3, major petitions on both sides of the question had been presented to Congress. How much these petitions influenced the final vote of 59 to 32 in favor of repeal is impossible to know. But with one exception the division was strictly on party lines. All 59 members who voted in favor of repeal were Republicans; of the 32 members voting against the measure, all but one was a Federalist. Only William Eustis, a Massachusetts Republican, crossed party lines in the vote.[48]

There is some indication in the contemporary records that the movements to petition Congress in regard to the repeal of the judiciary act of 1801 received encouragement, if not inspiration, from members of Congress. While the proposed repeal was before the Senate, Representative Bayard, writing to his father-in-law, Richard Bassett, one of the circuit judges appointed by President Adams under the 1801 act, declared: "I am surprized at the public apathy upon the subject. Why do not those who are opposed to the project, express in the public papers or by petitions their disapprobation of the measure? The majority affect to pay great deference to public sentiment, and it is likely that a public movement

---

[43] Burr to Charles Biddle, Feb. 2, 1802, Charles Biddle Papers, Hist. Soc. Pa.

[44] *Annals of Congress*, 7 Cong., 1 Sess., 183.

[45] Petition presented Feb. 16, 1802, House Records, RG 233, Natl. Archives.

[46] Presented Feb. 16, 1802, *ibid.*   [47] Presented Feb. 17, 1802, *ibid.*

[48] *House Journal*, IV, 119-120.

would have great effect."[49] While the measure was being debated in the House, Senator Morris wrote to a New York Federalist friend that "unless some strong Memorials should come forward soon the Repeal will certainly go thro the other House."[50] It is rarely possible to trace the process through which petitions originated, but at times the initiative for petitions came from members of Congress. Legislators hinted, if they did not openly suggest, that petitions expressing public support for the positions they were taking in Congress would be useful. Sometimes, they were specific in their suggestions. "The project is on foot to repeal the laws relative to internal revenue," Congressman Bayard wrote to his cousin Andrew Bayard, a Philadelphia banker and merchant, in January 1802. "This is the moment for your merchants to come forward if they wish the duties lowered upon any articles of importation."[51]

While some petitions may have been inspired by members of Congress, the independency of constituents produced others, as Senator Mitchill indicated in the following note to Gallatin:

> The inclosed memorial arrived from New York by the last Mail. The Citizens have taken this step without consulting me or regarding what I wrote them. The first disposition I make of them is to forward them to you for inspection. You will observe that the Directors of the Manhattan Company and the Members of the new City-Corporation are the leading Subscribers. But there is a numerous list besides, of our good republicans as well as others. After you shall have read the Paper, I shall be glad to have it again, that I may make some disposition of them.[52]

Two days later, Mitchill presented to the Senate "the petition of sundry merchants of the city of New York, praying that the period for the payment of bonds given for the duties on goods imported from South America and the West Indies, may be extended."[53]

A flood of petitions began when the House of Representatives adopted a resolution early in the Seventh Congress directing the

[49] Bayard to Bassett, Jan. 25, 1802, Donnan, ed., *Bayard Papers*, pp. 146-147.

[50] Morris to Nicholas Low, Feb. 12, 1802, Letter Book, Papers of Gouverneur Morris, Lib. Cong.

[51] James A. Bayard to Andrew Bayard, Jan. 9, 1802, Donnan, ed., *Bayard Papers*, p. 145.

[52] Mitchill to Gallatin, Jan. 15, 1805, Gallatin Papers, N.-Y. Hist. Soc.

[53] *Annals of Congress*, 8 Cong., 2 Sess., 36.

Committee of Commerce and Manufactures "to inquire whether any, and what alterations may be necessary in the acts laying duties on goods, wares, and merchandise, imported into the United States."[54] The petitions prompted by this inquiry provide an excellent opportunity to examine the role of petitions in the legislative process. A month after the adoption of the House resolution the first petition from hat manufacturers seeking protective duties was presented, and for the next six weeks from two to seven petitions from hatters were received each week. Among others petitioning for higher import duties on the products which they produced were starch manufacturers of Philadelphia, papermakers of Pennsylvania and Delaware, papermakers of Essex County, New Jersey, shoemakers of Lynn, Massachusetts, calico printers of Philadelphia and neighboring villages, cordwainers of Wilmington, Delaware, gunpowder manufacturers in the vicinity of Baltimore, and umbrella manufacturers of Philadelphia and vicinity.[55] A common argument of the petitions was the need to encourage the development of American industry. "Your petitioners would not be understood by this application to Congress as calling for a further restraint on the importation of Stone Ware with a view to obtain a monopoly of the home manufacture, and thereby to enhance its price," a group of manufacturers of stoneware explained, "but only to afford to domestic industry that encouragement which good policy requires, and which all wise Governments feel disposed to shew towards the members of their own Community."[56] Kentucky hemp growers prayed "that Congress will lay a duty on hemp, cordage and sail-duck, imported from abroad, adequate to prevent or lessen the importation of it, and to give encouragement to the husbandmen and manufacturers of our own country. . . . Your petitioners need not remark, that it has been the policy of all nations to give such a preference to the productions of their own countries, as might enable them to form a successful competition with those of foreigners."[57] A petition signed by fifty hatters in the City of Philadelphia seeking higher duties on hats imported from Europe remonstrated:

[54] *Ibid.*, 7 Cong., 1 Sess. (Dec. 11, 1801), 317-318.

[55] Copies of these petitions are in House Records, RG 233, Natl. Archives.

[56] Thomas and Joel Morgan, John Reynolds, William Chambers, and James Johnson, petition presented Jan. 5, 1802, *ibid.*

[57] Petition of sundry inhabitants of Kentucky presented Feb. 9, 1802, *ibid.*

Your petitioners will not dwell upon the painful reverse which has resulted from the want of competent protection and encouragement; but . . . they cannot, without great concern, view the manufacturing institutions of their country prostrated before a foreign commerce, which imposes upon the Citizens of the United States the ungracious and unpatriotic task of supporting workmen in foreign manufactories, when, at the same time, their own fellow-citizens at home are neglected, and for want of adequate support, threatened with ruin.[58]

Besides seeking protective duties, petitioners sought other changes in import duties to aid particular industries. The brush-makers of Philadelphia wanted the duties on bristles removed. Printers in Baltimore, New York, Philadelphia, Boston, and Charleston prayed for no higher duties on types. Glassmakers in Philadelphia wanted duties on coal reduced. Papermakers wanted the elimination of duties on imported rags.[59] As these petitions poured in, the House directed them to the Committee of Commerce and Manufactures, to whom the resolution to consider revisions in import duties had been referred. Although the committee reported in favor of providing relief for the petitioners, the House became so engaged in debating the repeal of the judiciary act of 1801 that no action was taken, and consideration was postponed until the following session of Congress.[60]

At the next session additional petitions were presented, among them a petition from the cordwainers of Philadelphia with eleven pages of signatures of the 556 subscribers.[61] These petitions were referred to the Committee of Commerce and Manufactures, which reported, February 21, 1803, that "justice to the petitioners and sound policy point to the necessity of granting governmental aid for the protection of such manufactures as are obviously capable of affording to the United States an adequate supply of their several and respective objects." The committee found that existing duties did not operate "as protecting duties to our infant manufactures," since there was inadequate discrimination between articles that competed with American manufactures and those that were not produced in the United States. With the Seventh Congress drawing to a close, the committee recommended that import duties be

---

[58] Petition of hatters of Philadelphia, Jan. 6, 1802, presented Jan. 14, 1802, *ibid.*

[59] Petitions are in *ibid.*

[60] *Annals of Congress*, 7 Cong., 1 Sess., 493, 1194; *ASP, Finance*, i, 730.

[61] Petitions are in House Records, RG 233, Natl. Archives.

revised at the next session and proposed that the Secretary of the Treasury be directed to prepare a plan for levying new and more specific duties which would neither increase nor diminish the existing revenue from imports.[62] The House adopted the committee's proposal, and ten days later Gallatin sent a circular to collectors transmitting the House resolution and asking for recommendations.[63]

Gallatin submitted his report—based on the suggestions from the collectors—to the House of Representatives on January 24, 1804.[64] On the following day, Samuel L. Mitchill, chairman of the Committee of Commerce and Manufactures, submitted the committee's report on the various memorials and petitions "praying for legislative patronage to several domestic arts, trades, and manufactures." Largely written by Mitchill,[65] the report provided a review of the various actions taken by the House in regard to the petitions during the preceding Congress and an examination of the existing level of encouragement to manufactures. Arguing that Congress had already done much to help domestic industry, the report pointed out that "there may be some danger in refusing to admit the manufactures of foreign countries; for, by the adoption of such a measure, we should have no market abroad for our produce, and industry would lose one of its chief incentives at home." However, the committee concluded that Congress might take additional steps to encourage domestic manufactures and presented a plan "to suit the wishes of the petitioners as far as seems reasonable, and as actual circumstances warrant." The committee offered a list of proposed alterations in import duties that would give some relief or further encouragement to most of the petitioners.[66]

After considering the report, the House referred it to the Committee of Ways and Means to bring in a bill,[67] thus taking the matter out of the hands of a committee composed largely of members with commercial connections and experience and placing it in the hands of a less sympathetic committee headed by Randolph. The bill reported by the Ways and Means Committee and subsequently passed by the House, though subjected to some amend-

[62] *Report of the Committee of Commerce and Manufactures, 21st February, 1803*, Rare Book Division, Lib. Cong.

[63] Circular, Treasury Department, Mar. 31, 1803, U. S. Finance Collection, Manuscript Division, Lib. Cong.

[64] *ASP, Finance*, II, 78-79.

[65] Mitchill to his wife, Feb. 19, 1804, Mitchill Papers, Museum C.N.Y.

[66] *ASP, Finance*, II, 80-81.

[67] *Annals of Congress*, 8 Cong., 1 Sess. (Mar. 2, 1804), 1086-1087.

ments from the floor, did not go as far in answering the requests of the petitioners as the recommendations of the Committee of Commerce and Manufactures. Even so, Representative Benjamin Huger, a South Carolina Federalist, opposed the bill as designed "to promote the manufactures of the Eastern and Middle States, to the great detriment of the Southern States."[68] In the vote on the bill, however, the opposition was less from the South than from the Federalists. Of the forty-one votes cast against the bill, only eighteen came from representatives of states south of Maryland. On the other hand, twenty-four of the forty-one opponents were Federalists.[69]

Despite the pleas of the petitioners and the support of the Committee of Commerce and Manufactures for greater protection for American industries, the act as finally passed did not provide much additional protection. The appeals of petitioners which received the most sympathetic hearing were those which sought the elimination of duties on materials used in manufacturing processes. The act thus answered the appeals of the papermakers, brushmakers, printfounders, and corkcutters by exempting from import duties various materials used in their industries. Changes were also made in the duties on starch and gunpowder. But the act did not in general provide for higher protective duties on manufactured products. No additional protection was provided to hatters despite a massive petitioning effort and the recommendation of the Committee of Commerce and Manufactures that the duty on hats be raised from 15 to 20 percent.[70] Nor was the duty raised on umbrellas, shoes, or printed calicoes—manufacturers of which had all petitioned for protection. The act showed that the pleas of numerous petitioners for protective duties did not move Congress in that direction. The petitions received the careful attention of Congress and played a part in determining the provisions of the act which finally emerged, but petitions from special-interest groups were weighed by members against other constituent and party pressures.

The issue that provoked the most widespread petitioning during Jefferson's presidency was the embargo act passed by Congress in December 1807. By the spring of 1808, Congress was receiving petitions seeking exemptions from the embargo, particularly from a number of towns in Massachusetts asking relief for the fishing

68 *Ibid.* (Mar. 21, 1804), 1205.
69 The vote is recorded in *ibid.*, 1205-1206.
70 *ASP, Finance*, II, 81.

industry.[71] In August a petition adopted at a town meeting in Boston and directed to the President called upon him to suspend the embargo or, if he doubted his authority to do so, to call Congress into special session. The meeting also instructed the selectmen of Boston to send a copy of the proceedings to the selectmen of every town in Massachusetts for their concurrence. This touched off a major petitioning campaign, which in turn provoked counterpetitions and revealed how deeply the embargo petitions were enmeshed in partisan politics. On the day after the Boston memorial against the embargo was adopted in August 1808, the Republican central committee of Massachusetts sent a circular to the chairmen of county Republican committees warning them to be "on your guard against the designs of the enemies of our present Administration. We proudly recognize the Constitutional Right of the Citizens to petition their Rulers for redress of grievances," the committee declared, "but, when the *united* wisdom of all departments of our National Councils have deliberately adopted a measure of *Defence*, against the unprincipled aggressions of foreign powers, it evinces a want of patriotism for the People to interpose their petitions against it."[72] The central committee charged that the Boston petitioners were seeking "to render the Administration unpopular;—to induce the people to clamour against their measures, and by these and other means, to place in the Presidential Chair of the nation a man of their own political views." The county committees were thus urged to take steps to counteract these efforts. "It will not be sufficient for the Republican towns to treat the application, from the town of Boston, with silent indifference," the central committee concluded, "—*they ought to act*; and in the most pointed terms disapprove of this interference with our National Councils, as impolitic, premature and hazardous to the peace of our country."[73]

As petitions and counterpetitions inundated the President at his summer office at Monticello during August and September 1808, Jefferson found it difficult to keep up with replies. Between August 26 and September 10 he responded to the petitions from thirty-

[71] Petitions from Plymouth County, Massachusetts, Newburyport, Massachusetts, presented Apr. 5, 1808; four petitions from Barnstable, Massachusets, presented Apr. 11, 1808, petition from Essex County, Massachusetts, presented Apr. 16, 1808, House Records, RG 233, Natl. Archives.

[72] Circular, Boston, Aug. 10, 1808, signed by Aaron Hill, Perez Morton, Samuel Brown, James Prince, Charles P. Sumner, and William Jarvis; Broadside Collection, Rare Book Division, Lib. Cong.

[73] *Ibid.*

eight towns.[74] At this point he decided to have printed copies of his reply prepared. Sending an order to Samuel Harrison Smith, he explained: "I am overwhelmed with petitions from Massachusetts. I give the same answer to them all, but as it is pretty long it requires more writing than I can get done in the country. I therefore inclose you a copy and must pray you to have 150 printed on good quarto writing paper and a large good type, and to send them to me by the post which leaves Washington for Milton this day sennight, as the petitions will be accumulating on me till then."[75] A few days later, Jefferson sent Smith a copy of an "answer to the Counter-Addresses, which being not likely to be so numerous, I will pray you to print me 50 copies."[76] Between August and December 1808 Jefferson recorded the receipt of 199 petitions against the embargo and 46 counterpetitions.[77] Jefferson's papers not only reveal the volume of the petitions directed to the President but also show the attention he gave to them, continuing the practice that he had followed since taking office of responding to all addresses and petitions sent to him.

Soon after Congress assembled in November 1808, petitions seeking the repeal of the embargo poured into the legislature. The largest petitioning effort came from Essex County, Massachusetts, which sent petitions from sixteen towns. The petitions were in printed form with the name of each town written in and each petition accompanied by from two to fifteen pages of signatures. The eighty-six pages of signatures appended to the sixteen petitions contained 4,101 names.[78] Other petitions calling for the repeal of the embargo came from Dutchess County, New York; Woodbridge, Connecticut; Lincoln County, North Carolina; various wards in the City of New York; Westmoreland County, Pennsylvania; and elsewhere. From Ontario County, New York, came fifty-seven copies of a printed petition each with signatures attached.[79] Many

[74] The covering form letter, with names of towns and correspondents to which his answers were sent, is in Jefferson Papers, Aug. 26, 1808, Lib. Cong. Copies of Jefferson's answer to both the petitions and counterpetitions are also in the same collection.

[75] Jefferson to Smith, Sept. 9, 1808, Jonathan Bayard Smith Papers, Lib. Cong.

[76] Jefferson to Smith, Sept. 13, 1808, Jefferson Papers, Lib. Cong.

[77] Jefferson's indexes to letters sent and received, *ibid.*

[78] These petitions are in House Records, RG 233, Natl. Archives. The petitions appear to have been originally stitched together into a booklet with a cover page addressed "Mr. Livermore." Representative Edward Livermore presented the petitions to the House, Nov. 17, 1808, *House Journal*, VI, 355.

[79] Petitions are in House Records, RG 233, Natl. Archives.

of the antiembargo petitions originated in strongly Federalist areas, and Republicans warned that the petitions did not represent all of the people. One Republican in Newburyport, in Essex County, Massachusetts, supplied Madison with information to lay before the President regarding a petition received from Newburyport. "I wish him to know," he wrote, "that this town contains between 9 and 10 hundred voters; at the last General Election there was 615 styling themselves federalists and 368 republicans. The number who attended the meeting in which this petition was ordered to be presented is said to be from 3 to 400, and all federalists except perhaps 6 or 8 in number. It is said many of that number did not vote. These matters managed by a small number of violent federalists, by whom the petition is supposed to have been prepared before the meeting, and some of violent persons seem to be determined to break through the Embargo Law at all hazards."[80]

The growing volume of attacks on the embargo led other Republicans to seek to assure the President that, if he did not have Federalist support, he retained the confidence of Republicans and the majority of Americans. During the months of December 1808 and January 1809, the legislatures of Georgia, South Carolina, North Carolina, Virginia, and New York all passed resolutions of support for the measures adopted by the government.[81]

If the petitions did not give an accurate reflection of support on either side of the embargo issue, they unmistakably conveyed to the President and to Congress the division in the country on the measure and the depth of feeling surrounding it. The language of many of the petitions showed the frustration, concern, and partisanship of opponents and friends alike. The Essex County, Massachusetts, petitioners spoke of "a season of uncommon publick danger and alarm" in which millions of Americans found themselves "deprived of the exercise of invaluable rights, the higher security and more perfect enjoyment of which, was, as they conceive, a principal motive of the establishment of the Union of the States, and of our excellent Constitution." They indicated that in a time of peace they had been "plunged from a state of unexampled pros-

[80] Stephen Cross to Madison, Aug. 11, 1808, Gallatin Papers, N.-Y. Hist. Soc. See also Josiah Batchelder, Jr., to Jefferson, Aug. 20, 1808, in which Batchelder assured Jefferson that the petition from Beverly, Massachusetts, did not represent the town. Jefferson Papers, Lib. Cong.

[81] Resolutions of Georgia, Dec. 6, 1808; South Carolina, Dec. 16, 1808; Virginia, Jan. 6, 1809; New York, Jan. 31, 1809, Jefferson Papers, Lib. Cong. *Resolutions of the Legislature of North Carolina, Communicated by Mr. Turner, December 30th, 1808.*

perity into deep distress; and this by the constituted Guardians of their liberty and safety." They accused the President of being "unconcerned at the wide spreading calamity," insisting that he "has answered the humble petitions of the people for relief, by a declared intention to persevere in a system of measures which threatens our utter ruin." They denied that the only alternative to the embargo was a war with Great Britain, charged that the embargo represented a total abandonment of the commercial interest of the nation, and appealed to Congress "for that relief and redress which they alone are competent to bestow."[82]

On the other hand, the legislature of North Carolina charged that the great clamor raised against the embargo had led foreign nations to believe that the nation was divided, "unable or unwilling to carry into effect any energetic measures of their government," and concluded that "though the laws laying an embargo have borne hard upon a great part of the citizens of the United States, the Legislature of North Carolina consider them as the best means which could have been devised to preserve our citizens and property from the devouring grasp of the belligerent powers." "Sooner than submit to unjust and vexatious restrictions on our commerce; to the impressment of our seamen; and to the taxation of the cargoes of our vessels, at the pleasure of foreign nations, we will live to ourselves, and have no connexion with any of them."[83]

Although Congress could find support in the petitions and resolutions laid before it for whatever course it might take in regard to the embargo, it could not but sense the nation's concern and distress. On the embargo issue, as on other questions, petitions were but one source of pressure on the legislature; but on this issue more than any other that came before the Jeffersonian Congresses, the torment of the nation as revealed in petitions moved the Congress to act to repeal the embargo.

While the petitions produced by the embargo constituted the most impressive volume of public petitions on any issue during Jefferson's presidency and contributed to the most dramatic reversal of public policy, petitions routinely played a role in the legislative process. Petitions were never mistaken for the voice of the nation, and members were more aware than historians can ever be of the special interests, partisan aims, and personal ambitions

[82] Petition of Newburyport, Essex County, Massachusetts, Oct. 15, 1808, presented Nov. 17, 1808, House Records, RG 233, Natl. Archives.

[83] *Resolutions of the Legislature of North Carolina, Communicated by Mr. Turner, December 30th, 1808.*

represented in appeals that came before Congress; but the attention and respect which petitions received and the place that they were afforded in the daily business of the legislature indicate that members of Congress regarded the process of petition as a legitimate and necessary part of the process of government.

XIV. The Jeffersonian Experience

"MR. JEFFERSON IS WELL CALCULATED TO PULL down any political edifice and those will not be disappointed who have feared he would employ himself as industriously and indefatigably in taking to pieces stone by stone the national building as Washington employed himself in putting them together. Even the foundation will be razed in less than four years."[1] Thus did one Virginia Federalist assess the prospects of Jefferson's presidency early in 1802. But Jefferson did not tear down the edifice of government. Indeed, soon after taking office he wrote privately: "When we reflect how difficult it is to move or inflect the great machine of society, how impossible to advance the notions of a whole people suddenly to ideal right, we see the wisdom of Solon's remark that no more good must be attempted than the nation can bear, and that will be chiefly to reform the waste of public money, and thus drive away the vultures who prey on it, and improve some little on old routines. Some new fences for securing constitutional rights may, with the aid of a good legislature, perhaps be attainable."[2] Jefferson was overly modest in anticipating what he might accomplish as President, but the structure of government changed little during his eight years in office.

The process of government was a continuing one, and the patterns and precedents of the Federalist era, while not always binding, had a persisting influence. The executive departments created under the Federalists remained basically the same, and most of the clerks and lesser functionaries in government offices stayed at their posts. The Cabinet mechanism introduced by Washington continued. In Congress the committee system continued to evolve and some changes were made in the rules of procedure, but most of the legislative rules had been worked out during the six Congresses that preceded Jefferson's inauguration. Nor did the Jeffersonians alter the judicial branch in any fundamental way, although they repealed the Federalist judiciary act of 1801 and substituted a revised act of their own making.

[1] Charles Lee to Leven Powell, Feb. 11, 1802, Tucker Family Papers, Univ. of N. C.

[2] Jefferson to Walter Jones, Mar. 31, 1801, Thomas Jefferson Miscellany, Manuscript Division, Lib. Cong.

What changed when the Republicans took power in 1801 was not the structure of government but the management of the machinery of government. For the first time in the nation's history there was a change in party control of the executive and legislative branches of the national government. For the first time since Washington had taken office twelve years before, there was an entirely new Cabinet. A new President and a new party in power brought new direction to both executive and legislative branches. While neither the Congress nor the executive branch was to become a model of efficiency, Jefferson's government was better managed than either of the two preceding administrations. It was also a government that was more open and more in harmony with the majority of the nation, and Jefferson was more fully trusting of the people than either of his predecessors. As Jefferson's first year in office drew to a close, New York's Republican Senator DeWitt Clinton affirmed: "I am much pleased with our President. Never did I before see realized a perfect view of the first Magistrate of a republican nation."[3]

But Jefferson carried into office more than a trust in the people and a devotion to republican government. Contrary to the direful predictions of the Federalists about the dangers of putting philosophers into power and embarking on "the tempestuous sea of liberty," Jefferson brought to the presidency the most system in administration and the strongest leadership that the office had yet experienced. He was both a policymaker and a working administrator who was in command of the daily operation of his administration. As President, Jefferson halted the decline in the vigor of the presidency that had occurred under Adams. He worked harder at his job than his predecessor, spending long hours at his desk, and even on vacation at Monticello he moved his office with him. He also reversed the trend toward pomp and ceremony in the presidential office that had begun under Washington.

Despite the fears of executive power that had characterized Republican opposition in the 1790s, executive influence was strong in the Jeffersonian government, but it was balanced by accountability. It is significant that Jefferson began his presidency by directing the compilation of a complete register of government employees in order to provide the public with a full view of "the true extent of the machine of government." He felt strongly that

[3] Clinton to Horatio Gates, Feb. 25, 1802, Emmett Collection, N. Y. Pub. Lib.

it was vital to keep this information under the eyes of both the officers of government and their constituents.

Jefferson was the first President to make the Cabinet system really work. It is true that in explaining to his colleagues the administrative procedures that he intended to follow he claimed merely to be returning to the practices followed by Washington. But Jefferson's own papers, written while he was a member of Washington's Cabinet, testify that this was less than an accurate historical recollection. Washington's Cabinet—important as it was in the establishment of the institution—never developed the effectiveness of Jefferson's. From the outset, Washington's council was divided by the cleavage between Hamilton and Jefferson; and before the end of his presidency, with both Hamilton and Jefferson out of the Cabinet, Washington had become so unsuccessful in filling the vacant posts with effective advisers that he turned outside the government for assistance. Looking to his ex-Secretary of the Treasury for continuing help and guidance, Washington sent him government papers and documents and even counted on him to draft his annual addresses to Congress.[4] Hamilton—a private citizen—had more influence during the last two years of Washington's presidency than any official inside the government. Such conditions never existed under Jefferson.

In retaining Washington's Cabinet, President Adams inherited Washington's problems, and he compounded them by virtually delegating administrative control to department heads. Once during one of Adams's long absences from the capital, a Federalist friend warned him: "The people elected you to administer the government. They did not elect your officers, nor do they . . . think them equal to govern, without your presence and control."[5] But Adams was slow to assert command. Throughout much of his presidency, he did not have control over his Cabinet, the leading members of which looked for direction to Hamilton—a party leader outside the government.[6] Secretary of War James McHenry regu-

[4] Washington to Hamilton, May 8, June 26, Aug. 10, Nov. 2, 12, 1796; Hamilton to Washington, May 20, Nov. 4 and 10, 1796; Hamilton's draft of Washington's Eighth Annual Address to Congress, Nov. 10, 1796, Syrett, ed., *Papers of Alexander Hamilton*, xx, 162-166, 237-240, 292-293, 362-366, 393-394, 190-195, 372-373, 381-382, 382-388.

[5] Uriah Forrest to Adams, Apr. 28, 1799, Charles Francis Adams, ed., *The Works of John Adams*, 10 vols. (Boston, 1850-1856), viii, 637-638.

[6] Stephen G. Kurtz, *The Presidency of John Adams* (Philadelphia, 1957), pp. 271-283.

larly sent Adams's Cabinet communications directly to Hamilton for recommendations and then gave Hamilton's replies to the President as his own.[7] Similar circumstances cannot be found during Jefferson's presidency. As chief executive, Jefferson presented a stark contrast to Adams in supplying administrative leadership.

In making the Cabinet function effectively as the central mechanism of executive administration, Jefferson succeeded in what neither of his predecessors had accomplished and in what Madison as his successor would likewise fail to achieve. Soon after the close of Madison's presidency, John Quincy Adams observed: "I am aware that by the experience of our history under the present Constitution, Mr. Jefferson alone of our four Presidents has had the good fortune of a Cabinet, harmonizing with each other, and with him through the whole period of his Administration."[8] The keys to Jefferson's success may be found in his talent for system and organization, his reliance on discussion and persuasion rather than authority to achieve his ends, and his ability to keep men of conflicting temperaments working together effectively. Jefferson was readily accessible to members of his Cabinet, genuinely solicitous of his advisers' opinions, and fully tolerant of dissenting views. All members of his Cabinet felt free to speak frankly and to oppose the President in Cabinet meetings, in private consultations, and in written communications. Jefferson included all members of the Cabinet in his decisionmaking process, never replaced his Cabinet with advisers outside the government, and—except for the final months of his administration after his successor had been elected —never left the Cabinet leaderless.

That Jefferson's presidency ended with the Cabinet and the Congress floundering over the embargo policy was due less to Jefferson's failure as a leader than to the sensitivity of his character that made him reluctant to commit his successor to a future course. So strongly had he resented the actions taken by Adams during the last months of his presidency that Jefferson became overly cautious not to make decisions for his successor as his own presidency came to an end. Jefferson's leadership, moreover, had been weakened

[7] McHenry to Hamilton, Apr. 14, 19, 1797; Jan. 26, 1798; Hamilton to McHenry, Apr. 29, 1797 [Jan. 27-Feb. 11], 1798, Syrett, ed., *Papers of Alexander Hamilton*, xxi, 48-49, 51-52, 339-341, 61-71, 341-346.

[8] John Quincy Adams to his mother, Apr. 23-May 16, 1817, Adams Papers, microfilm edition, reel 437. I am indebted to Julian P. Boyd for calling this letter to my attention.

by the growing opposition to the embargo during his final year in office, and he left Washington on a note of declining presidential power. Nevertheless, the overall record of his administration was one of strong presidential leadership. While Congress was not the subservient tool of the President pictured by his enemies, the record of presidential direction is persuasive. Most of major legislation passed by Congress developed from presidential proposals or recommendations.

Jefferson was in a powerful position to exert leadership. As the unchallenged leader of the Republican party and a President with wide popular support, he wielded an influence that Adams never approached and an influence that was different from that of Washington, whose popular support was admittedly unrivaled. While Washington never accepted a role as party leader, Jefferson did, and he was remarkably successful in maintaining the confidence of his party. Even when Republicans became critically divided in several states, virtually all sides claimed loyalty to Jefferson. As a party leader, Jefferson displayed the same qualities that characterized his executive leadership and relied on persuasion rather than dictation to accomplish his purposes.

By the end of Jefferson's presidency, the nation's population was approaching seven million, the area of the country had been nearly doubled by the purchase of Louisiana, and the membership in Congress had increased to 176 representatives and senators. Yet the size of the central administrative apparatus had grown not at all during Jefferson's eight years in office. In fact, the total of 123 officers, clerks, and other employees who staffed the departmental offices and the General Post Office in the capital was actually down slightly from the 127 persons employed in the same offices in 1801. The executive offices not only administered the laws but also provided the staff services for the legislature, whose members, having no staffs of their own, were dependent upon departmental offices for information and other assistance. While the role of the national government was limited—and by abolishing internal taxes and the revenue service to collect them the Republicans further reduced its operation—the size of the country and its continuing growth required a competency of central administration which the Republicans demonstrated that they could provide. They showed their administrative abilities following the Louisiana Purchase by successfully incorporating the populated area of lower Louisiana, including the city of New Orleans, into the nation. By reducing the national debt even while purchasing Louisiana, they also proved that they could manage the Treasury. The overall record of the administration under Jefferson demonstrated that the Republicans were capable managers of the machinery of government.

The workings of the Jeffersonian Congresses in their day-by-day operations were rarely exciting and may in retrospect seem a familiar pattern of committees, legislative maneuvers, and circuitous debates. But what emerges from the detailed record is a pattern of self-government which, with all its imperfections, displayed a firm commitment to a government of laws and a rationality and a practicality of procedure well suited to the new nation. The records of Congress abound with evidence of a careful process of legislating, of consistent practices of obtaining information and varying views before acting, and of providing access for constituent opinion to be heard. Not always efficient, Congress nevertheless followed orderly procedures and was responsive to a national constituency. The process of petition afforded direct access to the highest levels of government by individuals and groups. While the pleas of petitioners were never mistaken for the voice of the electorate, the process promoted openness and responsiveness in government and showed that the central government was not remote from those it governed.

There is indeed little evidence in the contemporary records to suggest that the government in Washington was isolated from the people. The capital city itself at the beginning of the nineteenth century was remote and largely inhabited by those in the government. But the members of Congress kept in close contact with their constituents; in fact, they spent the greater part of each year at home in their districts and resided only temporarily in Washington while Congress was in session. Most members corresponded with friends in their districts, and some attempted extensive communication with their constituents by mailing printed circular letters reporting on the proceedings of Congress. In the absence of any official register of debates, newspapers throughout the country reported the proceedings of Congress in more detail than they do today. Newspapers also published presidential messages, the texts of laws, and various governmental reports. Most members of Congress distributed copies of documents among their constituents, and Congress regularly authorized the printing of documents in numbers to permit such distribution. Public concern with the affairs of the nation was evident in the press in all parts of the country.

A close look at the operation of the executive and legislative branches of government during Jefferson's presidency does not indicate an isolation of the different branches of government from each other that has sometimes been suggested. The distance that separated the legislative halls on Capitol Hill and the government offices around the President's mansion should not be exaggerated. In an age when it took eighteen hours to go by stage from Philadelphia to New York,[9] the twenty-minute ride from the Capitol to the President's house was hardly a barrier between the legislative and the executive branches. Gallatin, who lived on Capitol Hill, made the trip daily to the Treasury.[10] Both the President and the Congress recognized and attempted to protect the constitutional separation of powers in the national government. But neither the President nor the Congress conceived of the separation of powers as designed to promote the isolation of the branches of the government.

The emphasis that Jefferson and his contemporaries placed on the theory of separation of powers between the executive and legislative branches has obscured the close working relationships between the two branches. President Jefferson was always careful to emphasize that he did not presume to tell the legislators what they should do, while putting before them the major programs for legislative action and confidentially sending drafts of bills to key members. Congress regularly asserted its independence and guarded its final legislative power, while calling upon department heads for information and recommendations. Cabinet members were responsive to congressional requests, appeared before congressional committees, and informally conferred with and advised individual legislators. They regularly assisted in the drafting of legislation and in reviewing matters before congressional committees. The fact that the departmental offices provided the staff services for both the executive and legislative branches is a condition that must not be overlooked in considering the relationships between the branches of government. Surely that circumstance not only blurred the lines of separation of powers but constituted a major factor in the process of government.

The functioning of government under Jefferson rested on a party foundation. Republicans in Congress and throughout the country looked to the President as the national leader of the party, and the

[9] Brown, ed., *Plumer's Memorandum*, Apr. 26, 1806, p. 492.
[10] Gallatin to Jefferson, Aug. 18, 1801, Jefferson Papers, Lib. Cong.

strength of his leadership depended heavily on the fact that the President and a majority of Congress belonged to the same party. By the time of Jefferson's election, virtually all members of Congress were openly identified with a political party, and the influence of party remained strong throughout the eight years of his presidency. In the boardinghouses of the capital, where most representatives and senators lived while Congress was in session, partisan affiliation was the most important single determinant of boardinghouse grouping. Except for the Seventh Congress, Federalist opposition was so weak that a considerable amount of individual independence and lack of party regularity could be tolerated within Republican ranks, but no decline in the sense of Republican party identity is evident. In the House of Representatives the election of a Republican Speaker and his appointment of Republican majorities to all standing committees and key select committees maintained party control. In the Senate the composition of committees was likewise dominated by party. Republican control there ranged from 76 percent of all committees elected during the first session of the Seventh Congress to 94 percent of the committees elected during the first session of the Tenth Congress.[11] The importance of party loyalty to the President was demonstrated by the demotion of John Randolph from his leadership position in the House after his break with Jefferson in 1806 and the removal of his close friend and supporter, Nathaniel Macon, from the speakership. The Republican nominating caucus also displayed the close connection between party and Congress; and the caucus successfully resolved the difficult problems of dropping an incumbent Vice-President in 1804 and deciding the presidential succession upon Jefferson's retirement.

The process of government would not persist unchanged under Jefferson's successor. The strong presidential leadership, Cabinet effectiveness, party viability, and successful working relationships between the executive and Congress that characterized Jefferson's administration are conditions that do not describe Madison's presidency. Although Madison, Gallatin, and Smith had worked together in Jefferson's Cabinet, they were unable to do so under the changed circumstances of Madison's presidency, when Smith became Secretary of State and Gallatin remained at the Treasury. The system that developed under Jefferson rested upon a complex set of interrelationships within and between the executive and leg-

[11] See Table 13, p. 252 above.

islative branches. Changes in any of a number of circumstances were bound to alter the system and did so under Madison. But for Jefferson the system worked remarkably well. Although historical judgments may differ concerning the policies that resulted, the Jeffersonian experience gave new strength to the process of republican government in the United States.

Appendix I

	1801	1808
The President	1	1
President's Private Secretary	1	1
Total President's Office	2	2
Department of State		
Secretary of State	1	1
Chief Clerk	1	1
Clerk in charge of Patent Office		1
Clerks	6	5
Messenger	1	1
Total Department of State	9	9
Department of the Treasury		
Secretary of the Treasury	1	1
Chief Clerk	1	2
Clerks	5	4
Clerks, Land Office	1	5
Messenger	1	1
Commissioner of the Revenue	1	
Clerks	3	1
Messenger	1	
Superintendent of Stamps	1	
Clerks	2	
Messenger	1	
Stampers[2]	3	
Comptroller	1	1
Chief Clerk	1	1
Clerks	10	12
Messenger	1	1
Auditor	1	1
Chief Clerk	1	1
Clerks	10	10
Messenger	1	1
Treasurer	1	1
Clerks	3	3
Messenger	1	1

Executive Branch Officers and Employees (*cont.*)

	1801	1808
Register	1	1
Clerks[3]	16	15
Messenger	1	1
Building Superintendent	1	1
Watchmen	2	2
Total Department of the Treasury	73	67
Department of War		
Secretary of War	1	1
Chief Clerk	1	1
Clerks	4	4
Messenger	1	1
Accountant	1	1
Chief Clerk	1	1
Clerks	8	7
Messenger	1	1
Total Department of War	18	17
Department of the Navy		
Secretary of the Navy	1	1
Chief Clerk	1	1
Clerks	3	3
Messenger	1	1
Accountant	1	1
Chief Clerk	1	1
Clerks	8	7
Messenger	1	1
Total Department of the Navy	17	16
Total Four Departments	117	109
General Post Office		
Postmaster General	1	1
Assistant Postmaster General	1	1
Chief Clerk	1	1
Clerks	6	10
Messenger	1	1
Total General Post Office	10	14
Total Four Departments and General Post Office	127	123
Attorney General	1	1
TOTAL EXECUTIVE BRANCH	130	126

¹ The figures for 1801 are based on the "Roll of the Officers, Civil, Military, and Naval of the United States," transmitted to the Senate and House of Representatives by Jefferson, Feb. 17, 1802, printed in *ASP, Misc.*, I, 304-305. The original of this report is in Senate Records, RG 46, Natl. Archives. No similar list exists for 1808. The figures for 1808 are based on departmental reports, which list only clerks. Messengers, building superintendent, and watchmen are presumed to have remained the same unless the office for which they worked was abolished. The following sources were used in compiling the figures for 1808:

Report of the names and salaries of the persons employed in the Department of State, enclosed in James Madison to the Speaker of the House of Representatives, Jan. 22, 1808, Original Reports, State Department, House Records, RG 233, Natl. Archives.

Letter from the Secretary of the Treasury, Transmitting a Report of the Clerks in the Treasury Department during the Year 1808 (Washington, D.C., 1809), Rare Book Division, Lib. Cong.

Reports of the Names of the Clerks Employed in the Office of the Secretary of War and the Accountant of the War Department during the Year 1808, enclosed in Henry Dearborn to the Speaker of the House of Representatives, Feb. 16, 1809, Reports, War Department, IV, 219-221, House Records, RG 233, Natl. Archives.

Statements of the Names of the Clerks Employed in the Office of the Secretary of the Navy and the Accountant of the Navy for the Year 1808, enclosed in Robert Smith to the Speaker of the House of Representatives, Feb. 10, 1809, Reports, Navy Department, I, 267-268, House Records, RG 233, Natl. Archives.

Letter from the Postmaster General of the United States, Enclosing a Report Respecting the Salaries Allowed to the Clerks Employed in that Department, during the Year 1808, Jan. 19, 1809, Original Reports, Post Office, House Records, RG 233, Natl. Archives.

² Six stampers are listed in the roll for 1801, but their compensation indicates that only one was full time. On the basis of compensation, the remaining five have been assigned the equivalent of two positions.

³ This figure does not include one temporary clerk in 1801.

Appendix II

(*Italics* indicate persons appointed prior to Jefferson's taking office on March 4, 1801.)[2]

DEPARTMENT OF STATE

Chief Clerk	*Jacob Wagner*
Clerks	*Stephen Pleasonton*
	Daniel Brent
	Christopher Thom
	Bernard Smith
	Richard Forrest
Clerk, Head of Patent Office	William Thornton

DEPARTMENT OF THE TREASURY

Office of the Secretary of the Treasury

Chief Clerk	*Edward Jones*
Clerks	*Daniel Sheldon*
	David Harper
	John Banks
	John B. Pickford
	James Murray
Clerk, Late Commissioner of the Revenue	*Joseph Thaw*
Clerks, Land Office	Joshua J. Moore
	Robert King
	John Gardiner

Comptroller of the Treasury   Gabriel Duvall

Chief Clerk	*Nathan Lufborough*[3]
Clerks	*Andrew Ross*
	Thomas Hewitt
	John Laub
	John Woodside

	Lund Washington
	John Knapp
	Alexander S. Smoot
	Jacob Laub
	Charles J. Polk
	Isaac D. Hodges
	Robert Polk
	Edward W. Duvall

Auditor — *Richard Harrison*

   Chief Clerk — *Patrick Ferrall*

   Clerks — *Robert Underwood*

William Parker

Charles Shoemaker

David Easton

Thomas G. Slye

Joseph W. Harrison

John Smith

John Coyle

Ezekiel King

Thomas Barclay

Treasurer — Thomas Tudor Tucker

   Clerks — *Samuel Brook*

Richard Wilson

Thomas B. Dashiell

Register — *Joseph Nourse*

   Clerks — *Joshua Dawson*

Michael Nourse

Joseph Stretch

William James

Richard Freeman

William Mackey

John McGowan

William Doughty

John Litle

Henry Kramer

James McClery

James Laurie

Charles J. Nourse

John B. Rittenhouse

George Mitchell

DEPARTMENT OF WAR

Office of the Secretary of War

Chief Clerk	John Smith
Clerks	*Hezekiah Rogers* Andrew McClary Joseph B. Varnum, Jr. Nicholas de Munn

Accountant of the War Department	*William Simmons*
Chief Clerk	*Peter Hagner*
Clerks	*James Eakin* *John Abbott* *Benjamin Betterton* Samuel Lewis John Wilson *Robert Ellis* *James Hodnett*

DEPARTMENT OF THE NAVY

Office of the Secretary of the Navy

Chief Clerk	*Charles W. Goldsborough*[4]
Clerks	Samuel T. Anderson John K. Smith Conrad Schwartz

Accountant of the Navy	*Thomas Turner*
Chief Clerk	*Thomas H. Gillis*
Clerks	*George G. Macdaniel* *Joseph Mechlin* *Samuel Turner, Jr.* *John Macdaniel, Jr.* *John Craven* *Henry Forrest* Ezekiel Macdaniel

GENERAL POST OFFICE

Postmaster General	Gideon Granger
Assistant Postmaster General	*Abraham Bradley, Jr.*

Chief Clerk   *Robert F. How*

Clerks   Phineas Bradley
                                         William P. Gardner
                                         Jacob Cist
                                         David Shoemaker
                                         Toppan Webster
                                         Horace H. Edwards
                                         James Hewitt
                                         Andrew Coyle
                                         Harvey Bestor
                                         Henry Aborn

¹ This roster has been compiled from the following sources:

Department of State

Statement of the Application of the Appropriations for Clerk-hire in the Department of State for the Years 1799, 1800 and 1801, enclosed in James Madison to the Speaker of the House of Representatives, Mar. 30, 1802, Original Reports of the Secretary of State, House Records, RG 233, Natl. Archives.

List of Persons Employed as Clerks in the Department of State in the Year 1807, enclosed in James Madison to the Speaker of the House of Representatives, Jan. 22, 1808, Original Reports, State Department, House Records, RG 233, Natl. Archives.

Department of the Treasury

Statement of the Application of the Appropriations made by Congress for Clerk-hire in the Treasury Department for the Years 1799, 1800 and 1801, enclosed in Albert Gallatin to the Speaker of the House of Representatives, Apr. 6, 1802, Original Reports, Treasury Department, House Records, RG 233, Natl. Archives.

A Statement of the Whole Amount Received by Each Clerk in the Several Offices of the Treasury Department for Services Rendered during the Year 1807, enclosed in Albert Gallatin to the Speaker of the House of Representatives, Jan. 15, 1808, Original Reports, Treasury Department, House Records, RG 233, Natl. Archives.

Department of War

Statements of the Applications of the Appropriations Made by Congress for Clerk-hire in the War Department for the Years 1799, 1800 and 1801, enclosed in Henry Dearborn to the Speaker of the House of Representatives, Mar. 27, 1802, Original Reports, War Department, House Records, RG 233, Natl. Archives.

Reports of the Names of the Clerks Employed in the Office of the Secretary of War and Office of the Accountant of the War Department during the Year 1807, enclosed in Henry Dearborn to the Speaker of the House of Representatives, Jan. 23, 1808, Reports, War Department, IV, 198-199, House Records, RG 233, Natl. Archives.

Department of the Navy

Statement of the Application of the Appropriations Made by Congress for Clerk-hire in the Navy Department for the Years 1799, 1800 and 1801, enclosed in Robert Smith to the Speaker of the House of Representatives, Mar. 26, 1802, Reports, Navy Department, i, 85-93, House Records, RG 233, Natl. Archives.

Statements Exhibiting the Names of the Clerks Employed in the Office of the Secretary of the Navy and the Accountant of the Navy for the Year 1807, enclosed in Robert Smith to the Speaker of the House of Representatives, Jan. 9, 1808, Original Reports, Navy Department, House Records, RG 233, Natl. Archives.

General Post Office

[List of Clerks], endorsed "Clerks in office given by W. Duane," William Duane to Albert Gallatin [1801], Gallatin Papers, N.-Y. Hist. Soc., microfilm edition.

Report of the Postmaster General to the House of Representatives, Jan. 7, 1808, Original Reports, Post Office, House Records, RG 233, Natl. Archives.

[2] Names of clerks in office on Jan. 1, 1807, have been listed except in cases of vacancies that were subsequently filled.

If the job classification of an individual differed in 1801 and 1807 (such as a clerk in 1801 who was a chief clerk in 1807), this has been indicated in a footnote. Otherwise, the person held the same title in 1801 and 1807 and was employed in the same department, though not always in the same office within that department. The latter condition applies mainly to the Treasury Department, where at times clerks were shifted among the offices.

In addition to those holding office on Mar. 4, 1801, the names of the following clerks on the 1807 list also appear in the records for 1801 as having been employed for short periods at some time during the year 1801. Treasury Department: John B. Pickford, Joshua J. Moore, Ezekiel King, and Charles Nourse (assuming this to be the same person as Charles J. Nourse). Navy Department: Samuel T. Anderson.

[3] Lufborough was a clerk in the Comptroller's office in 1801.

[4] Goldsborough was a clerk in the Navy Department in 1801.

Bibliographical Note

The records of Congress and of the executive departments of the national government in the National Archives, Washington, D. C., have been key sources for this study. The most important of these are the extensive collections of House and Senate records, which contain much material that historians of the early national period have not fully utilized. These collections are the Records of the United States House of Representatives, Record Group 233, and the Records of the United States Senate, Record Group 46. Indispensable aids to using these records are the *Preliminary Inventory of the Records of the United States House of Representatives, 1789-1946*, Volume I, compiled by Buford Rowland, Handy B. Fant, and Harold E. Hufford (National Archives, Washington, D. C., 1959) and *Preliminary Inventory of the Records of the United States Senate*, compiled by Harold E. Hufford and Watson G. Caudill (National Archives, Washington, D. C., 1950). The House and Senate records include the legislative journals, bill files, committee reports and papers, messages from the President, reports and communications from heads of the executive departments, petitions, memorials, resolutions of state legislatures, election records, records of the Clerk of the House and the Secretary of the Senate, and other records. These collections have not been microfilmed and permission to use the House Records must be obtained from the Clerk of the House of Representatives. Some of these records, which were printed for the use of members, are available in other depositories, and a guide to these documents is provided in A. W. Greeley, ed., *Public Documents of the First Fourteen Congresses, 1789-1817* (Washington, D. C., 1900). A microfilm compilation of printed House and Senate bills, beginning with the Seventh Congress, has been prepared by the Library of Congress. Many documents from the House and Senate records have been published in *American State Papers: Documents, Legislative and Executive of the United States*, 38 vols. (Washington, D. C., 1832-1861). Additional documents are in *The New American State Papers*, 176 vols. (Wilmington, Del., 1972-1973).

Legislative proceedings are recorded in *Journal of the House of Representatives of the United States*, 1st Congress-13th Congress, 9 vols. (Washington, D. C., 1826); *Journal of the Senate of the United States of America*, 1st Congress-13th Congress, 5 vols.

(Washington, D. C., 1820-1821); *Journal of the Executive Proceedings of the Senate of the United States: From the Commencement of the First to the Termination of the Nineteenth Congress*, 3 vols. (Washington, D. C., 1828); *The Debates and Proceedings in the Congress of the United States, 1789-1824* (half-title: *Annals of the Congress of the United States*), 42 vols. (Washington, D. C., 1834-1856).

The most valuable departmental records for this study were the following collections in the National Archives: Domestic Letters of the Department of State, microcopy M-40; Treasury Department, Letters and Reports to Congress, "E" Series, RG 56; Register's Office, Estimates and Statements, RG 56; Letters Sent by the Secretary of the Treasury to Collectors of Customs, microcopy M-175; Reports to Congress from the Secretary of War, microcopy M-220; Miscellaneous Letters Sent by the Secretary of War, microcopy M-370; Letters Sent by the Secretary of War to the Secretary of the Treasury, RG 203; Letters from the Secretary of the Navy to Executive Agents (includes separate volumes of Letters from the Secretary of the Navy to the President, to the Secretary of State, to the Secretary of War, and to the Secretary of the Treasury), RG 45; Letters from the Secretary of the Navy to Congress, RG 45; Miscellaneous Letters Sent by the Secretary of the Navy, microcopy M-209; Letters from and Opinions of Attorneys General, microcopy T-326; Letter Book of the Postmaster General, RG 28; Letters of Application and Recommendation during the Administration of Thomas Jefferson, 1801-1809, RG 59.

The Rare Book Division of the Library of Congress has copies of many documents printed by executive departments and by Congress during Jefferson's presidency.

The most essential manuscript collections for this study have been the magnificent collections of the Papers of Thomas Jefferson and the Papers of James Madison in the Manuscript Division of the Library of Congress, and the Papers of Albert Gallatin in the New-York Historical Society. The microfilm edition of the Papers of Albert Gallatin, edited by Carl E. Prince, is invaluable. Among the substantial manuscript holdings of the Library of Congress the following additional collections were the most useful: Breckinridge Family Papers, William A. Burwell Papers, George W. Campbell Papers, Papers of Gabriel Duvall, William Eustis Papers, Albert Gallatin Papers, Nicholas Gilman Papers, Papers of Joseph Hiester in Gregg Collection, James Monroe Papers, Papers of Gouverneur Morris, Joseph H. Nicholson Papers, William Plumer Papers, Jonathan Bayard Smith Papers, Samuel Smith Papers, Mrs. Samuel Harrison Smith Papers, Richard Stanford Personal Papers Miscellaneous, William Thornton Papers, Thomas Tudor Tucker Papers.

Other manuscript collections which have yielded useful material include the following, listed by depositories: *Chicago Historical Society*: Henry Dearborn Papers, Thomas Jefferson Papers; *College of William and Mary*: Tucker-Coleman Collection; *Columbia University*: DeWitt Clinton Papers; *Duke University*: Joseph Jones Papers, Ephraim Kirby Papers; *Historical Society of Delaware*: H. F. Brown Collection, Rodney Collection; *Historical Society of Pennsylvania*: Charles Biddle Papers, Leib-Harrison Family Papers, Thomas McKean Papers; *Maryland Historical Society*: Robert and William Smith Papers; *Massachusetts Historical Society*: Jefferson Papers (Coolidge Collection), Levi Lincoln Papers, Timothy Pickering Papers; *Museum of the City of New York*: Samuel Latham Mitchill Papers; *New York Public Library*: James Madison Papers, James Monroe Papers; *North Carolina Department of Archives and History*: Hayes Collection, Nathaniel Macon Papers; *University of Georgia*: Abraham Baldwin Papers; *University of North Carolina*: Walter Alves Papers, Cameron Family Papers, Ernest Haywood Collection, John Rutledge Papers; *University of Virginia*: Edgehill-Randolph Papers, Thomas Jefferson Papers, Wilson Cary Nicholas Papers; *Virginia Historical Society*: Archibald Stuart Papers; *Yale University*: Baldwin Family Papers, William Griswold Lane Collection, Park Family Papers.

Among the printed collections of papers of leading figures, the most useful for the period of Jefferson's presidency are: Paul L. Ford, ed., *The Writings of Thomas Jefferson*, 10 vols. (New York, 1892-1899); Henry Adams, ed., *The Writings of Albert Gallatin*, 3 vols. (Philadelphia, 1879); and Gaillard Hunt, ed., *The Writings of James Madison*, 9 vols. (New York, 1900-1910). The most valuable contemporary journals or diaries are Charles Francis Adams, ed., *Memoirs of John Quincy Adams, Comprising Portions of His Diary from 1795 to 1848*, 12 vols. (Philadelphia, 1874-1877), and Everett S. Brown, ed., *William Plumer's Memorandum of Proceedings in the United States Senate, 1803-1807* (New York, 1923). Much official correspondence and other papers are published in Clarence E. Carter, ed., *The Territorial Papers of the United States*, 26 vols. (Washington, D. C., 1934-1962).

Also useful is Gaillard Hunt, ed., *The First Forty Years of Washington Society, Portrayed by the Family Letters of Mrs. Samuel Harrison Smith* (New York, 1906).

The major secondary work on Thomas Jefferson as President is the distinguished biography by Dumas Malone, who has treated Jefferson's presidential years in two masterly volumes, *Jefferson the President: First Term, 1801-1805* (Boston, 1970) and *Jefferson the President: Second Term, 1805-1809* (Boston, 1974), works of great insight and exemplary scholarship. Henry Adams, *History of the United States of America during the Administrations of Thomas Jefferson and James Madison*, 9 vols. (New York, 1889-1891) provides a detailed history of Jefferson's administration but has been much revised by Dumas Malone and by the following works: Merrill D. Peterson, *Thomas Jefferson and the New Nation: A Biography* (New York, 1970); Marshall Smelser, *The Democratic Republic, 1801-1815* (New York, 1968); Richard E. Ellis, *The Jeffersonian Crisis: Courts and Politics in the Young Republic* (New York, 1971); Bradford Perkins, *Prologue to War: England and the United States, 1805-1812* (Berkeley, Calif., 1961); and Ralph Ketcham, *James Madison: A Biography* (New York, 1971). The role of the Republican party during Jefferson's presidency is examined in Noble E. Cunningham, Jr., *The Jeffersonian Republicans in Power: Party Operations, 1801-1809* (Chapel Hill, N. C., 1963).

Two useful background studies for the Jeffersonian Congresses are Roy Swanstrom, *The United States Senate, 1787-1801*, Senate Document No. 64, 87th Cong., 1st Sess. (Washington, D. C., 1962), and Patrick J. Furlong, "The Evolution of Political Organization in the House of Representatives, 1789-1801" (Ph.D. Dissertation, Northwestern University, 1966). For the background of Federalist administrative practices, Leonard White's *The Federalists: A Study in Administrative History* (New York, 1948) is most useful. White's *The Jeffersonians: A Study in Administrative History, 1801-1829* (New York, 1951) devotes most attention to the changes that Republicans made in administrative practices after Jefferson's presidency and neglects Jefferson's administration. White also used fewer archival sources in the volume on the Jeffersonians than in his earlier volume on the Federalists; much of the material in the National Archives relating to Jefferson's administration apparently was not examined. James Sterling Young's *The Washington Community, 1800-1828* (New York, 1966) raised important questions relating to the conduct of government under the Republicans, but in the present investigation a number of his major conclusions have been found to be insupportable by the evidence relating to the period of Jefferson's presidency. Ralph V. Harlow, *The History of Legislative Methods in the Period before 1825* (New Haven, Conn., 1917) is much outdated. Still valuable is Wesley E. Rich, *The History of the United States Post Office to the Year 1829* (Cambridge, Mass., 1924), a detailed and sound study. Useful also is Everett L. Long, "Jefferson and Congress: A Study of the Jeffersonian Legislative System, 1801-1809" (Ph.D. Dissertation, University of Missouri, 1966), and Malcolm J. Rohrbough, *The Land Office Business: The Settlement and Administration of American Public Lands, 1789-1837* (New York, 1968).

Members of Jefferson's Cabinet have been most carefully studied in Irving Brant, *James Madison, Secretary of State, 1800-1809* (Indianapolis, 1953); Raymond Walters, Jr., *Albert Gallatin: Jeffersonian Financier and Diplomat* (New York, 1957); and Richard A. Erney, "The Public Life of Henry Dearborn" (Ph.D. Dissertation, Columbia University, 1957). Henry Adams, *The Life of Albert Gallatin* (Philadelphia, 1879) also is still useful. Gallatin's fiscal theories and their application while he was Secretary of the Treasury are examined in Alexander Balinky, *Albert Gallatin: Fiscal Theories and Policies* (New Brunswick, N. J., 1958). Pertinent biographies of secondary figures include Lowell H. Harrison, *John Breckinridge: Jeffersonian Republican* (Louisville, Ky., 1969); Frank A. Cassell, *Merchant Congressman in the Young Republic: Samuel Smith of Maryland, 1752-1839* (Madison, Wisc., 1971); John S. Pancake, *Samuel Smith and the Politics of Business, 1752-1839* (University, Ala., 1972); Lynn W. Turner, *William Plumer of New Hampshire, 1759-1850* (Chapel Hill, N. C., 1962); Edmund Berkeley and Dorothy Smith Berkeley, *John Beckley* (Philadelphia, 1973); and Robert Ernst, *Rufus King: American Federalist* (Chapel Hill, N. C., 1968).

Index

Library of Congress Cataloging in Publication Data

Cunningham, Noble E.   1926-
   The process of government under Jefferson.

   Includes index.
   1.   United States—Politics and government—1801-1809.
2.   Jefferson, Thomas, Pres. U.S., 1743-1826.   I.   Title.
JK180.C86   320.9'73'046   77-85535
ISBN 0-691-04651-4